M000216638

Sources in American Constitutional History

Sources in American Constitutional History

Edited by MICHAEL LES BENEDICT

ROWMAN & LITTLEFIELD
Lanham • Boulder • New York • London

Published by Rowman & Littlefield
A wholly owned subsidiary of The Rowman & Littlefield Publishing Group, Inc.
4501 Forbes Boulevard, Suite 200, Lanham, Maryland 20706
www.rowman.com

Unit A, Whitacre Mews, 26-34 Stannary Street, London SE11 4AB

Copyright © 2016 by Rowman & Littlefield
Originally published in 1996 by D. C. Heath and Company

All rights reserved. No part of this book may be reproduced in any form or by any electronic or mechanical means, including information storage and retrieval systems, without written permission from the publisher, except by a reviewer who may quote passages in a review.

British Library Cataloguing in Publication Information Available

Library of Congress Cataloging-in-Publication Data

Library of Congress Control Number: 2015948290

ISBN: 978-1-4422-5670-5

♾™ The paper used in this publication meets the minimum requirements of American National Standard for Information Sciences—Permanence of Paper for Printed Library Materials, ANSI/NISO Z39.48-1992.

Printed in the United States of America

To my wife, Karen, and to our dear friends,
who bring such joy to our lives.

Preface

T HE PEOPLE of the United States are united not by an ancient, inherited culture or by ancient ties of blood. Instead, they are bound together by a common allegiance, voluntarily adopted by themselves or their forbears, to a system of democratic government articulated in written state and federal constitutions. These constitutions define the fundamental structure of our governments and embody the basic principles of American public life. They are principles of democratic self-government, restrained in the interest of individual liberty and of civil and political equality.

American historians have paid far more attention to the history of the Constitution of the United States than to those of individual states. This document collection reflects this national focus, but it is slowly changing. Future collections of constitutional documents may well include more state materials, especially for the modern period, as state courts pay more attention to their own constitutions as sources of constitutional principles. However, the basic documents reprinted or excerpted in this volume embody the general American constitutional heritage, from its British and colonial origins to the present day. This book is a basic rather than an exhaustive collection, drawn from a canon that nearly all constitutional scholars recognize; yet it is limited in length to be appropriate for a one-semester course in American constitutional history. As a basic collection reflecting the canon of American constitutional history, this volume consists for the most part of formal, governmental records—the records of constitutional conventions, legislative proceedings, presidential addresses·and proclamations, and court cases.

The documents reflect disagreements over the nature of the federal system, the boundaries of state and federal jurisdiction within that system, the relations among the three branches of the federal government, the scope of the rights that the Constitution secures against government infringement, and the role of the federal courts in defining and enforcing constitutional mandates. Many of the documents are judicial opinions, deciding specific cases. In our system such decisions have broad impact. The principles that a court articulates in such cases govern how it and lower courts will decide similar cases in the future. In effect, they establish what the law governing a subject is. If the law of one state is ruled unconstitutional in a particular case, all similar laws will be held unconstitutional if legally challenged unless the precedent itself is overturned. (In practice, things are a bit messier, but in general the principle holds true.) Over time, the courts have established their primary role in interpreting the meaning of the Constitution. Their statement of the law has a profound influence on the other branches of the federal and state governments.

The documents here are organized into chapters corresponding to those in Michael Les Benedict, *The Blessings of Liberty: A Concise History of the Constitution of the United States.* However, since they reflect the generally accepted canon of American constitutional history, they may supplement any textbook or other readings. The brief introductory headnotes provide information about the social, political, and intellectual context in which each document first appeared. By their nature, historical interpretations are subject to debate; teachers, students, and general readers are of course free to disagree with the author.

I owe an intellectual debt to the host of scholars who have illuminated the American constitutional tradition, determining the content of this documentary collection. They range from the great nineteenth and early twentieth-century authors of classic constitutional histories—George Bancroft, George Ticknor Curtis, James Schouler, Charles Warren, Andrew C. McLaughlin, and others—to the founders of more modern approaches and their present-day intellectual heirs—Charles A. Beard, Edward S. Corwin, James G. Randall, Alpheus T. Mason, Alfred H. Kelly, Paul L. Murphy, and Harold M. Hyman. Melvin Urofsky and Herman Belz, authors of the standard textbooks in American constitutional history, deserve special mention; they have defined the field for a generation of students. The document headnotes in this volume draw on the insights of all these scholars and on those of many others who have studied the institutions of American governance and events of constitutional significance. It is impossible to name all of them here; I have alluded to some in the Further Readings sections of *The Blessings of Liberty*, previously noted, but there are many more. They have my deepest gratitude, and, I hope, the gratitude of all who learn something of the great American constitutional heritage through this work.

M. L. B.

Contents

12   The Progressive Era

13   Liberal versus Conservative Constitutionalism in the 1920s

14   The New Deal and the Constitution

15   Liberal Constitutionalism

16 *Liberal Constitutionalism and Equality*

17 *Curbing Presidential Power*

18 *The Revival of Constitutional Conservatism*

19 *The Supreme Court and Conservative Constitutionalism*

Appendix

Introduction

As I have noted in the Preface to this collection of documents, the people of the United States are united not by an ancient, inherited culture or by ancient ties of blood. Instead, they are bound together by a common allegiance, voluntarily adopted by themselves or their forbears, to a system of democratic government articulated in written constitutions, state and federal. These constitutions define the fundamental structure of our governments and embody the basic principles of American public life. They are principles of democratic self-government, restrained in the interest of individual liberty and civil and political equality.

In most modern polities, a constitution is understood to serve the underlying nation. It may even be suspended in the interests of the nation. Similar ideas have sometimes been expressed in the United States. During the Civil War, some leaders argued that constitutional provisions that put the Union at risk must be suspended in order to preserve the nation. They drew on a new sense of American nationality, reflected in Lincoln's comment that the Union was older than any of the states and that Americans were tied together by "mystic chords of memory." But few Americans accepted the idea that the war had suspended the Constitution; instead they searched for and found sources of constitutional authority equal to the task of preserving the nation. In the United States, the rule seems to be, "No federal constitution, no nation; no state constitution, no state." The polities of the United States are founded on the principle of a social compact, in which people unite voluntarily to promote the common good, with their agreements expressed in written constitutions.

Historians have paid far more attention to the Constitution of the United States and its history than they have to the constitutions of the individual states. This collection of documents reflects this national focus, and is limited with a few exceptions to material that most American constitutional historians recognize as central to American constitutional development.

However, readers should be aware that the history of constitutional government in America transcends such documents. They are the formal articulations of constitutional ideas to which Americans have been deeply and emotionally committed, over which they have fought not only with words but twice, in the American Revolution and the Civil War, with weapons.

Readers may wonder how much the theories of government and liberty represented in these documents have mattered compared to the economic interests, racial identification, ethnic rivalries and other factors that lead to conflict in American society. The answer is, quite a bit. It is certainly true that few people will make great sacrifices for principles alone, although we know that some do and we often admire them for it. But convictions of right and wrong play a powerful role in disputes over practical matters. Americans expended far more in blood and treasure to resist British efforts to tax them than the taxes themselves ever would have cost. The conviction that they had a constitutional right to take their slaves into United States territories made southerners far more uncompromising than they might have been had they conceded the right of Congress to decide the issue. As legal scholars have put it, a constitutional right is a "trump"; it outweighs mere interests.

Because Americans are committed to constitutionalism, the principle that we are obligated to obey the Constitution as fundamental law, claiming some privilege or immunity as a constitutional right is a powerful weapon. To the degree that the claim is persuasive, neutrals come to one's side and opponents waver. That is why Americans so often translate claims of interest into claims of constitutional right.

The Constitution of the United States was framed in 1787 and ratified in 1788, going into operation the following year. However, its origins lay in an Anglo-American tradition of government and liberty. The documents in Chapters One and Two of this sourcebook are central to that tradition. Those reproduced in Chapters Three and Four document the struggle over the nature of the British Constitution, which culminated in the Declaration of Independence; the establishment of a confederation embodying the American understanding of the proper relationship among self-governing peoples belonging to a common empire; and finally the creation of a new kind of federal system, embodied in the Constitution of the United States and designed to establish effective central government without sacrificing liberty and local self-government.

Documents in immediately succeeding chapters are central to the acceptance of organized political dissent, the rise of judicial review, and the development of rival theories of the federal system—constitutional nationalism, state sovereignty, and state rights. Conflict over the nature of the federal system combined with the explosive issue of slavery and led to many events—the Civil War; the great expansion of federal power that attended the struggle; the death of state-sovereignty theories of federalism; and a redefinition of American citizenship to include all races and ultimately to incorporate political rights irrespective of gender. These developments are documented in Chapters Eight through Ten.

With the abolition of slavery, the constitutional questions surrounding state-federal relations and individual rights became entwined with the social and economic changes that accompanied the rise of the industrial economy. The documents in Chapters Eleven through Thirteen indicate how the courts tried to contain public policy within a traditional constitutional structure that tried to separate state and federal jurisdiction and to distinguish legislation that served the general interest from legislation that privileged some groups at the expense of others. The constraints that this effort placed on Americans' struggle to cope with the problems of a modern economy led to a crisis during the Great Depression of the 1930s and resulted in the New Deal transformation of the American constitutional system, illustrated by the sources in Chapters Fourteen and Fifteen. That transformation encouraged the development of broader concepts of civil liberty and a renewed commitment to equality of rights from the 1930s through the early 1970s, and a concomitant expansion of the role of the courts in protecting them. These developments are documented in Chapters Fifteen and Sixteen. The sources in Chapter Seventeen involve the growth of presidential power and the reaction to it.

The last two chapters include documents relating to the renaissance of conservative constitutionalism from the 1970s to the present—a revival of state-rights theories of federalism, a commitment to protecting rights in property, and a reaction against the perceived excesses of "rights consciousness" since the 1960s.

Americans share a commitment to ideas of democracy, liberty, and equality at the same time that they struggle over their exact meaning and application. These documents are the concrete manifestations of both the commitment and the conflict. I hope that by explicating the history of the conflicts, this sourcebook will reinforce the commitment to the ideals.

Sources in American Constitutional History

CHAPTER 1

English Origins of American Constitutionalism

1

In the seventeenth and eighteenth centuries, British subjects throughout the world considered the *Magna Carta,* or Great Charter, to be the most important statement of the liberties of Englishmen and women. It was forced from the arbitrary and autocratic King John by powerful barons in 1215. Although John soon repudiated it, his successors reissued it in varying versions through the centuries. In 1628, the great judge and legal writer Sir Edward Coke called the charter "the fountain of all the fundamental Laws of the Realm," and this remained the general view all through the American colonial era and for a century following the American Revolution. Not until the late nineteenth century did many people realize that the Great Charter was designed more to protect the feudal rights of the English aristocracy than the rights of ordinary subjects. John had manipulated his feudal prerogatives to bring in more money than he was entitled to by custom. As an examination of the excerpts below makes clear, the charter manifested a conviction that the king could not act arbitrarily but must govern according to the law and custom. That principle, articulated to protect the rights of the great barons of England, could protect ordinary subjects as well.

The *Magna Carta* (1215)

[1]   IN THE FIRST place we have granted to God, and by this our present charter confirmed for us and our heirs forever that the English Church shall be free, and shall have her rights entire, and her liberties inviolate. . . .

[2]   If any of our earls or barons, or others holding of us in chief by military

Samuel E. Thorne et. al, *The Great Charter: Four Essays on the* Magna Carta *and the History of Our Liberty* (N.Y.: Pantheon Books, 1965), Appendix, 113–118, 120, 124, 127–128, 131–132.

service shall have died, and at the time of his death his heir shall be full of age and owe "relief," he shall have his inheritance on payment of the ancient relief. . . .*

] If, however, the heir of any one of the aforesaid has been under age and in wardship, let him have his inheritance without relief and without fine when he comes of age.

] The guardian of the land of an heir who is thus under age, shall take from the land of the heir nothing but reasonable produce, reasonable customs, and reasonable services, and that without destruction or waste of men or goods. . . .

] A widow, after the death of her husband, shall forthwith and without difficulty have her marriage portion and inheritance. . . .

] No widow shall be compelled to marry, so long as she prefers to live without a husband. . . .

] Neither we nor our bailiffs shall seize any land or rent for any debt, so long as the chattels of the debtor are sufficient to repay the debt. . . .

] No scutage nor aid† shall be imposed on our kingdom, unless by common counsel of our kingdom, except for ransoming our person, for making our eldest son a knight, and for once marrying our eldest daughter. . . .

] And the city of London shall have all its ancient liberties and free customs, as well by land as by water; furthermore, we decree and grant that all other cities, boroughs, towns, and ports shall have all their liberties and free customs.

] A freeman shall not be amerced‡ for a slight offense, except in accordance with the degree of the offense; and for a grave offense he shall be amerced in accordance with the gravity of the offense. . . .

] Earls and barons shall not be amerced except through their peers, and only in accordance with the degree of the offense.

] No constable or other bailiff of ours shall take corn or other provisions from anyone without immediately tendering money therefor, unless he can have postponement thereof by permission of the seller.

] Neither we nor our bailiffs shall take, for our castles or for any other work of ours, wood which is not ours, against the will of the owner of that wood.

] No bailiff for the future shall, upon his own unsupported complaint, put anyone to his "law," without credible witnesses brought for this purpose.

] No freemen shall be taken or (and) imprisoned or disseised** or exiled or

---

*payment by an heir of an estate to a feudal lord in exchange for acknowledgment of the heir's right to inherit a "fief," or feudal estate

†money paid to feudal lords in lieu of military service

‡fined

**deprived of one's feudal right to property

[handwritten: King John kept ripping off people and taking money [from] noblemen]

in any way destroyed, nor will we go upon him nor send upon him, except by the lawful judgment of his peers or (and) by the law of the land.

[ɔ]   To no one will we sell, to no one will we refuse or delay, right or justice.

2 ∽

The seventeenth century witnessed a long and bitter struggle between those who tried to expand the power of the monarchy and those who sought to limit it and expand the power of Parliament instead. One side defended the royal prerogative, the other claimed to stand for the liberty of the monarch's subjects. The conflict culminated in the ouster of King James II in the "Glorious Revolution" of 1688 and the settlement of the throne upon William, Prince of Orange, and Mary. As part of the settlement, William and Mary agreed to a statement of the rights of Englishmen that became known as the Declaration of Rights, or the Bill of Rights. English people considered it second in importance only to the *Magna Carta* as a foundation of British liberty.

The Declaration of Rights (1689)

AN ACT FOR declaring the rights and liberties of the subject, and settling the succession of the crown. . . .

Whereas the late King *James* the Second, by the assistance of divers evil counsellors, judges, and ministers employed by him, did endeavour to subvert and extirpate the protestant religion, and the laws and liberties of this kingdom. . . .

All which are utterly and directly contrary to the known laws of statutes, and freedom of this realm.

And whereas the said late King *James* the Second having abdicated the government, and the throne being thereby vacant, his highness the Prince of Orange (whom it hath pleased Almighty God to make the glorious instrument of delivering this kingdom from popery and arbitrary power) did . . . cause letters to be written to the lords spiritual and temporal, being protestants; and other letters to the several counties, cities, universities, boroughs, and cinque-ports for the choosing of such persons to represent them, as were of right to be sent to parliament . . . in order to [assure] such an establishment, as that their religion, laws, and liberties might not again be in danger of being subverted. . . .

. . . [T]he said lords spiritual and temporal, and commons . . . do . . . (as their ancestors in like case have usually done) for the vindicating and asserting their ancient rights and liberties declare;

Danby Pickering (comp.), *Statutes at Large* (London: Joseph Bentham, 1764), 9: 67–69.

1. That the pretended power of suspending of laws, or the execution of laws, by regal authority, without consent of parliament, is illegal.

2. That the pretended power of dispensing with laws or the execution of laws, by regal authority, as it hath been assumed and executed of late, is illegal.

3. That the commission for erecting the late court of commissioners for ecclesiastical causes, and all other commissions and courts of like nature are illegal and pernicious.

4. That levying money for or to the use of the crown, by pretence of prerogative, without grant of parliament, for longer time, or in other manner than the same is or shall be granted, is illegal.

5. That it is the right of the subjects to petition the King, and all committments and prosecutions for such petitioning are illegal.

6. That the raising or keeping a standing army within the kingdom in time of peace, unless it be with consent of parliament, is against law.

7. That the subjects which are protestants, may have arms for their defence suitable to their conditions, and as allowed by law.

8. That election of members of parliament ought to be free.

9. That the freedom of speech, and debates or proceeding in parliament, ought not to be impeached or questioned in any court or place out of parliament.

10. That excessive bail ought not to be required, nor excessive fines imposed; nor cruel and unusual punishments inflicted.

11. That jurors ought to be duly impanelled and returned, and jurors which pass upon men in trials for high treason ought to be freeholders.

12. That all grants and promises of fines and forfeitures of particular persons before conviction, are illegal and void.

13. And that for redress of all grievances, and for the amending, strengthening, and preserving of the laws, parliaments ought to be held frequently.

And they do claim, demand, and insist upon all and singular the premises, as their undoubted rights and liberties; and that no declarations, judgments, doings or proceedings, to the prejudice of the people in any of the said premises, ought in any wise to be drawn hereafter into consequence or example.

3 ❧

The great philosopher John Locke provided the best statement of the justification for ousting King James and enthroning William and Mary. It represented the thinking of the so-called Whigs, who had argued since the late 1670s that the English people had the right to deny the throne to a king who threatened their liberty. The ideas that a social contract underlay government and that subjects had a right of resistance if a monarch tried to deprive them of liberty became fundamentals of eighteenth-century British constitutional thought. Whether the contract also limited Parliament, which was thought to represent the English people, was less clear. Ultimately, British constitutional thinkers would conclude that Parliament was sovereign because it represented the people; Americans would conclude that the people had the same right to resist arbitrary acts of Parliament that they had to resist those of a king. Compare Locke's statement of Whig principles to the justification for the American Revolution in the Declaration of Independence (Document 9).

John Locke, Second Treatise of Government (1690)

MAN BEING born . . . with a Title to perfect Freedom, and an uncontrouled enjoyment of all the Rights and Priviledges of the Law of Nature, equally with any other Man, or number of Men in the World, hath by Nature a Power, not only to preserve his Property, that is, his Life, Liberty and Estate, against the Injuries and Attempts of other Men; but to judge of, and punish the breaches of that Law in others, as he is perswaded the Offence deserves, even with Death it self, in Crimes where the heinousness of the Fact, in his Opinion, requires it. But because no *Political Society* can be, nor subsist without having in it self the Power to preserve the Property, and in order thereunto punish the Offences of all those of that Society; there, and there only is *Political Society,* where every one of the Members hath quitted this natural Power, resign'd it up into the hands of the Community in all cases that exclude him not from appealing for Protection to the Law established by it. And thus all private judgement of every particular Member being excluded, the Community comes to be Umpire, by settled standing Rules, indifferent, and the same to all Parties. . . .

MEN being . . . by Nature, all free, equal and independent, no one can be put out of this Estate, and subjected to the Political Power of another, without his own *Consent.* The only way whereby any one devests himself of his Natural Liberty, and *puts on the bonds of Civil Society* is by agreeing with

John Locke, *Two Treatises of Government,* ed. Peter Laslett (Cambridge: Cambridge University Press, 1963), 341–342, 348–349, 368–369, 374–377, 380.

other Men to joyn and unite into a Community, for their comfortable, safe, and peaceable living one amongst another, in a secure Enjoyment of their Properties, and a greater Security against any that are not of it. . . .

The great and *chief end* therefore, of Mens uniting into Commonwealths, and putting themselves under Government, *is the Preservation of their Property.** To which in the state of Nature there are many things wanting.

First, There wants an *establish'd,* settled, known *Law,* received and allowed by common consent to be the Standard of Right and Wrong, and the common measure to decide all Controversies between them. . . .

Secondly, In the State of Nature there wants *a known and indifferent Judge,* with Authority to determine all differences according to the established Law. For every one in that state being both Judge and Executioner of the Law of Nature, Men being partial to themselves, Passion and Revenge is very apt to carry them too far, and with too much heat, in their own Cases; as well as negligence, and unconcernedness, to make them too remiss, in other Mens.

Thirdly, In the state of Nature there often wants *Power* to back and support the Sentence when right, and to *give* it due *Execution. . . .*

The great end of Mens entring into Society, being the enjoyment of their Properties in Peace and Safety, and the great instrument and means of that being the Laws establish'd in that Society; the *first and fundamental positive Law* of all Commonwealths, *is the establishing of the Legislative Power;* as the *first and fundamental natural Law,* which is to govern even the Legislative it self, is *the preservation of the Society,* and (as far as will consist with the publick good) of every person in it. This *Legislative* is not only *the supream power* of the Common-wealth, but sacred and unalterable in the hands where the Community have once placed it. . . .

Though the *Legislative,* whether placed in one or more, whether it be always in being, or only by intervals, tho' it be the *Supream* Power in every Common-wealth; yet,

First, It is *not,* nor can possibly be absolutely *Arbitrary* over the Lives and Fortunes of the People. For it being but the joynt power of every Member of the Society given up to that Person, or Assembly, which is Legislator, it can be no more than those persons had in a State of Nature before they enter'd into Society, and gave up to the Community. For no Body can transfer to another more power than he has in himself; and no Body has an absolute Arbitrary Power over himself, or over any other, to destroy his own Life, or take away the Life or Property of another. A man, . . . having in the State of Nature no Arbitrary Power over the Life, Liberty, or Possession of another, but only so much as the Law of Nature gave him for the preservation of himself, and the rest of Mankind; this is all he doth, or can give up to the Common-wealth,

---

*In a previous paragraph, Locke defines property as "Lives, Liberties and Estates."

and by it to the *Legislative Power*, so that the Legislative can have no more than this. Their Power in the utmost Bounds of it, is *limited to the publick good* of the Society. It is a Power, that hath no other end but preservation, and therefore can never have a right to destroy, enslave, or designedly to impoverish the Subjects. . . .

Secondly, The *Legislative*, or Supream Authority, cannot assume to its self a power to Rule by extemporary Arbitrary Decrees, but *is bound to dispense Justice*, and decide the Rights of the Subject *by promulgated standing Laws, and known Authoris'd Judges*. . . .

[*Thirdly*,] Governments cannot be supported without great Charge, and 'tis fit every one who enjoys his share of the Protection, should pay out of his Estate his proportion for the maintenance of it. But still it must be with his own Consent, *i.e.* the Consent of the Majority, giving it either by themselves, or their Representatives chosen by them. . . . For what property have I in that which another may by right take, when he pleases to himself?

Fourthly, The *Legislative cannot transfer the Power of Making Laws* to any other hands. For it being but a delegated Power from the People, they, who have it, cannot pass it over to others. The People alone can appoint the Form of the Commonwealth, which is by Constituting the Legislative, and appointing in whose hands that shall be. . . .

. . . [T]he common Question will be made, *Who shall be Judge* whether the Prince or Legislative act contrary to their Trust? . . . To this I reply, *The People shall be Judge*; for who shall be *Judge* whether his Trustee or Deputy acts well, and according to the Trust reposed in him, but he who deputes him, and must, by having deputed him have still a Power to discard him, when he fails in his Trust? . . .

. . . The *Power that every individual gave the Society, which he entered into it, can never revert to the Individuals again, as long as the Society lasts, but will always remain in the Community*; because without this, there can be no Community, no Common-wealth, which is contrary to the original Agreement: So also when the Society hath placed the Legislative in any Assembly of Men, to continue in them and their Successors, with Direction and Authority for providing such Successors, *the Legislative can never revert to the People* whilst that Government lasts: Because having provided a Legislative with Power to continue for ever, they have given up their Political Power to the Legislative, and cannot resume it. But if they have set Limits to the Duration of their Legislative, and made this Supreme Power in any Person, or Assembly, only temporary: Or else when by the Miscarriages of those in Authority, it is forfeited; upon the Forfeiture of their Rulers, or at the Determination of the Time set, *it reverts to the Society*, and the People have a Right to act as Supreme, and continue the Legislative in themselves, or erect a new Form, or under the old form place it in new hands, as they think good.

CHAPTER 2

Colonial Origins of
American Constitutionalism

4 ❧

The kings of England encouraged the settlement of North America by granting charters
to companies of "merchant adventurers," authorizing them to plant and govern colonies
in the New World. The Virginia Company received such a charter in 1606; the Council of
New England received a similar charter in 1620. The Massachusetts Bay Company received its charter in 1629. It authorized the company's governor, assistants, and general
court to establish laws and ordinances to govern its colonies but did not specify where
they should meet. The company agreed to send the charter to the colony itself and to
hold the general court there, in effect turning government over to the colonists themselves.

The king gave similar charters to favored individuals, or *proprietors*, like Lord Baltimore and William Penn, who established Maryland and Pennsylvania, respectively.
Later, the king gave charters directly to the settlers of other colonies, retaining for himself
the right to name governors. As company and proprietary charters were revoked for various transgressions during the seventeenth century, nearly all the settlements received
such royal charters.

Charter of the Massachusetts Bay Company (1629)

CHARLES, BY THE GRACE OF GOD, Kinge of England, ... &c.
TO ALL to whome theis Presents shall come Greeting ... knowe yee ...
Wee ... give and graunte unto ... Sir Henry Rosewell, Sir John Younge, Sir
Richard Saltonstall ... all that Parte of Newe England in America, which

Ben Perley Poore (comp.), *Federal and State Constitutions, Colonial Charters, and Organic Laws of
the United States* (Washington, D.C.: Government Printing Office, 1878), part 1, pp. 932–942.

lyes . . . betweene a great River there, comonlie called Monomack River, alias Merrimack River, and a certen other River there, called Charles River, being in the Bottome of a certen Bay there, comonlie called Massachusetts . . . Bay; and also . . . those Landes . . . lying within . . . Three Englishe Myles on the South . . . of the . . . Charles River, or of any . . . Parte thereof. . . . TO BE HOLDEN of Us . . . as of our Manor of East Greenwich in our Countie of Kent . . . in free and common Soccage, and not in Capite, nor by Knights Service; . . . To the Ende that the Affaires and Buyssinesses which from tyme to tyme shall . . . arise concerning the saide Landes, and the Plantation of the same maie be the better mannaged and ordered . . . Wee will and ordeyne, that the saide Sir Henry Rosewell, Sir John Young . . . and all such others as shall hereafter be admitted and made free of the Company and Society hereafter mencoed, shall . . . be . . . one body corporate and politique . . . by the Name of the Governor and Company of the Massachusetts Bay in Newe-England . . . by the same Name they and their Successors shall . . . be . . . enabled . . . to implead, and to be impleaded, and to prosecute . . . all and singuler Suites, Causes Quarrels, and Accons, of what kinde or nature soever. And also to . . . acquire, and purchase any Landes . . . or any Goodes or Chattels, and the same to . . . sell, and dispose of, as . . . any other corporacon or Body politique of the same may lawfully doe . . . there shalbe one Governor, one Deputy Governor, and eighteene Assistants of the same Company, to be from tyme to tyme constituted, elected and chosen out of the Freemen of the saide Company, for the tyme being, . . . which said Officers shall applie themselves to take Care for the best disposeing and ordering of the generall buysines and Affaires of, for, and concerning the said Landes and Premisses hereby mencoed, to be graunted, and the Plantacion thereof, and the Government of the People there . . . and that there shall . . . be held . . . by the Governor, or Deputie Governor of the said Company, and seaven or more of the said Assistants for the tyme being, upon every last Wednesday in Hillary, Easter, Trinity, and Michas Termes respectivelie forever, one great generall and solempe assemblie, which foure generall assemblies shalbe stiled and called the foure greate and generall Courts of the saide Company; IN all of which saide greate and generall Courts soe assembled WEE DOE . . . graunte to the said Governor and Company . . . full Power and authoritie to choose . . . such . . . other as they . . . shall be willing to accept . . . to be free of the said Company and Body, and them into the same to admitt; and to elect and constitute such Officers as they shall thinke fitt . . . for the ordering . . . of the Affaires of the saide . . . Company. . . . And to make Lawes and Ordinances for the Good and Welfare of the saide Company, and for the Government and ordering of the saide Landes and Plantacion, and the People inhabiting . . . the same . . . soe as such Lawes and Ordinances be not contrarie or repugnant to the Lawes and Statuts of this our Realme of England. . . . That it shalbe lawfull and free for them and their Assignes . . . to . . . transport . . . into . . . the said Plantacon in Newe England . . . soe many of our loving Subjects, or any other strangers that will become our loving Subjects . . . as shall willinglie accompany them in the same Voyages and Plantacon; and also Shipping, Armour, Weapons . . . Corne, Victualls, and all Manner of Clothing, Implements . . . Beastes . . . and all other Thinges necessarie for the saide Plantacon, and for their Use and Defence, and for Trade with the People there. . . . AND, further our Will and Pleasure is . . . That all . . . Subjects of Us, . . . which shall goe to and inhabite within the saide Landes . . . and every of their Children . . . shall have and enjoy all liberties and Immunities of free and naturall Subjects within any of the Domynions of Us . . . to all Intents, . . . and Purposes whatsoever, as yf they . . . were borne within the Realme of England. . . . That it shall . . . be lawfull . . . for the Governor or Deputie Governor, and such of the Assistants and Freemen of the said Company for the Tyme being as shalbe assembled in any of their generall Courts aforesaide . . . to make . . . all Manner of wholesome and reasonable Orders, Lawes, Statutes, and Ordinances . . . not contrarie to the Lawes of this our Realme of England. . . . AND WEE DOE further . . . graunt to the said Governor and Company . . . that all . . . such Chiefe Comaunders, Captaines, Governors, and other Officers and Ministers, as by the said . . . Lawes . . . shalbe from Tyme to Tyme hereafter ymploied either in the Government of the saide Inhabitants and Plantacon, or in the Waye by Sea thither, or from thence . . . shall . . . have full and Absolute Power and Authoritie to correct, punishe, pardon, governe, and rule all . . . as shall . . . adventure themselves in any Voyadge thither or from thence, or that shall . . . inhabite within the Precincts . . . of Newe England aforesaid, according to the . . . Lawes . . . aforesaid.

5 ❧

In 1620 a group of radical Protestants who dissented from the tenets of the Church of England landed at Plymouth, outside the geographic boundaries specified by the charter of the company that had authorized their settlement. Without a charter establishing government, the so-called Pilgrims imitated the procedure by which they established their religious congregations: They entered a covenant, or compact, to establish a "Body Politick." Thus the Mayflower Compact represented a practical example of Locke's social compact, agreed to seventy years before the great philosopher wrote his *Two Treatises of Government.* New England colonists regularly entered into such agreements as they established towns beyond the boundaries of earlier settlements, putting into practice what Locke would later specify in theory.

The Mayflower Compact (1620)

IN THE NAME OF GOD, AMEN. We, whose names are underwritten, the Loyal Subjects of our dread Sovereign Lord King *James,* by the Grace of God, of *Great Britain* . . . Having undertaken for the Glory of God, and Advancement of the Christian Faith, and the Honour of our King and Country, a Voyage to plant the first Colony in the northern Parts of *Virginia;* Do by these Presents, solemnly and mutually, in the Presence of God and one another, covenant and combine ourselves together into a civil Body Politick, for our better Ordering and Preservation, and Furtherance of the Ends aforesaid: And by Virtue hereof do enact, constitute, and frame, such just and equal Laws, Ordinances, Acts, Constitutions, and Officers, from time to time, as shall be thought most meet and convenient for the general Good of the Colony; unto which we promise all due Submission and Obedience.

↳ *Built a Commonwealth*

Simple

Poore (comp.), *Federal and State Constitutions,* part 1, p. 931.

C H A P T E R   3

The American Revolution

6 ❧

In 1765 Parliament passed the Stamp Act, for the first time levying an internal tax upon the American colonies. (Parliament had previously placed duties on imports and exports.) Parliament also expanded the jurisdiction of the Admiralty courts, which did not provide jury trials. The colonial assemblies protested and called a general Stamp Act Congress, which presented the American constitutional argument against the tax and petitioned for the laws' repeal. To bring pressure to bear on the British government, colonial leaders organized a boycott of English trade.

Resolutions of the Stamp Act Congress (1765)

THE MEMBERS of this congress, sincerely devoted with the warmest sentiments of affection and duty to his Majesty's person and government, . . . esteem it our indispensable duty to make the following declarations, of our humble opinion, respecting the most essential rights and liberties of the colonists, and of the grievances under which they labour, by reason of several late acts of Parliament.

I. That his Majesty's subjects in these colonies, owe the same allegiance to the Crown of Great Britain that is owing from his subjects born within the realm, and all due subordination to that august body, the Parliament of Great Britain.

II. That his Majesty's liege subjects in these colonies are intitled to all the inherent rights and liberties of his natural born subjects within the kingdom of Great Britain.

III. That it is inseparably essential to the freedom of a people, and the un-

Hezekiah Niles (comp.), *Principles and Acts of the Revolution in America* (N.Y.: A. S. Barnes, 1876), p. 163.

doubted right of Englishmen, that no taxes be imposed on them, but with their own consent, given personally, or by their representatives.

IV. That the people of these colonies are not, and from their local circumstances cannot be, represented in the House of Commons in Great Britain.

V. That the only representatives of the people of these colonies, are persons chosen therein, by themselves, and that no taxes ever have been, or can be constitutionally imposed on them, but by their respective legislatures.

VI. That all supplies to the Crown, being free gifts of the people, it is unreasonable and inconsistent with the principles and spirit of the British constitution, for the people of Great Britain to grant to his Majesty the property of the colonists.

VII. That trial by jury is the inherent and invaluable right of every British subject in these colonies.

VIII. That the late Act of Parliament, entitled An Act for granting and applying certain Stamp Duties, and other Duties, in the British Colonies and Plantations in America, etc., by imposing taxes on the inhabitants of these colonies; and the said Act, and several other Acts, by extending the jurisdiction of the courts of Admiralty beyond its ancient limits, have a manifest tendency to subvert the rights and liberties of the colonists. . . .

XIII. That it is the right of the British subjects in these colonies, to petition the King or either House of Parliament.

Lastly, That it is the indispensable duty of these colonies to the best of sovereigns, to the mother country, and to themselves, to endeavour by a loyal and dutiful address to his Majesty, and humble applications to both houses of Parliament, to procure the repeal of the Act for granting and applying certain stamp duties, of all clauses of any other Acts of Parliament, whereby the jurisdiction of the admiralty is extended as aforesaid, and of the other late Acts for the restriction of American commerce.

7 ∽

Committed to the principle of parliamentary sovereig[n]
rejected the idea that its power could be limited. None
Whigs," a more liberal group of leaders sympathetic
Britain. The Rockingham ministry pushed a repeal of th[e]
but was forced to accompany it with the Declaratory A[ct]
sovereign power over the British empire.

The Declaratory Act (1766)

A N   A C T   F O R   the better securing the dependency of his Majesty's dominions in *America* upon the crown and parliament of *Great Britain*.

Whereas several of the houses of representatives in his Majesty's colonies and plantations in *America,* have of late, against law, claimed to themselves . . . the sole and exclusive right of imposing duties and taxes upon his Majesty's subjects in the said colonies and plantations; and have, in pursuance of such claim, passed certain votes, resolutions, and orders, derogatory to the legislative authority of parliament, and inconsistent with the dependency of the said colonies and plantations upon the crown of *Great Britain:* . . . be it declared . . . [t]hat the said colonies and plantations in *America* have been, are, and of right ought to be, subordinate unto, and dependent upon the imperial crown and parliament of *Great Britain;* and that the King's majesty, by and with the advice and consent of the lords spiritual and temporal, and commons of *Great Britain,* in parliament assembled, had, hath, and of right ought to have, full power and authority to make laws and statutes of sufficient force and validity to bind the colonies and people of *America,* subjects of the crown of *Great Britain, in all cases whatsoever. . . .*

II. And be it further declared . . . [t]hat all resolutions, votes, orders, and proceedings, in any of the said colonies or plantations, whereby the power and authority of the parliament of *Great Britain,* to make laws and statutes as aforesaid, is denied, or drawn into question, are, and are hereby declared to be, utterly null and void to all intents and purposes whatsoever.

8 ∾

After the fall of the Rockingham ministry, the British government renewed its efforts to increase the revenue it secured from the American colonies. It levied import duties on a wide variety of items and gave the East India Company a monopoly on the importation of tea to North America. Resistance to the laws in Boston led Parliament to pass the Coercive Acts, which suspended the operation of the colonial assembly and town governments in Massachusetts, altered the colony's charter to increase the power of the royal governor, and quartered troops in Boston. In response, the colonial assemblies called another Congress, which again claimed that the powers of Parliament were limited by the principles of the British constitution, as well as by the terms of the charters granted to the American colonists.

, *Statutes at Large,* 27: 19–20.

Resolutions of the First Continental Congress (1774)

... [T]HE DEPUTIES so appointed being now assembled, in a full and free representation of these Colonies, ... do, ... as Englishmen, their ancestors in like cases have usually done, for asserting and vindicating their rights and liberties, declare,

That the inhabitants of the English Colonies in North America, by the immutable laws of nature, the principles of the English constitution, and the several charters or compacts, have the following Rights:

Resolved, . . . 1. That they are entitled to life, liberty, & property, and they have never ceded to any sovereign power whatever, a right to dispose of either without their consent.

Resolved, . . . 2. That our ancestors, who first settled these colonies, were at the time of their emigration from the mother country, entitled to all the rights, liberties, and immunities of free and natural-born subjects, within the realm of England.

Resolved, . . . 3. That . . . their descendants now are, entitled to the exercise and enjoyment of all such of them, as their local and other circumstances enable them to exercise and enjoy.

Resolved, 4. That the foundation of English liberty, and of all free government, is a right in the people to participate in their legislative council: and as the English colonists are not represented, and from their local and other circumstances, cannot properly be represented in the British parliament, they are entitled to a free and exclusive power of legislation in their several provincial legislatures, where their right of representation can alone be preserved, in all cases of taxation and internal polity, subject only to the negative of their sovereign, in such manner as has been heretofore used and accustomed. But, from the necessity of the case, and a regard to the mutual interest of both countries, we cheerfully consent to the operation of such acts of the British parliament, as are bona fide, restrained to the regulation of our external commerce . . . ; excluding every idea of taxation, internal or external, for raising a revenue on the subjects in America, without their consent.

Resolved, . . . 5. That the respective colonies are entitled to the common law of England, and more especially to the great and inestimable privilege of being tried by their peers of the vicinage, according to the course of that law.

Resolved, 6. That they are entitled to the benefit of such of the English statutes as existed at the time of their colonization; and which they have, by experience, respectively found to be applicable to their several local and other circumstances.

Worthington Chauncey Ford (ed.), *Journals of the Continental Congress* (Washington, D.C.: Government Printing Office, 1904), 1: 66–71.

Resolved, . . . 7. That these, his majesty's colonies, are likewise entitled to all the immunities and privileges granted & confirmed to them by royal charters, or secured by their several codes of provincial laws.

Resolved, . . . 8. That they have a right peaceably to assemble, consider of their grievances, and petition the King; and that all prosecutions, prohibitory proclamations, and commitments for the same, are illegal.

Resolved, . . . 9. That the keeping [of] a Standing army in these colonies, in times of peace, without the consent of the legislature of that colony, in which such army is kept, is against law.

Resolved, . . . 10. It is indispensably necessary to good government, and rendered essential by the English constitution, that the constituent branches of the legislature be independent of each other; that, therefore, the exercise of legislative power in several colonies, by a council appointed, during pleasure, by the crown, is unconstitutional, dangerous, and destructive to the freedom of American legislation.

9 ∽

Radicals in the Massachusetts colonial assembly refused to dissolve, instead defying the Coercive Acts by organizing a provincial assembly that collected taxes and armaments for the colony itself. When British troops marched from Boston to suppress the assembly and arrest its leaders in 1775, militia loyal to the assembly took up arms.

Although the Continental Congress organized the militia into the Continental Army under the command of General George Washington, it delayed declaring independence. Prodded by the army and the colonial legislatures, the Congress appointed Thomas Jefferson, John Adams, and others to prepare a declaration justifying the repudiation of British authority. Jefferson prepared a statement, slightly modified by others, that applied the Whig philosophy of government and liberty to the revolutionary situation. Compare it to Locke's articulation of the Whig philosophy in Document 3.

The Declaration of Independence (1776)

The unanimous Declaration of the thirteen United States of America.

W HEN, IN THE Course of human events, it becomes necessary for one people to dissolve the political bands which have connected them with another, and to assume, among the Powers of the earth, the separate and equal station to which the Laws of Nature and of Nature's God entitle them, a decent respect to the opinions of mankind requires that they should declare the causes which impel them to the separation.

We hold these truths to be self-evident, that all men are created equal, that they are endowed by their Creator with certain unalienable Rights, that among these, are Life, Liberty, and the pursuit of Happiness. That, to secure these rights, Governments are instituted among Men, deriving their just Powers from the consent of the governed. That, whenever any form of Government becomes destructive of these ends, it is the Right of the People to alter or to abolish it, and to institute new Government, laying its foundation on such Principles, and organizing its Powers in such form, as to them shall seem most likely to effect their Safety and Happiness. Prudence, indeed, will dictate that Governments long established should not be changed for light and transient causes; and, accordingly, all experience hath shewn, that mankind are more disposed to suffer, while evils are sufferable, than to right themselves by abolishing the forms to which they are accustomed. But, when a long train of abuses and usurpations, pursuing invariably the same Object, evinces a design to reduce them under absolute Despotism, it is their right, it is their duty, to throw off such Government, and to provide new Guards for their future Security. Such has been the patient sufferance of these Colonies; and such is now the necessity which constrains them to alter their former Systems of Government. The history of the present King of Great Britain is a history of repeated injuries and usurpations, all having in direct object the establishment of an absolute Tyranny over these States. . . .

In every stage of these Oppressions, We have Petitioned for Redress, in the most humble terms: Our repeated Petitions, have been answered only by repeated injury. A Prince, whose character is thus marked by every act which may define a Tyrant, is unfit to be the ruler of a free People.

Nor have We been wanting in attentions to our Brittish brethren. We have warned them from time to time of attempts by their legislature to extend an unwarrantable jurisdiction over us. . . . They too have been deaf to the voice of justice and of consanguinity. We must, therefore, acquiesce in the necessity, which denounces our Separation, and hold them, as we hold the rest of mankind, Enemies in War, in Peace Friends.

We, therefore, the Representatives of the united States of America, in GENERAL CONGRESS assembled, appealing to the Supreme Judge of the World for the rectitude of our intentions, DO, in the Name, and by Authority of the good People of these Colonies, solemnly PUBLISH and DECLARE, That these United Colonies are, and of Right, ought to be free and Independent States; that they are Absolved from all Allegiance to the British Crown, and that all political connexion between them and the State of Great Britain, is and ought to be totally dissolved.

CHAPTER 4

Establishing New State and Federal Constitutions

10 ∾

Upon the break with Great Britain, most of the American states framed new constitutions, which generally included bills of rights. Many were influenced by Virginia's Declaration of Rights, which was prepared by George Mason and passed by Virginia's revolutionary convention shortly before the Continental Congress declared independence.

The Virginia Declaration of Rights (1776)

A DECLARATION of rights made by the representatives of the good people of Virginia, assembled in full and free convention; which rights do pertain to them and their posterity, as the basis and foundation of government.

Section 1. That all men are by nature equally free and independent, and have certain inherent rights, of which, when they enter into a state of society, they cannot, by any compact, deprive or divest their posterity; namely, the enjoyment of life and liberty, with the means of acquiring and possessing property, and pursuing and obtaining happiness and safety.

Sec. 2. That all power is vested in, and consequently derived from, the people; that magistrates are their trustees and servants, and at all times amenable to them.

Francis Newton Thorpe (comp.), *The Federal and State Constitutions, Colonial Charters, and Other Organic Laws of the States, Territories, and Colonies Now or Heretofore Forming the United States of America* (Washington, D.C.: Government Printing Office, 1909), 7: 3812–3814.

Sec. 3. That government is, or ought to be, instituted for the common benefit, protection, and security of the people, nation, or community; . . . and that, when any government shall be found inadequate or contrary to these purposes, a majority of the community hath an indubitable, inalienable, and indefeasible right to reform, alter, or abolish it, in such manner as shall be judged most conducive to the public weal.

Sec. 4. That no man, or set of men, are entitled to exclusive or separate emoluments or privileges from the community, but in consideration of public services. . . .

Sec. 5. That the legislative and executive powers of the State should be separate and distinct from the judiciary; and that the members of the two first may be restrained from oppression, by feeling and participating the burdens of the people, they should, at fixed periods, be reduced to a private station, return into that body from which they were originally taken, and the vacancies be supplied by frequent, certain, and regular elections. . . .

Sec. 6. That elections of members to serve as representatives of the people, in assembly, ought to be free; and that all men, having sufficient evidence of permanent common interest with, and attachment to, the community, have the right of suffrage, and cannot be taxed or deprived of their property for public uses, without their own consent, or that of their representatives so elected, nor bound by any law to which they have not, in like manner, assembled [assented], for the public good.

Sec. 7. That all power of suspending laws, or the execution of laws, by any authority, without consent of the representatives of the people, is injurious to their rights, and ought not to be exercised.

Sec. 8. That in all capital or criminal prosecutions a man hath a right to demand the cause and nature of his accusation, to be confronted with the accusers and witnesses, to call for evidence in his favor, and to a speedy trial by an impartial jury of twelve men of his vicinage, without whose unanimous consent he cannot be found guilty; nor can he be compelled to give evidence against himself; that no man be deprived of his liberty, except by the law of the land or the judgment of his peers.

Sec. 9. That excessive bail ought not to be required, nor excessive fines imposed, nor cruel and unusual punishments inflicted.

Sec. 10. That general warrants, whereby an officer or messenger may be commanded to search suspected places without evidence of [an act] committed, or to seize any person or persons not named, or whose offence is not particularly described and supported by evidence, are grievous and oppressive, and ought not to be granted.

Sec. 11. That in controversies respecting property, and in suits between man and man, the ancient trial by jury is preferable to any other, and ought to be held sacred.

Sec. 12. That the freedom of the press is one of the great bulwarks of liberty, and can never be restrained but by despotic governments.

Sec. 13. That a well-regulated militia, composed of the body of the people, trained to arms, is the proper, natural, and safe defence of a free State; that standing armies, in time of peace, should be avoided, as dangerous to liberty; and that in all cases the military should be under strict subordination to, and governed by, the civil power.

Sec. 14. That the people have a right to uniform government; and, therefore, that no government separate from, or independent of the government of Virginia, ought to be erected or established within the limits thereof.

Sec. 15. That no free government, or the blessings of liberty, can be preserved to any people, but by a firm adherence to justice, moderation, temperance, frugality, and virtue, and by frequent recurrence to fundamental principles.

Sec. 16. That religion, or the duty which we owe to our Creator, and the manner of discharging it, can be directed only by reason and conviction, not by force or violence; and therefore all men are equally entitled to the free exercise of religion, according to the dictates of conscience; and that it is the mutual duty of all to practise Christian forbearance, love, and charity towards each other.

11 ∾

Congress proposed the Articles of Confederation to the newly independent states in 1777, after watering down a draft that would have created a strong central government. The last of the thirteen new states did not ratify the proposal until 1781. Article II recognized the sovereignty of each state and limited the powers of Congress to those "expressly" delegated to it. These powers were primarily those Congress had come to exercise by 1777 in the course of the crisis with Britain.

"Continentalists," dissatisfied with the weak central government that the Articles created, consistently pressed the states to delegate more power to Congress, but the requirement that each state accede to any amendment frustrated their efforts.

The Articles of Confederation (1781)

Articles of Confederation and perpetual Union between the States of Newhampshire, Massachusetts-bay, Rhodeisland and Providence Plantations, Connecticut, New-York, New-Jersey, Pennsylvania, Delaware, Maryland, Virginia, North-Carolina, South-Carolina and Georgia.

Poore (comp.), *Federal and State Constitutions,* part 1, pp. 7–13.

ARTICLE I. The stile of this confederacy shall be "The United States of America."

ARTICLE II. Each State retains its sovereignty, freedom and independence, and every power, jurisdiction and right, which is not by this confederation expressly delegated to the United States, in Congress assembled.

ARTICLE III. The said States hereby severally enter into a firm league of friendship with each other, for their common defence, the security of their liberties, and their mutual and general welfare, binding themselves to assist each other, against all force offered to, or attacks made upon them, or any of them, on account of religion, sovereignty, trade, or any other pretence whatever.

ARTICLE IV. The better to secure and perpetuate mutual friendship and intercourse among the people of the different States in this Union, the free inhabitants of each of these States, paupers, vagabonds and fugitives from justice excepted, shall be entitled to all privileges and immunities of free citizens in the several States; and the people of each State shall have free ingress and regress to and from any other State, and shall enjoy therein all the privileges of trade and commerce, subject to the same duties, impositions and restrictions as the inhabitants thereof respectively. . . .

If any person guilty of, or charged with treason, felony, or other high misdemeanor in any State, shall flee from justice, and be found in any of the United States, he shall upon demand of the Governor or Executive power, of the State from which he fled, be delivered up and removed to the State having jurisdiction of his offence.

Full faith and credit shall be given in each of these States to the records, acts and judicial proceedings of the courts and magistrates of every other State.

ARTICLE V. For the more convenient management of the general interests of the United States, delegates shall be annually appointed in such manner as the legislature of each State shall direct, to meet in Congress on the first Monday in November, in every year. . . .

No State shall be represented in Congress by less than two, nor by more than seven members; and no person shall be capable of being a delegate for more than three years in any term of six years; nor shall any person, being a delegate, be capable of holding any office under the United States, for which he, or another for his benefit receives any salary, fees or emolument of any kind. . . .

In determining questions in the United States, in Congress assembled, each State shall have one vote.

Freedom of speech and debate in Congress shall not be impeached or questioned in any court, or place out of Congress, and the members of Congress shall be protected in their persons from arrests and imprisonments, during the time of their going to and from, and attendance on Congress, except for treason, felony, or breach of the peace.

ARTICLE VI. No State without the consent of the United States in Congress assembled, shall send any embassy to, or receive any embassy from, or enter into any conferrence, agreement, alliance or treaty with any king, prince or state; nor shall any person holding any office of profit or trust under the United States, or any of them, accept of any present, emolument, office or title of any kind whatever from any king, prince or foreign state; nor shall the United States in Congress assembled, or any of them, grant any title of nobility.

No two or more States shall enter into any treaty, confederation or alliance whatever between them, without the consent of the United States in Congress assembled. . . .

No vessels of war shall be kept up in time of peace by any State, except such number only, as shall be deemed necessary by the United States in Congress assembled, for the defence of such State, or its trade; nor shall any body of forces by kept up by any State, in time of peace, except such number only, as in the judgment of the United States, in Congress assembled, shall be deemed requisite to garrison the forts necessary for the defence of such State; but every State shall always keep up a well regulated and disciplined militia, sufficiently armed and accoutred. . . .

No State shall engage in any war without the consent of the United States in Congress assembled, unless such State be actually invaded by enemies, or shall have received certain advice of a resolution being formed by some nation of Indians to invade such State, and the danger is so imminent as not to admit of a delay, till the United States in Congress assembled can be consulted: nor shall any State grant commissions to any ships or vessels of war, nor letters of marque or reprisal, except it be after a declaration of war by the United States in Congress assembled. . . .

ARTICLE VII. When land-forces are raised by any State for the common defence, all officers of or under the rank of colonel, shall be appointed by the Legislature of each State respectively by whom such forces shall be raised. . . .

ARTICLE VIII. All charges of war, and all other expenses that shall be incurred for the common defence or general welfare, and allowed by the United States in Congress assembled, shall be defrayed out of a common treasury, which shall be supplied by the several States, in proportion to the value of all land within each State. . . .

The taxes for paying that proportion shall be laid and levied by the authority and direction of the Legislatures of the several States within the time agreed upon by the United States in Congress assembled.

ARTICLE IX. The United States in Congress assembled, shall have the sole and exclusive right and power of determining on peace and war, except in the cases mentioned in the sixth article—of sending and receiving ambassadors—entering into treaties and alliances, provided that no treaty of commerce shall be made whereby the legislative power of the respective States shall be restrained from imposing such imposts and duties on foreigners, as their own people are subjected to, or from prohibiting the exportation or importation, of any species of goods or commodities whatsoever—of establishing rules for deciding in all cases, what captures on land or water shall be legal, and in what manner prizes taken by land or naval forces in the service of the United States shall be divided or appropriated—of granting letters of marque and reprisal in times of peace—appointing courts for the trial of piracies and felonies committed on the high seas and establishing courts for receiving and determining finally appeals in all cases of captures, provided that no member of Congress shall be appointed a judge of any of the said courts.

The United States in Congress assembled shall also be the last resort on appeal in all disputes and differences now subsisting or that hereafter may rise between two or more States concerning boundary, jurisdiction or any other cause whatever; which authority shall always be exercised in the manner following. Whenever the legislative or executive authority or lawful agent of any State in controversy with another shall present a petition to Congress, stating the matter in question and praying for a hearing, notice thereof shall be given by order of Congress to the legislative or executive authority of the other State in controversy, and a day assigned for the appearance of the parties by their lawful agents, who shall then be directed to appoint by joint consent, commissioners or judges to constitute a court for hearing and determining the matter in question: but if they cannot agree, Congress shall name three persons out of each of the United States, and from the list of such persons each party shall alternately strike out one, the petitioners beginning, until the number shall be reduced to thirteen; and from that number not less than seven, nor more than nine names as Congress shall direct, shall in the presence of Congress be drawn out by lot, and the persons whose names shall be so drawn or any five of them, shall be commissioners or judges, to hear and finally determine the controversy. . . .

The United States in Congress assembled shall also have the sole and exclusive right and power of regulating the alloy and value of coin struck by their own authority, or by that of the respective States.—fixing the standard of weights and measures throughout the United States.—regulating the trade and managing all affairs with the Indians, not members of any of the States, provided that the legislative right of any State within its own limits be not infringed or violated—establishing and regulating post-offices from one State to another, throughout all the United States, and exacting such postage on the papers passing thro' the same as may be requisite to defray the expenses of the said office—appointing all officers of the land forces, in the service of the United States, excepting regimental officers—appointing all the officers of the naval forces, and commissioning all officers whatever in the service of the United States—making rules for the government and regulation of the said land and naval forces, and directing their operations.

The United States in Congress assembled shall have authority to appoint a committee, to sit in the recess of Congress, to be denominated "a Committee of the States," and to consist of one delegate from each State; and to appoint such other committees and civil officers as may be necessary for managing the general affairs of the United States under their direction—to appoint one of their number to preside, provided that no person be allowed to serve in the office of president more than one year in any term of three years; to ascertain the necessary sums of money to be raised for the service of the United States, and to appropriate and apply the same for defraying the public expenses—to borrow money, or emit bills on the credit of the United States, transmitting every half year to the respective States an account of the sums of money so borrowed or emitted,—to build and equip a navy—to agree upon the number of land forces, and to make requisitions from each State for its quota, in proportion to the number of white inhabitants in such State; which requisition shall be binding, and thereupon the Legislature of each State shall appoint the regimental officers, raise the men and cloath, arm and equip them in a soldier like manner, at the expense of the United States. . . .

The United States in Congress assembled shall never engage in a war, nor grant letters of marque and reprisal in time of peace, nor enter into any treaties or alliances, nor coin money, nor regulate the value thereof, nor ascertain the sums and expenses necessary for the defence and welfare of the United States, or any of them, nor emit bills, nor borrow money on the credit of the United States, nor appropriate money, nor agree upon the number of vessels of war, to be built or purchased, or the number of land or sea forces to be raised, nor appoint a commander in chief of the army or navy, unless nine States assent to the same: nor shall a question on any other point, except for adjourning from day to day be determined, unless by the votes of a majority of the United States in Congress assembled. . . .

ARTICLE X. The committee of the States, or any nine of them, shall be authorized to execute, in the recess of Congress, such of the powers of Congress as the United States in Congress assembled, by the consent of nine States, shall from time to time think expedient to vest them with. . . .

ARTICLE XI. Canada acceding to this confederation, and joining in the measures of the United States, shall be admitted into, and entitled to all the advantages of this Union: but no other colony shall be admitted into the same, unless such admission be agreed to by nine States.

ARTICLE XII. All bills of credit emitted, monies borrowed and debts contracted by, or under the authority of Congress, before the assembling of the

United States, in pursuance of the present confederation, shall be deemed and considered as a charge against the United States. . . .

ARTICLE XIII. Every State shall abide by the determinations of the United States in Congress assembled, on all questions which by this confederation are submitted to them. And the articles of this confederation shall be inviolably observed by every State, and the Union shall be perpetual; nor shall any alteration at any time hereafter be made in any of them; unless such alteration be agreed to in a Congress of the United States, and be afterwards confirmed by the Legislatures of every State.

12 ❧

The Articles of Confederation reflected the understanding of a federal system that was current in 1776: a federal system was one in which sovereign states bound themselves in a close alliance, acting together on matters of common concern. But such a system left the central government dependent on the individual states to carry out its directives. The failure of states to do so left the government created by the Articles starved for cash and unable to enforce its treaties and laws.

In an effort to strengthen the Union, the states in 1787 sent delegates to a constitutional convention at Philadelphia. Ultimately two plans emerged. The first, usually called the Virginia Plan, set up a national government and implicitly made the states subordinate to it. The New Jersey Plan, proposed in response, retained many of the elements of the Articles of Confederation but strengthened the central government. In the end, the delegates reached a compromise that established a new kind of federal government—one that had some features of a national government and others of a traditional federal government. For further discussion of the "compound" nature of the federal government, see James Madison's description in *Federalist No. 39* (Document 13).

The Virginia and New Jersey Plans (1787)

Resolutions proposed by Mr Randolph in Convention.

May 29. 1787.

1. Resolved that the articles of Confederation ought to be so corrected & enlarged as to accomplish the objects proposed by their institution; namely "common defence, security of liberty and general welfare."

Max Farrand (ed.), *The Records of the Federal Convention of 1787* (New Haven: Yale University Press, 1911), 1: 20–22, 242–245.

2. Resd. therefore that the rights of suffrage in the National Legislature ought to be proportioned to the Quotas of contribution, or to the number of free inhabitants, as the one or the other rule may seem best in different cases.

3. Resd. that the National Legislature ought to consist of two branches.

4. Resd. that the members of the first branch of the National Legislature ought to be elected by the people of the several States every   for the term of   . . . .

5. Resold. that the members of the second branch of the National Legislature ought to be elected by those of the first, out of a proper number of persons nominated by the individual Legislatures, to be of the age of   years at least; to hold their offices for a term sufficient to ensure their independency. . . .

6. Resolved that each branch ought to possess the right of originating Acts; that the National Legislature ought to be impowered to enjoy the Legislative Rights vested in Congress by the Confederation & moreover to legislate in all cases to which the separate States are incompetent, or in which the harmony of the United States may be interrupted by the exercise of individual Legislation; to negative all laws passed by the several States, contravening in the opinion of the National Legislature the articles of Union; and to call forth the force of the Union agst. any member of the Union failing to fulfill its duty under the articles thereof.

7. Resd. that a National Executive be instituted; to be chosen by the National Legislature for the term of   years, . . . and that besides a general authority to execute the National laws, it ought to enjoy the Executive rights vested in Congress by the Confederation.

8. Resd. that the Executive and a convenient number of the National Judiciary, ought to compose a council of revision with authority to examine every act of the National Legislature before it shall operate, & every act of a particular Legislature before a Negative thereon shall be final; and that the dissent of the said Council shall amount to a rejection, unless the Act of the National Legislature be again passed, or that of a particular Legislature be again negatived by   of the members of each branch.

9. Resd. that a National Judiciary be established to consist of one or more supreme tribunals, and of inferior tribunals to be chosen by the National Legislature, to hold their offices during good behaviour; . . . that the jurisdiction of the inferior tribunals shall be to hear & determine in the first instance, and of the supreme tribunal to hear and determine in the dernier resort, all piracies & felonies on the high seas, captures from an enemy; cases in which foreigners or citizens of other States applying to such jurisdictions may be in-

terested, or which respect the collection of the National revenue; impeach-ments of any National officers, and questions which may involve the national peace and harmony.

10. Resolvd. that provision ought to be made for the admission of States lawfully arising within the limits of the United States, whether from a volun-tary junction of Government & Territory or otherwise, with the consent of a number of voices in the National legislature less than the whole.

11. Resd. that a Republican Government & the territory of each State, ex-cept in the instance of a voluntary junction of Government & territory, ought to be guaranteed by the United States to each State. . . .

13. Resd. that provision ought to be made for the amendment of the Arti-cles of Union whensoever it shall seem necessary, and that the assent of the National Legislature ought not to be required thereto.

14. Resd. that the Legislative Executive & Judiciary powers within the sev-eral States ought to be bound by oath to support the articles of Union.

15. Resd. that the amendments which shall be offered to the Confedera-tion, by the Convention ought at a proper time, or times, after the approba-tion of Congress to be submitted to an assembly or assemblies of Representa-tives, recommended by the several Legislatures to be expressly chosen by the people, to consider & decide thereon.

Friday June 15th. (1787.)

Mr. Patterson, laid before the Convention the plan which he said several of the deputations wished to be substituted in place of that proposed by Mr. Randolp[h]. . . .

1. Resd. that the articles of Confederation ought to be so revised, corrected & enlarged, as to render the federal Constitution adequate to the exigences of Government, & the preservation of the Union.

2. Resd. that in addition to the powers vested in the U. States in Congress, by the present existing articles of Confederation, they be authorized to pass acts for raising a revenue, by levying a duty or duties on all goods or mer-chandizes of foreign growth or manufacture, imported into any part of the U. States, . . . and by a postage on all letters or packages passing through the general post-Office, to be applied to such federal purposes as they shall deem proper & expedient; to make rules & regulations for the collection thereof; . . . to pass Acts for the regulation of trade & commerce as well with foreign nations as with each other: provided that all punishments, fines, for-

feitures & penalties to be incurred for contravening such acts rules and regulations shall be adjudged by the Common law Judiciarys of the State in which any offence . . . shall have been committed or perpetrated, . . . subject nevertheless, for the correction of all errors, both in law & fact in rendering judgment, to an appeal to the Judiciary of the U. States[.]

3. Resd. that whenever requisitions shall be necessary, . . . the United States in Congs. be authorized to make such requisitions in proportion to the whole number of white & other free citizens & inhabitants of every age sex and condition including those bound to servitude for a term of years & three fifths of all other persons not comprehended in the foregoing description, except Indians not paying taxes; that if such requisitions be not complied with, in the time specified therein, to direct the collection thereof in the non complying States. . . .

4. Resd. that the U. States in Congs. be authorized to elect a federal Executive to consist of   persons, to continue in office for the term of
years . . . ; to be ineligible a second time, & removeable by Congs. on application by a majority of the Executives of the several States; that the Executives besides their general authority to execute the federal acts ought to appoint all federal officers not otherwise provided for, & to direct all military operations. . . .

5. Resd. that a federal Judiciary be established to consist of a supreme Tribunal the Judges of which to be appointed by the Executive, & to hold their offices during good behaviour . . . ; that the Judiciary so established shall have authority to hear & determine in the first instance on all impeachments of federal officers, & by way of appeal in the dernier resort in all cases touching the rights of Ambassadors, in all cases of captures from an enemy, in all cases of piracies & felonies on the high seas, in all cases in which foreigners may be interested, in the construction of any treaty or treaties, or which may arise on any of the Acts for regulation of trade, or the collection of the federal Revenue. . . .

6. Resd. that all Acts of the U. States in Congs. made by virtue & in pursuance of the powers hereby & by the articles of confederation vested in them, and all Treaties made & ratified under the authority of the U. States shall be the supreme law of the respective States so far forth as those Acts or Treaties shall relate to the said States or their Citizens, and that the Judiciary of the several States shall be bound thereby in their decisions, any thing in the respective laws of the Individual States to the contrary notwithstanding; and that if any State, or any body of men in any State shall oppose or prevent ye. carrying into execution such acts or treaties, the federal Executive shall be authorized to call forth ye power of the Confederated States . . . to enforce and compel an obedience to such Acts, or an Observance of such Treaties.

7. Resd. that provision be made for the admission of new States into the Union.

8. Resd. the rule for naturalization ought to be the same in every State[.]

13 ∾

Alexander Hamilton, James Madison, and John Jay wrote The Federalist Papers as part of the campaign to ratify the proposed Constitution. They appeared in New York newspapers over the signature "Publius." Although they were merely one group of arguments among many for ratification, by the nineteenth century they were recognized as profound statements of the political philosophy of the Constitution. The Federalist Papers remain among the most influential sources of constitutional interpretation today.

The Federalist Papers (1788)

Federalist No. 10 (Madison)

Federalist No. 10 is generally regarded as the most seminal of The Federalist Papers. In it Madison reversed traditional thinking, arguing that a large republic was more likely to solve the problems posed by factions than a small one. In traditional republican thought, a faction was a group that tried to gain control of government for its own purposes. Factions were the particular bane of republics.

Throughout history, republics had collapsed because of the disorder created by factional conflicts. Only populations with great public virtue could resist their blandishments. Initially optimistic about the public virtue of Americans, many revolutionary leaders were disillusioned by 1787. Everywhere, factional disputes seemed to rack the state governments. Many leaders hoped that a stronger central government might restore order. But opponents of the Constitution argued that factions would be even worse in a large republic, because there would be so many divergent economic interests, religions, and cultural traditions. Maintaining order in great empires had always required despotism; no large republic had ever retained liberty for long.

Madison challenged this conventional wisdom.

AMONG THE numerous advantages promised by a well-constructed Union, none deserves to be more accurately developed than its tendency to break and control the violence of faction. The friend of popular governments never finds himself so much alarmed for their character and fate as when he contemplates their propensity to this dangerous vice. . . . Complaints are everywhere heard from our most considerate and virtuous citizens, equally

Henry Cabot Lodge (ed.), *The Federalist: A Commentary on the Constitution of the United States* (N.Y. & London: G. P. Putman's Sons, 1888), 51–60, 232–239, 322–327.

the friends of public and private faith and of public and personal liberty, that our governments are too unstable, that the public good is disregarded in the conflicts of rival parties, and that measures are too often decided, not according to the rules of justice and the rights of the minor party, but by the superior force of an interested and overbearing majority. . . .

By a faction I understand a number of citizens, whether amounting to a majority or minority of the whole, who are united and actuated by some common impulse of passion, or of interest, adverse to the rights of other citizens, or to the permanent and aggregate interests of the community.

There are two methods of curing the mischiefs of faction: the one, by removing its causes; the other, by controlling its effects.

There are again two methods of removing the causes of faction: the one, by destroying the liberty which is essential to its existence; the other, by giving to every citizen the same opinions, the same passions, and the same interests.

It could never be more truly said than of the first remedy that it was worse than the disease. . . .

The second expedient is as impracticable as the first would be unwise. As long as the reason of man continues fallible, and he is at liberty to exercise it, different opinions will be formed. As long as the connection subsists between his reason and his self-love, his opinions and his passions will have a reciprocal influence on each other; and the former will be objects to which the latter will attach themselves. The diversity in the faculties of men, from which the rights of property originate, is not less an insuperable obstacle to a uniformity of interests. The protection of these faculties is the first object of government. From the protection of different and unequal faculties of acquiring property, the possession of different degrees and kinds of property immediately results; and from the influence of these on the sentiments and views of the respective proprietors ensues a division of the society into different interests and parties.

The latent causes of faction are thus sown in the nature of man; and we see them everywhere brought into different degrees of activity, according to the different circumstances of civil society. A zeal for different opinions concerning religion, concerning government, and many other points, as well of speculation as of practice; an attachment to different leaders ambitiously contending for pre-eminence and power; or to persons of other descriptions whose fortunes have been interesting to the human passions, have, in turn, divided mankind into parties, inflamed them with mutual animosity, and rendered them much more disposed to vex and oppress each other than to co-operate for their common good. . . . But the most common and durable source of factions has been the verious and unequal distribution of property. Those who hold and those who are without property have ever formed distinct interests in society. Those who are creditors, and those who are debtors, fall under a like discrimination. A landed interest, a manufacturing interest, a mercantile interest, a moneyed interest, with many lesser interests, grow up of necessity in civilized nations, and divide them into different classes, actuated by different sentiments and views. The regulation of these various and interfering interests forms the principal task of modern legislation and involves the spirit of party and faction in the necessary and ordinary operations of government. . . .

It is in vain to say that enlightened statesmen will be able to adjust these clashing interests, and render them all subservient to the public good. Enlightened statesmen will not always be at the helm. Nor, in many cases, can such an adjustment be made at all without taking into view indirect and remote considerations, which will rarely prevail over the immediate interest which one party may find in disregarding the rights of another or the good of the whole.

The inference to which we are brought is that the *causes* of faction cannot be removed, and that relief is only to be sought in the means of controlling its *effects*.

If a faction consists of less than a majority, relief is supplied by the republican principle, which enables the majority to defeat its sinister views by regular vote. . . . When a majority is included in a faction, the form of popular government, on the other hand, enables it to sacrifice to its ruling passion or interest both the public good and the rights of other citizens. To secure the public good and private rights against the danger of such a faction, and at the same time to preserve the spirit and the form of popular government, is then the great object to which our inquiries are directed. . . .

By what means is this object attainable? Evidently by one of two only. Either the existence of the same passion or interest in a majority at the same time must be prevented, or the majority, having such coexistent passion or interest, must be rendered, by their number and local situation, unable to concert and carry into effect schemes of oppression. . . .

From this view of the subject it may be concluded that a pure democracy, by which I mean a society consisting of a small number of citizens, who assemble and administer the government in person, can admit of no cure for the mischiefs of faction. A common passion or interest will, in almost every case, be felt by a majority of the whole; a communication and concert results from the form of government itself; and there is nothing to check the inducements to sacrifice the weaker party or an obnoxious individual. Hence it is that such democracies have ever been spectacles of turbulence and contention; have ever been found incompatible with personal security or the rights of property; and have in general been as short in their lives as they have been violent in their deaths. . . .

A republic, by which I mean a government in which the scheme of representation takes place, opens a different prospect and promises the cure for which we are seeking. Let us examine the points in which it varies from pure democracy, and we shall comprehend both the nature of the cure and the efficacy which it must derive from the Union.

The two great points of difference between a democracy and a republic are: first, the delegation of the government, in the latter, to a small number of citizens elected by the rest; secondly, the greater number of citizens, and greater sphere of country over which the latter may be extended.

The effect of the first difference is, on the one hand, to refine and enlarge the public views, by passing them through the medium of a chosen body of citizens, whose wisdom may best discern the true interest of their country, and whose patriotism and love of justice will be least likely to sacrifice it to temporary or partial considerations. Under such a regulation, it may well happen that the public voice, pronounced by the representatives of the people, will be more consonant to the public good than if pronounced by the people themselves, convened for the purpose. On the other hand, the effect may be inverted. Men of factious tempers, of local prejudices, or of sinister designs, may, by intrigue, by corruption, or by other means, first obtain the suffrages, and then betray the interests of the people. The question resulting is, whether small or extensive republics are most favorable to the election of proper guardians of the public weal; and it is clearly decided in favor of the latter by two obvious considerations. . . .

. . . [I]f the proportion of fit characters be not less in the large than in the small republic, the former will present a greater option, and consequently a greater probability of a fit choice.

In the next place, as each representative will be chosen by a greater number of citizens in the large than in the small republic, it will be more difficult for unworthy candidates to practise with success the vicious arts by which elections are too often carried; and the suffrages of the people being more free, will be more likely to center on men who possess the most attractive merit and the most diffusive and established characters. . . .

The other point of difference is the greater number of citizens and extent of territory which may be brought within the compass of republican than of democratic government; and it is this circumstance principally which renders factious combinations less to be dreaded in the former than in the latter. The smaller the society, the fewer probably will be the distinct parties and interests composing it; the fewer the distinct parties and interests, the more frequently will a majority be found of the same party; and the smaller the number of individuals composing a majority, and the smaller the compass within which they are placed, the more easily will they concert and execute their plans of oppression. Extend the sphere, and you take in a greater variety of parties and interests; you make it less probable that a majority of the whole will have a common motive to invade the rights of other citizens; or if such a common motive exists, it will be more difficult for all who feel it to discover their own strength and to act in unison with each other. . . .

Hence, it clearly appears, that the same advantage which a republic has over a democracy in controlling the effects of faction is enjoyed by a large over a small republic—is enjoyed by the Union over the States composing it. . . .

The influence of factious leaders may kindle a flame within their particular States, but will be unable to spread a general conflagration through the other States. A religious sect may degenerate into a political faction in a part of the Confederacy; but the variety of sects dispersed over the entire face of it must secure the national councils against any danger from that source. A rage for paper money, for an abolition of debts, for an equal division of property, or for any other improper or wicked project, will be less apt to pervade the whole body of the Union than a particular member of it, in the same proportion as such a malady is more likely to taint a particular county or district than an entire State.

In the extent and proper structure of the Union, therefore, we behold a republican remedy for the diseases most incident to republican government. And according to the degree of pleasure and pride we feel in being republicans ought to be our zeal in cherishing the spirit and supporting the character of federalists.

Federalist No. 39 (Madison)

Opponents of the Constitution charged that it would establish a national rather than a federal government. Again they warned that such a government, over so large an expanse of territory, would inevitably prove despotic. Liberty required that local affairs remain in local hands. Madison answered this charge in *Federalist No. 39*, pointing out that the proposed government contained both national and federal elements.

". . . **[I]**T WAS NOT sufficient," say the adversaries of the proposed Constitution, "for the convention to adhere to the republican form. They ought with equal care to have preserved the *federal* form, which regards the Union as a *Confederacy* of sovereign states; instead of which, they have framed a *national* government, which regards the Union as a *consolidation* of the States." And it is asked by what authority this bold and radical innovation was undertaken? The handle which has been made of this objection requires that it should be examined with some precision. . . .

In order to ascertain the real character of the government, it may be considered in relation to the foundation on which it is to be established; to the sources from which its ordinary powers are to be drawn; to the operation of those powers; to the extent of them; and to the authority by which future changes in the government are to be introduced.

On examining the first relation, it appears, on one hand, that the Constitution is to be founded on the assent and ratification of the people of America, given by deputies elected for the special purpose; but, on the other, that this assent and ratification is to be given by the people, not as individuals composing one entire nation, but as composing the distinct and independent States to which they respectively belong. It is to be the assent and ratification of the several States, derived from the supreme authority in each State—the authority of the people themselves. The act, therefore, establishing the Constitution will not be a *national* but a *federal* act.

That it will be a federal and not a national act, as these terms are understood by the objectors; the act of the people, as forming so many independent States, not as forming one aggregate nation, is obvious from this single consideration, that it is to result neither from the decision of a *majority* of the people of the Union, nor from that of a *majority* of the States. It must result from the *unanimous* assent of the several States that are parties to it. . . . Each State, in ratifying the Constitution, is considered as a sovereign body independent of all others, and only to be bound by its own voluntary act. In this relation, then, the new Constitution will, if established, be a *federal* and not a *national* constitution.

The next relation is to the sources from which the ordinary powers of government are to be derived. The House of Representatives will derive its powers from the people of America; and the people will be represented in the same proportion, and on the same principle as they are in the legislature of a particular State. So far the government is *national*, not *federal*. The Senate, on the other hand, will derive its powers from the States as political and coequal societies; and these will be represented on the principle of equality in the Senate, as they now are in the existing Congress. So far the government is *federal*, not *national*. The executive power will be derived from a very compound source. . . . From this aspect of the government it appears to be of a mixed character, presenting at least as many *federal* as *national* features.

The difference between a federal and national government, as it relates to the *operation of the government*, is by the adversaries of the plan of the convention supposed to consist in this, that in the former the powers operate on the political bodies composing the Confederacy in their political capacities; in the latter, on the individual citizens composing the nation in their individual capacities. On trying the Constitution by this criterion, it falls under the *national* not the *federal* character; though perhaps not so completely as has been understood. . . .

But if the government be national with regard to the *operation* of its powers, it changes its aspect again when we contemplate it in relation to the extent of its powers. The idea of a national government involves in it not only an authority over the individual citizens, but an indefinite supremacy over all persons and things, so far as they are objects of lawful government. Among a people consolidated into one nation, this supremacy is completely vested in the national legislature. Among communities united for particular purposes, it is vested partly in the general and partly in the municipal legislatures. In the former case, all local authorities are subordinate to the supreme; and may be controlled, directed, or abolished by it at pleasure. In the latter, the local or municipal authorities form distinct and independent portions of the supremacy, no more subject, within their respective spheres, to the general authority than the general authority is subject to them, within its own sphere. In this relation, then, the proposed government cannot be deemed a *national* one; since its jurisdiction extends to certain enumerated objects only, and leaves to the several States a residuary and inviolable sovereignty over all other objects. . . .

If we try the Constitution by its last relation to the authority by which amendments are to be made, we find it neither wholly *national* nor wholly *federal.* Were it wholly national, the supreme and ultimate authority would reside in the *majority* of the people of the Union; and this authority would be competent at all times, like that of a majority of every national society to alter or abolish its established government. Were it wholly federal, on the other hand, the concurrence of each State in the Union would be essential to every alteration that would be binding on all. The mode provided by the plan of the convention is not founded on either of these principles. In requiring more than a majority, and particularly in computing the proportion by *States,* not by *citizens,* it departs from the national and advances towards the *federal* character; in rendering the concurrence of less than the whole number of States sufficient, it loses again the *federal* and partakes of the *national* character.

The proposed Constitution, therefore, even when tested by the rules laid down by its antagonists, is, in strictness, neither a national nor a federal Constitution, but a composition of both. In its foundation it is federal, not national; in the sources from which the ordinary powers of the government are drawn, it is partly federal and partly national; in the operation of these powers, it is national, not federal; in the extent of them, again, it is federal, not national; and, finally in the authoritative mode of introducing amendments, it is neither wholly federal nor wholly national.

Federalist No. 51 (Madison)

In *Federalist No. 51* Madison pointed out how separation of powers and the compound of national and federal government would both protect liberty. The framers had created a new sort of federalism—one that retained its virtues but made possible a much more effective central government.

IN ORDER TO lay a due foundation for that separate and distinct exercise of the different powers of government, which to a certain extent is admitted on all hands to be essential to the preservation of liberty, it is evident that each department should have a will of its own; and consequently should be so constituted that the members of each should have as little agency as possible in the appointment of the members of the others. . . .

It is equally evident, that the members of each department should be as little dependent as possible on those of the others, for the emoluments annexed to their offices. Were the executive magistrate, or the judges, not independent of the legislature in this particular, their independence in every other would be merely nominal.

But the great security against a gradual concentration of the several powers in the same department, consists in giving to those who administer each department the necessary constitutional means and personal motives to resist encroachments of the others. The provision for defense must in this, as in all other cases, be made commensurate to the danger of attack. Ambition must be made to counteract ambition. The interest of the man must be connected with the constitutional rights of the place. It may be a reflection on human nature, that such devices should be necessary to control the abuses of government. But what is government itself but the greatest of all reflections on human nature? If men were angels, no government would be necessary. If angels were to govern men, neither external nor internal controls on government would be necessary. In framing a government which is to be administered by men over men, the great difficulty lies in this: you must first enable the government to control the governed; and in the next place oblige it to control itself. A dependence on the people is, no doubt, the primary control on the government; but experience has taught mankind the necessity of auxiliary precautions. . . .

But it is not possible to give to each department an equal power of self-defence. In republican government, the legislative authority necessarily predominates. The remedy for this inconveniency is to divide the legislature into different branches; and to render them, by different modes of election and different principles of action, as little connected with each other as the nature of their common functions and their common dependence on the society will admit. . . . As the weight of the legislative authority requires that it should be thus divided, the weakness of the executive may require, on the other hand, that it should be fortified. . . .

There are, moreover, . . . considerations particularly applicable to the federal system of America, which place that system in a very interesting point of view.

First. In a single republic, all the power surrendered by the people is submitted to the administration of a single government; and the usurpations are guarded against by a division of the government into distinct and separate departments. In the compound republic of America, the power surrendered by the people is first divided between two distinct governments, and then the portion allotted to each subdivided among distinct and separate departments. Hence a double security arises to the rights of the people. The different governments will control each other, at the same time that each will be controlled by itself.

CHAPTER 5

Constitutional Issues
in the Early Republic

14 ❧

Treasury Secretary Alexander Hamilton proposed creating a national bank as part of his ambitious plan to fund the national debt and promote economic development in the United States. Privately owned, although with government representatives among its directors, the bank would receive the deposits of the United States, creating a massive pool of capital to be lent for commercial purposes. The bank would be authorized to establish branches throughout the country.

Many Americans worried that such a bank would be an engine of corruption, as they believed the Bank of England to be in Great Britain. Not only would a national bank undermine republican virtue by promoting materialism and a taste for luxury, but it would tie the interests of its wealthy clientele to the politicians who controlled the government.

Doubting the power of the federal government to establish a national bank, President George Washington asked Secretary of State Thomas Jefferson, who opposed it, for an opinion as to its constitutionality. Jefferson obliged with an argument for the strict construction of federal power.

Thomas Jefferson, Opinion Against the Constitutionality of a National Bank (1791)

I CONSIDER the foundation of the Constitution as laid on this ground: That "all powers not delegated to the United States, by the Constitution, nor prohibited by it to the States, are reserved to the States or to the people." To

Paul Leicester Ford (ed.), *The Writings of Thomas Jefferson* (N.Y.: G. P. Putnam's Sons, 1985), 5: 145–153.

take a single step beyond the boundaries thus specially drawn around the powers of Congress, is to take possession of a boundless field of power, no longer susceptible of any definition.

The incorporation of a bank, and the powers assumed by this bill, have not, in my opinion, been delegated to the United States, by the Constitution.

I. They are not among the powers specially enumerated. . . .

II. Nor are they within either of the general phrases, which are the two following:—

1. To lay taxes to provide for the general welfare of the United States, that is to say, "to lay taxes for *the purpose* of providing for the general welfare."

For the laying of taxes is the *power,* and the general welfare the *purpose* for which the power is to be exercised. They are not to lay taxes *ad libitum for any purpose they please; but only to pay the debts or provide for the welfare of the Union.* In like manner, they are not *to do anything they please* to provide for the general welfare, but only to *lay taxes* for that purpose. To consider the latter phrase, not as describing the purpose of the first, but as giving a distinct and independent power to do any act they please, which might be for the good of the Union, would render all the preceding and subsequent enumerations of power completely useless.

It would reduce the whole instrument to a single phrase, that of instituting a Congress with power to do whatever would be for the good of the United States. . . .

. . . Certainly no such universal power was meant to be given them. It was intended to lace them up straitly within the enumerated powers, and those without which, as means, these powers could not be carried into effect. It is known that the very power now proposed *as a means* was rejected as *an end* by the Convention which formed the Constitution. . . .

2. The second general phrase is, "to make all laws *necessary* and proper for carrying into execution the enumerated powers." But they can all be carried into execution without a bank. A bank therefore is not *necessary,* and consequently not authorized by this phrase.

It has been urged that a bank will give great facility or convenience in the collection of taxes. Suppose this were true: yet the Constitution allows only the means which are "*necessary,*" not those which are merely "*convenient*" for effecting the enumerated powers. If such a latitude of construction be allowed to this phrase as to give any non-enumerated power, it will go to every one, for there is not one which ingenuity may not torture into a *convenience* in some instance *or other,* to *some one* of so long a list of enumerated powers. It would swallow up all the delegated powers, and reduce the whole to one power, as before observed. Therefore it was that the Constitution restrained them to the *necessary* means, that is to say, to those means without which the grant of power would be nugatory. . . .

Perhaps, indeed, bank bills may be a more *convenient* vehicle than treasury orders. But a little *difference* in the degree of *convenience,* cannot constitute the necessity which the Constitution makes the ground for assuming any non-enumerated power. . . .

Can it be thought that the Constitution intended that for a shade or two of *convenience,* more or less, Congress should be authorized to break down the most ancient and fundamental laws of the several States; such as those against Mortmain, the laws of Alienage, the rules of descent, the acts of distribution, the laws of escheat and forfeiture, the laws of monopoly? Nothing but a necessity invincible by any other means, can justify such a prostitution of laws, which constitute the pillars of our whole system of jurisprudence.

15 ⟳

Washington asked Hamilton to respond to Jefferson's argument. Hamilton did so with a powerful argument for broad construction of federal power. Washington came down on Hamilton's side and Congress passed the bill establishing the first Bank of the United States in 1791.

Alexander Hamilton, Opinion Sustaining the Constitutionality of a National Bank (1791)

. . . **[I]**T APPEARS to the Secretary of the Treasury that this *general principle* is *inherent* in the very *definition* of government, and *essential* to every step of the progress to be made by that of the United States, namely: That every power vested in a government is in its nature *sovereign,* and includes, by *force* of the *term,* a right to employ all the *means* requisite and fairly applicable to the attainment of the *ends* of such power, and which are not precluded by restrictions and exceptions specified in the Constitution, or not immoral, or not contrary to the *essential ends* of political society. . . .

If it would be necessary to bring proof to a proposition so clear, as that which affirms that the powers of the Federal Government, as to *its objects,* were sovereign, there is a clause of its Constitution which would be decisive. It is that which declares that the Constitution, and the laws of the United States made in

Henry Cabot Lodge (ed.), *The Works of Alexander Hamilton* (N.Y.: G. P. Putnam's Sons, 1904), 3: 445–494.

pursuance of it, and all treaties made, or which shall be made, under their authority, shall be the *supreme law of the land.* The power which can create the *supreme law of the land* in *any case,* is doubtless *sovereign* as to such case. . . .

[I]t is unquestionably incident to *sovereign power* to erect corporations, and consequently to *that* of the United States, in *relation* to the *objects* intrusted to the management of the government. The difference is this: where the authority of the government is general, it can create corporations in *all cases;* where it is confined to certain branches of legislation, it can create corporations *only* in those cases. . . .

For a more complete elucidation of the point, nevertheless, the arguments . . . against the power of the government to erect corporations, however foreign they are to the great and fundamental rule which has been stated, shall be particularly examined. . . .

The first of these arguments is, that the foundation of the Constitution is laid on this ground: "That all powers not delegated to the United States by the Constitution, nor prohibited by it to the States, are reserved to the States, or to the people." Whence it is meant to be inferred, that Congress can in no case exercise any power not included in those enumerated in the Constitution. And it is affirmed, that the power of erecting a corporation is not included in any of the enumerated powers. . . .

It is not denied that there are *implied,* as well as *express powers,* and that the *former* are as effectually delegated as the *latter.* . . .

Then it follows, that as a power of erecting a corporation may as well be *implied* as any other thing, it may as well be employed as an *instrument* or *means* of carrying into execution any of the specified powers, as any other *instrument* or *means* whatever. The only question must be in this, as in every other case, whether the means to be employed, or, in this instance, the corporation to be erected, has a natural relation to any of the acknowledged objects or lawful ends of the government. Thus a corporation may not be erected by Congress for superintending the police of the city of Philadelphia, because they are not authorized to *regulate* the *police* of that city. But one may be erected in relation to the collection of taxes, or to the trade with foreign countries, or to the trade between the States, or with the Indian tribes; because it is the province of the Federal Government to *regulate* those objects, and because it is incident to a general *sovereign* or *legislative* power to *regulate* a thing, to employ all the means which relate to its regulation to the best and greatest advantage. . . .

. . . [I]t is . . . be objected, that none but necessary and proper means are to be employed; and the Secretary of State maintains, that no means are to be considered *necessary* but those without which the grant of the power would be *nugatory.* . . .

It is essential to the being of the national government, that so erroneous a conception of the meaning of the word *necessary* should be exploded.

It is certain, that neither the grammatical nor popular sense of the term requires that construction. According to both, *necessary* often means no more than *needful, requisite, incidental, useful,* or *conducive to.* It is a common mode of expression to say, that it is *necessary* for a government or a person to do this or that thing, when nothing more is intended or understood, than that the interests of the government or person require, or will be promoted by, the doing of this or that thing. The imagination can be at no loss for exemplifications of the use of the word in this sense. And it is the true one in which it is to be understood as used in the Constitution. . . .

To understand the word as the Secretary of State does, would be to depart from its obvious and popular sense, and to give it a restrictive operation, an idea never before entertained. It would be to give it the same force as if the word *absolutely* or *indispensably* had been prefixed to it.

Such a construction would beget endless uncertainty and embarrassment. The cases must be palpable and extreme, in which it could be pronounced, with certainty, that a measure was absolutely necessary, or one, without which the exercise of a given power would be nugatory. There are few measures of any government which would stand so severe a test. . . .

The *degree* in which a measure is necessary can never be a *test* of the legal right to adopt it; that must be a matter of opinion, and can only be a *test* of expediency. The *relation* between the *measure* and the *end;* between the *nature* of the *means* employed towards the execution of a power, and the object of that power, must be the criterion of constitutionality, not the more or less of *necessity* or *utility.* . . .

But the doctrine which is contended for . . . does not affirm that the National Government is sovereign in all respects, but that it is sovereign to a certain extent—that is, to the extent of the objects of its specified powers.

It leaves, therefore, a criterion of what is constitutional, and of what is not so. This criterion is the *end,* to which the measure relates as a *means.* If the *end* be clearly comprehended within any of the specified powers, and if the measure have an obvious relation to that *end,* and is not forbidden by any particular provision of the Constitution, it may safely be deemed to come within the compass of the national authority. . . .

The Secretary of State introduces his opinion with an observation, that the proposed incorporation undertakes to create certain capacities, properties, or attributes, which are against the laws of *alienage, descents, escheat,* and *forfeiture, distribution* and *monopoly,* and to confer a power to make laws paramount to those of the States. . . .

But if it were even to be admitted that the erection of a corporation is a direct alteration of the stated laws, in the enumerated particulars, it would do nothing toward proving that the measure was unconstitutional. If the Government of the United States can do no act which amounts to an alteration of a State law, all its powers are nugatory; for almost every new law is an alteration, in some way or another, of an *old law,* either *common* or *statute.*

There are laws concerning bankruptcy in some States. Some States have laws regulating the values of foreign coins. Congress are empowered to establish uniform laws concerning bankruptcy throughout the United States, and to regulate the values of foreign coins. The exercise of either of these powers by Congress necessarily involves an alteration of the laws of those States. . . .

It can therefore never be good reasoning to say this or that act is unconstitutional, because it alters this or that law of a State. It must be shown that the act which makes the alteration is unconstitutional on other accounts; not *because* it makes the alteration.

16 ∾

favored Bank, Hamilton (Federa *Jefferson (Republic*

By the mid-1790s, two rival groups were fighting for control of the state and national governments. The Federalists endorsed Hamilton's economic policies, favored a pro-British foreign policy, worried about stability and order, and worked for a strong national government with broadly construed powers. The Republicans (often called Jeffersonian Republicans to distinguish them from the later antislavery party) opposed Hamilton's policies, favored a pro-French foreign policy, feared that Federalists were undermining liberty, and argued for state rights and a strict construction of the powers of the federal government.

In 1798, angry at bitter criticism from Republicans and worried about potential war with France, the Federalists passed the Alien and Sedition Acts. The Alien Act authorized the president to deport without trial any alien he considered dangerous. The Sedition Act made it a crime to falsely criticize government officials. Armed with these laws, Federalist district attorneys and judges began to prosecute Republican newspaper editors and publicists.

The Republican-controlled legislatures of Kentucky and Virginia passed resolutions, written by Jefferson and Madison respectively, declaring the laws unconstitutional. The resolutions not only defended state rights but claimed that the states were sovereign and thus had the final authority to determine the constitutionality of federal legislation. After Federalist-controlled state legislatures denounced the Republican position, Kentucky and Virginia passed even more trenchant statements.

The Kentucky and Virginia Resolutions laid the foundations for two related state-oriented theories of federalism. The first, most apparent in the resolutions, was the theory of state sovereignty, which suggested that the states retained ultimate sovereignty in the federal system and were therefore superior to the federal government. The Kentucky Resolutions of 1799 implied that as sovereignties, the states had the final say on constitutional issues and could nullify unconstitutional federal laws. In later decades, state-sovereignty theorists would elaborate upon this proposition to argue that the federal government was the agent of the states, bound to act in all their interests equally, with no independent interests or will of its own.

The second state-oriented theory of federalism, still embryonic in the Kentucky and

Virginia Resolutions, was the theory of state rights. State-rights theory posited a basic equality between the state and federal governments, both of which were sovereign. Advocates of state rights believed that this dual sovereignty created a tension between state and federal authority requiring that a line be drawn to separate the jurisdiction of one from the other—an idea scholars came to call "dual federalism." Note how the Kentucky Resolutions of 1798 warned that federal legislation had crossed the line and was undermining states' control of their own institutions.

The Kentucky Resolutions (1798, 1799)

Kentucky House of Representatives, November 10, 1798

1. *Resolved,* That the several states composing the United States of America are not united on the principle of unlimited submission to their general government; but that, by compact, under the style and title of a Constitution for the United States, and of amendments thereto, they constituted a general government for special purposes, delegated to that government certain definite powers, reserving, each state to itself, the residuary mass of right to their own self-government; and that whensoever the general government assumes undelegated powers, its acts are unauthoritative, void, and of no force; that to this compact each state acceded as a state, and is an integral party; that this government, created by this compact, was not made the exclusive or final judge of the extent of the powers delegated to itself, since that would have made its discretion, and not the Constitution, the measure of its powers; but that, as in all other cases of compact among parties having no common judge, *each party has an equal right to judge for itself, as well of infractions as of the mode and measure of redress. . . .*

3. *Resolved,* That it is true, as a general principle, and is also expressly declared by one of the amendments to the Constitution, that "the powers not delegated to the United States by the Constitution, nor prohibited by it to the states, are reserved to the states respectively, or to the people"; and that, no power over the freedom of religion, freedom of speech, or freedom of the press, being delegated to the United States by the Constitution, nor prohibited by it to the states, all lawful powers respecting the same did of right remain, and were reserved to the states, or to the people; that thus was manifested their determination to retain to themselves the right of judging how far the licentiousness of speech, and of the press, may be abridged without lessening their useful freedom, and how far those abuses which cannot be separated from their use,

Jonathan Elliot (ed.), *The Debates in the Several State Conventions on the Adoption of the Federal Constitution . . . Together with the . . . Virginia and Kentucky Resolutions of '98–'99* (Washington: Jonathan Elliot, 1836), 4: 540–545.

should be tolerated rather than the use be destroyed; . . . and that, in addition to this general principle and express declaration, another and more special provision, has been made by one of the amendments to the Constitution, which expressly declares, that "Congress shall make no laws respecting an establishment of religion, or prohibiting the free exercise thereof, or abridging the freedom of speech, or of the press," thereby guarding, in the same sentence, and under the same words, the freedom of religion, of speech, and of the press, insomuch that whatever violates either throws down the sanctuary which covers the others,—and that libels, falsehood, and defamation, equally with heresy and false religion, are withheld from the cognizance of federal tribunals. That therefore the act of the Congress of the United States, passed on the 14th of July, 1798, entitled "An Act in Addition to the Act entitled 'An Act for the Punishment of certain Crimes against the United States,'" which does abridge the freedom of the press, is not law, but is altogether void, and of no force. . . .

6. *Resolved*, That the imprisonment of a person under the protection of the laws of this commonwealth, on his failure to obey the simple order of the President to depart out of the United States, as is undertaken by the said act, entitled, "An Act concerning Aliens," is contrary to the Constitution, one amendment in which has provided, that "no person shall be deprived of liberty without due process of law"; and that another having provided, "that, in all criminal prosecutions, the accused shall enjoy the right of a public trial by an impartial jury, to be informed as to the nature and cause of the accusation, to be confronted with the witnesses against him, to have compulsory process for obtaining witnesses in his favor, and to have assistance of counsel for his defence," the same act undertaking to authorize the President to remove a person out of the United States who is under the protection of the law, on his own suspicion . . . —contrary to these provisions also of the Constitution—is therefore not law, but utterly void, and of no force. . . .

8. *Resolved*, That the preceding resolutions be transmitted to the senators and representatives in Congress from this commonwealth, who are enjoined to present the same to their respective houses, and to use their best endeavors to procure, at the next session of Congress, a repeal of the aforesaid unconstitutional and obnoxious acts.

9. *Resolved*, lastly, That the governor of this commonwealth be, and is, authorized and requested to communicate the preceding resolutions to the legislatures of the several states, to assure them that this commonwealth considers union for special national purposes, and particularly for those specified in their late federal compact, to be friendly to the peace, happiness, and prosperity, of all the states; that, faithful to that compact, according to the plain intent and meaning in which it was understood and acceded to by the several parties, it is sincerely anxious for its preservation; that it does also believe,

that, to take from the states all the powers of self-government, and transfer them to a general and consolidated government, without regard to the special government, and reservations solemnly agreed to in that compact, is not for the peace, happiness, or prosperity of these states; and that, therefore, this commonwealth is determined, as it doubts not its co-states are, to submit to undelegated and consequently unlimited powers in no man, or body of men, on earth. . . .

. . . That this commonwealth does therefore call on its co-states for an expression of their sentiments on the acts concerning aliens, and for the punishment of certain crimes herein before specified, plainly declaring whether these acts are or are not authorized by the federal compact . . . ; and that the co-states, recurring to their natural rights not made federal, will concur in declaring these void and of no force, and will each unite with this commonwealth in requesting their repeal at the next session of Congress.

The Kentucky House of Representatives, Thursday, November 17, 1799

. . . [T] HE SPEAKER resumed the chair, and Mr. Desha reported, that the committee had taken under consideration sundry resolutions passed by several state legislatures, on the subject of the Alien and Sedition Laws, and had come to a resolution thereupon, which he delivered in at the clerk's table, where it was read and *unanimously* agreed to by the house, as follows:—

The representatives of the good people of this commonwealth, in General Assembly convened, having maturely considered the answers of sundry states in the Union to their resolutions, passed the last session, respecting certain unconstitutional laws of Congress, commonly called the Alien and Sedition Laws, would be faithless, indeed, to themselves, and to those they represent, were they silently to acquiesce in the principles and doctrines attempted to be maintained in all those answers, that of Virginia only excepted. To again enter the field of argument, and attempt more fully or forcibly to expose the unconstitutionality of those obnoxious laws, would, it is apprehended, be as unnecessary as unavailing. We cannot, however, but lament that, in the discussion of those interesting subjects by sundry of the legislatures of our sister states, unfounded suggestions and uncandid insinuations, derogatory to the true character and principles of this commonwealth, have been substituted in place of fair reasoning and sound argument. Our opinions of these alarming measures of the general government, together with our reasons for those opinions, were detailed with decency and with temper, and submitted to the discussion and judgment of our fellow citizens throughout the Union.

Resolved, . . . That the principle and construction, contended for by sundry of the state legislatures, that the general government is the exclusive judge of the extent of the powers delegated to it, stop not short of *despotism*—since the discretion of those who administer the government, and not the *Constitution,* would be the measure of their powers: That the several states who formed that instrument, being sovereign and independent, have the unquestionable right to judge of the infraction; and, *That a nullification, by those sovereignties, of all unauthorized acts done under color of that instrument, is the rightful remedy:* That this commonwealth does, under the most deliberate reconsideration, declare, that the said Alien and Sedition Laws are, in their opinion, palpable violations of the said Constitution; . . That, although this commonwealth, as a party to the federal compact, will bow to the laws of the Union, yet it does, at the same time, declare, that it will not now, or ever hereafter, cease to oppose, in a constitutional manner, every attempt, at what quarter soever offered, to violate that compact: And finally, in order that no pretext or arguments may be drawn from a supposed acquiescence, on the part of this commonwealth, in the constitutionality of those laws, and be thereby used as precedents for similar future violations of the federal compact, this commonwealth does now enter against them its solemn PROTEST.

17

During their battle against the Federalists, the Republicans identified themselves as the defenders of freedom of speech and the press. Their leader, Thomas Jefferson, had long argued against government coercion of people's beliefs, especially in matters of religion. Elected president in 1800, Jefferson applied his insight to politics, while at the same time restating the basic principles of his Republican party, in his inaugural address.

Thomas Jefferson, First Inaugural Address (1801)

DURING THE contest of opinion through which we have passed the animation of discussions and of exertions has sometimes worn an aspect which might impose on strangers unused to think freely and to speak and to write what they think; but this being now decided by the voice of the nation, announced according to the rules of the Constitution, all will, of course, arrange themselves under the will of the law, and unite in common efforts for the common good. All, too, will bear in mind this sacred principle, that though the will of the majority is in all cases to prevail, that will to be rightful must be reasonable; that the minority possess their equal rights, which equal

James D. Richardson (ed.), *A Compilation of the Messages and Papers of the Presidents, 1789–1897* (Washington, D.C.: Government Printing Office, 1896–1897), 1: 321–324.

law must protect, and to violate would be oppression. Let us, then, fellow-citizens, unite with one heart and one mind. Let us restore to social intercourse that harmony and affection without which liberty and even life itself are but dreary things. And let us reflect that, having banished from our land that religious intolerance under which mankind so long bled and suffered, we have yet gained little if we countenance a political intolerance as despotic, as wicked, and capable of as bitter and bloody persecutions. During the throes and convulsions of the ancient world, during the agonizing spasms of infuriated man, seeking through blood and slaughter his long-lost liberty, it was not wonderful that the agitation of the billows should reach even this distant and peaceful shore; that this should be more felt and feared by some and less by others, and should divide opinions as to measures of safety. But every difference of opinion is not a difference of principle. We have called by different names brethren of the same principle. We are all Republicans, we are all Federalists. If there be any among us who would wish to dissolve this Union or to change its republican form, let them stand undisturbed as monuments of the safety with which error of opinion may be tolerated where reason is left free to combat it. . . .

About to enter, fellow-citizens, on the exercise of duties which comprehend everything dear and valuable to you, it is proper you should understand what I deem the essential principles of our Government, and consequently those which ought to shape its Administration. I will compress them within the narrowest compass they will bear, stating the general principle, but not all its limitations. Equal and exact justice to all men, of whatever state or persuasion, religious or political; peace, commerce, and honest friendship with all nations, entangling alliances with none; the support of the State governments in all their rights, as the most competent administrations for our domestic concerns and the surest bulwarks against antirepublican tendencies; the preservation of the General Government in its whole constitutional vigor . . . ; a jealous care of the right of election by the people . . . ; absolute acquiescence in the decisions of the majority, the vital principle of republics . . . ; a well-disciplined militia, our best reliance in peace and for the first moments of war, till regulars may relieve them; the supremacy of the civil over the military authority; economy in the public expense, that labor may be lightly burthened; the honest payment of our debts and sacred preservation of the public faith; encouragement of agriculture, and of commerce as its handmaid; the diffusion of information and arraignment of all abuses at the bar of the public reason; freedom of religion; freedom of the press, and freedom of person under the protection of the habeas corpus, and trial by juries impartially selected.

C H A P T E R 6

Judicial Review, Nationalism, and State Sovereignty

18 ∾

By 1800 the belief was widespread, although not universal, that judges must refuse to enforce laws that violated constitutional limitations, in effect declaring them unconstitutional. Federalists believed that such "judicial review" was essential to preserving liberty. Republicans were more ambivalent, especially as Federalists passed a law increasing the size of the federal judiciary immediately after their defeat in 1800 and named Federalist partisans to the bench. Republicans feared that the judges would arbitrarily overturn Republican legislation, and they had difficulty reconciling the principle of judicial review with their commitment to legislative democracy.

In this environment, John Marshall, newly named chief justice of the Supreme Court, engineered the case of *Marbury v. Madison.* Marbury had been nominated and confirmed as a justice of the peace in Washington. As secretary of state, the Federalist Marshall had himself signed Marbury's commission and left it on the desk of the incoming Republican secretary of state, James Madison. Madison refused to deliver it, expecting the new Republican Congress to repeal the law creating Marbury's position. Encouraged by Marshall, Marbury sought a writ of mandamus from the Supreme Court to force Madison to deliver his commission. Section 13 of the Judiciary Act of 1789 authorized the Court to issue such writs.

Speaking for a unanimous Court, Marshall first held that Marbury was entitled to his writ if the Court were authorized to issue it. But he then held that the law empowering the Court to issue the writ was unconstitutional, making a powerful and almost unanswerable argument in favor of judicial review. Given the facts of the case, there was no way for the Jefferson administration to defy the ruling.

In fact, Congress had never intended to authorize the Court to issue the writ in cases like Marbury's, and Marshall could have simply ruled that Marbury had misinterpreted the Judiciary Act. But Marshall had wanted the opportunity to endorse judicial review, and he took advantage of Marbury's case to make a ringing declaration that remains the leading Court opinion on the matter to this day.

Marbury v. Madison (1803)

THIS . . . IS a plain case for a mandamus, either to deliver the commission, or a copy of it from the record; and it only remains to be inquired,

Whether it can issue from this court.

The act to establish the judicial courts of the United States authorizes the Supreme Court "to issue writs of mandamus in cases warranted by the principles and usages of law, to any courts appointed, or persons holding office, under the authority of the United States." . . .

The constitution vests the whole judicial power of the United States in one Supreme Court, and such inferior courts as congress shall, from time to time, ordain and establish. . . .

In the distribution of this power it is declared that "the Supreme Court shall have original jurisdiction in all cases affecting ambassadors, other public ministers and consuls, and those in which a state shall be a party. In all other cases, the Supreme Court shall have appellate jurisdiction." . . .

When an instrument organizing fundamentally a judicial system, divides it into one supreme, and so many inferior courts as the legislature may ordain and establish; then enumerates its powers, and proceeds so far to distribute them, as to define the jurisdiction of the Supreme Court by declaring the cases in which it shall take original jurisdiction, and that in others it shall take appellate jurisdiction; the plain import of the words seems to be, that in one class of cases its jurisdiction is original, and not appellate; in the other it is appellate, and not original. . . .

To enable this court, then, to issue a mandamus, it must be shown to be an exercise of appellate jurisdiction, or to be necessary to enable them to exercise appellate jurisdiction.

. . . [T]o issue such a writ to an officer for the delivery of a paper . . . seems not to belong to appellate but to original jurisdiction. Neither is it necessary in such a case as this, to enable the court to exercise its appellate jurisdiction.

The authority, therefore, given to the Supreme Court, by the act establishing the judicial courts of the United States, to issue writs of mandamus to public officers, appears not to be warranted by the constitution; and it becomes necessary to inquire whether a jurisdiction so conferred can be exercised.

The question, whether an act, repugnant to the constitution, can become the law of the land, is a question deeply interesting to the United States; but, happily, not of an intricacy proportioned to its interest. It seems only neces-

5 U.S. (1 Cranch) 137 (1803).

sary to recognize certain principles, supposed to have been long and well established, to decide it.

That the people have an original right to establish, for their future government, such principles, as, in their opinion, shall most conduce to their own happiness is the basis on which the whole American fabric has been erected. The exercise of this original right is a very great exertion; nor can it, nor ought it, to be frequently repeated. The principles, therefore, so established, are deemed fundamental. And as the authority from which they proceed is supreme, and can seldom act, they are designed to be permanent.

This original and supreme will organizes the government, and assigns to different departments their respective powers. It may either stop here, or establish certain limits not to be transcended by those departments.

The government of the United States is of the latter description. The powers of the legislature are defined and limited; and that those limits may not be mistaken, or forgotten, the constitution is written. To what purpose are powers limited, and to what purpose is that limitation committed to writing, if these limits may, at any time, be passed by those intended to be restrained? The distinction between a government with limited and unlimited powers is abolished, if those limits do not confine the persons on whom they are imposed, and if acts prohibited and acts allowed, are of equal obligation. It is a proposition too plain to be contested, that the constitution controls any legislative act repugnant to it; or, that the legislature may alter the constitution by an ordinary act.

Between these alternatives there is no middle ground. The constitution is either a superior paramount law, unchangeable by ordinary means, or it is on a level with ordinary legislative acts, and, like other acts, is alterable when the legislature shall please to alter it.

If the former part of the alternative be true, then a legislature act contrary to the constitution is not law; if the latter part be true, then written constitutions are absurd attempts, on the part of the people, to limit a power in its own nature illimitable.

Certainly all those who have framed written constitutions contemplate them as forming the fundamental and paramount law of the nation, and, consequently, the theory of every such government must be, that an act of the legislature, repugnant to the constitution, is void. . . .

If an act of the legislature, repugnant to the constitution, is void, does it, notwithstanding its invalidity, bind the courts, and oblige them to give it effect? Or, in other words, though it be not law, does it constitute a rule as operative as if it was a law? This would be to overthrow in fact what was established in theory; and would seem, at first view, an absurdity too gross to be insisted on. It shall, however, receive a more attentive consideration.

It is emphatically the province and duty of the judicial department to say what the law is. Those who apply the rule to particular cases, must of necessity expound and interpret that rule. If two laws conflict with each other, the courts must decide on the operation of each.

So if a law be in opposition to the constitution; if both the law and the constitution apply to a particular case, so that the court must either decide that case conformably to the law, disregarding the constitution; or conformably to the constitution, disregarding the law; the court must determine which of these conflicting rules governs the case. This is of the very essence of judicial duty.

If, then, the courts are to regard the constitution, and the constitution is superior to any ordinary act of the legislature, the constitution, and not such ordinary act, must govern the case to which they both apply.

Those, then, who controvert the principle that the constitution is to be considered, in court, as a paramount law, are reduced to the necessity of maintaining that courts must close their eyes on the constitution, and see only the law.

This doctrine would subvert the very foundation of all written constitutions. It would declare that an act which, according to the principles and theory of our government, is entirely void, is yet, in practice, completely obligatory. It would declare that if the legislature shall do what is expressly forbidden, such act, notwithstanding the express prohibition, is in reality effectual. It would be given to the legislature a practical and real omnipotence, with the same breath which professes to restrict their powers within narrow limits. It is prescribing limits, and declaring that those limits may be passed at pleasure....

The rule must be discharged.

19 ∾

In the Dartmouth College Case, the Supreme Court interpreted the Obligation of Contracts Clause of Article I, section 10 of the constitution in a way that expanded the protection of property rights. In 1769 a royal charter had established New Hampshire's Dartmouth College, donating land to support it and authorizing a self-sustaining board of trustees to administer it. By the early 1800s, the oligarchical board was a pillar of the state's Federalist establishment, with Republicans criticizing its special privileges. In 1816 a newly elected Republican governor and state legislature intervened in a dispute between the trustees and the college's president by revising the charter and opening the board up to new members selected by the state. The old trustees challenged the law in the New Hampshire courts, saying that it deprived them of property without due process of law. The state courts rejected the argument, holding that Dartmouth was a public institution and thus subject to legislative control.

The trustees, represented by Daniel Webster, appealed to the Supreme Court, arguing that the original charter amounted to a contract, which the state was forbidden to impair by the Obligations of Contracts Clause. Denying that Dartmouth was a public institution, Marshall and a unanimous Court endorsed Webster's argument. The decision meant that states would be unable to alter any charters they had issued to private groups.

The implications of the decision were enormous, because states were beginning to issue corporate charters to businesses to help foster economic development. State legislatures minimized the impact by inserting provisions into new charters reserving the right to make future modifications. But many companies retained old charters that vested them with rights that could obstruct government efforts to regulate them or promote economic development. Moreover, Marshall's opinion reinforced the tendency of judges to see themselves as the protectors of property rights against heedless legislatures.

Dartmouth College v. Woodward (1819)

THE OPINION of the Court was delivered by Mr. Chief Justice Marshall. . . .

The Superior Court of Judicature of New-Hampshire rendered a judgment upon this verdict for the defendant, which judgment has been brought before this Court by writ of error. The single question now to be considered is, do the acts to which the verdict refers violate the constitution of the United States?

This Court can be insensible neither to the magnitude nor delicacy of this question. . . . On more than one occasion, this Court has expressed the cautious circumspection with which it approaches the consideration of such questions; and has declared, that, in no doubtful case, would it pronounce a legislative act to be contrary to the constitution. . . .

The points for consideration are,

1. Is this contract protected by the constitution of the United States?

2. Is it impaired by the acts under which the defendant holds? . . .

. . . If the act of incorporation be a grant of political power, if it create[s] a civil institution to be employed in the administration of the government, or if the funds of the college be public property, or if the State of New-Hampshire, as a government, be alone interested in its transactions, the subject is one in which the legislature of the State may act according to its own judgment, unrestrained by any limitation of its power imposed by the constitution of the United States. . . .

17 U.S. (4 Wheaton) 518 (1819).

. . . Dartmouth College is really endowed by private individuals, who have bestowed their funds for the propagation of the christian religion among the Indians, and for the promotion of piety and learning generally. From these funds the salaries of the tutors are drawn; and these salaries lessen the expense of education to the students. It is then eleemosynary, and, as far as respects its funds, a private corporation. . . .

. . . It is no more a State instrument, than a natural person exercising the same powers would be. . . .

From this review of the charter, it appears, that Dartmouth College is an eleemosynary institution, incorporated for the purpose of perpetuating the application of the bounty of the donors, to the specified objects of that bounty; that its trustees or governors were originally named by the founder, and invested with the power of perpetuating themselves; that they are not public officers, nor is it a civil institution, participating in the administration of government; but a charity school, or a seminary of education, incorporated for the preservation of its property, and the perpetual application of that property to the objects of its creation. . . .

[The charter] is plainly a contract to which the donors, the trustees, and the crown, (to whose rights and obligations New-Hampshire succeeds,) were the original parties. It is a contract made on a valuable consideration. It is a contract for the security and disposition of property. It is a contract, on the faith of which, real and personal estate has been conveyed to the corporation. . . .

We next proceed to the inquiry, whether its obligation has been impaired by those acts of the legislature of New-Hampshire, to which the special verdict refers.

From the review of this charter, which has been taken, it appears, that the whole power of governing the college, of appointing and removing tutors, of fixing their salaries, of directing the course of study to be pursued by the students, and of filling up vacancies created in their own body, was vested in the trustees. On the part of the crown it was expressly stipulated, that this corporation, thus constituted, should continue forever; and that the number of trustees should forever consist of twelve, and no more. By this contract the crown was bound, and could have made no violent alteration in its essential terms, without impairing its obligation.

. . . It is too clear to require the support of argument, that all contracts, and rights, respecting property, remained unchanged by the revolution. The obligations then, which were created by the charter to Dartmouth College, were the same in the new, that they had been in the old government. The power of the government was also the same. A repeal of this charter at any time prior to the adoption of the present constitution of the United States, would have been an extraordinary and unprecedented act of power, but one which could have been contested only by the restrictions upon the legislature, to be found in the constitution of the State. But the constitution of the United States has imposed this additional limitation, that the legislature of a State shall pass no act "impairing the obligation of contracts."

It has been already stated, that the act "to amend the charter, and enlarge and improve the corporation of Dartmouth College," increases the number of trustees to twenty-one, gives the appointment of the additional members to the executive of the State, and creates a board of overseers, to consist of twenty-five persons, of whom twenty-one are also appointed by the executive of New-Hampshire, who have power to inspect and control the most important acts of the trustees.

On the effect of this law, two opinions cannot be entertained. . . . The whole power of governing the college is transferred from trustees appointed according to the will of the founder, expressed in the charter, to the executive of New-Hampshire. . . . The will of the State is substituted for the will of the donors, in every essential operation of the college. . . . The charter of 1769 exists no longer. It is reorganized; and reorganized in such a manner, as to convert a literary institution, moulded according to the will of its founders, and placed under the control of private literary men, into a machine entirely subservient to the will of government. . . .

It results from this opinion, that the acts of the legislature of New-Hampshire . . . are repugnant to the constitution of the United States; and that the judgment on this special verdict ought to have been for the plaintiffs. The judgment of the State Court must, therefore, be reversed.

20 ⌒∿

The charter of the first Bank of the United States expired in 1811. After some hesitation, nationalist Republicans passed a bill chartering a second national bank in 1816. State rights–oriented Republicans opposed the measure, and the legislatures of several states tried to prevent the bank from opening branches within their boundaries. Among them was Maryland, which imposed a stiff tax on branches of banks not chartered by the state. McCulloch, chief officer of the U.S. bank's Maryland branch, refused to pay. The state courts upheld the Maryland law, and McCulloch appealed to the Supreme Court. Maryland challenged the constitutionality of the law establishing the national bank. Even if the bank were constitutional, Maryland insisted, the state had the sovereign power to levy a tax on any property within its boundaries.

The case raised the issue of strict versus broad construction that Hamilton and Jefferson had argued nearly thirty years earlier and that still separated nationalist from state-rights constitutionalism. In another powerful opinion, one that is still the leading statement of the Court on the powers of the federal government, Marshall upheld national supremacy and the broad-constructionist position.

McCulloch v. Maryland (1819)

M R . C H I E F Justice Marshall delivered the opinion of the Court.

In the case now to be determined, the defendant, a sovereign State, denies the obligation of a law enacted by the legislature of the Union, and the plaintiff, on his part, contests the validity of an act which has been passed by the legislature of that State. The constitution of our country, in its most interesting and vital parts, is to be considered; the conflicting powers of the government of the Union and of its members, as marked in that constitution, are to be discussed; and an opinion given, which may essentially influence the great operations of the government. No tribunal can approach such a question without a deep sense of its importance, and of the awful responsibility involved in its decision. . . .

The first question made in the cause is, has Congress power to incorporate a bank? . . .

In discussing this question, the counsel for the State of Maryland have deemed it of some importance, in the construction of the constitution, to consider that instrument not as emanating from the people, but as the act of sovereign and independent States. The powers of the general government, it has been said, are delegated by the States, who alone are truly sovereign; and must be exercised in subordination to the States, who alone possess supreme dominion.

It would be difficult to sustain this proposition. The Convention which framed the constitution was indeed elected by the State legislatures. But the instrument, when it came from their hands, was a mere proposal, without obligation, or pretensions to it. . . . [T]he instrument was submitted to the people. They acted upon it in the only manner in which they can act safely, effectively, and wisely, on such a subject, by assembling in Convention. It is true, they assembled in their several States—and where else should they have assembled? No political dreamer was ever wild enough to think of breaking down the lines which separate the States, and of compounding the American people into one common mass. . . .

From these Conventions the constitution derives its whole authority. . . .

. . . To the formation of a league, such as was the confederation, the State sovereignties were certainly competent. But when, "in order to form a more perfect union," it was deemed necessary to change this alliance into an effective government, possessing great and sovereign powers, and acting directly on the people, the necessity of referring it to the people, and of deriving its powers directly from them, was felt and acknowledged by all.

The government of the Union, then, (whatever may be the influence of this fact on the case,) is, emphatically, and truly, a government of the people. In form and in substance it emanates from them. Its powers are granted by them, and are to be exercised directly on them, and for their benefit.

This government is acknowledged by all to be one of enumerated powers. . . . That principle is now universally admitted. But the question respecting the extent of the powers actually granted, is perpetually arising, and will probably continue to arise, as long as our system shall exist.

In discussing these questions, the conflicting powers of the general and State governments must be brought into view, and the supremacy of their respective laws, when they are in opposition, must be settled.

If any one proposition could command the universal assent of mankind, we might expect it would be this—that the government of the Union, though limited in its powers, is supreme within its sphere of action. This would seem to result necessarily from its nature. It is the government of all; its powers are delegated by all; it represents all, and acts for all. . . . But this question is not left to mere reason: the people have, in express terms, decided it, by saying, "this constitution, and the laws of the United States, which shall be made in pursuance thereof," "shall be the supreme law of the land," and by requiring that the members of the State legislatures, and the officers of the executive and judicial departments of the States, shall take the oath of fidelity to it.

The government of the United States, then, though limited in its powers, is supreme; and its laws, when made in pursuance of the constitution, form the supreme law of the land, "any thing in the constitution or laws of any State to the contrary notwithstanding."

Among the enumerated powers, we do not find that of establishing a bank or creating a corporation. But there is no phrase in the instrument which, like the articles of confederation, excludes incidental or implied powers; and which requires that every thing granted shall be expressly and minutely described. Even the 10th amendment, which was framed for the purpose of quieting the excessive jealousies which had been excited, omits the word "expressly," and declares only that the powers "not delegated to the United States, nor prohibited to the States, are reserved to the States or to the people;" thus leaving the question, whether the particular power which may become the subject of contest has been delegated to the one government, or prohibited to the other, to depend on a fair construction of the whole instrument. . . . A constitution, to contain an accurate detail of all the subdivisions of which its great powers will admit, and of all the means by which they may be carried into execution, would partake of the prolixity of a legal code, and could scarcely be embraced by the human mind. It would probably never be understood by the public. Its nature, therefore, requires, that only its great outlines should be marked, its important objects designated, and the minor ingredients which compose those objects be deduced from the nature of the objects themselves. . . . In considering this question, then, we must never forget, that it is *a constitution* we are expounding.

Although, among the enumerated powers of government, we do not find the word "bank" or "incorporation," we find the great powers to lay and collect taxes; to borrow money; to regulate commerce; to declare and conduct a war; and to raise and support armies and navies. The sword and the purse, all the external relations, and no inconsiderable portion of the industry of the nation, are entrusted to its government. . . . [A] government, entrusted with such ample powers, on the due execution of which the happiness and prosperity of the nation so vitally depends, must also be entrusted with ample means for their execution. The power being given, it is the interest of the nation to facilitate its execution. It can never be their interest, and cannot be presumed to have been their intention, to clog and embarrass its execution by withholding the most appropriate means. . . .

But the constitution of the United States has not left the right of Congress to employ the necessary means, for the execution of the powers conferred on the government, to general reasoning. To its enumeration of powers is added that of making "all laws which shall be necessary and proper, for carrying into execution the foregoing powers, and all other powers vested by this constitution, in the government of the United States, or in any department thereof."

The counsel for the State of Maryland have urged various arguments, to prove that this clause, though in terms a grant of power, is not so in effect; but is really restrictive of the general right, which might otherwise be implied, of selecting means for executing the enumerated powers. . . .

. . . [T]he argument on which most reliance is placed, is drawn from the peculiar language of this clause. Congress is not empowered by it to make all laws, which may have relation to the powers conferred on the government, but such only as may be "*necessary and proper*" for carrying them into execution. The word "*necessary*," is considered as controlling the whole sentence, and as limiting the right to pass laws for the execution of the granted powers, to such as are indispensable, and without which the power would be nugatory. That it excludes the choice of means, and leaves to Congress, in each case, that only which is most direct and simple.

Is it true, that this is the sense in which the word "necessary" is always used? Does it always import an absolute physical necessity, so strong, that one thing, to which another may be termed necessary, cannot exist without that other? We think it does not. If reference be had to its use, in the common affairs of the world, or in approved authors, we find that it frequently imports no more than that one thing is convenient, or useful, or essential to another. To employ the means necessary to an end, is generally understood as employing any means calculated to produce the end, and not as being confined to those single means, without which the end would be entirely unattainable. . . .

. . . The subject is the execution of those great powers on which the welfare of a nation essentially depends. It must have been the intention of those who gave these powers, to insure, as far as human prudence could insure, their beneficial execution. This could not be done by confiding the choice of means to such narrow limits as not to leave it in the power of Congress to adopt any which might be appropriate, and which were conducive to the end. This provision is made in a constitution intended to endure for ages to come, and, consequently, to be adapted to the various *crises* of human affairs. To have prescribed the means by which government should, in all future time, execute its powers, would have been to change, entirely, the character of the instrument, and give it the properties of a legal code. It would have been an unwise attempt to provide, by immutable rules, for exigencies which, if foreseen at all, must have been seen dimly, and which can be best provided for as they occur. . . .

We admit, as all must admit, that the powers of the government are limited, and that its limits are not to be transcended. But we think the sound construction of the constitution must allow to the national legislature that discretion, with respect to the means by which the powers it confers are to be carried into execution, which will enable that body to perform the high duties assigned to it, in the manner most beneficial to the people. Let the end be legitimate, let it be within the scope of the constitution, and all means which are appropriate, which are plainly adapted to that end, which are not prohibited, but consist with the letter and spirit of the constitution, are constitutional.

That a corporation must be considered as a means not less usual, not of higher dignity, not more requiring a particular specification than other means, has been sufficiently proved. If we look to the origin of corporations, to the manner in which they have been framed in that government from which we have derived most of our legal principles and ideas, or the uses to which they have been applied, we find no reason to suppose that a constitution, omitting, and wisely omitting, to enumerate all the means for carrying into execution the great powers vested in government, ought to have specified this. . . .

If a corporation may be employed indiscriminately with other means to carry into execution the powers of the government, no particular reason can be assigned for excluding the use of a bank, if required for its fiscal operations. To use one, must be within the discretion of Congress, if it be an appropriate mode of executing the powers of government. . . .

... Should Congress, in the execution of its powers, adopt measures which are prohibited by the constitution; or should Congress, under the pretext of executing its powers, pass laws for the accomplishment of objects not entrusted to the government; it would become the painful duty of this tribunal, should a case requiring such a decision come before it, to say that such an act was not the law of the land. But where the law is not prohibited, and is really calculated to effect any of the objects entrusted to the government, to undertake here to inquire into the degree of its necessity, would be to pass the line which circumscribes the judicial department, and to tread on legislative ground. This court disclaims all pretensions to such a power. . . .

It being the opinion of the Court, that the act incorporating the bank is constitutional; and that the power of establishing a branch in the State of Maryland might be properly exercised by the bank itself, we proceed to inquire—

2. Whether the State of Maryland may, without violating the constitution, tax that branch?

That the power of taxation is one of vital importance; that it is retained by the States; that it is not abridged by the grant of a similar power to the government of the Union; that it is to be concurrently exercised by the two governments: are truths which have never been denied. But, such is the paramount character of the constitution, that its capacity to withdraw any subject from the action of even this power, is admitted. . . .

. . . [T]he constitution and the laws made in pursuance thereof are supreme; . . . they control the constitution and laws of the respective States, and cannot be controlled by them. From this, which may be almost termed an axiom, other propositions are deduced as corollaries, on the truth or error of which, and on their application to this case, the cause has been supposed to depend. These are, 1st. that a power to create implies a power to preserve. 2nd. That a power to destroy, if wielded by a different hand, is hostile to, and incompatible with these powers to create and to preserve. 3d. That where this repugnancy exists, that authority which is supreme must control, not yield to that over which it is supreme. . . .

The power of Congress to create, and of course to continue, the bank, was the subject of the preceding part of this opinion; and is no longer to be considered as questionable.

That the power of taxing it by the States may be exercised so as to destroy it, is too obvious to be denied. . . .

The Court has bestowed on this subject its most deliberate consideration. The result is a conviction that the States have no power, by taxation or otherwise, to retard, impede, burden, or in any manner control, the operations of the constitutional laws enacted by Congress to carry into execution the powers vested in the general government. This is, we think, the unavoidable consequence of that supremacy which the constitution has declared.

We are unanimously of opinion, that the law passed by the legislature of Maryland, imposing a tax on the Bank of the United States, is unconstitutional and void.

21 ↜

[handwritten annotations: "commerce clause", "monopoly on", "steamboat"]

Seeking to promote commerce along the Hudson River, New York promised a monopoly on steam-driven river and coastal traffic to the first inventor who could produce a serviceable steam-propelled boat. In 1807 Robert Fulton succeeded in meeting the state's specifications and received the monopoly, which he exploited in partnership with the politically influential Robert Livingston. Anyone who wished to establish steamboat traffic on New York's rivers or coastal waters had to secure a license from the Fulton-Livingston tandem. By the 1820s steam shipping in New York was controlled by a patchwork of monopolies sublicensed from Fulton and Livingston.

Many entrepreneurs objected, but the state's courts upheld the system. Gibbons ran a steamboat line between New Jersey and New York in competition with Ogden, who held the Fulton-Livingston license. Gibbons held a federal license, required of all engaged in interstate coastal commerce. The license was simply a device to raise money, rather than part of a regulatory system.

Ogden secured an injunction against Gibbons in the New York courts, which once again upheld the monopoly system. Gibbons appealed to the Supreme Court. His lawyer, Daniel Webster, argued that the Constitution delegated exclusive power to Congress to regulate interstate commerce and that any state law that infringed on it must fall. New York's lawyers argued that Congress's powers should be construed strictly to preserve maximum state authority. Federal power over interstate commerce should be interpreted to extend only to establishing the rules of commerce and not to controlling the means (such as boats and wagons) by which trade was carried on. Moreover, New York was an independent state, older than the Union, with sovereign authority to regulate the state's internal trade and to promote invention; neither the simple delegation of authority over interstate commerce to Congress, nor Congress's exercise of that authority, could preclude the state from exercising its independent power.

For a unanimous Court, Marshall once again expounded on the broad powers of the federal government. He articulated a sweeping definition of commerce. But he withheld judgment on whether the simple delegation of the interstate commerce power to Congress precluded states from passing laws that touched upon it. Instead he ruled that the New York law was inconsistent with the federal licensing law. Where state and federal laws came into conflict, he held, federal law was supreme. But Marshall implied that Congress's power over interstate commerce was exclusive. Many state acts that seemed to regulate interstate commerce, he insisted, were really exercises of state police powers, which he carefully distinguished from Congress's power over commerce.

Gibbons v. Ogden (1824)

MR. CHIEF Justice Marshall delivered the opinion of the Court . . . as follows:

. . . [R]eference has been made to the political situation of these States, anterior to its formation. It has been said, that they were sovereign, were completely independent, and were connected with each other only by a league. This is true. But, when these allied sovereigns converted their league into a government, when they converted their Congress of Ambassadors, deputed to deliberate on their common concerns, and to recommend measures of general utility, into a Legislature, empowered to enact laws on the most interesting subjects, the whole character in which the States appear, underwent a change, the extent of which must be determined by a fair consideration of the instrument by which that change was effected.

This instrument contains an enumeration of powers expressly granted by the people to their government. It has been said, that these powers ought to be construed strictly. But why ought they to be so construed? Is there one sentence in the constitution which gives countenance to this rule? . . . We do not, therefore, think ourselves justified in adopting it. . . . We know of no rule for construing the extent of such powers, other than is given by the language of the instrument which confers them, taken in connexion with the purposes for which they were conferred.

The words are, "Congress shall have power to regulate commerce with foreign nations, and among the several States, and with the Indian tribes."

The subject to be regulated is commerce. . . . The counsel for the appellee would limit it to traffic, to buying and selling, or the interchange of commodities, and do not admit that it comprehends navigation. This would restrict a general term, applicable to many objects, to one of its significations. Commerce, undoubtedly, is traffic, but it is something more: it is intercourse. It describes the commercial intercourse between nations, and parts of nations, in all its branches, and is regulated by prescribing rules for carrying on that intercourse. . . .

To what commerce does this power extend? The constitution informs us, to commerce "with foreign nations, and among the several States, and with the Indian tribes."

It has, we believe, been universally admitted, that these words comprehend every species of commercial intercourse between the United States and foreign nations. No sort of trade can be carried on between this country and any other, to which this power does not extend. . . .

22 U.S. (9 Wheaton) 1 (1824).

If this be the admitted meaning of the word, in its application to foreign nations, it must carry the same meaning throughout the sentence, and remain a unit, unless there be some plain intelligible cause which alters it.

The subject to which the power is next applied, is to commerce "among the several States." The word "among" means intermingled with. A thing which is among others, is intermingled with them. Commerce among the States, cannot stop at the external boundary line of each State, but may be introduced into the interior. . . .

. . . [I]n regulating commerce with foreign nations, the power of Congress does not stop at the jurisdictional lines of the several States. It would be a very useless power, if it could not pass those lines. The commerce of the United States with foreign nations, is that of the whole United States. Every district has a right to participate in it. The deep streams which penetrate our country in every direction, pass through the interior of almost every State in the Union, and furnish the means of exercising this right. If Congress has the power to regulate it, that power must be exercised whenever the subject exists. If it exists within the States, if a foreign voyage may commence or terminate at a port within a State, then the power of Congress may be exercised within a State.

This principle is, if possible, still more clear, when applied to commerce "among the several States." They either join each other, in which case they are separated by a mathematical line, or they are remote from each other, in which case other States lie between them. What is commerce "among" them; and how is it to be conducted? Can a trading expedition between two adjoining States, commence and terminate outside of each? And if the trading intercourse be between two States remote from each other, must it not commence in one, terminate in the other, and probably pass through a third? Commerce among the States must, of necessity, be commerce with the States. . . . The power of Congress, then, whatever it may be, must be exercised within the territorial jurisdiction of the several States. . . .

We are now arrived at the inquiry—What is this power?

It is the power to regulate; that is, to prescribe the rule by which commerce is to be governed. This power, like all others vested in Congress, is complete in itself, may be exercised to its utmost extent, and acknowledges no limitations, other than are prescribed in the constitution. . . .

But it has been urged with great earnestness, that, although the power of Congress to regulate commerce with foreign nations, and among the several States, be co-extensive with the subject itself, and have no other limits than are prescribed in the constitution, yet the States may severally exercise the same power, within their respective jurisdictions. . . .

In discussing the question, whether this power is still in the States, in the case under consideration, we may dismiss from it the inquiry, whether it is surrendered by the mere grant to Congress, or is retained until Congress shall exercise the power. We may dismiss that inquiry, because it has been exercised, and the regulations which Congress deemed it proper to make, are now in full operation. The sole question is, can a State regulate commerce with foreign nations and among the States, while Congress is regulating it?

The counsel for the respondent answer this question in the affirmative. . . .

. . . [T]he inspection laws are said to be regulations of commerce, and are certainly recognised in the constitution, as being passed in the exercise of a power remaining with the States.

That inspection laws may have a remote and considerable influence on commerce, will not be denied; but that a power to regulate commerce is the source from which the right to pass them is derived, cannot be admitted. . . . They form a portion of that immense mass of legislation, which embraces every thing within the territory of a State, not surrendered to the general government: all which can be most advantageously exercised by the States themselves. Inspection laws, quarantine laws, health laws of every description, as well as laws for regulating the internal commerce of a State, and those which respect turnpike roads, ferries, &c., are component parts of this mass.

No direct general power over these objects is granted to Congress; and, consequently, they remain subject to State legislation. . . . So, if a State, in passing laws on subjects acknowledged to be within its control, and with a view to those subjects, shall adopt a measure of the same character with one which Congress may adopt, it does not derive its authority from the particular power which has been granted, but from some other, which remains with the State, and may be executed by the same means. All experience shows, that the same measures, or measures scarcely distinguishable from each other, may flow from distinct powers; but this does not prove that the powers themselves are identical. . . .

In our complex system, presenting the rare and difficult scheme of one general government, whose action extends over the whole, but which possesses only certain enumerated powers; and of numerous State governments, which retain and exercise all powers not delegated to the Union, contests respecting power must arise. Were it even otherwise, the measures taken by the respective governments to execute their acknowledged powers, would often be of the same description, and might, sometimes, interfere. This, however, does not prove that the one is exercising, or has a right to exercise, the powers of the other. . . .

. . . In argument, however, it has been contended, that if a law passed by a State, in the exercise of its acknowledged sovereignty, comes into conflict with a law passed by Congress in pursuance of the constitution, they affect the subject, and each other, like equal opposing powers.

But the framers of our constitution foresaw this state of things, and provided for it, by declaring the supremacy not only of itself, but of the laws made in pursuance of it. . . . In every such case, the act of Congress . . . is supreme; and the law of the State, though enacted in the exercise of powers not controverted, must yield to it.

22 ∾

Marshall's decisions were widely criticized by opponents of constitutional nationalism, who denied that the Supreme Court was the final authority on the constitutional system. Advocates of state sovereignty denied that *any* branch of the federal government, which was merely a compact among the states, could have the final say in disputes between state and national authority. They pointed out that Article VI of the Constitution mandated that state courts were to enforce the federal Constitution, laws, and treaties against conflicting state provisions. Thus, the state courts were the final judge of the constitutionality of state and federal laws, and section 25 of the the Judiciary Act of 1789, which authorized appeals from decisions of state courts to the Supreme Court, was unconstitutional.

Acting on these ideas, several state supreme courts ruled section 25 of the Judiciary Act void and ignored Supreme Court writs of error, refusing to forward court records or to honor Supreme Court decrees. Their officials refused to appear to defend state actions in Supreme Court cases. Among the most recalcitrant was the Virginia Court of Appeals, the state's highest court. In court opinions and unsigned newspaper essays, its chief justice, Spencer Roane, as well as other Virginians, articulated the state-sovereignty argument.

Cohens v. Virginia gave John Marshall an opportunity to reply forcefully. The case arose when Virginia arrested the Cohen brothers for selling Washington, D.C., lottery tickets in Virginia. The Cohens argued that the D.C. lottery law, as a federal enactment, overrode Virginia's ban on the sale of tickets of out-of-state lotteries. The Virginia courts denied that federal laws held such precedence and refused to recognize the Cohens' appeal to the Supreme Court under section 25.

Marshall once more made a powerful argument for national supremacy, holding section 25 constitutional. Then, to prevent Virginia from defying the decision, he ruled that it was right on the merits of the case: Congress had not intended the D.C. lottery law to supersede state enactments barring sales of out-of-state lottery tickets. Despite the force of Marshall's argument, many state courts, especially in the South, refused to recognize the Supreme Court's authority to hear appeals of state decisions until the Civil War discredited state-sovereignty constitutional arguments.

Cohens v. Virginia (1821)

THE COUNSEL for the defendant in error . . . have laid down the general proposition, that a sovereign independent State is not suable, except by its own consent. . . .

The American States, as well as the American people, have believed a close and firm Union to be essential to their liberty and to their happiness. They

19 U.S. (6 Wheaton) 264 (1821).

have been taught by experience, that this Union cannot exist without a government for the whole; and they have been taught by the same experience that this government would be a mere shadow, that must disappoint all their hopes, unless invested with large portions of that sovereignty which belongs to independent States. . . .

If it could be doubted, whether from its nature, it were not supreme in all cases where it is empowered to act, that doubt would be removed by the declaration, that "this constitution, and the laws of the United States, which shall be made in pursuance thereof, and all treaties made, or which shall be made, under the authority of the United States, shall be the supreme law of the land; and the judges in every State shall be bound thereby; any thing in the constitution or laws of any State to the contrary notwithstanding." . . .

The general government, though limited as to its objects, is supreme with respect to those objects. This principle is a part of the constitution; and if there be any who deny its necessity, none can deny its authority. . . .

With the ample powers confided to this supreme government . . . are connected many express and important limitations on the sovereignty of the States. . . . [T]he sovereignty of the States is surrendered in many instances where the surrender can only operate to the benefit of the people, and where, perhaps, no other power is conferred on Congress than a conservative power to maintain the principles established in the constitution. The maintenance of these principles in their purity, is certainly among the great duties of the government. One of the instruments by which this duty may be peaceably performed, is the judicial department. It is authorized to decide all cases of every description, arising under the constitution or laws of the United States. From this general grant of jurisdiction, no exception is made of those cases in which a State may be a party. When we consider the situation of the government of the Union and of a State, in relation to each other; the nature of our constitution; the subordination of the State governments to that constitution; the great purpose for which jurisdiction over all cases arising under the constitution and laws of the United States, is confided to the judicial department; are we at liberty to insert in this general grant, an exception of those cases in which a State may be a party? Will the spirit of the constitution justify this attempt to control its words? We think it will not. We think a case arising under the constitution or laws of the United States, is cognizable in the Courts of the Union, whoever may be the parties to that case. . . .

2d. The second objection to the jurisdiction of the Court is, that its appellate power cannot be exercised, in any case, over the judgment of a State Court.

This objection is sustained chiefly by arguments drawn from the supposed total separation of the judiciary of a State from that of the Union, and their entire independence of each other. . . .

This hypothesis is not founded on any words in the constitution, which might seem to countenance it, but on the unreasonableness of giving a contrary construction to words which seem to require it; and on the incompatibility of the application of the appellate jurisdiction to the judgments of State Courts, with that constitutional relation which subsists between the government of the Union and the governments of those States which compose it.

Let this unreasonableness, this total incompatibility, be examined.

That the United States form, for many, and for most important purposes, a single nation, has not yet been denied. In war, we are one people. In making peace, we are one people. In all commercial regulations, we are one and the same people. In many other respects, the American people are one, and the government which is alone capable of controlling and managing their interests in all these respects, is the government of the Union. It is their government, and in that character they have no other. America has chosen to be, in many respects, and to many purposes, a nation; and for all these purposes, her government is complete; to all these objects, it is competent. The people have declared, that in the exercise of all powers given for these objects, it is supreme. It can, then, in effecting these objects, legitimately control all individuals or governments within the American territory. The constitution and laws of a State, so far as they are repugnant to the constitution and laws of the United States, are absolutely void. These States are constituent parts of the United States. They are members of one great empire—for some purposes sovereign, for some purposes subordinate.

In a government so constituted, is it unreasonable that the judicial power should be competent to give efficacy to the constitutional laws of the legislature? That department can decide on the validity of the constitution or law of a State, if it be repugnant to the constitution or to a law of the United States. Is it unreasonable that it should also be empowered to decide on the judgment of a State tribunal enforcing such unconstitutional law? . . .

We think it is not. We think that in a government acknowledgedly supreme, with respect to objects of vital interest to the nation, there is nothing inconsistent with sound reason, nothing incompatible with the nature of government, in making all its departments supreme, so far as respects those objects, and so far as is necessary to their attainment. The exercise of the appellate power over those judgments of the State tribunals which may contravene the constitution or laws of the United States, is, we believe, essential to the attainment of those objects.

23 &

By the 1830s the reaction against constitutional nationalism had grown very strong. Southern state courts continued to challenge the Supreme Court, President Andrew Jackson defended state rights, and Vice-President John C. Calhoun had formulated a powerful state-sovereignty argument. From the mid-1820s on, the Marshall Court became more judicious about interfering with state legislation. *Barron v. Baltimore* called on the Supreme Court to decide whether the Bill of Rights bound the state governments as well as the federal government. Barron owned a wharf that was left in shallow water after the city of Baltimore diverted streams to improve roads around its harbor. Barron sued, arguing that the city had taken his property without the just compensation required by the Fifth Amendment. Although only the First Amendment specifically referred to Congress, Marshall, again speaking for a unanimous Court, eschewed this opportunity to expand radically the Court's jurisdiction. The Bill of Rights applied only to the federal government, he ruled. His argument would later have an important impact on the way Congress worded the Fourteenth Amendment, which was designed to protect rights against state infringement (see the Fourteenth Amendment, in the appendix, pp. A-13–A-14).

Barron v. Baltimore (1833)

M<small>R.</small> C<small>HIEF</small> Justice Marshall delivered the opinion of the Court. . . .

The question . . . presented is, we think, of great importance, but not of much difficulty.

The constitution was ordained and established by the people of the United States for themselves, for their own government, and not for the government of the individual States. Each State established a constitution for itself, and, in that constitution, provided such limitations and restrictions on the powers of its particular government as its judgment dictated. The people of the United States framed such a government for the United States as they supposed best adapted to their situation, and best calculated to promote their interests. The powers they conferred on this government were to be exercised by itself; and the limitations on power, if expressed in general terms, are naturally, and, we think, necessarily applicable to the government created by the instrument. . . .

If these propositions be correct, the fifth amendment must be understood as restraining the power of the general government, not as applicable to the States. In their several constitutions they have imposed such restrictions on their respective governments as their own wisdom suggested; such as they deemed most proper for themselves. . . .

The counsel for the plaintiff in error insists that the constitution was intended to secure the people of the several States against the undue exercise of power by their respective state governments, as well as against that which might be attempted by their general government. In support of this argument he relies on the inhibitions contained in the tenth section of the first article.

We think that section affords a strong if not a conclusive argument in support of the opinion already indicated by the court. . . .

. . . These restrictions . . . are by express words applied to the States. "No

State shall enter into any treaty," etc. Perceiving that in a constitution framed by the people of the United States for the government of all, no limitation of the action of government on the people would apply to the state government, unless expressed in terms; the restrictions contained in the tenth section are in direct words so applied to the States. . . .

If the original constitution, in the ninth and tenth sections of the first article, draws this plain and marked line of discrimination between the limitations it imposes on the powers of the general government, and on those of the States; if in every inhibition intended to act on state power, words are employed which directly express that intent; some strong reason must be assigned for departing from this safe and judicious course in framing the amendments, before that departure can be assumed.

Supreme court said the Bill of rights don't apply to local govt

CHAPTER 7

Jacksonian Democracy and State Rights

24 ❧

In the early nineteenth century, Blackstone's *Commentaries on the Laws of England* remained the primary source of information on the common law in the United States, augmented by Kent's *Commentaries on American Law* and a few other treatises. The rules Blackstone described as governing the legal status of married women remained in force until the 1830s and 1840s, when state legislatures began to pass Married Women's Property Acts, allowing wives to retain control of their property after marriage. However, states did not begin to permit married women to retain control over their earnings until the 1860s. Women remained subject to all sorts of discriminations and disqualifications, giving rise to the first women's rights movement.

Blackstone on the Rights of Married Women (1775)

BY MARRIAGE, the husband and wife are one person in law: that is, the very being or legal existence of the woman is suspended during the marriage, or at least is incorporated and consolidated into that of the husband: under whose wing, protection, and *cover*, she performs every thing; and is therefore called in our law-french a *feme-covert*; . . . and her condition during her marriage is called her *coverture*. . . . For this reason, a man cannot grant any thing to his wife, or enter into covenant with her: for the grant would be to suppose her separate existence; and to covenant with her, would be only to covenant with himself: and therefore it is also generally true, that all compacts made between husband and wife, when single, are voided by the intermarriage. A woman indeed may be attorney for her husband; for that implies no separation from, but is rather a representation of, her lord. And a hus-

William Blackstone, *Commentaries on the Laws of England* (Oxford, England: Clarendon Press, 1765), 1: 430–433.

band may also bequeath any thing to his wife by will; for that cannot take effect till the coverture is determined by his death. The husband is bound to provide his wife with necessaries by law, as much as himself; and if she contracts debts for them, he is obliged to pay them. . . . If the wife be injured in her person or her property, she can bring no action for redress without her husband's concurrence, and in his name, as well as her own: neither can she be sued, without making the husband a defendant. . . . In criminal prosecutions, it is true, the wife may be indicted and punished separately; for the union is only a civil union. But, in trials of any sort, they are not allowed to be evidence for, or against, each other: partly because it is impossible their testimony should be indifferent; but principally because of the union of person. . . . But where the offence is directly against the person of the wife, this rule has been usually dispensed with. . . .

But, though our law in general considers man and wife as one person, yet there are some instances in which she is separately considered; as inferior to him, and acting by his compulsion. And therefore all deeds executed, and acts done, by her, during her coverture, are void, or at least voidable. . . . And in some felonies, and other inferior crimes, committed by her, through constraint of her husband, the law excuses her: but this extends not to treason or murder.

The husband also (by the old law) might give his wife moderate correction. For, as he is to answer for her misbehaviour, the law thought it reasonable to intrust him with this power of restraining her, by domestic chastisement, in the same moderation that a man is allowed to correct his servants or children; for whom the master or parent is also liable in some cases to answer. But this power of correction was confined within reasonable bounds. . . . But, with us, in the politer reign of Charles the second, this power of correction began to be doubted: and a wife may now have security of the peace against her husband; or, in return, a husband against his wife. Yet the lower rank of people, who were always fond of the old common law, still claim and exert their ancient privilege: and the courts of law will still permit a husband to restrain a wife of her liberty, in case of any gross misbehaviour.

These are the chief legal effects of marriage during the coverture; upon which we may observe, that even the disabilities, which the wife lies under, are for the most part intended for her protection and benefit. So great a favourite is the female sex of the laws of England.

25 ❧

As in most Western societies, women in the United States were excluded from exercising political rights, such as voting, holding office, and serving on juries, and from accepting political responsibilities, such as serving in the militia. Therefore, it was considered inappropriate for them to participate in public life—for example, to speak at public meetings, petition legislatures, or organize political campaigns.

Under the common law, women lost their legal standing as independent individuals when they married. As stated in Blackstone (Document 24), they became *femes covert*—"covered women"—whose legal identities were subsumed into those of their husbands. The common-law rules giving husbands control over their wives' property applied, unless a formal prenuptial agreement made a different arrangement. Married women were unable to sue in their own names or make contracts. If a marital relationship broke down, it was extremely difficult to secure a divorce; and until the 1820s and 1830s, fathers were more likely to receive custody of children. Finally, women were not expected to attain the same educational levels as men nor to engage in professional occupations. Hardly any schools would train them, and no professional associations would accept them.

In the democratic, individualistic United States of the 1830s and 1840s, more and more women (and men) found this situation intolerable. Reform was made more urgent by social and economic changes. Women were especially vulnerable to the economic consequences of dependency when husbands proved incompetent or dissolute, or simply deserted their families.

By the 1830s, women were active in a variety of moral reform movements fueled by the religious revival known as the Second Great Awakening. They were particularly prominent in the fledgling abolitionist movement. In the 1830s and 1840s, legislatures began to consider Married Women's Property Acts, which would enable women to own and control property separately from their husbands. It was in this context that reformers organized the first women's rights convention in the United States, held at Seneca Falls, New York. Its "Declaration of Sentiments" forcefully demonstrated the inconsistency between women's position and the nation's founding principles.

The Declaration of Sentiments of the Seneca Falls Convention (1848)

W H E N , I N the course of human events, it becomes necessary for one portion of the family of man to assume among the people of the earth a position different from that which they have hitherto occupied, but one to which the laws of nature and of nature's God entitle them, a decent respect to the opinions of mankind requires that they should declare the causes that impel them to such a course.

We hold these truths to be self-evident: that all men and women are created equal; that they are endowed by their Creator with certain inalienable rights; that among these are life, liberty, and the pursuit of happiness; that to secure these rights governments are instituted, deriving their just powers

Elizabeth Cady Stanton, Susan B. Anthony, and Matilda Joslyn Gage (comps.), *The History of Woman Suffrage* (Rochester, N.Y.: Mann, 1881), 1: 70–71.

from the consent of the governed. Whenever any form of government becomes destructive of these ends, it is the right of those who suffer from it to refuse allegiance to it, and to insist upon the institution of a new government, laying its foundation on such principles, and organizing its powers in such form, as to them shall seem most likely to effect their safety and happiness. Prudence, indeed, will dictate that governments long established should not be changed for light and transient causes; and accordingly all experience hath shown that mankind are more disposed to suffer, while evils are sufferable, than to right themselves by abolishing the forms to which they were accustomed. But when a long train of abuses and usurpations, pursuing invariably the same object evinces a design to reduce them under absolute despotism, it is their duty to throw off such government, and to provide new guards for their future security. Such has been the patient sufferance of the women under this government, and such is now the necessity which constrains them to demand the equal situation to which they are entitled.

The history of mankind is a history of repeated injuries and usurpations on the part of man toward woman, having in direct object the establishment of an absolute tyranny over her. To prove this, let facts be submitted to a candid world.

He has never permitted her to exercise her inalienable right to the elective franchise.

He has compelled her to submit to laws, in the formation of which she had no voice.

He has withheld from her rights which are given to the most ignorant and degraded men—both natives and foreigners.

Having deprived her of this first right of a citizen, the elective franchise, thereby leaving her without representation in the halls of legislation, he has oppressed her on all sides.

He has made her, if married, in the eye of the law, civilly dead.

He has taken from her all right in property, even to the wages she earns.

He has made her, morally, an irresponsible being, as she can commit many crimes with impunity, provided they be done in the presence of her husband. In the covenant of marriage, she is compelled to promise obedience to her husband, he becoming, to all intents and purposes, her master—the law giving him power to deprive her of her liberty, and to administer chastisement.

He has so framed the laws of divorce, as to what shall be the proper causes, and in case of separation, to whom the guardianship of the children shall be given, as to be wholly regardless of the happiness of women. . . .

He has monopolized nearly all the profitable employments, and from those she is permitted to follow, she receives but a scanty remuneration. He closes against her all the avenues to wealth and distinction which he considers most honorable to himself. . . .

He has denied her the facilities for obtaining a thorough education, all colleges being closed against her.

He allows her in Church, as well as State, but a subordinate position. . . .

He has created a false public sentiment by giving to the world a different code of morals for men and women, by which moral delinquencies which exclude women from society, are not only tolerated, but deemed of little account in man.

He has usurped the prerogative of Jehovah himself, claiming it as his right to assign for her a sphere of action, when that belongs to her conscience and to her God.

He has endeavored, in every way that he could, to destroy her confidence in her own powers, to lessen her self-respect, and to make her willing to lead a dependent and abject life.

Now, in view of this entire disfranchisement of one-half the people of this country, their social and religious degradation . . . we insist that they have immediate admission to all the rights and privileges which belong to them as citizens of the United States.

26 ⌒

Andrew Jackson's political and constitutional views were not very well known when he was elected to the presidency in 1828, but it was generally understood that he did not sympathize with the constitutional nationalism of his predecessor, John Quincy Adams, and of Chief Justice John Marshall. His opinions became clearer after he vetoed the Maysville Road bill for exceeding the powers of Congress and sided with southern states seeking to take over Native American lands in defiance of Supreme Court decrees.

Jackson's veto of the bill rechartering the second Bank of the United States crystallized his constitutional and political philosophy. The veto came in response to legislation passed in 1832, extending the charter of the bank another twenty years from the time it was to expire in 1836. Jackson attacked the monopolistic features of the bill, its infringement of state rights, and especially its violation of the principle of equal rights. He insisted that the Supreme Court did not have the final word on issues of constitutionality; it was the duty of Congress and the president to act on their own understanding of the Constitution.

Andrew Jackson, Veto of the National Bank Bill (1832)

A BANK OF the United States is in many respects convenient for the Government and useful to the people. Entertaining this opinion, and deeply impressed with the belief that some of the powers and privileges possessed by

Richardson (ed.), *Messages and Papers of the Presidents*, 2: 576–591.

the existing bank are unauthorized by the Constitution, subversive of the rights of the States, and dangerous to the liberties of the people, I felt it my duty at an early period of my Administration to call the attention of Congress to the practicability of organizing an institution combining all its advantages and obviating these objections. I sincerely regret that in the act before me I can perceive none of those modifications of the bank charter which are necessary, in my opinion, to make it compatible with justice, with sound policy, or with the Constitution of our country.

The present corporate body ... enjoys an exclusive privilege of banking under the authority of the General Government, a monopoly of its favor and support, and, as a necessary consequence, almost a monopoly of the foreign and domestic exchange. The powers, privileges, and favors bestowed upon it in the original charter, by increasing the value of the stock far above its par value, operated as a gratuity of many millions to the stockholders. . . .

. . . The act before me proposes another gratuity to the holders of the same stock, and in many cases to the same men, of at least seven millions more. This donation finds no apology in any uncertainty as to the effect of the act. On all hands it is conceded that its passage will increase at least 20 or 30 per cent more the market price of the stock, subject to the payment of the annuity of $200,000 per year secured by the act, thus adding in a moment one-fourth to its par value. . . .

It is not conceivable how the present stockholders can have any claim to the special favor of the Government. The present corporation has enjoyed its monopoly during the period stipulated in the original contract. If we must have such a corporation, why should not the Government sell out the whole stock and thus secure to the people the full market value of the privileges granted? . . .

But this act does not permit competition in the purchase of this monopoly. It seems to be predicated on the erroneous idea that the present stockholders have a prescriptive right not only to the favor but to the bounty of Government. It appears that more than a fourth part of the stock is held by foreigners and the residue is held by a few hundred of our own citizens, chiefly of the richest class. For their benefit does this act exclude the whole American people from competition in the purchase of this monopoly and dispose of it for many millions less than it is worth. . . .

It is maintained by the advocates of the bank that its constitutionality in all its features ought to be considered as settled by precedent and by the decision of the Supreme Court. To this conclusion I can not assent. Mere precedent is a dangerous source of authority, and should not be regarded as deciding questions of constitutional power except where the acquiescence of the people and the States can be considered as well settled. So far from this being the case on this subject, an argument against the bank might be based on precedent. One Congress, in 1791, decided in favor of a bank; another, in 1811, decided against it. One Congress, in 1815, decided against a bank; another, in 1816, decided in its favor. Prior to the present Congress, therefore, the precedents drawn from that source were equal. If we resort to the States, the expressions of legislative, judicial, and executive opinions against the bank have been probably to those in its favor as 4 to 1. There is nothing in precedent, therefore, which, if its authority were admitted, ought to weigh in favor of the act before me.

If the opinion of the Supreme Court covered the whole ground of this act, it ought not to control the coordinate authorities of this Government. The Congress, the Executive, and the Court must each for itself be guided by its own opinion of the Constitution. Each public officer who takes an oath to support the Constitution swears that he will support it as he understands it, and not as it is understood by others. . . .

But in the case relied upon the Supreme Court have not decided that all the features of this corporation are compatible with the Constitution. It is true that the court have said that the law incorporating the bank is a constitutional exercise of power by Congress; but taking into view the whole opinion of the court and the reasoning by which they have come to that conclusion, I understand them to have decided that inasmuch as a bank is an appropriate means for carrying into effect the enumerated powers of the General Government, therefore the law incorporating it is in accordance with that provision of the Constitution which declares that Congress shall have power "to make all laws which shall be necessary and proper for carrying those powers into execution." . . .

. . . Under the decision of the Supreme Court, therefore, it is the exclusive province of Congress and the President to decide whether the particular features of this act are *necessary* and *proper* in order to enable the bank to perform conveniently and efficiently the public duties assigned to it as a fiscal agent, and therefore constitutional, or *unnecessary* and *improper*, and therefore unconstitutional. . . .

. . . [L]et us examine the details of this act in accordance with the rule of legislative action which they have laid down. It will be found that many of the powers and privileges conferred on it can not be supposed necessary for the purpose for which it is proposed to be created, and are not, therefore, means necessary to attain the end in view, and consequently not justified by the Constitution. . . .

The several States reserved the power at the formation of the Constitution to regulate and control titles and transfers of real property, and most, if not all, of them have laws disqualifying aliens from acquiring or holding lands within their limits. But this act . . . gives to alien stockholders in this bank an interest and title, as members of the corporation, to all the real property it may acquire within any of the States of this Union. This privilege granted to aliens is not *"necessary"* to enable the bank to perform its public duties, nor in any sense *"proper,"* because it is vitally subversive of the rights of the States. . . .

By its silence, considered in connection with the decision of the Supreme Court in the case of McCulloch against the State of Maryland, this act takes from the States the power to tax a portion of the banking business carried on within their limits, in subversion of one of the strongest barriers which secured them against Federal encroachments. . . .

Upon the formation of the Constitution the States guarded their taxing power with peculiar jealousy. . . . Nothing comes more fully within it than banks and the business of banking, by whomsoever instituted and carried on. Over this whole subject matter it is just as absolute, unlimited, and uncontrollable as if the Constitution had never been adopted, because in the formation of that instrument it was reserved without qualification. . . .

It can not be *necessary* to the character of the bank as a fiscal agent of the Government that its private business should be exempted from that taxation to which all the State banks are liable, nor can I conceive it *"proper"* that the substantive and most essential powers reserved by the States shall be thus attacked and annihilated as a means of executing the powers delegated to the General Government. . . .

If our power over means is so absolute that the Supreme Court will not call in question the constitutionality of an act of Congress the subject of which "is not prohibited, and is really calculated to effect any of the objects intrusted to the Government," although, as in the case before me, it takes away powers expressly granted to Congress and rights scrupulously reserved to the States, it becomes us to proceed in our legislation with the utmost caution. Though not directly, our own powers and the rights of the States may be indirectly legislated away in the use of means to execute substantive powers. . . .

It is to be regretted that the rich and powerful too often bend the acts of government to their selfish purposes. Distinctions in society will always exist under every just government. Equality of talents, of education, or of wealth can not be produced by human institutions. In the full enjoyment of the gifts of Heaven and the fruits of superior industry, economy, and virtue, every man is equally entitled to protection by law; but when the laws undertake to add to these natural and just advantages artificial distinctions, to grant titles, gratuities, and exclusive privileges, to make the rich richer and the potent more powerful, the humble members of society—the farmers, mechanics, and laborers—who have neither the time nor the means of securing like favors to themselves, have a right to complain of the injustice of their Government. There are no necessary evils in government. Its evils exist only in its abuses. If it would confine itself to equal protection, and, as Heaven does its rains, shower its favors alike on the high and the low, the rich and the poor, it would be an unqualified blessing. In the act before me there seems to be a wide and unnecessary departure from these just principles.

Nor is our Government to be maintained or our Union preserved by invasions of the rights and powers of the several States. In thus attempting to make our General Government strong we make it weak. Its true strength consists in leaving individuals and States as much as possible to themselves— in making itself felt, not in its power, but in its beneficence; not in its control, but in its protection; not in binding the States more closely to the center, but leaving each to move unobstructed in its proper orbit.

27 ◌

South Carolinian John C. Calhoun entered Congress in 1811 as a nationalist Republican. He joined with Henry Clay to advocate broad federal power to promote the national economy. But by the mid-1820s, South Carolina had reacted strongly against constitutional nationalism, and Calhoun took the lead in strengthening the state-sovereignty constitutional argument. Building upon Jefferson's Kentucky Resolutions and the reasoning of the Virginia critics of Marshall's nationalistic Supreme Court decisions, Calhoun devised a practical method for the states to exercise final authority in determining whether federal laws were constitutional—"nullification."

In his draft of the South Carolina Exposition, which the state legislature approved in a modified form in 1828, Calhoun repeated the state-sovereignty argument against the Supreme Court's final authority to interpret the Constitution. He insisted that this power resided in the people of the individual states, meeting in constitutional conventions just as they did when they ratified the Constitution. Calhoun reiterated his ideas in an address on federalism delivered in 1831 at Fort Hill, South Carolina.

John C. Calhoun on State Sovereignty (1828, 1831)

Draft of the South Carolina Exposition (1828)

THE POWERS of the General Government are particularly enumerated and specifically delegated; and all powers not expressly delegated, or which are not necessary and proper to carry into effect those that are so granted, are reserved expressly to the States or the people. . . .

Our system, then, consists of two distinct and independent Governments. The general powers, expressly delegated to the General Government, are subject to its sole and separate control; and the States cannot, without violating the constitutional compact, interpose their authority to check, or in any manner to counteract its movements, so long as they are confined to the proper sphere. So, also, the peculiar and local powers reserved to the States are subject to their exclusive control; nor can the General Government interfere, in any manner, with them, without violating the Constitution. . . .

. . . [T]here is, in our system, a striking distinction between *Government* and *Sovereignty*. The separate governments of the several States are vested in their Legislative, Executive, and Judicial Departments; while the sovereignty resides in the people of the States respectively. The powers of the General Government are also vested in its Legislative, Executive, and Judicial Departments, while the sovereignty resides in the people of the several States who created it. . . .

If we look to the history and practical operation of the system, we shall find, on the side of the States, no means resorted to in order to protect their reserved rights against the encroachments of the General Government; while the latter has, from the beginning, adopted the most efficient to prevent the States from encroaching on those delegated to them. The 25th section of the Judiciary Act . . . provides for an appeal from the State courts to the Supreme Court of the United States in all cases, in . . . which, the construction of the Constitution,—the laws of Congress, or treaties of the United States may be involved; thus giving to that high tribunal . . . the power, in reality, of nullifying the acts of the State Legislatures whenever, in their opinion, they may conflict with the powers delegated to the General Government. A more ample and complete protection against the encroachments of the governments of the several States cannot be imagined; and to this extent the power may be considered as indispensable and constitutional. But, by a strange misconception of the nature of our system, . . . it has been regarded as the ultimate power, not only of protecting the General Government against the encroachments of the governments of the States, but also of the encroachments of the former on the latter;—and as being, in fact, the only means provided by the Constitution . . . of determining the limits assigned to each. Such a construction of its powers would, in fact, raise one of the departments of the General Government above the parties who created the constitutional compact. . . . [I]t would, in effect, divest the people of the States of the sovereign authority, and clothe that department with the robe of supreme power. . . .

If it be conceded . . . that the sovereign powers delegated are divided between the General and State Governments, and that the latter hold their portion by the same tenure as the former, it would seem impossible to deny to the States the right of deciding on the infractions of their powers, and the proper remedy to be applied for their correction. The right of judging, in such cases, is an essential attribute of sovereignty,—of which the States cannot be divested without losing their sovereignty itself. . . .

. . . How is the remedy to be applied by the States? In this inquiry a question may be made,—whether a State can interpose its sovereignty through the ordinary Legislature. . . . [P]lausible reasons may be assigned against this mode of action. . . . [T]here can be none as to the fact that a Convention fully represents them for all purposes whatever. Its authority, therefore, must remove every objection as to form, and leave the question on the single point of the right of the States to interpose at all. When convened, it will belong to the Convention itself to determine, authoritatively, whether the acts of which we complain be unconstitutional; and, if so, whether they constitute a violation so deliberate, palpable, and dangerous, as to justify the interposition of the State to protect its rights. If this question be decided in the affirmative, the Convention will then determine in what manner they ought to be declared null and void within the limits of the State; which solemn declaration . . . would be obligatory, not only on her own citizens, but on the General Government itself; and thus place the violated rights of the State under the shield of the Constitution.

The Fort Hill Address (1831)

The great and leading principle is, that the General Government emanated from the people of the several States, forming distinct political communities, and acting in their separate and sovereign capacity, and not from all of the people forming one aggregate political community; that the Constitution of the United States is, in fact, a compact, to which each State is a party, in the character already described; and that the several States, or parties, have a right to judge of its infractions; and in case of a deliberate, palpable, and dangerous exercise of power not delegated, they have the right, in the last resort, to use the language of the Virginia Resolutions, "*to interpose for arresting the progress of the evil, and for maintaining, within their respective limits, the authorities, rights, and liberties appertaining to them.*" This right of interposition, thus solemnly asserted by the State of Virginia, be it called what it may,—State-right, veto, nullification, or by any other name,—I conceive to be the fundamental principle of our system.

28 ❧

In 1830 South Carolina senator Robert Y. Hayne articulated the view that state conventions not only could nullify federal legislation, but could also dissolve the state's connection to the Union by passing an ordinance of secession. Daniel Webster responded with a classic statement of constitutional nationalism. Note especially the way he linked the nationalist constitutional argument to the preservation of liberty. Webster was challenging the identification of liberty with state rights, the dominant view since the Federalist-Republican conflict of the 1790s.

Daniel Webster, Reply to Hayne (1830)

. . . THE GREAT question is, Whose prerogative is it to decide on the constitutionality or unconstitutionality of the laws? On that, the main debate hinges. The proposition, that, in case of a supposed violation of the Constitution by Congress, the States have a constitutional right to interfere and annul the law of Congress, is the proposition of the gentleman. I do not admit it. . . . I do not admit, that, under the Constitution and in conformity with it, there is any mode in which a State government, as a member of the Union, can interfere and stop the progress of the general government, by force of her own laws, under any circumstances whatever.

This leads us to inquire into the origin of this government and the source of its power. Whose agent is it? Is it the creature of the State legislatures, or the creature of the people? If the government of the United States be the agent of the State governments, then they may control it, provided they can agree in the manner of controlling it; if it be the agent of the people, then the people alone can control it, restrain it, modify, or reform it. It is observable enough, that the doctrine for which the honorable gentleman contends leads him to the necessity of maintaining, not only that this general government is the creature of the States, but that it is the creature of each of the States severally, so that each may assert the power for itself of determining whether it acts within the limits of its authority. It is the servant of four-and-twenty masters, of different wills and different purposes, and yet bound to obey all. This absurdity (for it seems no less) arises from a misconception as to the origin of this government and its true character. It is, Sir, the people's Constitution, the people's government, made for the people, made by the people, and answerable to the people. The people of the United States have declared that this Constitution shall be the supreme law. We must either admit the proposition, or dispute their authority. The States are, unequestionably, sovereign, so far as their sovereignty is not affected by this supreme law. But the State legislatures, as political bodies, however sovereign, are yet not sovereign over the people. So far as the people have given power to the general government, so far the grant is unquestionably good, and the government holds of the people, and not of the State governments. We are all agents of the same supreme power, the people. The general government and the State governments derive their authority from the same source. Neither can, in relation to

J. W. McIntyre (ed.), *The Writings and Speeches of Daniel Webster* (Boston: Little Brown, 1903), 6: 53–55, 67–68, 73–75.

the other, be called primary, though one is definite and restricted, and the other general and residuary. The national government possesses those powers which it can be shown the people have conferred on it, and no more. All the rest belongs to the State governments, or to the people themselves. So far as the people have restrained State sovereignty, by the expression of their will, in the Constitution of the United States, so far, it must be admitted, State sovereignty is effectually controlled. . . .

The people . . . erected this government. They gave it a Constitution, and in that Constitution they have enumerated the powers which they bestow on it. They have made it a limited government. They have defined its authority. They have restrained it to the exercise of such powers as are granted; and all others, they declare, are reserved to the States or the people. But, Sir, they have not stopped here. If they had, they would have accomplished but half their work. No definition can be so clear, as to avoid possibility of doubt; no limitation so precise, as to exclude all uncertainty. Who, then, shall construe this grant of the people? . . .

. . . [T]he people have wisely provided, in the Constitution itself, a proper, suitable mode and tribunal for settling questions of constitutional law. . . . The Constitution has itself pointed out, ordained, and established that authority. How has it accomplished this great and essential end? By declaring, Sir, that *"the Constitution, and the laws of the United States made in pursuance thereof, shall be the supreme law of the land, any thing in the Constitution or laws of any State to the contrary notwithstanding."*

This, Sir, was the first great step. By this the supremacy of the Constitution and laws of the United States is declared. The people so will it. No State law is to be valid which comes in conflict with the Constitution, or any law of the United States passed in pursuance of it. But who shall decide this question of interference? To whom lies the last appeal? This, Sir, the Constitution itself decides also, by declaring, *"that the judicial power shall extend to all cases arising under the Constitution and laws of the United States."* These two provisions cover the whole ground. They are, in truth, the keystone of the arch! With these it is a government; without them it is a confederation. . . .

If, Sir, the people in these respects had done otherwise than they have done, their Constitution could neither have been preserved, nor would it have been worth preserving. And if its plain provisions shall now be disregarded, and these new doctrines interpolated in it, it will become as feeble and helpless a being as its enemies, whether early or more recent, could possibly desire. It will exist in every State but as a poor dependent on State permission. . . .

Mr. President, I have thus stated the reasons of my dissent to the doctrines which have been advanced and maintained. I am conscious of having detained you and the Senate much too long. . . . But it is a subject of which my heart is full, and I have not been willing to suppress the utterance of its spontaneous sentiments. I cannot, even now, persuade myself to relinquish it, without expressing once more my deep conviction, that, since it respects nothing less than the Union of the States, it is of most vital and essential importance to the public happiness. . . . It is to that Union we owe our safety at home, and our consideration and dignity abroad. It is to that Union that we are chiefly indebted for whatever makes us most proud of our country. . . .

I have not allowed myself, Sir, to look beyond the Union, to see what might lie hidden in the dark recess behind. I have not coolly weighed the chances of preserving liberty when the bonds that unite us together shall be broken asunder. I have not accustomed myself to hang over the precipice of disunion, to see whether, with my short sight, I can fathom the depth of the abyss below; nor could I regard him as a safe counsellor in the affairs of this government, whose thoughts should be mainly bent on considering, not how the Union may be best preserved, but how tolerable might be the condition of the people when it should be broken up and destroyed. While the Union lasts, we have high, exciting, gratifying prospects spread out before us, for us and our children. Beyond that I seek not to penetrate the veil. God grant that in my day, at least, that curtain may not rise! God grant that on my vision never may be opened what lies behind! When my eyes shall be turned to behold for the last time the sun in heaven, may I not see him shining on the broken and dishonored fragments of a once glorious Union; on States dissevered, discordant, belligerent; on a land rent with civil feuds, or drenched, it may be, in fraternal blood! Let their last feeble and lingering glance rather behold the gorgeous ensign of the republic, now known and honored throughout the earth, still full high advanced, its arms and trophies streaming in their original lustre, not a stripe erased or polluted, nor a single star obscured, bearing for its motto, no such miserable interrogatory as "What is all this worth?" nor those other words of delusion and folly, "Liberty first and Union afterwards"; but everywhere, spread all over in characters of living light, blazing on all its ample folds, as they float over the sea and over the land, and in every wind under the whole heavens, that other sentiment, dear to every true American heart,—Liberty *and* Union, now and for ever, one and inseparable!

29 ॰

South Carolina put state-sovereignty ideas into practice in response to the Tariff of 1828, which set import duties so high that its opponents termed it the "Tariff of Abominations." The state legislature called a state convention, which passed an ordinance of nullification, declaring the tariff void and instructing the legislature to stop its collection in the state.

President Jackson carefully isolated the South Carolinians by reassuring key southern states that he would help them gain control of Native American lands and by negotiating a promised reduction in the tariff. Jackson then persuaded Congress to pass the Force Act of 1833, authorizing him to use the military to enforce the law in South Carolina if necessary, and he issued a proclamation calling on its citizens to obey the law. Declaring itself satisfied with the reduction of the tariff, South Carolina repealed the nullification ordinance—but then nullified the Force Act (which Congress allowed to expire anyway).

The Nullification Crisis made clear the difference between state sovereignty as formulated by Calhoun and the South Carolinians and state rights as articulated by Jackson and most northern Democrats. Jackson insisted that the United States was a nation, not a confederacy of sovereign states. He rejected the idea that the states could nullify federal laws or secede. Jackson did advocate strict construction of federal power, and he adhered to the idea that a clear line separated state and federal authority, with neither sovereignty authorized to encroach on the jurisdiction of the other. But in his Proclamation to the People of South Carolina, Jackson insisted that the Supreme Court, not the individual states, bore the responsibility for policing that line.

The Nullification Crisis (1832–1833)

South Carolina Ordinance of Nullification (1832)

WHEREAS the Congress of the United States, by various acts, purporting to be acts laying duties and imposts on foreign imports, but in reality intended for the protection of domestic manufactures, and the giving of bounties to classes and individuals engaged in particular employments, at the expense and to the injury and oppression of other classes and individuals, . . . hath exceeded its just powers under the Constitution . . . and hath violated the true meaning and intent of the Constitution, which provides for equality in imposing the burthens of taxation upon the several States and portions of the confederacy. . . .

We, therefore, the people of the State of South Carolina in Convention assembled, do declare and ordain, . . . that the several acts and parts of acts of . . . Congress . . . purporting to be laws for the imposing of duties and imports on the importation of foreign commodities . . . are unauthorized by the Constitution of the United States, and violate the true meaning and intent thereof, and are null, void, and no law, nor binding upon this State, its officers or citizens. . . .

And it is further ordained, that it shall not be lawful for any of the constituted authorities, whether of this State or of the United States, to enforce the payment of duties imposed by the said acts within the limits of this State; but it shall be the duty of the Legislature to adopt such measures and pass such acts as may be necessary to give full effect to this ordinance, and to prevent

S. C. Statutes at Large, 1 (1832): 329.

the enforcement and arrest the operation of the said acts and parts of acts of the Congress of the United States within the limits of this State. . . .

And we, the people of South Carolina, . . . do further declare that we will not submit to the application of force, on the part of the Federal Government, to reduce this State to obedience; but that we will consider . . . any . . . act on the part of the Federal Government, to coerce the State, shut up her ports, destroy or harrass her commerce, or to enforce the acts hereby declared to be null and void, otherwise than through the civil tribunals of the country, as inconsistent with the longer continuance of South Carolina in the Union: and that the people of this State will thenceforth hold themselves absolved from all further obligation to maintain or preserve their political connexion with the people of the other States.

Andrew Jackson, Proclamation to the People of South Carolina (1832)

THE ORDINANCE is founded, not on the indefeasible right of resisting acts which are plainly unconstitutional and too oppressive to be endured, but on the strange position that any one State may not only declare an act of Congress void, but prohibit its execution; that they may do this consistently with the Constitution; that the true construction of that instrument permits a State to retain its place in the Union and yet be bound by no other of its laws than those it may choose to consider as constitutional. It is true, they add, that to justify this abrogation of a law it must be palpably contrary to the Constitution; but it is evident that to give the right of resisting laws of that description, coupled with the uncontrolled right to decide what laws deserve that character, is to give the power of resisting all laws; for as by the theory there is no appeal, the reasons alleged by the State, good or bad, must prevail. . . . There are two appeals from an unconstitutional act passed by Congress—one to the judiciary, the other to the people and the States. . . . [O]ur social compact, in express terms, declares that the laws of the United States, its Constitution, and treaties made under it are the supreme law of the land, and, for greater caution, adds "that the judges in every State shall be bound thereby, anything in the constitution or laws of any State to the contrary notwithstanding." And it may be asserted without fear of refutation that no federative government could exist without a similar provision. . . .

I consider, then, the power to annul a law of the United States, assumed by one State, *incompatible with the existence of the Union, contradicted expressly by the letter of the Constitution, unauthorized by its spirit, inconsistent with*

Richardson (ed.), *Messages and Papers of the Presidents*, 2: 641–652.

every principle on which it was founded, and destructive of the great object for which it was formed. . . .

The Constitution declares that the judicial powers of the United States extend to cases arising under the laws of the United States, and that such laws, the Constitution, and treaties shall be paramount to the State constitutions and laws. The judiciary act prescribes the mode by which the case may be brought before a court of the United States by appeal when a State tribunal shall decide against this provision of the Constitution. The ordinance declares there shall be no appeal—makes the State law paramount to the Constitution and laws of the United States, forces judges and jurors to swear that they will disregard their provisions, and even makes it penal in a suitor to attempt relief by appeal. It further declares that it shall not be lawful for the authorities of the United States or of that State to enforce the payment of duties imposed by the revenue laws within its limits.

Here is a law of the United States, not even pretended to be unconstitutional, repealed by the authority of a small majority of the voters of a single State. Here is a provision of the Constitution which is solemnly abrogated by the same authority.

On such expositions and reasonings the ordinance grounds not only an assertion of the right to annul the laws of which it complains, but to enforce it by a threat of seceding from the Union if any attempt is made to execute them.

This right to secede is deduced from the nature of the Constitution, which, they say, is a compact between sovereign States who have preserved their whole sovereignty and therefore are subject to no superior; that because they made the compact they can break it when in their opinion it has been departed from by the other States. . . .

The Constitution of the United States . . . forms a *government*, not a league; and whether it be formed by compact between the States or in any other manner, its character is the same. It is a Government in which all the people are represented, which operates directly on the people individually, not upon the States; they retained all the power they did not grant. But each State, having expressly parted with so many powers as to constitute, jointly with the other States, a single nation, can not, from that period, possess any right to secede, because such secession does not break a league, but destroys the unity of a nation; and any injury to that unity is not only a breach which would result from the contravention of a compact, but it is an offense against the whole Union. To say that any State may at pleasure secede from the Union is to say that the United States are not a nation, because it would be a solecism to contend that any part of a nation might dissolve its connection with the other parts, to their injury or ruin, without committing any offense.

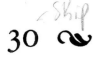

30 ☙

The Marshall Court had forcefully interpreted the Constitution to apply limits on the states. Its main vehicle for doing so was the Obligation of Contracts Clause of Article I, section 10. However, by 1835, when the great chief justice died, the constitutional nationalism he espoused was in eclipse. President Andrew Jackson and the triumphant Democratic party stood for state rights. Even while Marshall remained on the bench, the Supreme Court had begun to exercise more restraint in ruling state laws unconstitutional, as manifested in *Barron v. Baltimore* (Document 23). That trend continued when Jackson's former attorney general and treasury secretary, Roger Brooke Taney, became chief justice in 1836. Among the clearest consequences of growing Democratic influence was the Taney Court's willingness to interpret the constraints placed on the states by the Obligation of Contracts Clause more flexibly than the Marshall Court had, although it did not reverse any earlier Court decisions. The Charles River Bridge Case marked the change.

The case involved the modernization of transport in the Boston area and the rules governing corporate charters. In 1785 the Massachusetts state legislature had granted a charter of incorporation to the Charles River Bridge Company, authorizing it to build a bridge connecting Boston with the towns across the Charles River. The company was to maintain the bridge and receive tolls for a period of forty years, later extended to seventy years, after which the bridge was to revert to state ownership. Complaints soon arose over the monopoly, but the company successfully fended off challenges until 1828, when the legislature incorporated the Warren Bridge Company to build a second span across the river not far from the first. The new company was to collect tolls for only a short time, to recoup costs and make a reasonable profit. Then the state would maintain the span as a free bridge. The Charles River Bridge Company sued. Its attorney, Daniel Webster, argued that the law authorizing the Warren Bridge violated the Constitution's Obligation of Contracts Clause. Surely, Webster argued, a charter authorizing a company to build a bridge in exchange for tolls implied that the state would refrain from authorizing a competitor nearby. Losing in the state courts, the Charles River Bridge Company appealed to the Supreme Court.

Marshall's longtime ally Joseph Story would have found for Webster's client, but a 4–3 majority of the justices opposed such an extension of the principle of the Dartmouth College Case. Taney's opinion warned that interpreting corporate charters broadly to include implicit promises not to incorporate competitors would handcuff economic development. It would give corporations monopolies, in violation of the principle of equal rights, and would make their charters obstructions to growth rather than tools for promoting it.

Charles River Bridge v. Warren Bridge (1837)

MUCH HAS been said in the argument of the principles of construction by which this law is to be expounded, and what undertakings, on the part of the state, may be implied. The Court think there can be no serious

36 U.S. (11 Peters) 420 (1837).

difficulty on that head. It is the grant of certain franchises by the public to a private corporation, and in a matter where the public interest is concerned. The rule of construction in such cases is well settled, both in England, and by the decisions of our own tribunals. In . . . the case of the Proprietors of the Stourbridge Canal against Wheely and others, the court say, "the canal having been made under an act of parliament, the rights of the plaintiffs are derived entirely from that act. . . . [T]he rule of construction in all such cases, is now fully established to be this; that any ambiguity in the terms of the contract, must operate against the adventurers, and in favour of the public, and the plaintiffs can claim nothing that is not clearly given them by the act." . . .

Borrowing, as we have done, our system of jurisprudence from the English law; and having adopted, in every other case, civil and criminal, its rules for the construction of statutes; is there any thing in our local situation, or in the nature of our political institutions, which should lead us to depart from the principle where corporations are concerned? . . . We think not; and it would present a singular spectacle, if, while the courts in England are restraining, within the strictest limits, the spirit of monopoly, and exclusive privileges in nature of monopolies, and confining corporations to the privileges plainly given to them in their charter; the courts of this country should be found enlarging these privileges by implication; and construing a statute more unfavourably to the public, and to the rights of the community, than would be done in a like case in an English court of justice.

But we are not now left to determine, for the first time, the rules by which public grants are to be construed in this country. The subject has already been considered in this Court; and the rule of construction, above stated, fully established. . . .

. . . [T]he object and end of all government is to promote the happiness and prosperity of the community by which it is established; and it can never be assumed, that the government intended to diminish its power of accomplishing the end for which it was created. And in a country like ours, free, active, and enterprising, continually advancing in numbers and wealth; new channels of communication are daily found necessary, both for travel and trade; and are essential to the comfort, convenience, and prosperity of the people. A state ought never to be presumed to surrender this power, because . . . the whole community have an interest in preserving it undiminished. . . . No one will question that the interests of the great body of the people of the state, would, in this instance, be affected by the surrender of this great line of travel to a single corporation, with the right to exact toll, and exclude competition for seventy years. While the rights of private property are sacredly guarded, we must not forget that the community also have rights, and that the happiness and well being of every citizen depends on their faithful preservation.

Adopting the rule of construction above stated as the settled one, we proceed to apply it to the charter of 1785, to the proprietors of the Charles River Bridge. This act of incorporation ... confers on them the ordinary faculties of a corporation, for the purpose of building the bridge; and establishes certain rates of toll, which the company are authorized to take. This is the whole grant. There is no exclusive privilege given to them over the waters of Charles river, above or below their bridge. ...

... None of the faculties or franchises granted to that corporation, have been revoked by the legislature; and its right to take the tolls granted by the charter remains unaltered. In short, all the franchises and rights of property enumerated in the charter, and there mentioned to have been granted to it, remain unimpaired. But its income is destroyed by the Warren Bridge; which, being free, draws off the passengers and property which would have gone over it, and renders their franchise of no value. This is the gist of the complaint. ... In order then to entitle themselves to relief, it is necessary to show, that the legislature contracted not to do the act of which they complain; and that they impaired, or in other words, violated that contract by the erection of the Warren Bridge.

The inquiry then is, does the charter contain such a contract on the part of the state? Is there any such stipulation to be found in that instrument? It must be admitted on all hands, that there is none—no words that even relate to another bridge, or to the diminution of their tolls, or to the line of travel. If a contract on that subject can be gathered from the charter, it must be by implication; and cannot be found in the words used. Can such an agreement be implied? The rule of construction before stated is an answer to the question. ...

Indeed, the practice and usage of almost every state in the Union, old enough to have commenced the work of internal improvement, is opposed to the doctrine contended for on the part of the plaintiffs in error. Turnpike roads have been made in succession, on the same line of travel; the later ones interfering materially with the profits of the first. These corporations have, in some instances, been utterly ruined by the introduction of newer and better modes of transportation, and travelling. In some cases, rail roads have rendered the turnpike roads on the same line of travel so entirely useless, that the franchise of the turnpike corporation is not worth preserving. Yet in none of these cases have the corporations supposed that their privileges were invaded, or any contract violated on the part of the state. ...

And what would be the fruits of this doctrine of implied contracts on the part of the states, and of property in a line of travel by a corporation, if it should now be sanctioned by this Court? To what results would it lead us? ... Let it once be understood that such charters carry with them these implied contracts, and give this unknown and undefined property in a line of travelling; and you will soon find the old turnpike corporations awakening from their sleep, and calling upon this Court to put down the improvements which have taken their place. The millions of property which have been invested in rail roads and canals, upon lines of travel which had been before occupied by turnpike corporations, will be put in jeopardy. We shall be thrown back to the improvements of the last century, and obliged to stand still, until the claims of the old turnpike corporations shall be satisfied; and they shall consent to permit these states to avail themselves of the lights of modern science, and to partake of the benefit of those improvements which are now adding to the wealth and prosperity, and the convenience and comfort, of every other part of the civilized world. . . .

The judgment of the supreme judicial court of the commonwealth of Massachusetts, dismissing the plaintiffs' bill, must, therefore, be affirmed.

31 ⤳

Although the Taney Court was generally more sympathetic to state rights than the Marshall Court had been, in *Swift v. Tyson* it took a decidedly nationalistic position to maintain an environment conducive to commercial development. At issue was the negotiability of bills of exchange, notes that one person or business made out as a promise to pay some amount to another. These notes were often endorsed by successive payees and circulated like money. For such bills to circulate, it was essential that those accepting them have confidence that endorsers would pay off the bills if the original maker could not or would not. The general rule was that if one acquired such a note in good faith, without notice that the original maker or a subsequent endorser had grounds to refuse to pay, one was entitled to payment no matter how justified a maker or endorser might be in refusing to pay someone else. But the courts in New York held otherwise; the ultimate holder of the note stood in exactly the same relation to the maker or endorser as the earlier payee did. If that payee was not entitled to payment, then neither was the ultimate holder.

Swift v. Tyson, a suit for payment of such a note, was brought in the federal courts because the plaintiff who held the note was a citizen of a different state from the defendant who had endorsed it. Their transaction had occurred in New York; under New York law, the defendant would not be liable for paying the note. According to section 34 of the Judiciary Act of 1789, in such diversity-of-citizenship cases, federal courts were supposed to apply the law of the state in which a dispute arose. But in *Swift v. Tyson*, the Court followed the lead of the nationalistic and procommerce Justice Joseph Story. He interpreted section 34 to require the federal courts to apply state statutes, but to apply state court rulings only in cases that involved local, nontransportable property, such as land. As a result, the federal courts were free to create a uniform national law governing commercial transactions and other aspects of the economy. In the following hundred years, the federal courts did so aggressively, creating a body of economic law that often was more friendly to the interests of business than was the law enforced in state courts.

Swift v. Tyson (1842)

MR. JUSTICE Story delivered the opinion of the court. . . .

. . . [A]dmitting the doctrine to be fully settled in New York, it remains to be considered, whether it is obligatory upon this court, if it differs from the principles established in the general commercial law. It is observable that the courts of New York do not found their decisions upon this point upon any local statute, or positive, fixed, or ancient local usage; but they deduce the doctrine from the general principles of commercial law. It is, however, contended, that the 34th section of the Judiciary Act of 1789 (ch. 20) furnishes a rule obligatory upon this court to follow the decisions of the State tribunals, in all cases to which they apply. That section provides "that the laws of the several States, except where the Constitution, treaties, or statutes of the United States shall otherwise require or provide, shall be regarded as rules of decision in trials at common law in the courts of the United States, in cases where they apply." In order to maintain the argument, it is essential, therefore, to hold, that the word "laws," in this section, includes within the scope of its meaning the decisions of the local tribunals. In the ordinary use of language it will hardly be contended that the decisions of courts constitute laws. They are, at most, only evidence of what the laws are, and are not of themselves laws. They are often re-examined, reversed, and qualified by the courts themselves, whenever they are found to be either defective or ill-founded, or otherwise incorrect. The laws of a State are more usually understood to mean the rules and enactments promulgated by the legislative authority thereof, or long established local customs having the force of laws. In all the various cases, which have hitherto come before us for decision, this court have uniformly supposed that the true interpretation of the 34th section limited its application to State laws strictly local, that is to say, to the positive statutes of the State, and the construction thereof adopted by the local tribunals, and to rights and titles to things having a permanent locality, such as the rights and titles to real estate, and other matters immovable and intraterritorial in their nature and character. It never has been supposed by us, that the section did apply, or was designed to apply, to questions of a more general nature, not at all dependent upon local statutes or local usages of a fixed and permanent operation, as, for example, to the construction of ordinary contracts or other written instruments, and especially to questions of general commercial law. . . . And we have not now the slightest difficulty in holding, that this section, upon its true intendment and construction, is strictly limited to local statutes and local usages of the character before stated, and does not extend to contracts and other instruments of a commercial nature, the true interpretation and effect whereof are to be sought, not in the decisions of the local tribunals, but in the general principles and doctrines of commercial jurisprudence.

32 ᐁ

In Gibbons v. Ogden (Document 21), Marshall had implied that a state law might be unconstitutional for encroaching on Congress's exclusive power to regulate interstate commerce. In succeeding decades the Court had been unable to provide a coherent rule for deciding when a state law that affected interstate commerce was constitutional and when it was not. *Cooley v. Board of Wardens* tested the constitutionality of port ordinances requiring captains to hire local pilots to dock their vessels. In its decision, the Court finally established a workable formula. Reflecting the state-rights orientation of the mostly Democratic justices and noting that Congress itself had recognized the pilot laws in 1789, the Court rejected the proposition that the delegation of power over interstate and foreign commerce to Congress deprived states of any control over the subject. In the absence of conflicting congressional legislation, states could regulate local aspects of interstate commerce. That is still the rule today.

Cooley v. Board of Wardens of the Port of Philadelphia (1852)

... [**A**] MAJORITY of the court are of opinion, that a regulation of pilots is a regulation of commerce, within the grant to Congress of the commercial power, contained in the third clause of the eighth section of the first article of the Constitution.

It becomes necessary, therefore, to consider whether this law of Pennsylvania, being a regulation of commerce, is valid. . . .

. . . [W]e are brought directly and unavoidably to the consideration of the question, whether the grant of the commercial power to Congress, did *per se* deprive the States of all power to regulate pilots. This question has never been decided by this court, nor, in our judgment, has any case depending upon all the considerations which must govern this one, come before this court. The grant of commercial power to Congress does not contain any terms which expressly exclude the States from exercising an authority over its subject-matter. If they are excluded it must be because the nature of the power, thus

53 U.S. (12 Howard) 299 (1852).

granted to Congress, requires that a similar authority should not exist in the States. . . .

. . . Now the power to regulate commerce, embraces a vast field, containing not only many, but exceedingly various subjects, quite unlike in their nature; some imperatively demanding a single uniform rule, operating equally on the commerce of the United States in every port; and some, like the subject now in question, as imperatively demanding that diversity, which alone can meet the local necessities of navigation.

Either absolutely to affirm, or deny that the nature of this power requires exclusive legislation by Congress, is to lose sight of the nature of the subjects of this power, and to assert concerning all of them, what is really applicable but to a part. Whatever subjects of this power are in their nature national, or admit only of one uniform system, or plan of regulation, may justly be said to be of such a nature as to require exclusive legislation by Congress. That this cannot be affirmed of laws for the regulation of pilots and pilotage is plain. The act of 1789 contains a clear and authoritative declaration by the first Congress, that the nature of this subject is such, that until Congress should find it necessary to exert its power, it should be left to the legislation of the States; that it is local and not national; that it is likely to be the best provided for, not by one system, or plan of regulations, but by as many as the legislative discretion of the several States should deem applicable to the local peculiarities of the ports within their limits. . . .

We are of opinion that this State law was enacted by virtue of a power, residing in the State to legislate; that it is not in conflict with any law of Congress; that it does not interfere with any system which Congress has established by making regulations, or by intentionally leaving individuals to their own unrestricted action; that this law is therefore valid, and the judgment of the Supreme Court of Pennsylvania in each case must be affirmed.

CHAPTER 8

Slavery and the Constitution

33

In the mid-1830s, northern opponents of slavery organized the first societies devoted to the immediate abolition of slavery throughout the Union. The abolitionists urged Congress to end slavery where the federal government had clear authority to do so, in the federal territories and in Washington, D.C., and they launched an education campaign aimed at rekindling the flickering antislavery movement in the South. Proslavery Southerners drew on state-sovereignty ideas to argue not only that the federal government was obliged to sustain slavery in Washington and the territories, but that antislavery agitation itself violated the spirit of the Union. In 1837 John C. Calhoun expressed the proslavery position in a series of resolutions.

John C. Calhoun, Resolutions on State Sovereignty and Slavery (1837)

Resolved, That in the adoption of the Federal Constitution, the States adopting the same acted, severally, as free, independent, and sovereign States; and that each, for itself, by its own voluntary assent, entered the Union with the view to its increased security against all dangers, domestic as well as foreign. . . .

Resolved, That in delegating a portion of their powers to be exercised by the Federal Government, the States retained, severally, the exclusive and sole right over their own domestic institutions and police, and are alone responsible for them, and that any intermeddling of any one or more States, or a combination of their citizens, with the domestic institutions and police of the

Congressional Globe, 25th Cong., 2d sess., 55 (Dec. 27, 1837).

others, on any ground, or under any pretext whatever, political, moral, religious, with the view to their alteration, or subversion, is an assumption of superiority not warranted by the Constitution; insulting to the States interfered with, tending to endanger their domestic peace and tranquility, subversive of the objects for which the Constitution was formed, and, by necessary consequence, tending to weaken and destroy the Union itself.

Resolved, That this Government was instituted and adopted by the several States of this Union as a common agent, in order to carry into effect the powers which they had delegated by the Constitution for their mutual security and prosperity; and that, in fulfillment of this high and sacred trust, this Government is bound so to exercise its powers as to give, as far as may be practicable, increased stability and security to the domestic institutions of the States that compose the Union. . . .

Resolved, That domestic slavery, as it exists in the Southern and Western States of this Union, composes an important part of their domestic institutions, inherited from their ancestors, and existing at the adoption of the Constitution, by which it is recognised as constituting an essential element in the distribution of its powers among the States; and that no change of opinion, or feeling, on the part of the other States of the Union in relation to it can justify them or their citizens in open and systematic attacks thereon, with the view to its overthrow; and that all such attacks are in manifest violation of the mutual and solemn pledge to protect and defend each other, given by the States, respectively, on entering into the Constitutional compact. . . .

Resolved, That the intermeddling of any State or States, or their citizens, to abolish slavery in this District, or any of the Territories, on the ground, or under the pretext, that it is immoral or sinful; or the passage of any act or measure of Congress, with that view, would be a direct and dangerous attack on the institutions of all the slaveholding States.

Resolved, That the union of these States rest on an equality of rights and advantages among its members; and that whatever destroys that equality, tends to destroy the Union itself; and that it is the solemn duty of all, and more especially of this body, which represents the States in their corporate capacity, to resist all attempts to discriminate between the States in extending the benefits of the Government to the several portions of the Union; and that to refuse to extend to the Southern and Western States any advantage which would tend to strengthen, or render them more secure, or increase their limits or population by the annexation of new territory or States, on the assumption or under the pretext that the institution of slavery, as it exists among them, is immoral or sinful, or otherwise obnoxious, would be contrary to that equality of rights and advantages which the Constitution was intended to secure alike to all the members of the Union.

34 ‿

In reaction to pressure from abolitionists, slave-state legislatures took steps to suppress criticism of slavery within their boundaries. The following sections of the Virginia state code were originally passed in 1831–1832, 1835–1836, and 1847–1848. Note that they not only made it illegal to deny the right to hold people in slavery, but they required postmasters, who were *federal* officers, to enforce state laws denying freedom of the press. Such laws convinced many Northerners that slavery was inconsistent with the liberty of white as well as black Americans.

Virginia Sedition Laws (1860)

[Section] 26. If a free person, by speaking or writing, maintain that owners have not right of property in their slaves, he shall be confined in jail not more than one year, and fined not exceeding five hundred dollars. He may be arrested, and carried before a justice, by any white person.

[Section] 27. If a free person write, print, or cause to be written or printed, any book or other writing, with intent to advise or incite negroes in this state to rebel or make insurrection, or inculcating resistance to the right of property of masters in their slaves, or if he shall, with intent to aid the purpose of any such book or writing, knowingly, circulate the same, he shall be confined in the penitentiary not less than one nor more than five years.

[Section] 28. If a postmaster, or deputy postmaster, know that any such book or other writing has been received at his office in the mail, he shall give notice thereof to some justice, who shall enquire into the circumstances and have such book or writing burned in his presence; if it appear to him that the person to whom it was directed subscribed therefor, knowing its character, or agreed to receive it for circulation to aid the purposes of abolitionists, the justice shall commit such person to jail. If any postmaster, or deputy postmaster, violate this section, he shall be fined not exceeding two hundred dollars.

35 ‿

For decades southern slaveowners complained that northern state authorities failed to meet their obligation to return runaway slaves. Many Northerners, in turn, denied that the Fugitive Slave Clause of Article IV, section 2 of the Constitution authorized Congress to pass legislation on the subject, insisting that it merely enjoined northern states to do so.

Code of Virginia (1860), chap. 198, sec. 26–28, from *The Code of Virginia*, 2d ed. (Richmond: Ritchie, Dunnavant & Co., 1860), 809.

The Supreme Court rejected this argument in *Prigg v. Pennsylvania* [41 U.S. (16 Peters) 539] in 1842, sustaining the constitutionality of the Fugitive Slave Act of 1793. However, the Court said that Congress could not require state officers to help enforce the federal law, and northern legislatures quickly made it illegal to do so, rendering the law ineffective.

Congress passed a new, draconian Fugitive Slave Act as part of the Compromise of 1850, which was designed to settle slavery issues arising out of the acquisition of territory in the Mexican War. The effect of the law was to impose elements of the southern slave codes on the North, leading to bitter resentment that contributed to the formation of the antislavery Republican party in 1854–1855.

The Fugitive Slave Act (1850)

B E IT *enacted by the Senate and House of Representatives of the United States of America in congress assembled,*

Sec. 3. . . . . [T]he Circuit Courts of the United States, and the Superior Courts of each organized Territory of the United States, shall from time to time enlarge the number of commissioners, with a view to afford reasonable facilities to reclaim fugitives from labor, and to the prompt discharge of the duties imposed by this act.

Sec. 4. And be it further enacted, That the commissioners above named shall have concurrent jurisdiction with the judges of the Circuit and District Courts of the United States, . . . and shall grant certificates to such claimants, upon satisfactory proof being made, with authority to take and remove such fugitives from service or labor, under the restrictions herein contained, to the State or Territory from which such persons may have escaped or fled.

Sec. 5. And be it further enacted, That it shall be the duty of all marshals and deputy marshals to obey and execute all warrants and precepts issued under the provisions of this act, . . . and after arrest of such fugitive . . . should such fugitive escape, whether with or without the assent of such marshal or his deputy, such marshall shall be liable, on his official bond, to be prosecuted for the benefit of such claimant, for the full value of the service or labor of said fugitive . . . : and the better to enable the said commissioners, . . . to execute their duties faithfully and efficiently, . . . they are hereby authorized . . . to appoint, in writing . . . any . . . suitable persons, from time to time, to execute all such warrants . . . as may be issued by them in the lawful performance of their respective duties; with authority . . . to summon and call to their aid the bystanders, or *posse comitatus* of the proper county, when necessary . . . and all good citizens are hereby commanded to aid and assist in the prompt and efficient execution of this law, whenever their services may be required, as aforesaid, for that purpose. . . .

U.S. Statutes at Large, 9 (1850): 462.

Sec. 6. And be it further enacted, That when a person held to service or labor in any State or Territory of the United States, has heretofore or shall hereafter escape into another State or Territory of the United States, the . . . persons to whom such service or labor may be due, or . . . their agent or attorney, duly authorized, by power of attorney, . . . may pursue and reclaim such fugitive person, either by procuring a warrant from some one of the courts, judges, or commissioners aforesaid, . . . or by seizing and arresting such fugitive, where the same can be done without process, and by taking, . . . such person . . . forthwith before such court, judge, or commissioner, whose duty it shall be to hear and determine the case of such claimant in a summary manner; . . . and with proof, . . . by affidavit, of the identity of the person whose service or labor is claimed to be due as aforesaid, . . . to make out and deliver to such claimant, . . . a certificate . . . with authority to such claimant . . . to use such reasonable force and restraint as may be necessary, . . . to take and re-move such fugitive person back to the State or Territory whence he or she may have escaped as aforesaid. In no trial or hearing under this act shall the testimony of such alleged fugitive be admitted in evidence; and the certifi-cates . . . shall be conclusive of the right of the person or persons in whose favor granted, to remove such fugitive to the State or Territory from which he escaped. . . .

Sec. 8. And be it further enacted, That the marshals, deputies, and the clerks of the said District and Territorial Courts, shall be paid, for their services, the like fees as may be allowed to them for similar services in other cases; . . . and in all cases where the proceedings are before a commissioner, he shall be enti-tled to a fee of ten dollars in full for his services in each case, upon the deliv-ery of the said certificate to the claimant, his or her agent or attorney; or a fee of five dollars in cases where the proof shall not, in the opinion of such com-missioner, warrant such certificate and delivery. . . .

[handwritten note: payment of someone bringing slave back]

36 ❧

By the mid-1850s a powerful antislavery movement had developed in the North, embod-ied in the Republican party, which came close to winning the presidential election of 1856. Although most Republicans rejected the abolitionists' call for immediate emancipa-tion, they insisted that slavery be banned from the territories—a position known as "free soil"—making it unlikely that there would be any more slave states. As the party's plat-form of 1856 shows, Republicans argued both that Congress had sovereign jurisdiction over the territories and that the Due Process Clause of the Fifth Amendment precluded it from establishing slavery there.

The Antislavery Planks of the Republican National Platform (1856)

Resolved: That, with our Republican fathers, we hold it to be a self-evident truth, that all men are endowed with the inalienable right to life, liberty, and the pursuit of happiness, and that the primary object and ulterior design of our Federal Government were to secure these rights to all persons under its exclusive jurisdiction; that, as our Republican fathers, when they had abolished Slavery in all our National Territory, ordained that no person shall be deprived of life, liberty, or property, without due process of law, it becomes our duty to maintain this provision of the Constitution against all attempts to violate it for the purpose of establishing Slavery in the Territories of the United States by positive legislation, prohibiting its existence or extension therein. That we deny the authority of Congress, of a Territorial Legislation, of any individual, or association of individuals, to give legal existence to Slavery in any Territory of the United States, while the present Constitution shall be maintained.

Resolved: That the Constitution confers upon Congress sovereign powers over the Territories of the United States for their government; and that in the exercise of this power, it is both the right and the imperative duty of Congress to prohibit in the Territories those twin relics of barbarism—Polygamy, and Slavery.

37 ∾

Democrats responded to the Republicans' free-soil doctrine with two constitutional arguments. Most northern and many southern Democrats insisted that the spirit of the Constitution gave settlers in the territories the same right to control their local institutions that the states had. Therefore it was up to the settlers, not Congress, to decide whether to permit slavery in the territories. Its advocates called this doctrine "popular sovereignty." In effect, the doctrine treated the territories as protostates, with full state rights. Many southern Democrats took a more extreme position, based on the state-sovereignty doctrine Calhoun articulated in his resolutions of 1831 (Document 27). Because the federal government was created by the sovereign states, it was their agent and had to serve the interests of all of them equally. Therefore, the federal government was *obligated* to establish slave codes for the territories, so that Southerners would have the same protection for their property that Northerners did.

Related to the slavery question was the status of free African Americans. Many Republicans insisted that free blacks in the northern states were entitled to the same rights that the Constitution secured to white citizens. The southern states denied citizenship to the

Donald Bruce Johnson (ed.), *National Party Platforms* (Urbana: University of Illinois Press, 1978), 1: 27.

free African-American inhabitants of their own states and insisted that they were not obligated to recognize the rights of those living in the North.

The Dred Scott Case brought these questions before the Supreme Court. Scott had
been a slave whose master, John Emerson, had taken him into territory that Congress
had declared free as part of the Missouri Compromise of 1820. (The compromise drew a
line across the Louisiana Purchase at latitude 36°30′; it permitted slavery south of the line
and banned slavery north of it.) After his master's death, Scott sued Mrs. Emerson for his
freedom, arguing that he had been emancipated by living in free territory. Losing in the
Missouri courts, he instituted a new suit in the federal courts as a citizen of Missouri
suing Mrs. Emerson's brother, a resident of New York, whom she had put in charge of
her business affairs. Thus the case raised the question of whether an African American
was a citizen who could bring a diversity-of-citizenship case in federal court, and it also
raised the question of whether Congress could ban slavery from the territories.

With Chief Justice Taney delivering the opinion, the Court ruled that African Americans were not citizens of the United States, even if they were recognized as citizens in the
states where they resided. Reflecting the state-rights, dual-federalist orientation of most
of the judges, the Court separated state citizenship from United States citizenship, making each independent of the other. Although states could grant citizenship to whomever
they wished, citizenship in the United States was fixed in 1789 and required at least an act
of Congress to modify.

The Court then ruled unconstitutional any laws barring slavery from the territories.
Article IV's delegation of power over the territories to Congress referred only to territories held at the formation of the Union. Territories acquired since then had to be administered for the benefit of all states equally. In effect, the Court said that in governing the
territories, the state-sovereignty view that the federal government had to act as the agent
of all the states was correct. Moreover, a law barring slavery in the territories would deprive slaveholders of property in violation of the Due Process Clause of the Fifth Amendment—a clear repudiation of the Republican argument that the same amendment forbade Congress from establishing slavery in the territories.

The decision proved disastrous. It seemed to endorse the extreme proslavery position
that Congress was obligated to pass slave codes for the territories, undercutting the moderate Democratic position of popular sovereignty. In the presidential election of 1860 the
Democratic party divided over the issue, with Southerners demanding that the party endorse a territorial slave code and Northerners sustaining popular sovereignty. Each side
nominated its own candidate. The division enabled the Republicans to win the presidential election, precipitating secession and the Civil War.

Dred Scott v. Sandford (1857)

M R. C H I E F Justice Taney delivered the opinion of the court. . . .

The [first] question is simply this: Can a negro, whose ancestors were imported into this country, and sold as slaves, become a member of the political

60 U.S. (19 Howard) 393 (1857).

community formed and brought into existence by the Constitution of the United States, and as such become entitled to all the rights, and privileges, and immunities, guarantied by that instrument to the citizen? One of which rights is the privilege of suing in a court of the United States in the cases specified in the Constitution. . . .

The words "people of the United States" and "citizens" are synonymous terms, and mean the same thing. They both describe the political body who, according to our republican institutions, form the sovereignty, and who hold the power and conduct the Government through their representatives. They are what we familiarly call the "sovereign people," and every citizen is one of this people, and a constituent member of this sovereignty. The question before us is, whether the class of persons described in the plea in abatement compose a portion of this people, and are constituent members of this sovereignty? We think they are not, and that they are not included, and were not intended to be included, under the word "citizens" in the Constitution, and can therefore claim none of the rights and privileges which that instrument provides for and secures to citizens of the United States. On the contrary, they were at that time considered as a subordinate and inferior class of beings, who had been subjugated by the dominant race, and, whether emancipated or not, . . . had no rights or privileges but such as those who held the power and the Government might choose to grant them. . . .

In discussing this question, we must not confound the rights of citizenship which a State may confer within its own limits, and the rights of citizenship as a member of the Union. It does not by any means follow, because he has all the rights and privileges of a citizen of a State, that he must be a citizen of the United States. He may have all of the rights and privileges of the citizen of a State, and yet not be entitled to the rights and privileges of a citizen in any other State. For, previous to the adoption of the Constitution of the United States, every State had the undoubted right to confer on whomsoever it pleased the character of citizen, and to endow him with all its rights. But this character of course was confined to the boundaries of the State, and gave him no rights or privileges in other States beyond those secured to him by the laws of nations and the comity of States. Nor have the several States surrendered the power of conferring these rights and privileges by adopting the Constitution of the United States. Each State may still confer them upon an alien, or any one it thinks proper, or upon any class or description of persons; yet he would not be a citizen in the sense in which that word is used in the Constitution of the United States, nor entitled to sue as such in one of its courts, nor to the privileges and immunities of a citizen in the other States. The rights which he would acquire would be restricted to the State which gave them. . . .

. . . [N]o State can, by any act or law of its own, passed since the adoption of the Constitution, introduce a new member into the political community created by the Constitution of the United States. It cannot make him a member of this community by making him a member of its own. And for the same reason it cannot introduce any person, or description of persons, who were not intended to be embraced in this new political family, which the Constitution brought into existence, but were intended to be excluded from it.

The question then arises, whether the provisions of the Constitution, in relation to the personal rights and privileges to which the citizen of a State should be entitled, embraced the negro African race, at that time in this country, or who might afterwards be imported, who had then or should afterwards be made free in any State; and to put it in the power of a single State to make him a citizen of the United States, and endue [endow?] him with the full rights of citizenship in every other State without their consent? Does the Constitution of the United States act upon him whenever he shall be made free under the laws of a State, and raised there to the rank of a citizen, and immediately clothe him with all the privileges of a citizen in every other State, and in its own courts?

The court think the affirmative of these propositions cannot be maintained. And if it cannot, the plaintiff in error could not be a citizen of the State of Missouri, within the meaning of the Constitution of the United States, and, consequently, was not entitled to sue in its courts.

. . . [E]very person, and every class and description of persons, who were at the time of the adoption of the Constitution recognised as citizens in the several States, became also citizens of this new political body; but none other; it was formed by them, and for them and their posterity, but for no one else. . . .

In the opinion of the court, the legislation and histories of the times, and the language used in the Declaration of Independence, show, that neither the class of persons who had been imported as slaves, nor their descendants, whether they had become free or not, were then acknowledged as a part of the people, nor intended to be included in the general words used in that memorable instrument. . . .

They had for more than a century before been regarded as beings of an inferior order, and altogether unfit to associate with the white race, either in social or political relations; and so far inferior, that they had no rights which the white man was bound to respect; and that the negro might justly and lawfully be reduced to slavery for his benefit. . . .

This state of public opinion had undergone no change when the Constitution was adopted, as is equally evident from its provisions and language. . . .

. . . [T]here are two clauses in the Constitution which point directly and specifically to the negro race as a separate class of persons, and show clearly that they were not regarded as a portion of the people or citizens of the Government then formed.

One of these clauses reserves to each of the thirteen States the right to import slaves until the year 1808, if it thinks proper. . . . And by the other provision the States pledge themselves to each other to maintain the right of property of the master, by delivering up to him any slave who may have escaped from his service, and be found within their respective territories. . . . [T]hese two provisions show, conclusively, that neither the description of persons therein referred to, nor their descendants, were embraced in any of the other provisions of the Constitution. . . .

. . . [W]e may refer, in support of this proposition, to the plain and unequivocal language of the laws of the several States, some passed after the Declaration of Independence and before the Constitution was adopted, and some since the Government went into operation.

We need not refer, on this point, particularly to the laws of the present slaveholding States. . . . They have continued to treat them as an inferior class, and to subject them to strict police regulations, drawing a broad line of distinction between the citizen and the slave races, and legislating in relation to them upon the same principle which prevailed at the time of the Declaration of Independence. . . .

And if we turn to the legislation of the States where slavery had worn out, or measures taken for its speedy abolition, we shall find the same opinions and principles equally fixed and equally acted upon.

Thus, Massachusetts, in 1776, passed a law [that] . . . forbids the marriage of any white person with any negro, Indian, or mulatto, and inflicts a penalty of fifty pounds upon any one who shall join them in marriage; and declares all such marriages absolutely null and void, and degrades thus the unhappy issue of the marriage by fixing upon it the stain of bastardy. And this mark of degradation was renewed, and again impressed upon the race, in the careful and deliberate preparation of their revised code published in 1836. . . .

So, too, in Connecticut. . . .

By the laws of New Hampshire, collected and finally passed in 1815, no one was permitted to be enrolled in the militia of the State, but free white citizens; and the same provision is found in a subsequent collection of the laws, made in 1855. Nothing could more strongly mark the entire repudiation of the African race. . . .

The legislation of the States therefore shows, in a manner not to be mistaken, the inferior and subject condition of that race at the time the Constitution was adopted, and long afterwards, throughout the thirteen States by which that instrument was framed; and it is hardly consistent with the respect due to these States, to suppose that they regarded at that time, as fellow-citizens and members of the sovereignty, a class of beings whom they had thus stigmatized; ...

To all this mass of proof we have still to add, that Congress has repeatedly legislated upon the same construction of the Constitution that we have given. ...

We proceed ... to inquire whether the facts relied on by the plaintiff entitled him to his freedom. ...

The act of Congress, upon which the plaintiff relies, declares that slavery and involuntary servitude, except as a punishment for crime, shall be forever prohibited in all that part of the territory ceded by France, under the name of Louisiana, which lies north of thirty-six degrees thirty minutes north latitude, and not included within the limits of Missouri. And the difficulty which meets us at the threshold of this part of the inquiry is, whether Congress was authorized to pass this law under any of the powers granted to it by the Constitution. ...

The counsel for the plaintiff has laid much stress upon that article in the Constitution which confers on Congress the power "to dispose of and make all needful rules and regulations respecting the territory or other property belonging to the United States;" but, in the judgment of the court, that provision has no bearing on the present controversy, and the power there given, whatever it may be, is confined, and was intended to be confined, to the territory which at that time belonged to, or was claimed by, the United States, and was within their boundaries as settled by the treaty with Great Britain, and can have no influence upon a territory afterwards acquired from a foreign Government. It was a special provision for a known and particular territory, and to meet a present emergency, and nothing more. ...

... Consequently, the power which Congress may have lawfully exercised in this Territory, while it remained under a Territorial Government, and which may have been sanctioned by judicial decision, can furnish no justification and no argument to support a similar exercise of power over territory afterwards acquired by the Federal Government. ...

This brings us to examine by what provision of the Constitution the present Federal Government, under its delegated and restricted powers, is authorized to acquire territory outside of the original limits of the United States, and what powers it may exercise therein over the person or property of a citizen of the United States, while it remains a Territory, and until it shall be admitted as one of the States of the Union.

There is certainly no power given by the Constitution to the Federal Government to establish or maintain colonies bordering on the United States or at a distance, to be ruled and governed at its own pleasure; nor to enlarge its territorial limits in any way, except by the admission of new States. ...

... The power to expand the territory of the United States by the admission of new States is plainly given; and . . . this power . . . has been held to authorize the acquisition of territory, not fit for admission at the time, but to be admitted as soon as its population and situation would entitle it to admission. It is acquired to become a State, and not to be held as a colony and governed by Congress with absolute authority. . . . [A]s there is no express regulation in the Constitution defining the power which the General Government may exercise over the person or property of a citizen in a Territory thus acquired, the court must necessarily look to the provisions and principles of the Constitution, and its distribution of powers, for the rules and principles by which its decision must be governed.

Taking this rule to guide us, it may be safely assumed that citizens of the United States who migrate to a Territory belonging to the people of the United States, cannot be ruled as mere colonists, dependent upon the will of the General Government, and to be governed by any laws it may think proper to impose. The principle upon which our Governments rest . . . is the union of States, sovereign and independent within their own limits in their internal and domestic concerns, and bound together as one people by a General Government, possessing certain enumerated and restricted powers, delegated to it by the people of the several States, and exercising supreme authority within the scope of the powers granted to it, throughout the dominion of the United States. A power, therefore, in the General Government to obtain and hold colonies and dependent territories, over which they might legislate without restriction, would be inconsistent with its own existence in its present form. Whatever it acquires, it acquires for the benefit of the people of the several States who created it. It is their trustee acting for them, and charged with the duty of promoting the interests of the whole people of the Union in the exercise of the powers specifically granted.

At the time when the Territory in question was obtained by cession from France, it contained no population fit to be associated together and admitted as a State; and it therefore was absolutely necessary to hold possession of it, as a Territory belonging to the United States, until it was settled and inhabited by a civilized community capable of self-government, and in a condition to be admitted on equal terms with the other States as a member of the Union. . . .

But until that time arrives, it is undoubtedly necessary that some Government should be established, in order to organize society, and to protect the inhabitants in their persons and property. . . .

But the power of Congress over the person or property of a citizen can never be a mere discretionary power under our Constitution and form of Government. The powers of the Government and the rights and privileges of the citizen are regulated and plainly defined by the Constitution itself. . . . The Territory being a part of the United States, the Government and the citizen both enter it under the authority of the Constitution, with their respective rights defined and marked out; and the Federal Government can exercise no power over his person or property, beyond what that instrument confers, nor lawfully deny any right which it has reserved. . . .

. . . [T]he rights of property are united with the rights of person, and placed on the same ground by the fifth amendment to the Constitution, which provides that no person shall be deprived of life, liberty, and property, without due process of law. And an act of Congress which deprives a citizen of the United States of his liberty or property, merely because he came himself or brought his property into a particular Territory of the United States, and who had committed no offence against the laws, could hardly be dignified with the name of due process of law. . . .

It seems, however, to be supposed, that there is a difference between property in a slave and other property, and that different rules may be applied to it in expounding the Constitution of the United States. . . .

But . . . if the Constitution recognises the right of property of the master in a slave, and makes no distinction between that description of property and other property owned by a citizen, no tribunal, acting under the authority of the United States, whether it be legislative, executive, or judicial, has a right to draw such a distinction, or deny to it the benefit of the provisions and guarantees which have been provided for the protection of private property against the encroachments of the Government.

Now, . . . the right of property in a slave is distinctly and expressly affirmed in the Constitution. The right to traffic in it, like an ordinary article of merchandise and property, was guarantied to the citizens of the United States, in every State that might desire it, for twenty years. And the Government in express terms is pledged to protect it in all future time, if the slave escapes from his owner. This is done in plain words—too plain to be misunderstood. And no word can be found in the Constitution which gives Congress a greater power over slave property, or which entitles property of that kind to less protection than property of any other description. The only power conferred is the power coupled with the duty of guarding and protecting the owner in his rights.

Upon these considerations, it is the opinion of the court that the act of Congress which prohibited a citizen from holding and owning property of this kind in the territory of the United States north of the line therein mentioned, is not warranted by the Constitution, and is therefore void; and that neither Dred Scott himself, nor any of his family, were made free by being carried into this territory. . . .

Upon the whole, therefore, it is the judgment of this court, that it appears by the record before us that the plaintiff in error is not a citizen of Missouri, in the sense in which that word is used in the Constitution; and that the Circuit Court of the United States, for that reason, had no jurisdiction in the case, and could give no judgment in it. Its judgment for the defendant must, consequently, be reversed, and a mandate issued, directing the suit to be dismissed for want of jurisdiction.

38 ❧

The election of the Republican presidential candidate, Abraham Lincoln, led seven states of the Deep South to secede in the winter of 1860–1861. South Carolina, the foremost advocate of state-sovereignty constitutionalism since the 1820s, took the lead. Its *Declaration of the Immediate Causes* restated the state-sovereignty interpretation of the origins and nature of the Union.

South Carolina Secedes from the Union (1860)

[T HE REVOLUTION] established the two great principles asserted by the Colonies, namely: the right of a State to govern itself; and the right of a people to abolish a Government when it becomes destructive of the ends for which it was instituted. . . .

In 1787, Deputies were appointed by the States to revise the Articles of Confederation, and on 17th September, 1787, these Deputies recommended, for the adoption of the States, the Articles of Union, known as the Constitution of the United States.

The parties to whom this Constitution was submitted, were the several sovereign States. . . .

Thus was established, by compact between the States, a Government, with defined objects and powers, limited to the express words of the grant. . . .

We hold that the Government thus established is subject to the two great principles asserted in the Declaration of Independence; and we hold further, that the mode of its formation subjects it to a third fundamental principle, namely: the law of compact. We maintain that in every compact between two or more parties, the obligation is mutual; that the failure of one of the contracting parties to perform a material part of the agreement, entirely releases the obligation of the other; and that where no arbiter is provided, each party

South Carolina Convention, 1860–1861, *Declaration of the Immediate Causes which Induce and Justify the Secession of South Carolina from the Federal Union and the Ordinance of Secession* (Charleston: Evans and Cogswell, 1860).

is remitted to his own judgment to determine the fact of failure, with all its consequences.

In the present case, that fact is established with certainty. We assert, that fourteen of the States have deliberately refused for years past to fulfil their constitutional obligations. . . .

We affirm that [the] ends for which this Government was instituted have been defeated, and the Government itself has been made destructive of them by the action of the non-slaveholding States. . . .

We, therefore, the people of South Carolina, by our delegates, in Convention assembled, appealing to the Supreme Judge of the world for the rectitude of our intentions, have solemnly declared that the Union heretofore existing between this State and the other States of North America, is dissolved, and that the State of South Carolina has resumed her position among the nations of the world, as a separate and independent State.

An Ordinance

TO DISSOLVE THE UNION BETWEEN THE STATE OF SOUTH CAROLINA AND OTHER STATES UNITED WITH HER UNDER THE COMPACT ENTITLED "THE CONSTITUTION OF THE UNITED STATES OF AMERICA."

We, the People of the State of South Carolina in Convention assembled, do declare and ordain, . . .

That the Ordinance adopted by us in Convention, . . . whereby the Constitution of the United States of America was ratified, and also, all Acts and parts of Acts of the General Assembly of this State, ratifying amendments of the said Constitution, are hereby repealed; and that the union now subsisting between South Carolina and other States, under the name of "The United States of America," is hereby dissolved.

39 ∾

In his first inaugural address, Abraham Lincoln answered the state-sovereignty justification of secession, denying that the Union was created by sovereign states. Indeed, Lincoln argued, the Union predated even independence.

Abraham Lincoln, First Inaugural Address (1861)

. . . [**A**]   DISRUPTION of the Federal Union, heretofore only menaced, is now formidably attempted.

Richardson (ed.), *Messages and Papers of the Presidents*, 6: 5–12.

I hold that in contemplation of universal law and of the Constitution the Union of these States is perpetual. Perpetuity is implied, if not expressed, in the fundamental law of all national governments. It is safe to assert that no government proper ever had a provision in its organic law for its own termination. Continue to execute all the express provisions of our National Constitution, and the Union will endure forever, it being impossible to destroy it except by some action not provided for in the instrument itself.

Again: If the United States be not a government proper, but an association of States in the nature of contract merely, can it, as a contract, be peaceably unmade by less than all the parties who made it? One party to a contract may violate it—break it, so to speak—but does it not require all to lawfully rescind it?

Descending from these general principles, we find the proposition that in legal contemplation the Union is perpetual confirmed by the history of the Union itself. The Union is much older than the Constitution. It was formed, in fact, by the Articles of Association in 1774. It was matured and continued by the Declaration of Independence in 1776. It was further matured, and the faith of all the then thirteen States expressly plighted and engaged that it should be perpetual, by the Articles of Confederation in 1778. And finally, in 1787, one of the declared objects for ordaining and establishing the Constitution was *"to form a more perfect Union."*

But if destruction of the Union by one or by a part only of the States be lawfully possible, the Union is *less* perfect than before the Constitution, having lost the vital element of perpetuity.

It follows from these views that no State upon its own mere motion can lawfully get out of the Union, that *resolves* and *ordinances* to that effect are legally void, and that acts of violence within any State or States against the authority of the United States are insurrectionary or revolutionary, according to circumstances.

I therefore consider that in view of the Constitution and the laws the Union is unbroken, and to the extent of my ability I shall take care, as the Constitution itself expressly enjoins upon me, that the laws of the Union be faithfully executed in all the States.

C H A P T E R   9

The Constitution and the Civil War

40 ❧

When the Civil War began with South Carolina's shelling of Fort Sumter on April 12, 1861, Lincoln acted decisively. Ordering a special session of Congress for July, in the interim the president mobilized the state militias, called for volunteers to serve in the United States armed forces, proclaimed a blockade of Confederate ports, and issued a proclamation suspending the privilege of the writ of *habeas corpus*. He justified his actions by somewhat loose interpretations of preexisting laws and by citing the Constitution's mandate that the president "take Care that the Laws be faithfully executed," by his constitutional status as commander-in-chief of the armed forces, and by the oath of office specified in Article II, which obligated the president to "preserve, protect, and defend the Constitution of the United States." Lincoln argued that those provisions gave the president implied powers to carry out his responsibilities, subject to the final authority of Congress.

Chief Justice Roger Taney challenged Lincoln's views. When army officers, fighting their way through guerrillas and snipers in Maryland, arrested a leading Confederate sympathizer and held him without trial, Taney arranged personally to hear the petition for a writ of *habeas corpus* in his capacity as circuit court judge. (Each Supreme Court justice was responsible for traveling around a specific circuit, joining district court judges to hear various federal cases.) Despite Lincoln's proclamation, Taney issued the writ. When the arresting officer, obeying Lincoln's command, refused to produce the prisoner, Taney issued a blistering opinion denouncing the president's usurpation of power. Lincoln responded to Taney's argument in the message he sent to Congress when it convened in July.

Lincoln and Taney Clash over Presidential Power and *Habeas Corpus* (1861)

Ex Parte Merryman

AS THE CASE comes before me, . . . I understand that the President not only claims the right to suspend the writ of *habeas corpus* himself, at his discretion,

17 Federal Cases 144 (Circuit Ct. Maryland. 1861) (Case No. 9487).

but to delegate that discretionary power to a military officer, and to leave it to him to determine whether he will or will not obey judicial process that may be served upon him. . . .

. . . I had supposed it to be one of those points of constitutional law upon which there was no difference of opinion, and that it was admitted on all hands that the privilege of the writ could not be suspended except by an act of Congress. . . .

It is the second Article of the Constitution that provides for the organization of the Executive Department, and enumerates the powers conferred on it, and prescribes its duties. And if the high power over the liberty of the citizens now claimed was intended to be conferred on the President, it would undoubtedly be found in plain words in this article. But there is not a word in it that can furnish the slightest ground to justify the exercise of the power. . . .

And the only power, therefore, which the President possesses, where the "life, liberty and property" of a private citizen is concerned, is the power and duties prescribed in the third section of the Second Article which requires, "that he shall take care that the laws be faithfully executed." He is not authorized to execute them himself, or through agents or officers, civil or military, appointed by himself, but he is to take care that they be faithfully carried into execution as they are expounded and adjudged by the co-ordinate branch of the government, to which that duty is assigned by the Constitution. It is thus made his duty to come in aid of the judicial authority, if it shall be resisted by force too strong to be overcome without the assistance of the Executive arm. But in exercising this power, he acts in subordination to judicial authority, assisting it to execute its process and enforce its judgments.

With such provisions in the Constitution, expressed in language too clear to be misunderstood by anyone, I can see no ground whatever for supposing that the President in any emergency or in any state of things can authorize the suspension of the privilege of the writ of *habeas corpus,* or arrest a citizen except in aid of the judicial power.

Abraham Lincoln, Message to Congress (July 4, 1861)

SOON AFTER THE first call for militia it was considered a duty to authorize the Commanding General in proper cases, according to his discretion, to suspend the privilege of the writ of *habeas corpus,* or, in other words, to arrest and detain without resort to the ordinary processes and forms of law such individuals as he might deem dangerous to the public safety. This authority has purposely been exercised but very sparingly. Nevertheless, the legality and

Richardson (ed.), *Messages and Papers of the Presidents,* 6: 20–31.

propriety of what has been done under it are questioned, and the attention of the country has been called to the proposition that one who is sworn to "take care that the laws be faithfully executed" should not himself violate them. Of course some consideration was given to the questions of power and propriety before this matter was acted upon. The whole of the laws which were required to be faithfully executed were being resisted and failing of execution in nearly one-third of the States. Must they be allowed to finally fail of execution, even had it been perfectly clear that by the use of the means necessary to their execution some single law, made in such extreme tenderness of the citizen's liberty that practically it relieves more of the guilty than of the innocent, should to a very limited extent be violated? To state the question more directly, Are all the laws *but one* to go unexecuted, and the Government itself go to pieces lest that one be violated? Even in such a case, would not the official oath be broken if the Government should be overthrown when it was believed that disregarding the single law would tend to preserve it? But it was not believed that this question was presented. It was not believed that any law was violated. The provision of the Constitution that "the privilege of the writ of *habeas corpus* shall not be suspended unless when, in cases of rebellion or invasion, the public safety may require it" is equivalent to a provision—is a provision—that such privilege may be suspended when, in cases of rebellion or invasion, the public safety *does* require it. It was decided that we have a case of rebellion and that the public safety does require the qualified suspension of the privilege of the writ which was authorized to be made. Now it is insisted that Congress, and not the Executive, is vested with this power; but the Constitution itself is silent as to which or who is to exercise the power; and as the provision was plainly made for a dangerous emergency, it can not be believed the framers of the instrument intended that in every case the danger should run its course until Congress could be called together, the very assembling of which might be prevented, as was intended in this case, by the rebellion.

No more extended argument is now offered, as an opinion at some length will probably be presented by the Attorney-General. Whether there shall be any legislation upon the subject, and, if any, what, is submitted entirely to the better judgment of Congress.

41 ❧

By 1862 Lincoln was under intense pressure to make the abolition of slavery a war aim. He resisted doing so, afraid that it would alienate northern Democrats and southern Unionists. When a few military officers freed slaves in their theaters of operation, he countermanded their orders, insisting that the Constitution limited the government's war powers to actions directly related to winning the war. However, in the autumn of

1862, Lincoln announced that he would issue a proclamation freeing the slaves of those still in rebellion on January 1, 1863. On that day, justifying it as a war measure, he issued the Emancipation Proclamation, freeing all slaves behind enemy lines.

Abraham Lincoln, The Emancipation Proclamation (1863)

... **I,** ABRAHAM Lincoln, President of the United States, by virtue of the power in me vested as Commander in Chief of the Army and Navy of the United States in time of actual armed rebellion against the authority and Government of the United States, and as a fit and necessary war measure for suppressing said rebellion, . . . do order and declare that all persons held as slaves within said designated States and parts of States are and henceforward shall be free, and that the executive government of the United States, including the military and naval authorities thereof, will recognize and maintain the freedom of said persons.

And I hereby enjoin upon the people so declared to be free to abstain from all violence, unless in necessary self-defense; and I recommend to them that in all cases when allowed they labor faithfully for reasonable wages.

And I further declare and make known that such persons of suitable condition will be received into the armed service of the United States to garrison forts, positions, stations, and other places and to man vessels of all sorts in said service.

And upon this act, sincerely believed to be an act of justice, warranted by the Constitution upon military necessity, I invoke the considerate judgment of mankind and the gracious favor of Almighty God.

42

Abraham Lincoln was not the main speaker at the dedication of the cemetery at Gettysburg. Following Edward Everett's classical oration, Lincoln offered only a few words. But they summarized both the American mission—to prove to the world that people are capable of democratic self-government—and the nationalist understanding of federalism. Note that Lincoln once more dated the founding of the nation to before the ratification of the Constitution. His great allusion to government of, by, and for the people echoed Daniel Webster's reply to Robert Hayne (Document 28) and rebutted the state-sovereignty argument that the Union was created by and for the states.

Richardson (ed.), *Messages and Papers of the Presidents,* 6: 157–159.

Abraham Lincoln, The Gettysburg Address (1863)

FOURSCORE and seven years ago our fathers brought forth on this continent a new nation, conceived in liberty, and dedicated to the proposition that all men are created equal.

Now we are engaged in a great civil war, testing whether that nation, or any nation so conceived and so dedicated, can long endure. We are met on a great battlefield of that war. We have come to dedicate a portion of that field as a final resting-place for those who here gave their lives that that nation might live. It is altogether fitting and proper that we should do this.

But, in a larger sense, we cannot dedicate—we cannot consecrate—we cannot hallow—this ground. The brave men, living and dead, who struggled here, have consecrated it far above our poor power to add or detract. The world will little note nor long remember what we say here, but it can never forget what they did here. It is for us, the living, rather, to be dedicated here to the unfinished work which they who fought here have thus far so nobly advanced. It is rather for us to be here dedicated to the great task remaining before us—that from these honored dead we take increased devotion to that cause for which they gave the last full measure of devotion; that we here highly resolve that these dead shall not have died in vain; that this nation, under God, shall have a new birth of freedom; and that government of the people, by the people, for the people, shall not perish from the earth.

Roy P. Basler (ed.), *The Collected Works of Abraham Lincoln* (New Brunswick, N.J.: Rutgers University Press, 1953), 7: 23.

CHAPTER 10

Reconstruction and the Constitution

43 ❧

Upon the assassination of Abraham Lincoln just as the Civil War ended, Andrew Johnson became president. Johnson, a state rights–oriented Jacksonian Democrat, had been the only senator from a seceding state to remain loyal to the Union. Lincoln had secured his nomination as vice-president to represent the wartime coalition of Republicans and War Democrats in the Union party. Johnson hoped for a quick restoration of the southern states to normal relations in the Union. Claiming authority as commander-in-chief to control the Reconstruction process, Johnson appointed provisional governors who organized state constitutional conventions to reestablish loyal state governments. He required the conventions to repudiate secession, recognize emancipation, and ratify the Thirteenth Amendment. When they did so, the president urged Congress to recognize their restoration and seat those of their congressmen and senators who met loyalty requirements.

Republicans, however, were unwilling to end Reconstruction without taking action to protect the basic rights of the freed slaves. Their resolve stiffened as the southern state legislatures, counties, and towns passed "Black Codes" that in many cases severely restricted the freedom of African Americans. Hoping that Johnson would cooperate, Republicans passed the Civil Rights Bill in April 1866. Its first section, reproduced below, declared all persons born in the United States to be citizens, repudiating the Supreme Court's decision in *Dred Scott v. Sandford*. Other sections punished those who violated the act and authorized the transfer of cases from state to federal courts in any jurisdiction that enforced laws or customs denying the guaranteed rights. Republicans sustained the constitutionality of the Civil Rights Act as an exercise of the power granted by the second section of the Thirteenth Amendment or as an enforcement of the Privileges and Immunities Clause of Article IV, section 2 of the Constitution (see the appendix, p. A-9).

President Johnson broke with the party that had elected him vice-president and vetoed the Civil Rights Bill for invading the jurisdiction of the states. However, Congress overrode the veto and then proposed the Fourteenth Amendment, which incorporated the bill's fundamental principles (see appendix, pp. A-13–A-14).

Andrew Johnson Vetoes the Civil Rights Bill (1866)

The Civil Rights Act of 1866

ALL PERSONS born in the United States and not subject to any foreign power, excluding Indians not taxed, are hereby declared to be citizens of the United States; and such citizens, of every race and color, without regard to any previous condition of slavery or involuntary servitude, except as a punishment for crime whereof the party shall have been duly convicted, shall have the same right, in every State and Territory in the United States, to make and enforce contracts, to sue, be parties, and give evidence, to inherit, purchase, lease, sell, hold, and convey real and personal property, and to full and equal benefit of all laws and proceedings for the security of person and property, as is enjoyed by white citizens, and shall be subject to like punishment, pains and penalties, and to none other, any law, statute, ordinance, regulation, or custom, to the contrary notwithstanding.

Andrew Johnson, Veto of the Civil Rights Bill

IN ALL OUR history, in all our experience as a people living under Federal and State law, no such system as that contemplated by the details of this bill has ever before been proposed or adopted. They establish for the security of the colored race safeguards which go infinitely beyond any that the General Government has ever provided for the white race. In fact, the distinction of race and color is by the bill made to operate in favor of the colored and against the white race. They interfere with the municipal legislation of the States, with the relations existing exclusively between a State and its citizens, or between inhabitants of the same State—an absorption and assumption of power by the General Government which, if acquiesced in, must sap and destroy our federative system of limited powers and break down the barriers which preserve the rights of the States. It is another step, or rather stride, toward centralization and the concentration of all legislative power in the National Government.

44 ∾

With President Johnson encouraging their resistance, all the former Confederate states but Tennessee refused to ratify the Fourteenth Amendment. In response, Congress passed a Reconstruction law over Johnson's veto. The Reconstruction Act put all the

U.S. Statutes at Large, 14 (1866): 27.
Richardson (ed.), *Messages and Papers of the Presidents,* 6: 405–413.

southern states except Tennessee under military control, promising restoration to the Union when they held new state conventions, elected by black as well as white voters, ratified the Fourteenth Amendment, eliminated racial discrimination from their laws, and established equal voting rights without regard to race. All the states complied and were restored to the Union by 1870, most with Republican-run state governments.

The Reconstruction Act (1867)

W H E R E A S no legal State governments or adequate protection for life or property now exists in the rebel States of Virginia, North Carolina, South Carolina, Georgia, Mississippi, Alabama, Louisiana, Florida, Texas, and Arkansas; and whereas it is necessary that peace and good order should be enforced in said States until loyalty and republican State governments can be legally established: Therefore

Be it enacted, . . . That said rebel States shall be divided into military districts and made subject to the military authority of the United States. . . .

Sec. 3. . . . . It shall be the duty of each officer assigned as aforesaid to protect all persons in their rights of person and property, to suppress insurrection, disorder, and violence, and to punish, or cause to be punished, all disturbers of the public peace and criminals, and to this end he may allow local civil tribunals to take jurisdiction of and to try offenders, or, when in his judgment it may be necessary for the trial of offenders, he shall have power to organize military commissions or tribunals for that purpose. . . .

Sec. 5. . . . . When the people of any one of said rebel States shall have formed a constitution of government in conformity with the Constitution of the United States in all respects, framed by a convention of delegates elected by the male citizens of said State twenty-one years old and upward, of whatever race, color, or previous condition, . . . and when such constitution shall provide that the elective franchise shall be enjoyed by all such persons as have the qualifications herein stated for electors of delegates, and when such constitution shall be ratified by a majority of the persons voting on the question of ratification who are qualified as electors of delegates, and when such constitution shall have been submitted to Congress for examination and approval, and Congress shall have approved the same, and when said State, by a vote of its legislature elected under said constitution, shall have adopted the amendment to the Constitution of the United States, proposed by the thirty-ninth Congress, and known as article fourteen, and when said article shall have become a part of the Constitution of the United States, said State shall be declared entitled to representation in Congress, and senators and

U.S. Statues at Large, 14 (1867): 428.

representatives shall be admitted therefrom on their taking oaths prescribed by law, and then and thereafter the preceding sections of this act shall be inoperative in said State. . . .

Sec. 6. . . . Until the people of said rebel States shall be by law admitted to representation in the Congress of the United States, any civil governments which may exist therein shall be deemed provisional only, and in all respects subject to the paramount authority of the United States at any time to abolish, modify or control, or supersede the same.

45 ∽

President Johnson continued to oppose the Republican Reconstruction policy, using all his political and constitutional powers to do so. He used his patronage power to remove federal officers who opposed his course, replacing them with his supporters. Congress responded by passing the Tenure of Office Act in 1867 over Johnson's veto. The law restored ousted officers to their positions if Congress refused to confirm the nominations of their successors. Appointing military officers in accordance with the Reconstruction Act, Johnson interpreted their authority narrowly; he replaced commanders who enforced the law vigorously. Finally, in an effort to gain full control of the army, Johnson suspended Secretary of War Edwin M. Stanton, who sympathized with the Republicans, in accordance with procedures specified by the Tenure of Office Act. When the Senate refused to concur in the suspension, Johnson removed Stanton anyway, in apparent defiance of the law.

The House of Representatives, in December 1867, had already voted against impeaching Johnson for his general obstructiveness. Many Republicans had argued that a president could be impeached only for clear violations of law rather than for abuses of power. With Johnson now seeming to flout the law openly, the House voted impeachment resolutions, fearing that he was planning to defy the Reconstruction Acts as well. Most of the articles were variations of Articles I and III. Article X alleged a kind of seditious libel on Congress, while Article XI attempted to place Johnson's removal of Stanton in the context of the president's campaign to undermine the Reconstruction Acts. In the end, the Republicans fell one vote short of convicting Johnson in the Senate, in large part because it did not appear that Stanton was covered by the Tenure of Office Act after all.

Articles of Impeachment (1868)

ART. I. That said Andrew Johnson, President of the United States, on the 21st day of February, A. D. 1868, at Washington, in the District of Columbia, unmindful of the high duties of his office, of his oath of office, and of the require-

Richardson (ed.), *Messages and Papers of the Presidents*, 6: 709–718.

ment of the Constitution that he should take care that the laws be faithfully executed, did unlawfully and in violation of the Constitution and laws of the United States issue an order in writing for the removal of Edwin M. Stanton from the office of Secretary for the Department of War. . . . which order was unlawfully issued with intent then and there to violate the act entitled "An act regulating the tenure of certain civil offices," passed March 2, 1867, and with the further intent, contrary to the provisions of said act, in violation thereof, and contrary to the provisions of the Constitution of the United States, and without the advice and consent of the Senate of the United States, the said Senate then and there being in session, to remove said Edwin M. Stanton from the office of Secretary for the Department of War, the said Edwin M. Stanton being then and there Secretary for the Department of War, and being then and there in the due and lawful execution and discharge of the duties of said office; whereby said Andrew Johnson, President of the United States, did then and there commit and was guilty of a high misdemeanor in office.

ART. III. That said Andrew Johnson, President of the United States, on the 21st day of February, A. D. 1868, at Washington, in the District of Columbia, did commit and was guilty of a high misdemeanor in office in this, that without authority of law, while the Senate of the United States was then and there in session, he did appoint one Lorenzo Thomas to be Secretary for the Department of War *ad interim,* without the advice and consent of the Senate, and with intent to violate the Constitution of the United States, no vacancy having happened in said office of Secretary for the Department of War during the recess of the Senate, and no vacancy existing in said office at the time. . . .

ART. X. That said Andrew Johnson, President of the United States, unmindful of the high duties of his office and the dignity and proprieties thereof, and of the harmony and courtesies which ought to exist and be maintained between the executive and legislative branches of the Government of the United States, designing and intending to set aside the rightful authority and powers of Congress, did attempt to bring into disgrace, ridicule, hatred, contempt, and reproach the Congress of the United States and the several branches thereof, to impair and destroy the regard and respect of all the good people of the United States for the Congress and legislative power thereof (which all officers of the Government ought inviolably to preserve and maintain), and to excite the odium and resentment of all the good people of the United States against Congress and the laws by it duly and constitutionally enacted. . . .

. . . [B]y means whereof said Andrew Johnson has brought the high office of the President of the United States into contempt, ridicule, and disgrace, to the great scandal of all good citizens; whereby said Andrew Johnson, President of the United States, did commit and was then and there guilty of a high misdemeanor in office.

ART. XI. That said Andrew Johnson, President of the United States, unmindful of the high duties of his office and of his oath of office, and in disregard of the Constitution and laws of the United States, did heretofore, to wit, on the 18th day of August, A.D. 1866, at the city of Washington, in the District of Columbia, by public speech, declare and affirm in substance that the Thirty-ninth Congress of the United States was not a Congress of the United States authorized by the Constitution to exercise legislative power under the same, but, on the contrary, was a Congress of only part of the States; thereby denying and intending to deny that the legislation of said Congress was valid or obligatory upon him, the said Andrew Johnson, except in so far as he saw fit to approve the same, and also thereby denying and intending to deny the power of the said Thirty-ninth Congress to propose amendments to the Constitution of the United States; and in pursuance of said declaration the said Andrew Johnson, President of the United States, afterwards, to wit, on the 21st day of February, A.D. 1868, at the city of Washington, in the District of Columbia, did unlawfully, and in disregard of the requirement of the Constitution that he should take care that the laws be faithfully executed, attempt to prevent the execution of an act entitled "An act regulating the tenure of certain civil offices," passed March 2, 1867, by unlawfully devising and contriving, and attempting to devise and contrive, means by which he should prevent Edwin M. Stanton from forthwith resuming the functions of the office of Secretary for the Department of War, notwithstanding the refusal of the Senate to concur in the suspension theretofore made by said Andrew Johnson of said Edwin M. Stanton from said office of Secretary for the Department of War, and also by further unlawfully devising and contriving, and attempting to devise and contrive, means then and there to prevent the execution of an act entitled "An act making appropriations for the support of the Army for the fiscal year ending June 30, 1868, and for other purposes," approved March 2, 1867, and also to prevent the execution of an act entitled "An act to provide for the more efficient government of the rebel States," passed March 2, 1867, whereby the said Andrew Johnson, President of the United States, did then, to wit, on the 21st day of February, A.D. 1868, at the city of Washington, commit and was guilty of a high misdemeanor in office.

46 ⌇

The Civil War and Reconstruction marked a virtual revolution in the federal system. The Thirteenth, Fourteenth, and Fifteenth Amendments (see the appendix, pp. A-13–A-15) for the first time empowered the federal government to protect the rights of the people of the United States. But while the Civil War had discredited the old state-sovereignty theory of the Constitution, it did not kill the commitment to state rights. Now that constitutional nationalism was ascendant, people worried that taken to its logical consequences, it might destroy the contours of the federal system. During Reconstruction, therefore, Northerners only reluctantly concluded that the national government had to take on the responsibility for protecting rights, and they tried to preserve the basic structure of federalism. Reconstruction legislation was designed to encourage the states to fulfill their obligation to afford equal protection of fundamental rights.

The Supreme Court reflected the general desire to preserve federalism in *Texas v. White*. In this case the defendants challenged the right of Texas to bring a suit against them in federal court, arguing that its unreconstructed government did not represent a state in the Union. Chief Justice Chase's majority opinion echoed Lincoln's nationalistic argument that the Union was an organic development predating the Constitution. But Chase followed this panegyric to the Union with a paean to the place of the states within it, reconciling Lincoln's nationalistic rhetoric with a concern for state rights.

Texas v. White (1869)

T H E   C H I E F Justice delivered the opinion of the Court. . . .

The Union of the States never was a purely artificial and arbitrary relation. It began among the Colonies, and grew out of common origin, mutual sympathies, kindred principles, similar interests, and geographical relations. It was confirmed and strengthened by the necessities of war, and received definite form, and character, and sanction from the Articles of Confederation. By these the Union was solemnly declared to "be perpetual." And when these Articles were found to be inadequate to the exigencies of the country, the Constitution was ordained "to form a more perfect Union." It is difficult to convey the idea of indissoluble unity more clearly than by these words. What can be indissoluble if a perpetual Union, made more perfect, is not?

But the perpetuity and indissolubility of the Union, by no means implies the loss of distinct and individual existence, or of the right of self-government by the States. Under the Articles of Confederation each State retained its sovereignty, freedom, and independence, and every power, jurisdiction, and right not expressly delegated to the United States. Under the Constitution, though the powers of the States were much restricted, still, all powers not delegated to the United States, nor prohibited to the States, are reserved to the States respectively, or to the people. And we have already had occasion to remark at this term, that "the people of each State compose a State, having its own government, and endowed with all the functions essential to separate and independent existence," and that "without the States in union, there could be no

74 U.S.(7 Wallace) 700 (1869).

such political body as the United States." Not only, therefore, can there be no loss of separate and independent autonomy to the States, through their union under the Constitution, but it may be not unreasonably said that the preservation of the States, and the maintenance of their governments, are as much within the design and care of the Constitution as the preservation of the Union and the maintenance of the National government. The Constitution, in all its provisions, looks to an indestructible Union, composed of indestructible States. . . .

Considered therefore as transactions under the Constitution, the ordinance of secession, adopted by the convention and ratified by a majority of the citizens of Texas, and all the acts of her legislature intended to give effect to that ordinance, were absolutely null. They were utterly without operation in law. The obligations of the State, as a member of the Union, and of every citizen of the State, as a citizen of the United States, remained perfect and unimpaired. It certainly follows that the State did not cease to be a State, nor her citizens to be citizens of the Union.

47 ❧

The opinions in the Slaughterhouse Cases were the Supreme Court's first comprehensive interpretation of the Fourteenth Amendment. The facts of the case brought home the revolutionary potential of the Fourteenth Amendment for the federal system.

The case did not involve the rights of African Americans, for whose protection the amendment had been principally designed. Instead, the plaintiffs were New Orleans butchers, probably all white Democrats, who were attacking a health regulation passed by Louisiana's Republican state legislature, elected as a consequence of Reconstruction. In an effort to ward off recurrent epidemics, the law chartered a company to build a slaughterhouse downriver from the city and required all butchering to be done at its facilities. The butchers argued that the law fostered a monopoly, depriving them of one of the privileges of a citizen of the United States—to pursue freely their occupations—as well as depriving them of liberty without due process of law and denying them equal protection, all violations of the newly ratified Fourteenth Amendment.

If the Supreme Court agreed that such legislation came within the purview of the Fourteenth Amendment, it would mark a revolution in federalism. Not only would hosts of state laws be challenged in the courts, but Congress would have authority to review and counteract similar laws under the fifth section of the Amendment. To avoid these consequences, a narrow 5–4 majority of the justices fell back on state-rights conceptions of the Union. As in the *Dred Scott* decision, the Court separated state citizenship from national citizenship and defined each as embodying different privileges. Protection of ordinary rights was a privilege of state citizenship that remained within state jurisdiction; the privileges of United States citizenship referred to rights inherently national. The

Court dismissed the butchers' due-process and equal-protection arguments curtly, without much analysis.

The *Slaughterhouse* decision significantly narrowed the sorts of rights that the federal government could protect under the Fourteenth Amendment. It became extremely difficult to enforce Reconstruction-era laws protecting the civil and political rights of African Americans.

The Slaughterhouse Cases (1873)

M R . J U S T I C E Miller delivered the opinion of the Court. . . .

. . . [I]n the light of . . . events, almost too recent to be called history, but which are familiar to us all; and on the most casual examination of the language of these amendments, no one can fail to be impressed with the one pervading purpose found in them all, lying at the foundation of each, and without which none of them would have been even suggested; we mean the freedom of the slave race, the security and firm establishment of that freedom, and the protection of the newly-made freeman and citizen from the oppressions of those who had formerly exercised unlimited dominion over him. . . .

We do not say that no one else but the negro can share in this protection. Both the language and spirit of these articles are to have their fair and just weight in any question of construction. . . .

The first section of the fourteenth article, to which our attention is more specially invited, opens with a definition of citizenship—not only citizenship of the United States, but citizenship of the States. No such definition was previously found in the Constitution, nor had any attempt been made to define it by act of Congress. . . . But it had been held by this court, in the celebrated Dred Scott case, only a few years before the outbreak of the civil war, that a man of African descent, whether a slave or not, was not and could not be a citizen of a State or of the United States. . . .

. . . [T]o establish a clear and comprehensive definition of citizenship which should declare what should constitute citizenship of the United States, and also citizenship of a State, the first clause of the first section was framed.

"All persons born or naturalized in the United States, and subject to the jurisdiction thereof, are citizens of the United States and of the State wherein they reside." . . .

. . . It declares that persons may be citizens of the United States without regard to their citizenship of a particular State, and it overturns the Dred Scott decision by making *all persons* born within the United States and subject to its jurisdiction citizens of the United States. . . .

83 U.S. (16 Wallace) 36 (1873).

The next observation is more important in view of the arguments of counsel in the present case. It is, that the distinction between citizenship of the United States and citizenship of a State is clearly recognized and established. Not only may a man be a citizen of the United States without being a citizen of a State, but an important element is necessary to convert the former into the latter. He must reside within the State to make him a citizen of it, but it is only necessary that he should be born or naturalized in the United States to be a citizen of the Union.

It is quite clear, then, that there is a citizenship of the United States, and a citizenship of a State, which are distinct from each other, and which depend upon different characteristics or circumstances in the individual.

We think this distinction and its explicit recognition in this amendment of great weight in this argument, because the next paragraph of this same section, which is the one mainly relied on by the plaintiffs in error, speaks only of privileges and immunities of citizens of the United States, and does not speak of those of citizens of the several States. The argument, however, in favor of the plaintiffs rests wholly on the assumption that the citizenship is the same, and the privileges and immunities guaranteed by the clause are the same.

The language is, "No State shall make or enforce any law which shall abridge the privileges or immunities of citizens of *the United States*." It is a little remarkable, if this clause was intended as a protection to the citizen of a State against the legislative power of his own State, that the word citizen of the State should be left out when it is so carefully used, and used in contradistinction to citizens of the United States, in the very sentence which precedes it. It is too clear for argument that the change in phraseology was adopted understandingly and with a purpose.

Of the privileges and immunities of the citizen of the United States, and of the privileges and immunities of the citizen of the State, and what they respectively are, we will presently consider; but we wish to state here that it is only the former which are placed by this clause under the protection of the Federal Constitution, and that the latter, whatever they may be, are not intended to have any additional protection by this paragraph of the amendment.

If, then, there is a difference between the privileges and immunities belonging to a citizen of the United States as such, and those belonging to the citizen of the State as such, the latter must rest for their security and protection where they have heretofore rested; for they are not embraced by this paragraph of the amendment. . . .

In the Constitution of the United States . . . is found in section two of the fourth article, . . . the following words: "The citizens of each State shall be entitled to all the privileges and immunities of citizens of the several States." . . .

... [W]e are not without judicial construction of this clause of the Constitution. The first and the leading case on the subject is that of *Corfield* v. *Coryell,* decided by Mr. Justice Washington in the Circuit Court for the District of Pennsylvania in 1823.

"The inquiry," he says, "is, what are the privileges and immunities of citizens of the several States? We feel no hesitation in confining these expressions to those privileges and immunities which are *fundamental;* which belong of right to the citizens of all free governments, and which have at all times been enjoyed by citizens of the several States which compose this Union, from the time of their becoming free, independent, and sovereign. What these fundamental principles are, it would be more tedious than difficult to enumerate. They may all, however, be comprehended under the following general heads: protection by the government, with the right to acquire and possess property of every kind, and to pursue and obtain happiness and safety, subject, nevertheless, to such restraints as the government may prescribe for the general good of the whole."

This definition of the privileges and immunities of citizens of the States ... embraces nearly every civil right for the establishment and protection of which organized government is instituted. ...

It would be the vainest show of learning to attempt to prove by citations of authority, that up to the adoption of the recent amendments, no claim or pretence was set up that those rights depended on the Federal government for their existence or protection, beyond the very few express limitations which the Federal Constitution imposed upon the States—such, for instance, as the prohibition against ex post facto laws, bills of attainder, and laws impairing the obligation of contracts. But with the exception of these and a few other restrictions, the entire domain of the privileges and immunities of citizens of the States, as above defined, lay within the constitutional and legislative power of the States, and without that of the Federal government. Was it the purpose of the fourteenth amendment, by the simple declaration that no State should make or enforce any law which shall abridge the privileges and immunities of *citizens of the United States,* to transfer the security and protection of all the civil rights which we have mentioned, from the States to the Federal government? And where it is declared that Congress shall have the power to enforce that article, was it intended to bring within the power of Congress the entire domain of civil rights heretofore belonging exclusively to the States?

All this and more must follow, if the proposition of the plaintiffs in error be sound. For not only are these rights subject to the control of Congress whenever in its discretion any of them are supposed to be abridged by State legislation, but that body may also pass laws in advance, limiting and restricting the exercise of legislative power by the States, in their most ordinary and usual functions, as in its judgment it may think proper on all such subjects. And still further, such a construction followed by the reversal of the judgments of the Supreme Court of Louisiana in these cases, would constitute this court a perpetual censor upon all legislation of the States, on the civil rights of their own citizens, with authority to nullify such as it did not approve as consistent with those rights, as they existed at the time of the adoption of this amendment. The argument we admit is not always the most conclusive which is drawn from the consequences urged against the adoption of a particular construction of an instrument. But when, as in the case before us, these consequences are so serious, so far-reaching and pervading, so great a departure from the structure and spirit of our institutions; when the effect is to fetter and degrade the State governments by subjecting them to the control of Congress, in the exercise of powers heretofore universally conceded to them of the most ordinary and fundamental character; when in fact it radically changes the whole theory of the relations of the State and Federal governments to each other and of both these governments to the people; the argument has a force that is irresistible, in the absence of language which expresses such a purpose too clearly to admit of doubt.

We are convinced that no such results were intended by the Congress which proposed these amendments, nor by the legislatures of the States which ratified them. . . .

The argument has not been much pressed in these cases that the defendant's charter deprives the plaintiffs of their property without due process of law, or that it denies to them the equal protection of the law. The first of these paragraphs has been in the Constitution since the adoption of the fifth amendment, as a restraint upon the Federal power. It is also to be found in some form of expression in the constitutions of nearly all the States, as a restraint upon the power of the States. This law, then, has practically been the same as it now is during the existence of the government, except so far as the present amendment may place the restraining power over the States in this matter in the hands of the Federal government.

We are not without judicial interpretation, therefore, both State and National, of the meaning of this clause. And it is sufficient to say that under no construction of that provision that we have ever seen, or any that we deem admissible, can the restraint imposed by the State of Louisiana upon the exercise of their trade by the butchers of New Orleans be held to be a deprivation of property within the meaning of that provision.

"Nor shall any State deny to any person within its jurisdiction the equal protection of the laws."

In the light of the history of these amendments, and the pervading purpose of them, which we have already discussed, it is not difficult to give a meaning to this clause. The existence of laws in the States where the newly emancipated negroes resided, which discriminated with gross injustice and hardship against them as a class, was the evil to be remedied by this clause, and by it such laws are forbidden.

If, however, the States did not conform their laws to its requirements, then by the fifth section of the article of amendment Congress was authorized to enforce it by suitable legislation. We doubt very much whether any action of a State not directed by way of discrimination against the negroes as a class, or on account of their race, will ever be held to come within the purview of this provision. It is so clearly a provision for that race and that emergency, that a strong case would be necessary for its application to any other. . . .

In the early history of the organization of the government, its statesmen seem to have divided on the line which should separate the powers of the National government from those of the State governments, and though this line has never been very well defined in public opinion, such a division has continued from that day to this.

The adoption of the first eleven amendments to the Constitution so soon after the original instrument was accepted, shows a prevailing sense of danger at that time from the Federal power. And it cannot be denied that such a jealousy continued to exist with many patriotic men until the breaking out of the late civil war. It was then discovered that the true danger to the perpetuity of the Union was in the capacity of the State organizations to combine and concentrate all the powers of the State, and of contiguous States, for a determined resistance to the General Government.

Unquestionably this has given great force to the argument, and added largely to the number of those who believe in the necessity of a strong National government.

But, however pervading this sentiment, and however it may have contributed to the adoption of the amendments we have been considering, we do not see in those amendments any purpose to destroy the main features of the general system. Under the pressure of all the excited feeling growing out of the war, our statesmen have still believed that the existence of the States with powers for domestic and local government, including the regulation of civil rights—the rights of person and of property—was essential to the perfect working of our complex form of government, though they have thought proper to impose additional limitations on the States, and to confer additional power on that of the Nation.

But whatever fluctuations may be seen in the history of public opinion on this subject during the period of our national existence, we think it will be found that this court, so far as its functions required, has always held with a steady and an even hand the balance between State and Federal power, and we trust that such may continue to be the history of its relation to that subject so long as it shall have duties to perform which demand of it a construction of the Constitution, or of any of its parts.

The judgments of the Supreme Court of Louisiana in these cases are AF-FIRMED.

48 ⌒

Advocates of women's rights, disillusioned by Republicans' refusal to forbid gender discrimination as well as racial discrimination in voting rights during Reconstruction, nonetheless hoped that the Fourteenth Amendment would be interpreted to bar sexual discrimination in basic rights. Upon its ratification Myra Bradwell, the editor of the *Chicago Legal News*, sought admission to the Illinois bar. Although the law governing admissions did not refer to gender, the Illinois Supreme Court refused her application, saying that long custom restricted the bar to men and that only new legislation could reverse the tradition.

Bradwell appealed to the Supreme Court. The *Slaughterhouse* majority simply held that the right to practice one's profession was a privilege of state citizenship and therefore not protected by the Fourteenth Amendment. The dissenters in *Slaughterhouse* concurred in the judgment, even though they believed that the right to follow one's occupation *was* a privilege protected by the amendment. Justice Bradley, writing for the dissenters, argued that Illinois's discrimination was reasonable, given the sphere that society assigned to women. Only Chief Justice Chase would have ruled the discrimination unconstitutional.

Joseph P. Bradley, Concurring Opinion in *Bradwell v. Illinois* (1873)

MR. JUSTICE Bradley:

I concur in the judgment of the court in this case, by which the judgment of the Supreme Court of Illinois is affirmed, but not for the reasons specified in the opinion just read. . . .

The claim that, under the fourteenth amendment of the Constitution, which declares that no State shall make or enforce any law which shall abridge the privileges and immunities of citizens of the United States, the statute law of Illinois, or the common law prevailing in that State, can no longer be set up as a barrier against the right of females to pursue any lawful employment for a livelihood (the practice of law included), assumes that it is

83 U.S. (16 Wallace) 130, at 139 (1873) (Bradley, concurring).

one of the privileges and immunities of women as citizens to engage in any and every profession, occupation, or employment in civil life.

It certainly cannot be affirmed, as an historical fact, that this has ever been established as one of the fundamental privileges and immunities of the sex. On the contrary, the civil law, as well as nature herself, has always recognized a wide difference in the respective spheres and destinies of man and woman. Man is, or should be, woman's protector and defender. The natural and proper timidity and delicacy which belongs to the female sex evidently unfits it for many of the occupations of civil life. The constitution of the family organization, which is founded in the divine ordinance, as well as in the nature of things, indicates the domestic sphere as that which properly belongs to the domain and functions of womanhood. The harmony, not to say identity, of interests and views which belong, or should belong, to the family institution is repugnant to the idea of a woman adopting a distinct and independent career from that of her husband. . . .

The paramount destiny and mission of woman are to fulfil the noble and benign offices of wife and mother. This is the law of the Creator. And the rules of civil society must be adapted to the general constitution of things, and cannot be based upon exceptional cases.

The humane movements of modern society, which have for their object the multiplication of avenues for woman's advancement, and of occupations adapted to her condition and sex, have my heartiest concurrence. But I am not prepared to say that it is one of her fundamental rights and privileges to be admitted into every office and position, including those which require highly special qualifications and demanding special responsibilities. In the nature of things it is not every citizen of every age, sex, and condition that is qualified for every calling and position. It is the prerogative of the legislator to prescribe regulations founded on nature, reason, and experience for the due admission of qualified persons to professions and callings demanding special skill and confidence. This fairly belongs to the police power of the State; and, in my opinion, in view of the peculiar characteristics, destiny, and mission of woman, it is within the province of the legislature to ordain what offices, positions, and callings shall be filled and discharged by men, and shall receive the benefit of those energies and responsibilities, and that decision and firmness which are presumed to predominate in the sterner sex.

49 ❧

In the Civil Rights Cases, the Supreme Court continued to try to insulate the federal system from the revolutionary implications of the post–Civil War amendments. The federal Civil Rights Act of 1875 made it illegal for inns, public conveyances, theaters, and other amusement places to deny full and equal facilities to any person on account of race. But the act was defied throughout the South and much of the North. In 1883, the Supreme Court ruled the law unconstitutional.

Speaking for eight of the nine justices, Justice Bradley carefully distinguished between the powers delegated to Congress under the Thirteenth and Fourteenth Amendments (see the appendix, p. A-13–A-14). The Thirteenth Amendment authorized Congress to protect the fundamental rights of freedom against infringement by private individuals; the Fourteenth authorized Congress to protect a higher category of rights and to prevent arbitrary discriminations, but only against state actions. The State Action Rule became a key element of Fourteenth-Amendment law.

Justice John Marshall Harlan, a former slaveowner who became a leading Kentucky Republican, vigorously dissented. He insisted that racial discrimination was a "badge of servitude" inseparable from slavery, and that Congress could punish individuals for engaging in it.

In the wake of the decision, most of the northern states passed their own laws barring racial discrimination in public accommodations, although the new laws were often flouted. Southern states, in contrast, began to move towards state-enforced racial segregation.

The Civil Rights Cases (1883)

MR. JUSTICE Bradley delivered the opinion of the court. . . .

Has Congress constitutional power to make such a law? Of course, no one will contend that the power to pass it was contained in the Constitution before the adoption of the last three amendments. The power is sought, first, in the Fourteenth Amendment. . . .

The first section of the Fourteenth Amendment (which is the one relied on), after declaring who shall be citizens of the United States, and of the several States, is prohibitory in its character, and prohibitory upon the States. It declares that:

> "No State shall make or enforce any law which shall abridge the privileges or immunities of citizens of the United States; nor shall any State deprive any person of life, liberty, or property without due process of law; nor deny to any person within its jurisdiction the equal protection of the laws."

It is State action of a particular character that is prohibited. Individual invasion of individual rights is not the subject-matter of the amendment. It has a deeper and broader scope. It nullifies and makes void all State legislation, and State action of every kind, which impairs the privileges and immunities of citizens of the United States, or which injures them in life, liberty or prop-

109 U.S. 3 (1883).

erty without due process of law, or which denies to any of them the equal protection of the laws. It not only does this, but, in order that the national will, thus declared, may not be a mere *brutum fulmen* [an empty noise], the last section of the amendment invests Congress with power to enforce it by appropriate legislation. To enforce what? To enforce the prohibition. To adopt appropriate legislation for correcting the effects of such prohibited State laws and State acts, and thus to render them effectually null, void, and innocuous. This is the legislative power conferred upon Congress, and this is the whole of it. It does not invest Congress with power to legislate upon subjects which are within the domain of State legislation; but to provide modes of relief against State legislation, or State action, of the kind referred to. It does not authorize Congress to create a code of municipal law for the regulation of private rights; but to provide modes of redress against the operation of State laws, and the action of State officers executive or judicial, when these are subversive of the fundamental rights specified in the amendment. Positive rights and privileges are undoubtedly secured by the Fourteenth Amendment; but they are secured by way of prohibition against State laws and State proceedings affecting those rights and privileges, and by power given to Congress to legislate for the purpose of carrying such prohibition into effect. . . .

But the power of Congress to adopt direct and primary, as distinguished from corrective legislation, on the subject in hand, is sought, in the second place, from the Thirteenth Amendment, which abolishes slavery. . . .

This amendment, as well as the Fourteenth, is undoubtedly self-executing without any ancillary legislation, so far as its terms are applicable to any existing state of circumstances. By its own unaided force and effect it abolished slavery, and established universal freedom. Still, legislation may be necessary and proper to meet all the various cases and circumstances to be affected by it, and to prescribe proper modes of redress for its violation in letter or spirit. And such legislation may be primary and direct in its character; for the amendment is not a mere prohibition of State laws establishing or upholding slavery, but an absolute declaration that slavery or involuntary servitude shall not exist in any part of the United States. . . .

. . . [I]t is assumed, that the power vested in Congress to enforce the article by appropriate legislation, clothes Congress with power to pass all laws necessary and proper for abolishing all badges and incidents of slavery in the United States: and upon this assumption it is claimed, that this is sufficient authority for declaring by law that all persons shall have equal accommodations and privileges in all inns, public conveyances, and places of amusement; the argument being, that the denial of such equal accommodations and privileges is, in itself, a subjection to a species of servitude within the meaning of the amendment. Conceding the major proposition to be true, that Congress has a right to enact all necessary and proper laws for the obliteration and prevention of slavery with all its badges and incidents, is the minor proposition also true, that the denial to any person of admission to the accommodations and privileges of an inn, a public conveyance, or a theatre, does subject that person to any form of servitude, or tend to fasten upon him any badge of slavery? If it does not, then power to pass the law is not found in the Thirteenth Amendment. . . .

The long existence of African slavery in this country gave us very distinct notions of what it was, and what were its necessary incidents. Compulsory service of the slave for the benefit of the master, restraint of his movements except by the master's will, disability to hold property, to make contracts, to have a standing in court, to be a witness against a white person, and such like burdens and incapacities, were the inseparable incidents of the institution. Severer punishments for crimes were imposed on the slave than on free persons guilty of the same offences. Congress, as we have seen, by the Civil Rights Bill of 1866, passed in view of the Thirteenth Amendment, before the Fourteenth was adopted, undertook to wipe out these burdens and disabilities, the necessary incidents of slavery, constituting its substance and visible form. . . .

. . . Can the act of a mere individual, the owner of the inn, the public conveyance or place of amusement, refusing the accommodation, be justly regarded as imposing any badge of slavery or servitude upon the applicant, or only as inflicting an ordinary civil injury, properly cognizable by the laws of the State, and presumably subject to redress by those laws until the contrary appears?

After giving to these questions all the consideration which their importance demands, we are forced to the conclusion that such an act of refusal has nothing to do with slavery or involuntary servitude, and that if it is violative of any right of the party, his redress is to be sought under the laws of the State. . . . It would be running the slavery argument into the ground to make it apply to every act of discrimination which a person may see fit to make as to the guests he will entertain, or as to the people he will take into his coach or cab or car, or admit to his concert or theatre, or deal with in other matters of intercourse or business. . . .

When a man has emerged from slavery, and by the aid of beneficent legislation has shaken off the inseparable concomitants of that state, there must be some stage in the progress of his elevation when he takes the rank of a mere citizen, and ceases to be the special favorite of the laws, and when his rights as a citizen, or a man, are to be protected in the ordinary modes by which other men's rights are protected. There were thousands of free colored people in this country before the abolition of slavery, enjoying all the essential rights of life, liberty and property the same as white citizens; yet no one, at that time, thought that it was any invasion of his personal status as a freeman because he was not admitted to all the privileges enjoyed by white citizens, or because he was subjected to discriminations in the enjoyment of accommodations in inns, public conveyances and places of amusement. Mere discriminations on account of race or color were not regarded as badges of slavery. . . .

Mr. Justice Harlan dissenting.

The opinion in these cases proceeds, it seems to me, upon grounds entirely too narrow and artificial. I cannot resist the conclusion that the substance and spirit of the recent amendments of the Constitution have been sacrificed by a subtle and ingenious verbal criticism. . . .

The terms of the Thirteenth Amendment are absolute and universal. They embrace every race which then was, or might thereafter be, within the United States. No race, as such, can be excluded from the benefits or rights thereby conferred. Yet, it is historically true that that amendment was suggested by the condition, in this country, of that race which had been declared, by this court, to have had—according to the opinion entertained by the most civilized portion of the white race, at the time of the adoption of the Constitution—"no rights which the white man was bound to respect," none of the privileges or immunities secured by that instrument to citizens of the United States. . . .

These are the circumstances under which the Thirteenth Amendment was proposed for adoption. They are now recalled only that we may better understand what was in the minds of the people when that amendment was considered, and what were the mischiefs to be remedied and the grievances to be redressed by its adoption. . . .

. . . When . . . it was determined, by a change in the fundamental law, to uproot the institution of slavery wherever it existed in the land, and to establish universal freedom, there was a fixed purpose to place the authority of Congress in the premises beyond the possibility of a doubt. Therefore, . . . power to enforce the Thirteenth Amendment, by appropriate legislation, was expressly granted. Legislation for that purpose, my brethren concede, may be direct and primary. But to what specific ends may it be directed? . . .

The Thirteenth Amendment, it is conceded, did something more than to prohibit slavery as an *institution,* resting upon distinctions of race, and upheld by positive law. My brethren admit that it established and decreed universal *civil freedom* throughout the United States. But did the freedom thus established involve nothing more than exemption from actual slavery? Was nothing more intended than to forbid one man from owning another as property? Was it the purpose of the nation simply to destroy the institution, and then remit the race, theretofore held in bondage, to the several States for such protection, in their civil rights, necessarily growing out of freedom, as those States, in their discretion, might choose to provide? Were the States against whose protest the institution was destroyed, to be left free, so far as national interference was concerned, to make or allow discriminations against that race, as such, in the enjoyment of those fundamental rights which by universal concession, inhere in a state of freedom? . . .

That there are burdens and disabilities which constitute badges of slavery and servitude, and that the power to enforce by appropriate legislation the Thirteenth Amendment may be exerted by legislation of a direct and primary character, for the eradication, not simply of the institution, but of its badges and incidents, are propositions which ought to be deemed indisputable. . . . I do not contend that the Thirteenth Amendment invests Congress with authority, by legislation, to define and regulate the entire body of the civil rights which citizens enjoy, or may enjoy, in the several States. But I hold that since slavery, as the court has repeatedly declared, . . . was the moving or principal cause of the adoption of that amendment, and since that institution rested wholly upon the inferiority, as a race, of those held in bondage, their freedom necessarily involved immunity from, and protection against, all discrimination against them, because of their race, in respect of such civil rights as belong to freemen of other races. Congress, therefore, under its express power to enforce that amendment, by appropriate legislation, may enact laws to protect that people against the deprivation, *because of their race,* of any civil rights granted to other freemen in the same State; and such legislation may be of a direct and primary character, operating upon States, their officers and agents, and also, upon, at least, such individuals and corporations as exercise public functions and wield power and authority under the State. . . .

It remains now to consider these cases with reference to the power Congress has possessed since the adoption of the Fourteenth Amendment. . . .

. . . [W]hen, under what circumstances, and to what extent, may Congress, by means of legislation, exert its power to enforce the provisions of this amendment? . . .

. . . The Fourteenth Amendment presents the first instance in our history of the investiture of Congress with affirmative power, by *legislation,* to *enforce* an express prohibition upon the States. It is not said that the *judicial* power of the nation may be exerted for the enforcement of that amendment. No enlargement of the judicial power was required, for it is clear that had the fifth section of the Fourteenth Amendment been entirely omitted, the judiciary could have stricken down all State laws and nullified all State proceedings in hostility to rights and privileges secured or recognized by that amendment. The power given is, in terms, by congressional *legislation,* to enforce the provisions of the amendment.

The assumption that this amendment consists wholly of prohibitions upon State laws and State proceedings in hostility to its provisions, is unauthorized by its language. The first clause of the first section—"All persons born or naturalized in the United States, and subject to the jurisdiction thereof, are citizens of the United States, and of the State wherein they reside"—is of a distinctly affirmative character. . . .

The citizenship thus acquired, by that race, in virtue of an affirmative grant from the nation, may be protected, not alone by the judicial branch of the government, but by congressional legislation of a primary direct character. . . .

It is, therefore, an essential inquiry what, if any, right, privilege or immunity was given, by the nation, to colored persons, when they were made citizens of the State in which they reside? . . .

. . . [W]hat was secured to colored citizens of the United States—as between them and their respective States—by the national grant to them of State citizenship? With what rights, privileges, or immunities did this grant invest them? There is one, if there be no other—exemption from race discrimination in respect of any civil right belonging to citizens of the white race in the same State. . . . [S]uch must be their constitutional right, . . . unless the recent amendments be splendid baubles, thrown out to delude those who deserved fair and generous treatment at the hands of the nation. . . .

This court has always given a broad and liberal construction to the Constitution, so as to enable Congress, by legislation, to enforce rights secured by that instrument. The legislation which Congress may enact, in execution of its power to enforce the provisions of this amendment, is such as may be appropriate to protect the right granted. The word appropriate was undoubtedly used with reference to its meaning, as established by repeated decisions of this court. Under given circumstances, that which the court characterizes as corrective legislation might be deemed by Congress appropriate and entirely sufficient. Under other circumstances primary direct legislation may be required. But it is for Congress, not the judiciary, to say what legislation is appropriate—that is—best adapted to the end to be attained. . . .

This construction does not in any degree intrench upon the just rights of the States in the control of their domestic affairs. It simply recognizes the enlarged powers conferred by the recent amendments upon the general government. . . .

My brethren say, that when a man has emerged from slavery, and by the aid of beneficent legislation has shaken off the inseparable concomitants of that state, there must be some stage in the progress of his elevation when he takes the rank of a mere citizen, and ceases to be the special favorite of the laws, and when his rights as a citizen, or a man, are to be protected in the ordinary modes by which other men's rights are protected. It is, I submit, scarcely just to say that the colored race has been the special favorite of the laws. The statute of 1875, now adjudged to be unconstitutional, is for the benefit of citizens of every race and color. What the nation, through Congress, has sought to accomplish in reference to that race, is—what had already been done in every State of the Union for the white race—to secure and protect rights belonging to them as freemen and citizens; nothing more. . . . Today, it is the colored race which is denied, by corporations and individuals wielding public authority, rights fundamental in their freedom and citizenship. At some future time, it may be that some other race will fall under the ban of race discrimination. If the constitutional amendments be enforced, according to the intent with which, as I conceive, they were adopted, there cannot be, in this republic, any class of human beings in practical subjection to another class, with power in the latter to dole out to the former just such privileges as they may choose to grant. The supreme law of the land has decreed that no authority shall be exercised in this country upon the basis of discrimination, in respect of civil rights, against freemen and citizens because of their race, color, or previous condition of servitude. To that decree—for the due enforcement of which, by appropriate legislation, Congress has been invested with express power—every one must bow.

50 ❧

The flickering commitment of the Republican party to protecting black rights in the South sputtered out with the failure to pass the so-called Force Act of 1890. Within a few years a racist reaction was in full swing, spreading to the North as well as the South. Southern states began to institute mandatory racial segregation and took the first steps towards disfranchising African-American voters.

Trying to stem the tide, African-American leaders and a few white allies tested the new segregation laws in court. Homer Plessy challenged an 1890 Louisiana law requiring racial segregation in railway transportation, arguing that it deprived him of the equal protection of the law in violation of the Fourteenth Amendment. Eight of the nine justices rejected the plea. Justice Harlan filed a dissent that is now considered a classic call for a color-blind Constitution.

Plessy v. Ferguson (1896)

M R. J U S T I C E Brown . . . delivered the opinion of the court. . . .

The object of the [Fourteenth] amendment was undoubtedly to enforce the absolute equality of the two races before the law, but in the nature of things it could not have been intended to abolish distinctions based upon color, or to enforce social, as distinguished from political equality, or a commingling of the two races upon terms unsatisfactory to either. Laws permitting, and even requiring, their separation in places where they are liable to be brought into contact do not necessarily imply the inferiority of either race to the other, and have been generally, if not universally, recognized as within the competency of the state legislatures in the exercise of their police power. The most common instance of this is connected with the establishment of separate schools for white and colored children, which has been held to be a valid exercise of the legislative power even by courts of States where the political rights of the colored race have been longest and most earnestly enforced. . . .

. . . [E]very exercise of the police power must be reasonable, and extend only to such laws as are enacted in good faith for the promotion for the public good, and not for the annoyance or oppression of a particular class. . . .

So far, then, as a conflict with the Fourteenth Amendment is concerned, the case reduces itself to the question whether the statute of Louisiana is a reasonable regulation, and with respect to this there must necessarily be a large discretion on the part of the legislature. In determining the question of reasonableness it is at liberty to act with reference to the established usages, customs and traditions of the people, and with a view to the promotion of their comfort, and the preservation of the public peace and good order. Gauged by this standard, we cannot say that a law which authorizes or even requires the separation of the two races in public conveyances is unreasonable, or more obnoxious to the Fourteenth Amendment than the acts of Congress requiring separate schools for colored children in the District of Columbia, the constitutionality of which does not seem to have been questioned, or the corresponding acts of state legislatures.

We consider the underlying fallacy of the plaintiff's argument to consist in the assumption that the enforced separation of the two races stamps the colored race with a badge of inferiority. If this be so, it is not by reason of anything found in the act, but solely because the colored race chooses to put that construction upon it. . . . The argument also assumes that social prejudices may be overcome by legislation, and that equal rights cannot be secured to the negro except by an enforced commingling of the two races. We cannot accept this proposition. If the two races are to meet upon terms of social equality, it must be the result of natural affinities, a mutual appreciation of each other's merits and a voluntary consent of individuals. . . . Legislation is powerless to eradicate racial instincts or to abolish distinctions based upon physical differences, and the attempt to do so can only result in accentuating the difficulties of the present situation. If the civil and political rights of both races be equal one cannot be inferior to the other civilly or politically. If one race be inferior to the other socially, the Constitution of the United States cannot put them upon the same plane.

Mr. Justice Harlan dissenting. . . .

. . . [W]e have before us a state enactment that compels, under penalties, the separation of the two races in railroad passenger coaches, and makes it a crime for a citizen of either race to enter a coach that has been assigned to citizens of the other race.

Thus the State regulates the use of a public highway by citizens of the United States solely upon the basis of race. . . .

In respect of civil rights, common to all citizens, the Constitution of the United States does not, I think, permit any public authority to know the race of those entitled to be protected in the enjoyment of such rights. Every true man has pride of race, and under appropriate circumstances when the rights of others, his equals before the law, are not to be affected, it is his privilege to express such pride and to take such action based upon it as to him seems proper. But I deny that any legislative body or judicial tribunal may have regard to the race of citizens when the civil rights of those citizens are involved. . . .

It was said in argument that the statute of Louisiana does not discriminate against either race, but prescribes a rule applicable alike to white and colored citizens. But this argument does not meet the difficulty. Every one knows that the statute in question had its origin in the purpose, not so much to exclude white persons from railroad cars occupied by blacks, as to exclude colored people from coaches occupied by or assigned to white persons. . . . No one would be so wanting in candor as to assert the contrary. . . .

. . . If a State can prescribe, as a rule of civil conduct, that whites and blacks shall not travel as passengers in the same railroad coach, why may it not so regulate the use of the streets of its cities and towns as to compel white citizens to keep on one side of a street and black citizens to keep on the other? Why may it not, upon like grounds, punish whites and blacks who ride together in street cars or in open vehicles on a public road or street? Why may it not require sheriffs to assign whites to one side of a court-room and blacks to the other? And why may it not also prohibit the commingling of the two races in the galleries of legislative halls or in public assemblages convened for the consideration of the political questions of the day? Further, if this statute of Louisiana is consistent with the personal liberty of citizens, why may not the State require the separation in railroad coaches of native and naturalized citizens of the United States, or of Protestants and Roman Catholics? . . .

The white race deems itself to be the dominant race in this country. And so it is, in prestige, in achievements, in education, in wealth and in power. So, I doubt not, it will continue to be for all time, if it remains true to its great heritage and holds fast to the principles of constitutional liberty. But in view of the Constitution, in the eye of the law, there is in this country no superior, dominant, ruling class of citizens. There is no caste here. Our Constitution is color-blind, and neither knows nor tolerates classes among citizens. . . . It is, therefore, to be regretted that this high tribunal, the final expositor of the fundamental law of the land, has reached the conclusion that it is competent for a State to regulate the enjoyment by citizens of their civil rights solely upon the basis of race.

In my opinion, the judgment this day rendered will, in time, prove to be quite as pernicious as the decision made by this tribunal in the *Dred Scott case.* . . . The present decision, it may well be apprehended, will not only stimulate aggressions, more or less brutal and irritating, upon the admitted rights of colored citizens, but will encourage the belief that it is possible, by means of state enactments, to defeat the beneficent purposes which the people of the United States had in view when they adopted the recent amendments of the Constitution.

CHAPTER 11

The Industrial State, Laissez-Faire Constitutionalism, and State Rights

51 ❧

Despite the Supreme Court's refusal to accept the job of reviewing state exercises of the police power in the Slaughterhouse Cases, businesses and individuals continued to complain that the various regulations deprived them of liberty or property without due process of law in violation of the Fourteenth Amendment. Railroad companies were particularly vocal, as a number of states, pressured by the Patrons of Husbandry—an organization of farmers also known as the Grange—created so-called Granger commissions to regulate the business practices and rates of railroads and warehouses. In the mid-1870s a group of lawsuits challenging the constitutionality of such legislation reached the Supreme Court.

Counsel for the railroads drew upon laissez-faire economic principles to argue that business practices and prices were most efficiently established by the free market in response to supply and demand. Government interference was either fruitless or harmful to the economy. The lawyers also articulated a moral view identified with laissez faire: It was wrong for one interest group, in this case farmers, to use the power of government to secure advantages at the expense of the community or another interest, like railroad entrepreneurs and warehousemen.

The Court decided the Granger Cases in 1877, the lead case being *Munn v. Illinois*. Influenced by Justice Bradley, who had dissented in *Slaughterhouse*, the Court pointed out that some types of business had long been recognized as "affected with a public interest" and therefore subject to such regulations. Two other dissenters in *Slaughterhouse*, Justices Stephen J. Field and William Strong, continued to argue that the Fourteenth Amendment mandated that the Court overturn such legislation.

Munn v. Illinois (1877)

M R . C H I E F Justice Waite delivered the opinion of the court. . . .
It is claimed that such a law is repugnant— . . .

. . . To that part of amendment 14 which ordains that no State shall "deprive any person of life, liberty, or property, without due process of law." . . .

When one becomes a member of society, he necessarily parts with some rights or privileges which, as an individual not affected by his relations to others, he might retain. "A body politic," as aptly defined in the preamble of the Constitution of Massachusetts, "is a social compact by which the whole people covenants with each citizen, and each citizen with the whole people, that all shall be governed by certain laws for the common good." This does not confer power upon the whole people to control rights which are purely and exclusively private, . . . but it does authorize the establishment of laws requiring each citizen to so conduct himself, and so use his own property, as not unnecessarily to injure another. This is the very essence of government. . . . From this source come the police powers, which, as was said by Mr. Chief Justice Taney in the *License Cases,* 5 How. 583, "are nothing more or less than the powers of government inherent in every sovereignty, . . . that is to say, . . . the power to govern men and things." Under these powers the government regulates the conduct of its citizens one towards another, and the manner in which each shall use his own property, when such regulation becomes necessary for the public good. In their exercise it has been customary in England from time immemorial, and in this country from its first colonization, to regulate ferries, common carriers, hackmen, bakers, millers, wharfingers, innkeepers, [etc.], and in so doing to fix a maximum of charge to be made for services rendered, accommodations furnished, and articles sold. To this day, statutes are to be found in many of the States upon some or all these subjects; and we think it has never yet been successfully contended that such legislation came within any of the constitutional prohibitions against interference with private property. . . .

This brings us to inquire as to the principles upon which this power of regulation rests, in order that we may determine what is within and what without its operative effect. Looking, then, to the common law, from whence came the right which the Constitution protects, we find that when private property is "affected with a public interest, it ceases to be *juris privati* only." This was said by Lord Chief Justice Hale more than two hundred years ago, in his treatise *De Portibus Maris,* . . . and has been accepted without objection as an essential

94 U.S. 113 (1877).

element in the law of property ever since. Property does become clothed with a public interest when used in a manner to make it of public consequence, and affect the community at large. When, therefore, one devotes his property to a use in which the public has an interest, he, in effect, grants to the public an interest in that use, and must submit to be controlled by the public for the common good, to the extent of the interest he has thus created. . . .

Common carriers exercise a sort of public office, and have duties to perform in which the public is interested. . . . Their business is, therefore, "affected with a public interest," within the meaning of the doctrine which Lord Hale has so forcibly stated.

But we need not go further. Enough has already been said to show that, when private property is devoted to a public use, it is subject to public regulation. . . .

It is insisted, however, that the owner of property is entitled to a reasonable compensation for its use, even though it be clothed with a public interest, and that what is reasonable is a judicial and not a legislative question.

As has already been shown, the practice has been otherwise. In countries where the common law prevails, it has been customary from time immemorial for the legislature to declare what shall be a reasonable compensation under such circumstances, or, perhaps more properly speaking, to fix a maximum beyond which any charge made would be unreasonable. . . . The controlling fact is the power to regulate at all. If that exists, the right to establish the maximum of charge, as one of the means of regulation, is implied. . . .

We know that this is a power which may be abused; but that is no argument against its existence. For protection against abuses by legislatures the people must resort to the polls, not to the courts.

52 ⚬⚬

By the 1890s more and more Americans were demanding that the state and federal government intervene to limit the growing power of corporations. Conservatives were particularly alarmed by the growth of the People's, or Populist, party, which by 1892 was rapidly emerging as a powerful political force in the West and South. It advocated government ownership of transportation and communications facilities, regulation of working hours and conditions, introduction of a progressive income tax (one that taxed the wealthy at a higher rate than the poor), and the free coinage of silver in order to inflate the currency.

Advocates of laissez faire denounced such proposals as socialistic "class legislation"— laws for the benefit of one part of the community at the expense of another. They argued that such legislation deprived its victims of property without due process of law and urged judges to hold it unconstitutional. Judge John F. Dillon, a highly respected federal judge, reflected these views in his presidential address at the 1892 convention of the American Bar Association.

John F. Dillon, Presidential Address to the American Bar Association (1892)

W E C A N N O T close our eyes to the fact that the institution of private property is menaced, both by open and covert attacks. It is attacked openly by the advocates . . . of socialism or communism, who seek to array the body of the community against individual right to exclusive property, and in favor of the right of the community *in some form*, to deprive the owner of it, or of its full enjoyment.

Property, or its rightful enjoyment, is also covertly invaded, not by the socialist, but at the instance of a . . . supposedly popular demand; in which case the attack is directed against particular owners or forms of ownership, and generally take the insidious, more specious and dangerous shape of an attempt to deprive the owners . . . of their property by unjust or discriminatory legislation in the exercise of the power of taxation, or of eminent domain, or of that elastic power known as the police power. . . .

The era of the despotism of the monarch, or of an oligarchy, has passed away. If we are not struck by judicial blindness, we cannot fail to see that what is now to be feared and guarded against is the despotism of the many— of the majority. . . .

The great, paramount, overshadowing duty of the legal profession in this country, in our day, is to defend, protect and preserve our legal institutions unimpaired. . . . If there is any problem yet unsettled, it is whether the bench is able to bear the burden of supporting under all circumstances, the fundamental law against popular, or supposedly popular, demands for enactments in conflict with it.

53 ↭

Laissez-faire arguments for closer judicial scrutiny of economic regulations comported with the traditional view among judges that class legislation deprived its victims of property without due process of law. However, judges rarely had found any challenged legislation that was so devoid of community benefit as to justify ruling it unconstitutional. However, in the 1890s the Supreme Court, influenced by laissez-faire beliefs, began to scrutinize such regulations more closely.

In Minnesota, the state legislature had given the state's railroad commission final authority to set reasonable freight rates. The state courts were permitted to make certain that the commission followed fair procedures in doing so but were not allowed to review the rates themselves. In *Chicago, Milwaukee and St. Paul Railway Co. v. Minnesota*, the Supreme Court held for the first time that the reasonableness of the rate set by a commission must be subject to judicial review, lest it deprive people of property without due process of law. Justice Bradley dissented, complaining that the decision practically reversed *Munn v. Illinois*.

The Court followed the logic of its position a few years later in *Smyth v. Ames*, 169 U.S. 466 (1897), overturning a rate set by the Iowa state legislature on the grounds that it did not provide what the justices thought was a reasonable return on investment.

Chicago, Milwaukee and St. Paul Railway Co. v. Minnesota (1890)

M R . J U S T I C E Blatchford . . . delivered the opinion of the court. . . .

The construction put upon the statute by the Supreme Court of Minnesota must be accepted by this court, for the purposes of the present case, as conclusive and not to be reexamined here as to its propriety or accuracy. The Supreme Court authoritatively declares that it is the expressed intention of the legislature of Minnesota, by the statute, that the rates recommended and published by the commission, if it proceeds in the manner pointed out by the act, are not simply advisory, nor merely *prima facie* equal and reasonable, but final and conclusive as to what are equal and reasonable charges. . . . In other words, . . . there is no power in the courts to stay the hands of the commission, if it chooses to establish rates that are unequal and unreasonable.

This being the construction of the statute by which we are bound in considering the present case, we are of opinion that, so construed, it conflicts with the Constitution of the United States. . . . It deprives the company of its right to a judicial investigation, by due process of law, . . . and substitutes therefor, as an absolute finality, the action of a railroad commission which . . . cannot be regarded as clothed with judicial functions or possessing the machinery of a court of justice. . . .

Mr. Justice Bradley (with whom concurred Mr. Justice Gray and Mr. Justice Lamar) dissenting.

⊏ I cannot agree to the decision of the court in this case. It practically overrules *Munn v. Illinois* . . . and the several railroad cases that were decided at the same time. The governing principle of those cases was that the regulation and settlement of the fares of railroads and other public accommodations is a legislative prerogative and not a judicial one. . . . When a railroad company is

134 U.S. 418 (1890).

chartered, it is for the purpose of performing a duty which belongs to the State itself. It is chartered as an agent of the State for furnishing public accommodation. The State might build its railroads if it saw fit. . . . And this duty is devolved upon the legislative department. If the legislature commissions private parties, whether corporations or individuals, to perform this duty, it is its prerogative to fix the fares and freights which they may charge for their services. . . .

But it is said that all charges should be reasonable, and that none but reasonable charges can be exacted; and it is urged that what is a reasonable charge is a judicial question. On the contrary, it is preeminently a legislative one, involving considerations of policy as well as of remuneration; and is usually determined by the legislature, by fixing a maximum of charges in the charter of the company, or afterwards, if its hands are not tied by contract. . . .

It may be that our legislatures are invested with too much power, open, as they are, to influences so dangerous to the interests of individuals, corporations and society. But such is the Constitution of our republican form of government; and we are bound to abide by it until it can be corrected in a legitimate way. If our legislatures become too arbitrary in the exercise of their powers, the people always have a remedy in their hands; they may at any time restrain them by constitutional limitations.

54 ❧

The Supreme Court traditionally had taken an expansive view of Congress's power to regulate interstate commerce. But as pressure grew on Congress to take steps to combat the growing power of big business, the Court attempted to draw a line between permissible and impermissible federal regulation.

Congress had passed the Sherman Anti-Trust Act in 1890 to punish conspiracies to monopolize interstate commerce. When the American Sugar Refining Co. acquired the stock of its leading competitors, including the E. C. Knight Co., putting the stock in the hands of a trust company, it gained control of more than 90 percent of the sugar refining in the country. The government moved to break up the monopoly, but the company's lawyers argued that refining was not part of commerce; it was manufacturing conducted within the boundaries of a state. As the following excerpt makes clear, the Court feared that if it interpreted production-related activity to be part of interstate commerce simply because the products would later be shipped out of state, then Congress would be able to regulate virtually all the significant businesses in the country. To avoid such a consequence, eight justices articulated the most explicit statement of state-rights constitutionalism yet from the Supreme Court, relying on the Tenth Amendment as a touchstone of federalism. Only the great dissenter, Justice Harlan, disagreed.

In holding that the government could not break up American Sugar's monopoly, the Court implicitly but clearly rejected the idea that federal action under the Commerce

Clause could be justified to combat what scholars came to call "federal effects"—that is, the fact that one state's refusal to guard against cheap and shoddy products, low wages, poor working conditions, or monopolistic actions put pressure on neighboring states to permit the same practices in order to keep their industries competitive. This was at most an "indirect" effect of production on interstate commerce; Congress could only regulate those aspects of business that directly affected such commerce.

U.S. v. E. C. Knight Co. (1895)

M R . C H I E F Justice Fuller . . . delivered the opinion of the court. . . .

The fundamental question is, whether conceding that the existence of a monopoly in manufacture is established by the evidence, that monopoly can be directly suppressed under the act of Congress in the mode attempted by this bill.

It cannot be denied that the power of a State to protect the lives, health, and property of its citizens, and to preserve good order and the public morals, . . . is a power originally and always belonging to the States, not surrendered by them to the general government, nor directly restrained by the Constitution of the United States, and essentially exclusive. The relief of the citizens of each State from the burden of monopoly and the evils resulting from the restraint of trade among such citizens was left with the States to deal with. . . . On the other hand, the power of Congress to regulate commerce among the several States is also exclusive. . . .

The argument is that the power to control the manufacture of refined sugar is a monopoly over a necessary of life, to the enjoyment of which by a large part of the population of the United States interstate commerce is indispensable, and that, therefore, the general government in the exercise of the power to regulate commerce may repress such monopoly directly and set aside the instruments which have created it. But this argument cannot be confined to necessaries of life merely, and must include all articles of general consumption. Doubtless the power to control the manufacture of a given thing involves in a certain sense the control of its disposition, but this is a secondary and not the primary sense; and although the exercise of that power may result in bringing the operation of commerce into play, it does not control it, and affects it only incidentally and indirectly. Commerce succeeds to manufacture, and is not a part of it. The power to regulate commerce is the power to prescribe the rule by which commerce shall be governed, and is a power independent of the power to suppress monopoly. . . .

It is vital that the independence of the commercial power and of the police power, and the delimitation between them, however sometimes perplexing, should always be recognized and observed, for while the one furnishes the strongest bond of union, the other is essential to the preservation of the autonomy of the States as required by our dual form of government; and acknowledged evils, however grave and urgent they may appear to be, had better be borne, than the risk be run, in the effort to suppress them, of more serious consequences by resort to expedients of even doubtful constitutionality.

It will be perceived how far-reaching the proposition is that the power of dealing with a monopoly directly may be exercised by the general government whenever interstate or international commerce may be ultimately affected. The regulation of commerce applies to the subjects of commerce and not to matters of internal police. Contracts to buy, sell, or exchange goods to be transported among the several States, the transportation and its instrumentalities, and articles bought, sold, or exchanged for the purposes of such transit among the States, or put in the way of transit, may be regulated, but this is because they form part of interstate trade or commerce. The fact that an article is manufactured for export to another State does not of itself make it an article of interstate commerce, and the intent of the manufacturer does not determine the time when the article or product passes from the control of the State and belongs to commerce.

55 ☙

Reflecting laissez-faire ideas, the Supreme Court held in the 1897 case of *Allgeyer v. Louisiana,* 165 U.S. 578, that the liberties protected by the Due Process Clause of the Fifth and Fourteenth Amendments included "liberty of contract"—the right of individuals to negotiate freely for goods, services, and labor. In effect, this circumvented the Court's decision in the Slaughterhouse Cases that the right to work was not a privilege of U.S. citizenship protected by the Fourteenth Amendment.

Advocates of laissez faire argued that government intervention in labor contracts was class legislation for the benefit of particular workers at the expense of employers and other workers who would be willing to take their jobs at longer hours or lower pay. Influenced by this idea, several state supreme courts ruled that laws establishing maximum hours of labor violated the Fourteenth Amendment's Due Process Clause. But in *Holden v. Hardy,* the Court upheld such legislation because it pertained to miners. Labor legislation was a justifiable exercise of the state's police powers if it protected the safety, health, or morals of members of the community.

Holden v. Hardy (1898)

M R . J U S T I C E Brown delivered the opinion of the court. . . .

[The] right of contract . . . is . . . subject to certain limitations which the state may lawfully impose in the exercise of its police powers. While this

169 U.S. 366 (1898).

power is inherent in all governments, it has doubtless been greatly expanded in its application during the past century, owing to an enormous increase in the number of occupations which are dangerous, or so far detrimental to the health of employees as to demand special precaution for their well-being and protection, or the safety of adjacent property. While this court has held ... that the police power cannot be put forward as an excuse for oppressive and unjust legislation, it may be lawfully resorted to for the purpose of preserving the public health, safety, or morals, or the abatement of public nuisances, and a large discretion "is necessarily vested in the legislature to determine, not only what the interests of the public require, but what measures are necessary for the protection of such interests." ...

While the business of mining coal and manufacturing iron began in Pennsylvania as early as 1716, and in Virginia, North Carolina, and Massachusetts even earlier than this, both mining and manufacturing were carried on in such a limited way and by such primitive methods that no special laws were considered necessary, prior to the adoption of the Constitution, for the protection of the operatives, but, in the vast proportions which these industries have since assumed, it has been found that they can no longer be carried on with due regard to the safety and health of those engaged in them, without special protection against the dangers necessarily incident to these employments. In consequence of this, laws have been enacted in most of the states designed to meet these exigencies and to secure the safety of persons peculiarly exposed to these dangers. ...

These statutes have been repeatedly enforced by the courts of the several states; their validity assumed, and, so far as we are informed, they have been uniformly held to be constitutional. ...

... [I]f it be within the power of a legislature to adopt such means for the protection of the lives of its citizens, it is difficult to see why precautions may not also be adopted for the protection of their health and morals. It is as much for the interest of the state that the public health should be preserved as that life should be made secure. ...

Upon the principles above stated, we think the act in question may be sustained as a valid exercise of the police power of the state. The enactment does not profess to limit the hours of all workmen, but merely those who are employed in underground mines, or in the smelting, reduction, or refining of ores or metals. These employments when too long pursued the legislature has judged to be detrimental to the health of the employees, and, so long as there are reasonable grounds for believing that this is so, its decision upon this subject cannot be reviewed by the Federal courts.

While the general experience of mankind may justify us in believing that men may engage in ordinary employments more than eight hours per day without injury to their health, it does not follow that labor for the same length of time is innocuous when carried on beneath the surface of the earth, when the operative is deprived of fresh air and sunlight, and is frequently subjected to foul atmosphere and a very high temperature, or to the influence of noxious gases, generated by the processes of refining or smelting. . . .

The legislature has also recognized the fact, which the experience of legislators in many states has corroborated, that the proprietors of these establishments and their operatives do not stand upon an equality, and that their interests are, to a certain extent, conflicting. The former naturally desire to obtain as much labor as possible from their employees, while the latter are often induced by the fear of discharge to conform to regulations which their judgment, fairly exercised, would pronounce to be detrimental to their health or strength. In other words, the proprietors lay down the rules and the laborers are practically constrained to obey them. In such cases self-interest is often an unsafe guide, and the legislature may promptly interpose its authority. . . .

. . . [T]he fact that both parties are of full age and competent to contract does not necessarily deprive the state of the power to interfere where the parties do not stand upon an equality, or where the public health demands that one party to the contract shall be protected against himself. . . .

. . . The question in each case is whether the legislature has adopted the statute in exercise of a reasonable discretion, or whether its action be a mere excuse for an unjust discrimination, or the oppression, or spoliation of a particular class. . . .

We are of opinion that the act in question was a valid exercise of the police power of the state. . . .

56 ꙮ

Despite its ruling in *Holden v. Hardy,* the Supreme Court overturned a New York law regulating working hours in the bakery industry in *Lochner v. New York.* In this classic example of laissez-faire constitutionalism, the Court made clear that freedom of contract was the rule and regulation the exception, putting in jeopardy labor laws that had been passed throughout the nation. Note that it was the substance of the law itself, rather than the procedure by which it had been passed or administered, that violated due process. The notion that the Due Process Clause applied to the substance of laws as well as to the procedures for adopting and enforcing them came to be called "substantive due process of law."

The *Lochner* decision was denounced in two vigorous dissents. Justice Harlan and two other dissenters argued powerfully that reasonable legislators easily could have concluded that the regulations served the community's interests in promoting safety, health, and moral well-being. Thus they called for judicial restraint within the traditional paradigm of judicial review, in which judges guarded against class legislation.

In contrast, Justice Oliver Wendell Holmes attacked the whole concept of substantive due process and, implicitly, the concept of class legislation. He cautioned judges against reading particular economic or moral philosophies into the Constitution. Holmes derided the idea that there was a "natural law" that could be applied to specific cases through logical reasoning. People created law rather than "discovering" it, he insisted, articulating the doctrine known as Legal Positivism. When judges thought they were applying natural economic laws that dictated liberty of contract, they were, in fact, reading their own opinions into the Constitution.

Lochner v. New York (1905)

M R. J U S T I C E Peckham . . . delivered the opinion of the court. . . .

The statute necessarily interferes with the right of contract between the employer and employés, concerning the number of hours in which the latter may labor in the bakery of the employer. The general right to make a contract in relation to his business is part of the liberty of the individual protected by the Fourteenth Amendment of the Federal Constitution. . . . Under that provision no State can deprive any person of life, liberty or property without due process of law. . . . There are, however, certain powers, existing in the sovereignty of each State in the Union, somewhat vaguely termed police powers. . . . Those powers, broadly stated, . . . relate to the safety, health, morals and general welfare of the public. Both property and liberty are held on such reasonable conditions as may be imposed by the governing power of the State in the exercise of those powers, and with such conditions the Fourteenth Amendment was not designed to interfere. . . .

It must, of course, be conceded that there is a limit to the valid exercise of the police power by the State. . . . Otherwise the Fourteenth Amendment would have no efficacy and the legislatures of the States would have unbounded power, and it would be enough to say that any piece of legislation was enacted to conserve the morals, the health or the safety of the people; such legislation would be valid, no matter how absolutely without foundation the claim might be. The claim of the police power would be a mere pretext—become another and delusive name for the supreme sovereignty of the State to be exercised free from constitutional restraint. . . . In every case that comes before this court, therefore, where legislation of this character is concerned and where the protection of the Federal Constitution is sought, the

198 U.S. 45 (1905).

question necessarily arises: Is this a fair, reasonable and appropriate exercise of the police power of the State, or is it an unreasonable, unnecessary and arbitrary interference with the right of the individual to his personal liberty or to enter into those contracts in relation to labor which may seem to him appropriate or necessary for the support of himself and his family? . . .

The question whether this act is valid as a labor law, pure and simple, may be dismissed in a few words. There is no reasonable ground for interfering with the liberty of person or the right of free contract, by determining the hours of labor, in the occupation of a baker. There is no contention that bakers as a class are not equal in intelligence and capacity to men in other trades or manual occupations, or that they are not able to assert their rights and care for themselves without the protecting arm of the State, interfering with their independence of judgment and of action. They are in no sense wards of the State. Viewed in the light of a purely labor law, with no reference whatever to the question of health, we think that a law like the one before us involves neither the safety, the morals nor the welfare of the public, and that the interest of the public is not in the slightest degree affected by such an act. The law must be upheld, if at all, as a law pertaining to the health of the individual engaged in the occupation of a baker. . . .

We think the limit of the police power has been reached and passed in this case. There is, in our judgment, no reasonable foundation for holding this to be necessary or appropriate as a health law to safeguard the public health or the health of the individuals who are following the trade of a baker. . . .

We think that there can be no fair doubt that the trade of a baker, in and of itself, is not an unhealthy one to that degree which would authorize the legislature to interfere with the right to labor, and with the right of free contract on the part of the individual, either as employer or employé. . . . It might be safely affirmed that almost all occupations more or less affect the health. There must be more than the mere fact of the possible existence of some small amount of unhealthiness to warrant legislative interference with liberty. It is unfortunately true that labor, even in any department, may possibly carry with it the seeds of unhealthiness. But are we all, on that account, at the mercy of legislative majorities? . . . No trade, no occupation, no mode of earning one's living, could escape this all-pervading power. . . .

This interference on the part of the legislatures of the several States with the ordinary trades and occupations of the people seems to be on the increase. . . .

It is impossible for us to shut our eyes to the fact that many of the laws of this character, while passed under what is claimed to be the police power for the purpose of protecting the public health or welfare, are, in reality, passed from other motives. . . .

. . . It seems to us that the real object and purpose were simply to regulate the hours of labor between the master and his employés (all being men, *sui juris*), in a private business, not dangerous in any degree to morals or in any real and substantial degree, to the health of the employés. Under such circumstances the freedom of master and employé to contract with each other in relation to their employment, and in defining the same, cannot be prohibited or interfered with, without violating the Federal Constitution.

Mr. Justice Harlan, with whom Mr. Justice White and Mr. Justice Day concurred, dissenting.

While this court has not attempted to mark the precise boundaries of what is called the police power of the State, the existence of the power has been uniformly recognized, both by the Federal and state courts.

All the cases agree that this power extends at least to the protection of the lives, the health and the safety of the public against the injurious exercise by any citizen of his own rights. . . .

Granting then that there is a liberty of contract which cannot be violated even under the sanction of direct legislative enactment, but assuming, as according to settled law we may assume, that such liberty of contract is subject to such regulations as the State may reasonably prescribe for the common good and the well-being of society, what are the conditions under which the judiciary may declare such regulations to be in excess of legislative authority and void? Upon this point there is no room for dispute; for, the rule is universal that a legislative enactment, Federal or state, is never to be disregarded or held invalid unless it be, beyond question, plainly and palpably in excess of legislative power. . . .

Let these principles be applied to the present case. . . .

It is plain that this statute was enacted in order to protect the physical well-being of those who work in bakery and confectionery establishments. It may be that the statute had its origin, in part, in the belief that employers and employés in such establishments were not upon an equal footing, and that the necessities of the latter often compelled them to submit to such exactions as unduly taxed their strength. Be this as it may, the statute must be taken as expressing the belief of the people of New York that, as a general rule, and in the case of the average man, labor in excess of sixty hours during a week in such establishments may endanger the health of those who thus labor. Whether or not this be wise legislation it is not the province of the court to inquire. Under our systems of government the courts are not concerned with the wisdom or policy of legislation. . . . Therefore I submit that this court will transcend its functions if it assumes to annul the statute of New York.

Mr. Justice Holmes dissenting. . . .

This case is decided upon an economic theory which a large part of the country does not entertain. If it were a question whether I agreed with that theory, I should desire to study it further and long before making up my mind. But I do not conceive that to be my duty, because I strongly believe that my agreement or disagreement has nothing to do with the right of a majority to embody their opinions in law. It is settled by various decisions of this court that state constitutions and state laws may regulate life in many ways which we as legislators might think as injudicious or if you like as tyrannical as this, and which equally with this interfere with the liberty to contract. Sunday laws and usury laws are ancient examples. A more modern one is the prohibition of lotteries. The liberty of the citizen to do as he likes so long as he does not interfere with the liberty of others to do the same, which has been a shibboleth for some well-known writers, is interfered with by school laws, by the Post Office, by every state or municipal institution which takes his money for purposes thought desirable, whether he likes it or not. The Fourteenth Amendment does not enact Mr. Herbert Spencer's Social Statics. . . . [A] constitution is not intended to embody a particular economic theory, whether of paternalism and the organic relation of the citizen to the State or of *laissez faire*. It is made for people of fundamentally differing views, and the accident of our finding certain opinions natural and familiar or novel and even shocking ought not to conclude our judgment upon the question whether statutes embodying them conflict with the Constitution of the United States.

General propositions do not decide concrete cases. The decision will depend on a judgment or intuition more subtle than any articulate major premise. But I think that the proposition just stated, if it is accepted, will carry us far toward the end. Every opinion tends to become a law. I think that the word liberty in the Fourteenth Amendment is perverted when it is held to prevent the natural outcome of a dominant opinion, unless it can be said that a rational and fair man necessarily would admit that the statute proposed would infringe fundamental principles as they have been understood by the traditions of our people and our law. It does not need research to show that no such sweeping condemnation can be passed upon the statute before us.

CHAPTER 12

The Progressive Era

57 ❧

Theodore Roosevelt was in many ways the first modern president. Seizing the leadership of the progressive movement, he made the presidency the focal point of public attention, taking bold executive action to enforce laws on the books or, in some cases, to go beyond the laws. In his *Autobiography,* Roosevelt briefly explained his "stewardship theory" of the presidency, which he dated back to Jackson and Lincoln. Roosevelt began the process by which the president came to dominate American policy making in the twentieth century.

Theodore Roosevelt on the Presidency (1913)

VERY MUCH the most important action I took as regards labor had nothing to do with legislation, and represented executive action which was not required by the Constitution. It illustrated as well as anything that I did the theory which I have called the Jackson-Lincoln theory of the presidency; that is, that occasionally great national crises arise which call for immediate and vigorous executive action, and that in such cases it is the duty of the President to act upon the theory that he is the steward of the people, and that the proper attitude for him to take is that he is bound to assume that he has the legal right to do whatever the needs of the people demand, unless the Constitution or the laws explicitly forbid him to do it.

Theodore Roosevelt, *Autobiography,* in *The Works of Theodore Roosevelt* (N.Y.: Charles Scribner's Sons, 1913), 20: 455.

58 ⌒⌒

As interstate commerce grew in the United States, state legislators became frustrated by the effect of the federal system on state efforts to regulate various aspects of their societies. Prohibition of the production and sale of alcoholic beverages, for example, was undermined by the ease with which alcohol could be brought in from other states. The same was true of state efforts to prohibit the sale of lottery tickets. Yet states did not have constitutional authority to interfere with interstate trade.

Responding to state requests, Congress began to pass laws banning the transportation of various goods through the mail and interstate commerce. Lewd and pornographic materials were among the first items banned, by the so-called Comstock law. In 1895 Congress acted to suppress the interstate transportation of lottery tickets. Opponents challenged the action as a regulation of morals, a subject within the police powers of the states and not part of interstate commerce.

Justice Harlan, who had dissented in *E. C. Knight,* spoke for a narrow 5–4 majority in this case. Harlan's opinion justified a substantial increase in federal economic regulation, which the Court would later sustain when it endorsed the constitutionality of the federal Pure Food and Drug Act in *Hipolite Egg Co. v. U.S.,* 220 U.S. 45 (1911).

The Lottery Case (*Champion v. Ames*) (1903)

M R . J U S T I C E Harlan . . . delivered the opinion of the court. . . .

We are of opinion that lottery tickets are subjects of traffic and therefore are subjects of commerce, and the regulation of the carriage of such tickets from State to State . . . is a regulation of commerce among the several States.

. . . [I]t is said that the statute in question does not regulate the carrying of lottery tickets from State to State, but by punishing those who cause them to be so carried Congress in effect prohibits such carrying; that in respect of the carrying from one State to another of articles or things that are, in fact, or according to usage in business, the subjects of commerce, the authority given Congress was not to *prohibit,* but only to *regulate.* . . .

. . . Are we prepared to say that a provision which is, in effect, a *prohibition* of the carriage of such articles from State to State is not a fit or appropriate mode for the *regulation* of that particular kind of commerce? If lottery traffic, *carried on through interstate commerce,* is a matter of which Congress may take cognizance and over which its power may be exerted, can it be possible that it must tolerate the traffic, and simply regulate the manner in which it may be carried on? Or may not Congress, for the protection of the people of

188 U.S. 321 (1903).

all the States, and under the power to regulate interstate commerce, devise such means, within the scope of the Constitution, and not prohibited by it, as will drive that traffic out of commerce among the States? . . .

If a State, when considering legislation for the suppression of lotteries within its own limits, may properly take into view the evils that inhere in the raising of money, in that mode, why may not Congress, invested with the power to regulate commerce among the several States, provide that such commerce shall not be polluted by the carrying of lottery tickets from one State to another? In this connection it must not be forgotten that the power of Congress to regulate commerce among the States is plenary, is complete in itself, and is subject to no limitations except such as may be found in the Constitution. What provision in that instrument can be regarded as limiting the exercise of the power granted? What clause can be cited which, in any degree, countenances the suggestion that one may, of right, carry or cause to be carried from one State to another that which will harm the public morals? . . .

. . . As a State may, for the purpose of guarding the morals of its own people, forbid all sales of lottery tickets within its limits, so Congress, for the purpose of guarding the people of the United States against the "widespread pestilence of lotteries" and to protect the commerce which concerns all the States, may prohibit the carrying of lottery tickets from one State to another. In legislating upon the subject of the traffic in lottery tickets, as carried on through interstate commerce, Congress only supplemented the action of those States—perhaps all of them—which, for the protection of the public morals, prohibit the drawing of lotteries, as well as the sale or circulation of lottery tickets, within their respective limits. It said, in effect, that it would not permit the declared policy of the States, which sought to protect their people against the mischiefs of the lottery business, to be overthrown or disregarded by the agency of interstate commerce. We should hesitate long before adjudging that an evil of such appalling character, carried on through interstate commerce, cannot be met and crushed by the only power competent to that end. . . .

It is said, however, that if, in order to suppress lotteries carried on through interstate commerce, Congress may exclude lottery tickets from such commerce, that principle leads necessarily to the conclusion that Congress may arbitrarily exclude from commerce among the States any article, commodity or thing, of whatever kind or nature, or however useful or valuable, which it may choose, no matter with what motive, to declare shall not be carried from one State to another. It will be time enough to consider the constitutionality of such legislation when we must do so.

Mr. Chief Justice Fuller, with whom concur Mr. Justice Brewer, Mr. Justice Shiras and Mr. Justice Peckham, dissenting. . . .

It is urged . . . that because Congress is empowered to regulate commerce between the several States, it, therefore, may suppress lotteries by prohibiting the carriage of lottery matter. Congress may indeed make all laws necessary and proper for carrying the powers granted to it into execution, and doubtless an act prohibiting the carriage of lottery matter would be necessary and proper to the execution of a power to suppress lotteries; but that power belongs to the States and not to Congress. To hold that Congress has general police power would be to hold that it may accomplish objects not entrusted to the General Government, and to defeat the operation of the Tenth Amendment, declaring that: "The powers not delegated to the United States by the Constitution, nor prohibited by it to the States, are reserved to the States respectively, or to the people."

59 ～

By the 1900s it was obvious that the Supreme Court had to be convinced that economic regulations, especially of labor relations, served a traditional police-power purpose before it would sustain their constitutionality. This stance forced lawyers to present the Court with the sort of evidence that was more appropriately provided to legislatures. Indeed, legal analysts such as young Roscoe Pound of Nebraska, who would have a long and brilliant career at Harvard Law School, urged the Court to adopt a "sociological jurisprudence"—to look at the actual workings of the law rather than relying solely upon theoretical legal logic.

Among the first lawyers to put this advice into practice was Louis D. Brandeis. The legal brief he presented in *Muller v. Oregon*, defending an Oregon law that set maximum working hours for women in factories and laundries, was filled with data documenting the toll that long hours took on women's health and morals. The "Brandeis Brief" proved persuasive, and the Court sustained the law.

Feminist leaders had mixed reactions. Some denounced the decision for taking the position that women, as the "weaker" sex, needed the special protection of the law. Such a position justified legislation that discriminated against women, even though it was supposedly for their own good. Other feminist leaders supported the decision, lauding regulations that protected women from economic exploitation and urging similar laws protecting men.

Muller v. Oregon (1908)

MR. JUSTICE Brewer delivered the opinion of the court. . . .

. . . It is the law of Oregon that women, whether married or single, have equal contractual and personal rights with men. . . .

208 U.S. 212 (1908).

It thus appears that, putting to one side the elective franchise, in the matter of personal and contractual rights they stand on the same plane as the other sex. Their rights in these respects can no more be infringed than the equal rights of their brothers. . . .

. . . It may not be amiss, in the present case, before examining the constitutional question, to notice the course of legislation, as well as expressions of opinion from other than judicial sources. In the brief filed by Mr. Louis D. Brandeis for the defendant in error is a very copious collection of all these matters. . . .

The legislation and opinions referred to . . . may not be, technically speaking, authorities, and in them is little or no discussion of the constitutional question presented to us for determination, yet they are significant of a widespread belief that woman's physical structure, and the functions she performs in consequence thereof, justify special legislation restricting or qualifying the conditions under which she should be permitted to toil. Constitutional questions, it is true, are not settled by even a consensus of present public opinion. . . . At the same time, when a question of fact is debated and debatable, and the extent to which a special constitutional limitation goes is affected by the truth in respect to that fact, a widespread and long-continued belief concerning it is worthy of consideration. We take judicial cognizance of all matters of general knowledge.

It is undoubtedly true, as more than once declared by this court, that the general right to contract in relation to one's business is part of the liberty of the individual, protected by the 14th Amendment to the Federal Constitution; yet it is equally well settled that this liberty is not absolute and extending to all contracts, and that a state may, without conflicting with the provisions of the 14th Amendment, restrict in many respects the individual's power of contract. . . .

That woman's physical structure and the performance of maternal functions place her at a disadvantage in the struggle for subsistence is obvious. This is especially true when the burdens of motherhood are upon her. Even when they are not, by abundant testimony of the medical fraternity continuance for a long time on her feet at work, repeating this from day to day, tends to injurious effects upon the body, and, as healthy mothers are essential to vigorous offspring, the physical well-being of woman becomes an object of public interest and care in order to preserve the strength and vigor of the race.

Still again, history discloses the fact that woman has always been dependent upon man. He established his control at the outset by superior physical strength, and this control in various forms, with diminishing intensity, has continued to the present. . . . [I]t is still true that in the struggle for subsistence she is not an equal competitor with her brother. Though limitations upon personal and contractual rights may be removed by legislation, there is that in her disposition and habits of life which will operate against a full assertion of those rights. She will still be where some legislation to protect her seems necessary to secure a real equality of right. . . . [H]er physical structure and a proper discharge of her maternal functions—having in view not merely her own health, but the well-being of the race—justify legislation to protect her from the greed as well as the passion of man. The limitations which this statute places upon her contractual powers, upon her right to agree with her employer as to the time she shall labor, are not imposed solely for her benefit, but also largely for the benefit of all.

60 ⌯

As the Supreme Court became more sympathetic to economic regulation during the Progressive era, it also took a more expansive view of federal power. In *McCray v. U.S.*, 195 U.S. 27 (1904), the Court upheld Congress's use of the taxing power to suppress the production of goods that Congress found damaging to the public welfare. The power to tax and the power to regulate interstate commerce became the twin pillars of federal economic and social regulation.

In *Hoke v. U.S.* the Court considered the constitutionality of the so-called White Slave Act, enacted to suppress the transportation of women across state lines "for immoral purposes." The law clearly used a power expressly delegated by the Constitution for a purpose that was not delegated. It looked more like an exercise of the police power to protect safety, health, and morals than a regulation of interstate commerce. But the justices sustained the law anyway, explicitly recognizing the existence of a kind of national police power. The Court seemed to have fully accepted the radical implications of the nationalist conception of the federal system.

Hoke v. U.S. (1913)

M R . J U S T I C E McKenna delivered the opinion of the court. . . .

Plaintiffs in error admit that the States may control the immoralities of its citizens. Indeed, this is their chief insistence, and they especially condemn the act under review as a subterfuge and an attempt to interfere with the police power of the States to regulate the morals of their citizens and assert that it is in consequence an invasion of the reserved powers of the States. There is unquestionably a control in the States over the morals of their citizens, and, it

227 U.S. 308 (1913).

may be admitted, it extends to making prostitution a crime. It is a control, however, which can be exercised only within the jurisdiction of the States, but there is a domain which the States cannot reach and over which Congress alone has power; and if such power be exerted to control what the States cannot it is an argument for—not against—its legality. Its exertion does not encroach upon the jurisdiction of the States. . . .

Our dual form of government has its perplexities, State and Nation having different spheres of jurisdiction, as we have said, but it must be kept in mind that we are one people; and the powers reserved to the States and those conferred on the Nation are adapted to be exercised, whether independently or concurrently, to promote the general welfare, material and moral. This is the effect of the decisions, and surely if the facility of interstate transportation can be taken away from the demoralization of lotteries, the debasement of obscene literature, the contagion of diseased cattle or persons, the impurity of food and drugs, the like facility can be taken away from the systematic enticement to and the enslavement in prostitution and debauchery of women, and, more insistently, of girls. . . .

The principle established by the cases is the simple one, when rid of confusing and distracting considerations, that Congress has power over transportation "among the several States"; that the power is complete in itself, and that Congress, as an incident to it, may adopt not only means necessary but convenient to its exercise, and the means may have the quality of police regulations.

61 ॐ

A number of Americans opposed the entry of the United States into World War I on the side of the Allies. Most Americans of German and Scandinavian descent sympathized with Germany; many Irish Americans resented continued British rule of Ireland; socialists and other radicals agreed with left-wing European socialists that workers were being used as cannon fodder in a war among capitalists for the control of world trade and resources. To unite the nation in a total war against the Germans and the Austro-Hungarian empire, the administration of President Woodrow Wilson tried to suppress dissent. Congress helped by passing the Espionage Act of 1917 and the Sedition Act of 1918. The Espionage Act made it illegal to give false information with the intent of aiding the enemy, to foment disloyalty or mutiny in the armed services, and to obstruct recruiting. The Sedition Act went much further. It amended the Espionage Act to make it illegal to use "disloyal, profane, scurrilous, or abusive language" about the United States or to say or publish anything tending to bring the government into disrepute, or to promote the cause of its enemies, or to discourage production, with the intent to cripple the war effort.

The government used the Espionage and Sedition Acts to suppress radical labor and political organizations throughout the nation. It jailed both well-known figures (like the eminent labor leader Eugene v. Debs, who had received nearly a million votes as the Socialist candidate for president in 1912) and ordinary Americans who criticized the war. In response, civil libertarians formed the Civil Liberties Bureau to challenge the laws' constitutionality.

The first case to reach the Supreme Court involved the conviction of the general secretary of the Socialist party for violating the Espionage Act by arranging for the distribution of antiwar pamphlets to potential draftees. Under the traditional Bad Tendency Test, which most courts used to decide whether one could be punished for what one said or wrote, Schenck was sure to be convicted. It held that speech could be punished if it had the mere tendency to incite unlawful conduct. Speaking for a unanimous Supreme Court, Justice Oliver Wendell Holmes sustained the constitutionality of the Espionage Act while articulating what seemed to be a more demanding criterion, the Clear and Present Danger Test.

Schenck v. U.S. (1919)

M R . J U S T I C E Holmes delivered the opinion of the court. . . .

. . . Of course the document would not have been sent unless it had been intended to have some effect, and we do not see what effect it could be expected to have upon persons subject to the draft except to influence them to obstruct the carrying of it out. The defendants do not deny that the jury might find against them on this point.

But it is said, suppose that that was the tendency of this circular, it is protected by the First Amendment to the Constitution. . . . We admit that in many places and in ordinary times the defendants in saying all that was said in the circular would have been within their constitutional rights. But the character of every act depends upon the circumstances in which it is done. . . . The most stringent protection of free speech would not protect a man in falsely shouting fire in a theatre and causing a panic. . . . The question in every case is whether the words used are used in such circumstances and are of such a nature as to create a clear and present danger that they will bring about the substantive evils that Congress has a right to prevent. It is a question of proximity and degree. When a nation is at war many things that might be said in time of peace are such a hindrance to its effort that their utterance will not be endured so long as men fight and that no Court could regard them as protected by any constitutional right.

249 U.S. 47 (1919).

62 ᕗ

While World War I continued, radical socialist opponents of the conflict seized power in Russia. The Communists' success shocked American business and political leaders and led them to redouble their efforts to crush antiwar and labor radicalism in the United States, precipitating the Red Scare of 1919–1920. At the same time, President Wilson sent soldiers to Russia to try to help counterrevolutionaries overthrow the Communist government. American radicals reacted with outrage. Abrams and his tiny group of anarchist confederates distributed leaflets in New York City's garment district; printed in Yiddish and English, the handouts denounced the intervention and called for a general strike. The dissidents were arrested under the Sedition Act and sentenced to prison for fifteen to twenty years.

By the time Abrams's appeal was argued before the Supreme Court, Wilson's attorney general, A. Mitchell Palmer, had launched the so-called Palmer Raids, breaking up the headquarters of radical publications, labor unions, and political organizations, and rounding up immigrant radicals for deportation. In the midst of the hysteria, the majority of the justices sustained the constitutionality of the Sedition Act and Abrams's conviction, bringing Holmes's formulation into closer alignment with the Bad Tendency Test. Holmes and the recently appointed Louis D. Brandeis dissented. In the process Holmes made his Clear and Present Danger Test much more pointed and protective of free speech. He also argued eloquently that the jailed anarchists had not manifested the intent to aid the enemy that the law required for conviction. The Holmes-Brandeis dissent laid the foundation for twentieth-century civil libertarianism in the area of freedom of speech.

Abrams v. U.S. (1919)

M R. J U S T I C E Clarke delivered the opinion of the court. . . .

It will not do to say, as is now argued, that the only intent of these defendants was to prevent injury to the Russian cause. Men must be held to have intended, and to be accountable for, the effects which their acts were likely to produce. Even if their primary purpose and intent was to aid the cause of the Russian Revolution, the plan of action which they adopted necessarily involved, before it could be realized, defeat of the war program of the United States, for the obvious effect of this appeal, if it should become effective, as they hoped it might, would be to persuade persons of character such as those whom they regarded themselves as addressing, not to aid government loans and not to work in ammunition factories, where their work would produce

250 U.S. 616 (1919).

"bullets, bayonets, cannon" and other munitions of war, the use of which would cause the "murder" of Germans and Russians. . . .

. . . [W]hile the immediate occasion for this particular outbreak of lawlessness, on the part of the defendant alien anarchists, may have been resentment caused by our Government sending troops into Russia as a strategic operation against the Germans on the eastern battle front, yet the plain purpose of their propaganda was to excite, at the supreme crisis of the war, disaffection, sedition, riots, and, as they hoped, revolution, in this country for the purpose of embarrassing and if possible defeating the military plans of the Government in Europe. . . .

Mr. Justice Holmes dissenting. . . .

. . . I do not doubt for a moment that by the same reasoning that would justify punishing persuasion to murder, the United States constitutionally may punish speech that produces or is intended to produce a clear and imminent danger that it will bring about forthwith certain substantive evils that the United States constitutionally may seek to prevent. The power undoubtedly is greater in time of war than in time of peace because war opens dangers that do not exist at other times.

But as against dangers peculiar to war, as against others, the principle of the right to free speech is always the same. It is only the present danger of immediate evil or an intent to bring it about that warrants Congress in setting a limit to the expression of opinion where private rights are not concerned. Congress certainly cannot forbid all effort to change the mind of the country. Now nobody can suppose that the surreptitious publishing of a silly leaflet by an unknown man, without more, would present any immediate danger that its opinions would hinder the success of the government arms or have any appreciable tendency to do so. Publishing those opinions for the very purpose of obstructing however, might indicate a greater danger and at any rate would have the quality of an attempt. So I assume that the second leaflet if published for the purposes alleged in the fourth count might be punishable. . . .

[But] I do not see how anyone can find the intent required by the statute in any of the defendants' words. The second leaflet is the only one that affords even a foundation for the charge, and there . . . it is evident from the beginning to the end that the only object of the paper is to help Russia and stop American intervention there against the popular government—not to impede the United States in the war that it was carrying on. . . .

In this case sentences of twenty years imprisonment have been imposed for the publishing of two leaflets that I believe the defendants had as much right to publish as the Government has to publish the Constitution of the United

States now vainly invoked by them. Even if I am technically wrong and enough can be squeezed from these poor and puny anonymities to turn the color of legal litmus paper; I will add, even if what I think the necessary intent were shown; the most nominal punishment seems to me all that possibly could be inflicted, unless the defendants are to be made to suffer not for what the indictment alleges but for the creed that they avow—a creed that I believe to be the creed of ignorance and immaturity when honestly held, as I see no reason to doubt that it was held here, but which, although made the subject of examination at the trial, no one has a right even to consider in dealing with the charges before the Court.

Persecution for the expression of opinions seems to me perfectly logical. If you have no doubt of your premises or your power and want a certain result with all your heart you naturally express your wishes in law and sweep away all opposition. . . . But when men have realized that time has upset many fighting faiths, they may come to believe even more than they believe the very foundations of their own conduct that the ultimate good desired is better reached by free trade in ideas—that the best test of truth is the power of the thought to get itself accepted in the competition of the market, and that truth is the only ground upon which their wishes safely can be carried out. That at any rate is the theory of our Constitution. It is an experiment, as all life is an experiment. Every year if not every day we have to wager our salvation upon some prophecy based upon imperfect knowledge. While that experiment is part of our system I think that we should be eternally vigilant against attempts to check the expression of opinions that we loathe and believe to be fraught with death, unless they so imminently threaten immediate interference with the lawful and pressing purposes of the law that an immediate check is required to save the country. . . .

Mr. Justice Brandeis concurs with the foregoing opinion.

CHAPTER 13

Liberal versus Conservative Constitutionalism in the 1920s

63 ❧

The revival of conservatism in the United States was signaled by Warren G. Harding's election to the presidency in 1920 on a promise to return the country to "normalcy." The Supreme Court reflected the general trend with decisions that revived laissez-faire constitutionalism, especially in the area of labor relations.

The Court confirmed its new course in the 1923 case *Adkins v. Children's Hospital*, in which it rejected the evidence presented in a Brandeis-type legal brief and overturned legislation establishing minimum wages for female workers. There was no persuasive evidence linking low wages to the health, safety, and moral concerns to justify the exercise of the police power, the majority held. Laws infringing on "liberty of contract" were subject to heightened judicial scrutiny, and minimum-wage laws—and many other regulations of labor relations—were off limits.

As in *Muller v. Oregon* (Document 59), the feminist response was divided. Many applauded the decision for recognizing the equality of women. Others denounced the decision for encouraging the exploitation of women's labor.

Adkins v. Children's Hospital (1923)

M R. JUSTICE Sutherland delivered the opinion of the Court....
There is, of course, no such thing as absolute freedom of contract. It is sub-

261 U.S. 525 (1923).

ject to a great variety of restraints. But freedom of contract is, nevertheless, the general rule and restraint the exception; and the exercise of legislative authority to abridge it can be justified only by the existence of exceptional circumstances. . . .

. . . [T]he statute in question . . . is simply and exclusively a price-fixing law, confined to adult women . . . who are legally as capable of contracting for themselves as men. It forbids two parties having lawful capacity—under penalties as to the employer—to freely contract with one another in respect of the price for which one shall render service to the other in a purely private employment where both are willing, perhaps anxious, to agree, even though the consequence may be to oblige one to surrender a desirable engagement and the other to dispense with the services of a desirable employee. The price fixed by the board need have no relation to the capacity or earning power of the employee, the number of hours which may happen to constitute the day's work, the character of the place where the work is to be done, or the circumstances or surroundings of the employment; and, while it has no other basis to support its validity than the assumed necessities of the employee, it takes no account of any independent resources she may have. It is based wholly on the opinions of the members of the board and their advisers . . . as to what will be necessary to provide a living for a woman, keep her in health and preserve her morals. . . .

The standard furnished by the statute for the guidance of the board is so vague as to be impossible of practical application with any reasonable degree of accuracy. . . . The relation between earnings and morals is not capable of standardization. It cannot be shown that well paid women safeguard their morals more carefully than those who are poorly paid. Morality rests upon other considerations than wages. . . . As a means of safeguarding morals the attempted classification, in our opinion, is without reasonable basis. . . .

The law takes account of the necessities of only one party to the contract. It ignores the necessities of the employer by compelling him to pay not less than a certain sum, not only whether the employee is capable of earning it, but irrespective of the ability of his business to sustain the burden. . . . It compels him to pay at least the sum fixed in any event, because the employee needs it, but requires no service of equivalent value from the employee. . . . To the extent that the sum fixed exceeds the fair value of the services rendered, it amounts to a compulsory exaction from the employer for the support of a partially indigent person, for whose condition there rests upon him no peculiar responsibility, and therefore, in effect, arbitrarily shifts to his shoulders a burden which, if it belongs to anybody, belongs to society as a whole. . . .

. . . The ethical right of every worker, man or woman, to a living wage may be conceded. . . . [B]ut the fallacy of the proposed method of attaining it is that it assumes that every employer is bound at all events to furnish it. . . .

... We have ... been furnished with a large number of printed opinions approving the policy of the minimum wage, and our own reading has disclosed a large number to the contrary. These are all proper enough for the consideration of the lawmaking bodies, since their tendency is to establish the desirability or undesirability of the legislation; but they reflect no legitimate light upon the question of its validity, and that is what we are called upon to decide. The elucidation of that question cannot be aided by counting heads. . . .

It has been said that legislation of the kind now under review is required in the interest of social justice, for whose ends freedom of contract may lawfully be subjected to restraint. The liberty of the individual to do as he pleases, even in innocent matters, is not absolute. It must frequently yield to the common good, and the line beyond which the power of interference may not be pressed in neither definite nor unalterable. . . . Any attempt to fix a rigid boundary would be unwise as well as futile. But, nevertheless, there are limits to the power, and when these have been passed, it becomes the plain duty of the courts in the proper exercise of their authority to so declare. To sustain the individual freedom of action contemplated by the Constitution, is not to strike down the common good but to exalt it; for surely the good of society as a whole cannot be better served than by the preservation against arbitrary restraint of the liberties of its constituent members.

64 ∿

The revival of conservative constitutionalism implied a return not only to laissez faire but to state-rights constitutional doctrines as well. The Supreme Court demonstrated its renewed commitment to distinguishing federal from state concerns in the First Child Labor Case, *Hammer v. Dagenhart*. In a case financed by business interests, the father of two children forbidden to work at a southern cotton mill sued to enjoin the enforcement of the Child Labor Act, which banned the interstate shipment of goods made in factories employing children under sixteen. All understood that if the Court sustained the act, Congress might exercise its interstate commerce power to regulate labor relations in other ways. Attempting to find some limit to Congress's power to regulate society and the economy through the interstate commerce power, the Court ruled the law unconstitutional for crossing the boundary into state jurisdiction protected by the Tenth Amendment. Although the federal government might help states suppress dangerous or immoral products by barring them from interstate commerce, Congress could not bar inoffensive products. Relying on the precedents of the previous decade, Holmes and Brandeis issued a classic, blistering dissent.

The Child Labor Cases (1918, 1922)

Hammer v. Dagenhart (1918)

MR. JUSTICE Day delivered the opinion of the court. . . .

The power essential to the passage of this act, the Government contends, is found in the commerce clause of the Constitution which authorizes Congress to regulate commerce with foreign nations and among the States. . . .

. . . [I]t is insisted that adjudged cases in this court establish the doctrine that the power to regulate given to Congress incidentally includes the authority to prohibit the movement of ordinary commodities and therefore that the subject is not open for discussion. The cases demonstrate the contrary. They rest upon the character of the particular subjects dealt with. . . .

In each of these instances the use of interstate transportation was necessary to the accomplishment of harmful results. In other words, although the power over interstate transportation was to regulate, that could only be accomplished by prohibiting the use of the facilities of interstate commerce to effect the evil intended.

This element is wanting in the present case. The thing intended to be accomplished by this statute is the denial of the facilities of interstate commerce to those manufacturers in the States who employ children within the prohibited ages. The act in its effect does not regulate transportation among the States, but aims to standardize the ages at which children may be employed in mining and manufacturing within the States. The goods shipped are of themselves harmless. . . .

Commerce "consists of intercourse and traffic . . . and includes the transportation of persons and property, as well as the purchase, sale and exchange of commodities." The making of goods and the mining of coal are not commerce, nor does the fact that these things are to be afterwards shipped or used in interstate commerce, make their production a part thereof. . . .

Over interstate transportation, or its incidents, the regulatory power of Congress is ample, but the production of articles, intended for interstate commerce, is a matter of local regulation. . . .

. . . If it were otherwise, all manufacture intended for interstate shipment would be brought under federal control to the practical exclusion of the authority of the States, a result certainly not contemplated by the framers of the Constitution when they vested in Congress the authority to regulate commerce among the States. . . .

The grant of power to Congress over the subject of interstate commerce

247 U.S. 251 (1918).

was to enable it to regulate such commerce and not to give it authority to control the states in their exercise of the police power over local trade and manufacture.

The grant of authority over a purely federal matter was not intended to destroy the local power always existing and carefully reserved to the States in the Tenth Amendment to the Constitution. . . .

In interpreting the Constitution it must never be forgotten that the Nation is made up of States to which are entrusted the powers of local government. And to them and to the people the powers not expressly delegated to the National Government are reserved.

Mr. Justice Holmes, dissenting. . . .

. . . [I]f an act is within the powers specifically conferred upon Congress, it seems to me that it is not made any less constitutional because of the indirect effects that it may have, however obvious it may be that it will have those effects, and that we are not at liberty upon such grounds to hold it void. . . .

. . . I should have thought that the most conspicuous decisions of this Court had made it clear that the power to regulate commerce and other constitutional powers could not be cut down or qualified by the fact that it might interfere with the carrying out of the domestic policy of any State. . . .

The notion that prohibition is any less prohibition when applied to things now thought evil I do not understand. But if there is any matter upon which civilized countries have agreed—far more unanimously than they have with regard to intoxicants and some other matters over which this country is now emotionally aroused—it is the evil of premature and excessive child labor. I should have thought that if we were to introduce our own moral conceptions where in my opinion they do not belong, this was preeminently a case for upholding the exercise of all its powers by the United States.

But I had thought that the propriety of the exercise of a power admitted to exist in some cases was for the consideration of Congress alone and that this Court always had disavowed the right to intrude its judgment upon questions of policy or morals. It is not for this Court to pronounce when prohibition is necessary to regulation if it ever may be necessary—to say that it is permissible as against strong drink but not as against the product of ruined lives.

The act does not meddle with anything belonging to the States. They may regulate their internal affairs and their domestic commerce as they like. But when they seek to send their products across the state line they are no longer within their rights. . . . Under the Constitution such commerce belongs not to the States but to Congress to regulate. It may carry out its views of public policy whatever indirect effect they may have upon the activities of the States. . . .

Mr. Justice McKenna, Mr. Justice Brandeis and Mr. Justice Clarke concur in this opinion.

After the Court ruled the first Child Labor Act unconstitutional, Congress immediately passed a second act, levying a punitive tax on the products of child labor. In the Second Child Labor Case, the Supreme Court ruled that this effort to exercise a national police power, violated the Tenth Amendment as well.

Bailey v. Drexel Furniture Co. (1922)

Mr. Chief Justice Taft delivered the opinion of the court. . . .

. . . [T]his act . . . provides a heavy exaction for a departure from a detailed and specified course of conduct in business. . . . If an employer departs from this prescribed course of business, he is to pay to the Government one-tenth of his entire net income in the business for a full year. The amount is not to be proportioned in any degree to the extent or frequency of the departures, but is to be paid by the employer in full measure whether he employs five hundred children for a year, or employs only one for a day. . . . The employer's factory is to be subject to inspection at any time not only by the taxing officers of the Treasury, the Department normally charged with the collection of taxes, but also by the Secretary of Labor and his subordinates whose normal function is the advancement and protection of the welfare of the workers. In the light of these features of the act, a court must be blind not to see that the so-called tax is imposed to stop the employment of children within the age limits prescribed. Its prohibitory and regulatory effect and purpose are palpable. All others can see and understand this. How can we properly shut our minds to it? . . .

. . . Grant the validity of this law, and all that Congress would need to do, hereafter, in seeking to take over to its control any one of the great number of subjects of public interest, jurisdiction of which the States have never parted with, and which are reserved to them by the Tenth Amendment, would be to enact a detailed measure of complete regulation of the subject and enforce it by a so-called tax upon departures from it. To give such magic to the word "tax" would be to break down all constitutional limitation of the powers of Congress and completely wipe out the sovereignty of the States.

259 U.S. 20 (1922).

CHAPTER 14

The New Deal and the Constitution

65

In 1929 the United States economy went into an accelerating decline that by 1932 had put 25 percent of Americans out of work, with another 25 percent underemployed. With so many unemployed and the future so bleak, demand for goods declined dramatically, forcing more layoffs and reducing purchases of raw materials, which led to further declines in demand, in an apparently endless downward spiral. Prices collapsed and debtors were unable to repay creditors. Businesses went bankrupt. Farmers lost their land and families lost their homes. Banks teetered on the edge of insolvency; if they failed, they would take the savings of millions of Americans with them.

President Herbert Hoover, committed to limited government, went as far as his principles would allow to combat the Great Depression, but that was not far enough. In the presidential election of 1932, the voters turned to the Democratic candidate, Franklin Delano Roosevelt. Upon taking office, Roosevelt launched a program of sweeping change, a "New Deal" for the American people. Following his lead, Congress passed a series of laws creating agencies, boards, and commissions to regulate production, marketing, and labor relations in various industries. It passed the Agricultural Adjustment Act, authorizing the Department of Agriculture to develop production quotas for different crops. It created public work projects to employ the jobless and established a federal program of relief. In 1935 Congress established the Social Security system to provide income to the aged and the National Labor Relations Board to ensure employment practices that would permit unions to organize freely. States established New Deal–type programs of their own. At the same time many of the federal programs encouraged cooperation between federal and state authorities.

Although some elements of the business community supported Roosevelt's first emergency measures, by 1935 big business was overwhelmingly hostile, objecting especially to the provisions encouraging labor organization. Companies that processed food, taxed to compensate farmers for reducing production, also turned against the New Deal. Conservatives argued that the New Deal broke down the traditional boundaries between state and federal authorities and amounted to a massive system of class legislation, transferring wealth from the thrifty and hardworking to the underemployed.

The New Deal came under general attack in the courts. Much of its legislation plainly violated the laissez-faire and state-rights tenets of conservative constitutionalism. Many state and federal judges enjoined enforcement of various New Deal programs. People who refused to obey the regulations were sustained by courts that ruled the guidelines unconstitutional. In the first of these cases to reach the Supreme Court, the majority of the justices seemed sympathetic to efforts to deal with the crisis. They sustained emergency state legislation suspending the collection of debts. In *Nebbia v. New York,* 291 U.S. 502 (1934), the justices upheld stringent state regulation of milk production. The Court seemed to be expanding its definition of businesses that were affected with a public interest and thus subject to close state supervision.

But in *Schechter Poultry Corp. v. U.S.,* 295 U.S. 495 (1935), the justices unanimously declared the National Industrial Recovery Act, the New Deal's main vehicle for regulating industry, unconstitutional. Congress had delegated too much authority to the executive branch to establish industrial codes, providing too little substantive guidance. Congress could not so delegate its legislative powers to the president, the Court declared. The delegation problem could be remedied by more carefully drawn laws. More serious, however, was the justices' concern that the act covered activities remote from interstate commerce.

U.S. v. Butler challenged the constitutionality of the New Deal's agricultural program, which was based on the federal government's taxing and spending power. The Agricultural Adjustment Act taxed food processors and used the money to pay farmers to adhere to production limits. After agreeing that Congress could tax and spend for purposes beyond the powers expressly delegated by the Constitution, six of the justices declared that it could not exercise the power in ways that encroached on matters reserved to state jurisdiction by the Tenth Amendment. The case is famous for Justice Roberts's naive expression of judicial formalism. Overturning legislation passed by huge legislative majorities to deal with the greatest crisis since the Civil War, Roberts insisted that the Court was merely comparing the challenged laws to the words of the Constitution. The three liberal justices, Brandeis, Harlan Fiske Stone, and Benjamin N. Cardozo, dissented.

U.S. v. Butler (1936)

M R . J U S T I C E Roberts delivered the opinion of the Court. . . .

. . . The Government asserts that . . . Article I, §8 of the Constitution authorizes the contemplated expenditure of the funds raised by the tax. This contention presents the great and the controlling question in the case. . . .

There should be no misunderstanding as to the function of this court in such a case. It is sometimes said that the court assumes a power to overrule or control the action of the people's representatives. This is a misconception. The Constitution is the supreme law of the land ordained and established by the people. All legislation must conform to the principles it lays down. When

297 U.S. 1 (1936).

an act of Congress is appropriately challenged in the courts as not conforming to the constitutional mandate the judicial branch of the Government has only one duty,—to lay the article of the Constitution which is invoked beside the statute which is challenged and to decide whether the latter squares with the former. . . .

The Congress is expressly empowered to lay taxes to provide for the general welfare. . . .

. . . While . . . the power to tax is not unlimited, its confines are set in the clause which confers it, and not in those of §8 which bestow and define the legislative powers of the Congress. It results that the power of Congress to authorize expenditure of public moneys for public purposes is not limited by the direct grants of legislative power found in the Constitution.

But the adoption of the broader construction leaves the power to spend subject to limitations. . . .

. . . Story says that if the tax be not proposed for the common defence or general welfare, but for other objects wholly extraneous, it would be wholly indefensible upon constitutional principles. . . .

We are not now required to ascertain the scope of the phrase "general welfare of the United States" or to determine whether an appropriation in aid of agriculture falls within it. Wholly apart from that question, another principle embedded in our Constitution prohibits the enforcement of the Agricultural Adjustment Act. The act invades the reserved rights of the states. It is a statutory plan to regulate and control agricultural production, a matter beyond the powers delegated to the federal government. The tax, the appropriation of the funds raised, and the direction for their disbursement, are but parts of the plan. They are but means to an unconstitutional end.

From the accepted doctrine that the United States is a government of delegated powers, it follows that those not expressly granted, or reasonably to be implied from such as are conferred, are reserved to the states or to the people. To forestall any suggestion to the contrary, the Tenth Amendment was adopted. The same proposition, otherwise stated, is that powers not granted are prohibited. None to regulate agricultural production is given, and therefore legislation by Congress for that purpose is forbidden.

It is an established principle that the attainment of a prohibited end may not be accomplished under the pretext of the exertion of powers which are granted. . . .

The power of taxation, which is expressly granted, may, of course, be adopted as a means to carry into operation another power also expressly granted. But resort to the taxing power to effectuate an end which is not legitimate, not within the scope of the Constitution, is obviously inadmissible. . . .

If the act before us is a proper exercise of the federal taxing power, evidently the regulation of all industry throughout the United States may be accomplished by similar exercises of the same power. . . .

Until recently no suggestion of the existence of any such power in the Federal Government has been advanced. The expressions of the framers of the Constitution, the decisions of this court interpreting that instrument, and the writings of great commentators will be searched in vain for any suggestion that there exists in the clause under discussion or elsewhere in the Constitution, the authority whereby every provision and every fair implication from that instrument may be subverted, the independence of the individual states obliterated, and the United States converted into a central government exercising uncontrolled police power in every state of the Union, superseding all local control or regulation of the affairs or concerns of the states.

66 ⮌

Carter v. Carter Coal Co. challenged another of the government's industrial codes, this one covering production, marketing, and working conditions in the coal industry. Adhering to the distinction between production and interstate commerce that was central to state-rights constitutionalism, the majority of the justices ruled that the regulations invaded jurisdiction reserved to the states. It was irrelevant that the coal was intended for interstate commerce and that wages and working conditions in one state clearly affected those in other states. This time Chief Justice Charles Evans Hughes joined the three liberal justices in dissent.

A month later, the Court raised the stakes even higher, once again overturning a state law establishing a minimum wage for women and children. It was now clear that little, if any, federal New Deal legislation could pass the scrutiny of the Supreme Court; nor would state regulation of wages be upheld. Republicans, preparing for the presidential and congressional election of 1936, pointed to the Court's decisions as evidence that the New Deal had transgressed the bounds of constitutional government.

Carter v. Carter Coal Co. (1936)

M R . J U S T I C E Sutherland delivered the opinion of the Court. . . .

The proposition, often advanced and as often discredited, that the power of the federal government inherently extends to purposes affecting the nation as a whole with which the states severally cannot deal or cannot adequately deal, and the related notion that Congress, entirely apart from those powers delegated by the Constitution, may enact laws to promote the general welfare, have never been accepted but always definitely rejected by this court. . . .

298 U.S. 238 (1936).

The general rule with regard to the respective powers of the national and the state governments under the Constitution, is not in doubt. The states were before the Constitution; and, consequently, their legislative powers antedated the Constitution. Those who framed and those who adopted that instrument meant to carve from the general mass of legislative powers, then possessed by the states, only such portions as it was thought wise to confer upon the federal government. . . .

The determination of the Framers Convention and the ratifying conventions to preserve complete and unimpaired state self-government in all matters not committed to the general government is one of the plainest facts which emerge from the history of their deliberations. . . . Every journey to a forbidden end begins with the first step; and the danger of such a step by the federal government in the direction of taking over the powers of the states is that the end of the journey may find the states so despoiled of their powers, or—what may amount to the same thing—so relieved of the responsibilities which possession of the powers necessarily enjoins, as to reduce them to little more than geographical subdivisions of the national domain. . . .

. . . [T]he validity of the act depends upon whether it is a regulation of interstate commerce. . . .

. . . [T]he word "commerce" is the equivalent of the phrase "intercourse for the purposes of trade." Plainly, the incidents leading up to and culminating in the mining of coal do not constitute such intercourse. The employment of men, the fixing of their wages, hours of labor and working conditions, the bargaining in respect of these things—whether carried on separately or collectively—each and all constitute intercourse for the purposes of production, not of trade. . . .

But §1 (the preamble) of the act now under review declares that all production and distribution of bituminous coal "bear upon and directly affect its interstate commerce"; and that regulation thereof is imperative for the protection of such commerce. The contention of the government is that the labor provisions of the act may be sustained in that view.

That the production of every commodity intended for interstate sale and transportation has some effect upon interstate commerce may be, if it has not already been, freely granted; and we are brought to the final and decisive inquiry, whether here that effect is direct, as the "preamble" recites, or indirect. . . .

Whether the effect of a given activity or condition is direct or indirect is not always easy to determine. The word "direct" implies that the activity or condition invoked or blamed shall operate proximately—not mediately, remotely, or collaterally—to produce the effect. It connotes the absence of an efficient intervening agency or condition. And the extent of the effect bears no logical relation to its character. The distinction between a direct and an indirect effect turns, not upon the magnitude of either the cause or the effect, but entirely upon the manner in which the effect has been brought about. If the production by one man of a single ton of coal intended for interstate sale and shipment, and actually so sold and shipped, affects interstate commerce indirectly, the effect does not become direct by multiplying the tonnage, or increasing the number of men employed, or adding to the expense or complexities of the business, or by all combined. . . .

Much stress is put upon the evils which come from the struggle between employers and employees over the matter of wages, working conditions, the right of collective bargaining, etc., and the resulting strikes, curtailment and irregularity of production and effect on prices; and it is insisted that interstate commerce is *greatly* affected thereby. But . . . the conclusive answer is that the evils are all local evils over which the federal government has no legislative control.

67 ∽

The election of 1936 was, in effect, a referendum on conservative versus liberal constitutionalism. Democrats argued that government had broad responsibilities to promote the general welfare and that modern economic developments required the federal government to take an active role. Republicans argued that the New Deal deprived Americans of constitutional rights and usurped the jurisdiction of the states.

The Democratic and Republican National Platforms (1936)

The Democratic National Platform

WE HOLD *this truth to be self-evident*—that government in a modern civilization has certain inescapable obligations to its citizens, among which are:

(1) Protection of the family and the home.

(2) Establishment of a democracy of opportunity for all the people.

(3) Aid to those overtaken by disaster.

These obligations, neglected through 12 years of the old leadership, have once more been recognized by American Government. Under the new leadership they will never be neglected. . . .

Johnson (ed.), *National Party Platforms*, 1: 360, 362.

The Constitution

The REPUBLICAN platform proposes to meet many pressing national problems solely by action of the separate States. We know that drought, dust storms, floods, minimum wages, maximum hours, child labor, and working conditions in industry, monopolistic and unfair business practices cannot be adequately handled exclusively by 48 separate State legislatures, 48 separate State administrations, and 48 separate State courts. Transactions and activities which inevitably overflow State boundaries call for both State and Federal treatment.

We have sought and will continue to seek to meet these problems through legislation within the Constitution.

If these problems cannot be effectively solved by legislation within the Constitution, we shall seek such clarifying amendment as will assure to the legislatures of the several States and to the Congress of the United States, each within its proper jurisdiction, the power to enact those laws which the State and Federal legislatures, within their respective spheres, shall find necessary, in order adequately to regulate commerce, protect public health and safety and safeguard economic security. Thus we propose to maintain the letter and spirit of the Constitution.

The Republican National Platform

AMERICA IS in peril. The welfare of American men and women and the future of our youth are at stake. We dedicate ourselves to the preservation of their political liberty, their individual opportunity and their character as free citizens, which today for the first time are threatened by Government itself.

For three long years the New Deal Administration has dishonored American traditions and flagrantly betrayed the pledges upon which the Democratic Party sought and received public support.

The powers of Congress have been usurped by the President.

The integrity and authority of the Supreme Court have been flouted.

The rights and liberties of American citizens have been violated.

Regulated monopoly has displaced free enterprise.

The New Deal Administration constantly seeks to usurp the rights reserved to the States and to the people.

It has insisted on the passage of laws contrary to the Constitution. . . .

It has created a vast multitude of new offices, filled them with its favorites, set up a centralized bureaucracy, and sent out swarms of inspectors to harass our people.

Johnson (ed.), *National Party Platforms*, 1: 365–366.

It has bred fear and hesitation in commerce and industry, thus discouraging new enterprises, preventing employment and prolonging the depression. . . .

It has destroyed the morale of our people and made them dependent upon government. . . .

Constitutional Government and Free Enterprise

WE PLEDGE ourselves:

1. To maintain the American system of Constitutional and local self government, and to resist all attempts to impair the authority of the Supreme Court of the United States, the final protector of the rights of our citizens against the arbitrary encroachments of the legislative and executive branches of government. There can be no individual liberty without an independent judiciary.

2. To preserve the American system of free enterprise, private competition, and equality of opportunity, and to seek its constant betterment in the interests of all.

68 ✌

In the election of 1936, American voters overwhelmingly endorsed President Roosevelt, the Democratic party, and the New Deal. Faced with the apparent intransigence of the Supreme Court, Roosevelt proposed to add a new justice for each one over seventy years of age, thereby adding six new justices. But the Court surprised observers by changing direction in 1937. Denying that they were influenced by the court-packing scheme, Hughes and Roberts joined the liberal justices to sustain New Deal legislation against further challenges.

The first indication of the change came with the Court's decision in *West Coast Hotel Co. v. Parrish*. The case involved a minimum-wage law for women that seemed indistinguishable from the one that the Court had just overturned during the previous term. Nonetheless, Hughes, Roberts, and the three liberal justices proceeded to find enough difference to say that the prior decision was not determinative. They then took the rare step of overturning the lead case on the issue, *Adkins v. Children's Hospital* (Document 63), arguing that it had been a departure from the true constitutional rule established in *Muller v. Oregon* (Document 59). Liberty of contract *was* subject to the restraints that legislatures reasonably considered to benefit the community, the justices opined. The Supreme Court would not again overturn an economic regulation on substantive due process grounds, although in the 1980s and 1990s it began to substitute other reasons for doing so.

West Coast Hotel Co. v. Parrish (1937)

M R . C H I E F Justice Hughes delivered the opinion of the Court. . . .

The Constitution does not speak of freedom of contract. It speaks of liberty and prohibits the deprivation of liberty without due process of law. In prohibiting that deprivation the Constitution does not recognize an absolute and uncontrollable liberty. Liberty in each of its phases has its history and connotation. But the liberty safeguarded is liberty in a social organization which requires the protection of law against the evils which menace the health, safety, morals and welfare of the people. Liberty under the Constitution is thus necessarily subject to the restraints of due process, and regulation which is reasonable in relation to its subject and is adopted in the interests of the community is due process. . . .

It is manifest that this established principle is peculiarly applicable in relation to the employment of women in whose protection the State has a special interest. That phase of the subject received elaborate consideration in *Muller v. Oregon* (1908), . . . where the constitutional authority of the State to limit the working hours of women was sustained. . . .

We think that . . . the decision in the *Adkins* case was a departure from the true application of the principles governing the regulation by the State of the relation of employer and employed. . . .

. . . What can be closer to the public interest than the health of women and their protection from unscrupulous and overreaching employers? And if the protection of women is a legitimate end of the exercise of state power, how can it be said that the requirement of the payment of a minimum wage fairly fixed in order to meet the very necessities of existence is not an admissible means to that end? The legislature of the State was clearly entitled to consider the situation of women in employment, the fact that they are in the class receiving the least pay, that their bargaining power is relatively weak, and that they are the ready victims of those who would take advantage of their necessitous circumstances. . . .

There is an additional and compelling consideration which recent economic experience has brought into a strong light. The exploitation of a class of workers who are in an unequal position with respect to bargaining power and are thus relatively defenceless against the denial of a living wage is not only detrimental to their health and well being but casts a direct burden for their support upon the community. What these workers lose in wages the taxpayers are called upon to pay. The bare cost of living must be met. We may take judicial notice of the unparalleled demands for relief which arose

300 U.S. 379 (1937).

during the recent period of depression and still continue to an alarming extent despite the degree of economic recovery which has been achieved. . . . The community is not bound to provide what is in effect a subsidy for unconscionable employers. The community may direct its law-making power to correct the abuse which springs from their selfish disregard of the public interest.

69 ❧

Having repudiated laissez-faire constitutionalism in *West Coast Hotel Co. v. Parrish,* the new liberal majority on the Supreme Court next rejected the state-rights doctrine of federalism. The shift came with the Court's decision in *National Labor Relations Board v. Jones & Laughlin Steel Corp.,* in which the five justices sustained federal authority to regulate labor relations in industries affecting interstate commerce. That the employees were engaged in production rather than interstate commerce was of no moment, the Court held. The Depression had proven that wages, work rules, and other elements affecting production in one state profoundly affected production in others. Only the blindest formalism could ignore the reality of such federal effects.

NLRB v. Jones & Laughlin Steel Corp. (1937)

M R . C H I E F Justice Hughes delivered the opinion of the Court. . . .

. . . The Act is challenged in its entirety as an attempt to regulate all industry, thus invading the reserved powers of the States over their local concerns. . . .

. . . Respondent says that . . . the industrial relations and activities in the manufacturing department of respondent's enterprise are not subject to federal regulation. The argument rests upon the proposition that manufacturing in itself is not commerce. . . . *Schechter Corp.* v. *United States* . . . ; *Carter* v. *Carter Coal Co.* . . .

. . . The fundamental principle is that the power to regulate commerce is the power to enact "all appropriate legislation" for "its protection and advancement" . . . ; to adopt measures "to promote its growth and insure its safety" . . . ; "to foster, protect, control and restrain." . . . That power is plenary and may be exerted to protect interstate commerce "no matter what the source of the dangers which threaten it." . . . Undoubtedly the scope of this power must be considered in the light of our dual system of government and

301 U.S. 1 (1937).

may not be extended so as to embrace effects upon interstate commerce so indirect and remote that to embrace them, in view of our complex society, would effectually obliterate the distinction between what is national and what is local and create a completely centralized government. . . . The question is necessarily one of degree. . . .

That intrastate activities, by reason of close and intimate relation to interstate commerce, may fall within federal control is demonstrated in the case of carriers who are engaged in both interstate and intrastate transportation. There federal control has been found essential to secure the freedom of interstate traffic from interference or unjust discrimination and to promote the efficiency of the interstate service. . . .

The close and intimate effect which brings the subject within the reach of federal power may be due to activities in relation to productive industry although the industry when separately viewed is local. . . .

It is thus apparent that the fact that the employees here concerned were engaged in production is not determinative. The question remains as to the effect upon interstate commerce of the labor practice involved. In the *Schechter* case . . . we found that the effect there was so remote as to be beyond the federal power. . . . In the *Carter* case, . . . the Court was of the opinion that the provisions of the statute relating to production were invalid upon several grounds. . . . These cases are not controlling here. . . .

. . . Giving full weight to respondent's contention with respect to a break in the complete continuity of the "stream of commerce" by reason of respondent's manufacturing operations, the fact remains that the stoppage of those operations by industrial strife would have a most serious effect upon interstate commerce. In view of respondent's far-flung activities, it is idle to say that the effect would be indirect or remote. It is obvious that it would be immediate and might be catastrophic. We are asked to shut our eyes to the plainest facts of our national life and to deal with the question of direct and indirect effects in an intellectual vacuum. . . . When industries organize themselves on a national scale, making their relation to interstate commerce the dominant factor in their activities, how can it be maintained that their industrial labor relations constitute a forbidden field into which Congress may not enter when it is necessary to protect interstate commerce from the paralyzing consequences of industrial war? . . .

. . . It is not necessary again to detail the facts as to respondent's enterprise. Instead of being beyond the pale, we think that it presents in a most striking way the close and intimate relation which a manufacturing industry may have to interstate commerce and we have no doubt that Congress had constitutional authority to safeguard the right of respondent's employees to self-organization and freedom in the choice of representatives for collective bargaining.

70 ॰ॐ

The new majority on the Supreme Court soon made it clear that Congress had almost unbounded power to exercise its constitutionally delegated interstate commerce, taxing, and spending powers to regulate society and the economy. In *Steward Machine Co. v. Davis,* 301 U.S. 548 (1937), and *Helvering v. Davis,* 301 U.S. 619 (1937), the Court repudiated the idea that the Tenth Amendment limited the taxing and spending powers. In *U.S. v. Darby* the Court, now completely dominated by the old liberal justices and Roosevelt's appointees, unanimously sustained the Fair Labor Standards Act of 1938, which established minimum wages and maximum hours of labor in industries whose products were shipped through interstate commerce or that affected interstate commerce.

The lower federal court had quashed the indictment of Darby Lumber Co. for violating the act, citing *Hammer v. Dagenhart's* state-rights denial of Congress's power to regulate production by banning otherwise inoffensive goods from interstate commerce. The justices took advantage of the appeal to disavow state-rights constitutionalism, specifically overruling the decision in *Hammer v. Dagenhart* and endorsing Holmes's dissent. As a leading constitutional scholar observed, the opinion was designed to be "the death-knell of dual federalism."

U.S. v. Darby (1941)

MR. JUSTICE Stone delivered the opinion of the Court. . . .

The power of Congress over interstate commerce "is complete in itself, may be exercised to its utmost extent, and acknowledges no limitations other than are prescribed in the Constitution." *Gibbons v. Ogden,* . . . That power can neither be enlarged nor diminished by the exercise or non-exercise of state power. . . . Congress, following its own conception of public policy concerning the restrictions which may appropriately be imposed on interstate commerce, is free to exclude from the commerce articles whose use in the states for which they are destined it may conceive to be injurious to the public health, morals or welfare, even though the state has not sought to regulate their use. . . . *Lottery Case* . . . ; *Hipolite Egg Co.* v. *United States* . . . ; *Hoke* v. *United States.* . . .

Such regulation is not a forbidden invasion of state power merely because either its motive or its consequence is to restrict the use of articles of commerce within the states of destination; and is not prohibited unless by other Constitutional provisions. It is no objection to the assertion of the power to regulate interstate commerce that its exercise is attended by the same incidents which attend the exercise of the police power of the states. . . .

312 U.S. 100 (1941).

... The motive and purpose of a regulation of interstate commerce are matters for the legislative judgment upon the exercise of which the Constitution places no restriction and over which the courts are given no control. ...

In the more than a century which has elapsed since the decision of *Gibbons* v. *Ogden,* these principles of constitutional interpretation have been so long and repeatedly recognized by this Court as applicable to the Commerce Clause, that there would be little occasion for repeating them now were it not for the decision of this Court twenty-two years ago in *Hammer* v. *Dagenhart.* ... In that case it was held by a bare majority of the Court over the powerful and now classic dissent of Mr. Justice Holmes setting forth the fundamental issues involved, that Congress was without power to exclude the products of child labor from interstate commerce. The reasoning and conclusion of the Court's opinion there cannot be reconciled with the conclusion which we have reached, that the power of Congress under the Commerce Clause is plenary to exclude any article from interstate commerce subject only to the specific prohibitions of the Constitution.

Hammer v. *Dagenhart* has not been followed. The distinction on which the decision was rested that Congressional power to prohibit interstate commerce is limited to articles which in themselves have some harmful or deleterious property—a distinction which was novel when made and unsupported by any provision of the Constitution—has long since been abandoned. ...

The conclusion is inescapable that *Hammer* v. *Dagenhart* was a departure from the principles which have prevailed in the interpretation of the Commerce Clause both before and since the decision and that such vitality, as a precedent, as it then had has long since been exhausted. It should be and now is overruled. ...

There remains the question whether [direct] ... restriction on the production of goods for commerce is a permissible exercise of the commerce power. The power of Congress over interstate commerce is not confined to the regulation of commerce among the states. It extends to those activities intrastate which so affect interstate commerce or the exercise of the power of Congress over it as to make regulation of them appropriate means to the ... exercise of the granted power of Congress to regulate interstate commerce. ...

Congress, having by the present Act adopted the policy of excluding from interstate commerce all goods produced for the commerce which do not conform to the specified labor standards, it may choose the means reasonably adapted to the attainment of the permitted end, even though they involve control of intrastate activities. ...

Our conclusion is unaffected by the Tenth Amendment which provides: "The powers not delegated to the United States by the Constitution, nor prohibited by it to the States, are reserved to the States respectively, or to the people." The amendment states but a truism that all is retained which has not been surrendered. There is nothing in the history of its adoption to suggest that it was more than declaratory of the relationship between the national and state governments as it had been established by the Constitution before the amendment or that its purpose was other than to allay fears that the new national government might seek to exercise powers not granted, and that the states might not be able to exercise fully their reserved powers.

71 ∿

Although the Supreme Court had repudiated the idea that the Tenth Amendment restricted Congress's power to regulate interstate commerce, the question remained: Just how expansively should one define interstate commerce? In *Wickard v. Filburn,* the Court defined it extremely broadly, rejecting old efforts to keep regulation of production within the sole jurisdiction of the states. Filburn was an Ohio dairy farmer who grew a small amount of wheat that he fed to his livestock and ground into flour for home consumption. He was assessed a fine for sowing twelve acres more wheat than allotted to him under the second Agricultural Adjustment Act, passed in 1938. Filburn protested the assessment, arguing that none of his small, domestic production was intended for interstate commerce or could be said to affect it significantly.

A unanimous Court disagreed, pointing out the substantial effect that similar activities by millions of farmers would have on the national agricultural economy. The decision meant that congressional regulation could reach virtually anything that might affect interstate commerce, no matter how remote. Since then, Congress has used its authority to regulate anything affecting interstate commerce so as to exercise wide-ranging national police powers over the economy, public health, and the environment.

Wickard v. Filburn (1942)

M R . J U S T I C E Jackson delivered the opinion of the court. . . .

. . . We believe that a review of the course of decision under the Commerce Clause will make plain . . . that questions of the power of Congress are not to be decided by reference to any formula which would give controlling force to nomenclature such as "production" and "indirect" and foreclose consideration of the actual effects of the activity in question upon interstate commerce. . . .

. . . [Q]uestions of federal power cannot be decided simply by finding the activity in question to be "production," nor can consideration of its economic effects be foreclosed by calling them "indirect." . . .

317 U.S. 111 (1942).

Whether the subject of the regulation in question was "production," "consumption," or "marketing" is, therefore, not material for purposes of deciding the question of federal power before us. That an activity is of local character may help in a doubtful case to determine whether Congress intended to reach it. The same consideration might help in determining whether in the absence of Congressional action it would be permissible for the state to exert its power on the subject matter, even though in so doing it to some degree affected interstate commerce. But even if appellee's activity be local and though it may not be regarded as commerce, it may still, whatever its nature, be reached by Congress if it exerts a substantial economic effect on interstate commerce, and this irrespective of whether such effect is what might at some earlier time have been defined as "direct" or "indirect." . . .

The effect of consumption of homegrown wheat on interstate commerce is due to the fact that it constitutes the most variable factor in the disappearance of the wheat crop. Consumption on the farm where grown appears to vary in an amount greater than 20 per cent of average production. . . .

It is well established by decisions of this Court that the power to regulate commerce includes the power to regulate the prices at which commodities in that commerce are dealt in and practices affecting such prices. One of the primary purposes of the Act in question was to increase the market price of wheat, and to that end to limit the volume thereof that could affect the market. It can hardly be denied that a factor of such volume and variability as home-consumed wheat would have a substantial influence on price and market conditions. . . . This record leaves us in no doubt that Congress may properly have considered that wheat consumed on the farm where grown, if wholly outside the scheme of regulation, would have a substantial effect in defeating and obstructing its purpose to stimulate trade therein at increased prices.

72 ∽

Although the so-called Roosevelt Court sustained nationalist constitutionalism in general, it rejected the doctrine of *Swift v. Tyson.* That doctrine, which limited the application of section 34 of the Judiciary Act, required federal courts to follow state law in diversity-of-citizenship cases only with regard to certain local statutes and real-estate laws (see Document 31). It had been used to create national laws, friendly to business interests, on contracts and other economic matters.

Tompkins had been injured by a train as he walked beside the tracks. Under Pennsylvania law, he was deemed a trespasser and ineligible for compensation. Tompkins's lawyers argued that based on *Swift v. Tyson,* the Court should ignore Pennsylvania's rule and apply a general one more sympathetic to those injured through railroad negligence.

The Court not only overruled *Swift v. Tyson,* but delivered an exegesis on the philosophy of Legal Positivism that had led it to repudiate laissez-faire constitutionalism. (For an explanation of Legal Positivism, see the introduction to *Lochner v. New York,* Document 56.)

Erie Railroad Co. v. Tompkins (1938)

M R . J U S T I C E Brandeis delivered the opinion of the Court. . . .

Except in matters governed by the Federal Constitution or by Acts of Congress, the law to be applied in any case is the law of the State. And whether the law of the State shall be declared by its Legislature in a statute or by its highest court in a decision is not a matter of federal concern. There is no federal general common law. Congress has no power to declare substantive rules of common law applicable in a State whether they be local in their nature or "general," be they commercial law or a part of the law of torts. . . . As stated by Mr. Justice Field when protesting . . . against ignoring the Ohio common law of fellow servant liability: . . .

". . . [N]otwithstanding the great names which may be cited in favor of the doctrine [of *Swift v. Tyson*], and notwithstanding the frequency with which the doctrine has been reiterated, there stands, as a perpetual protest against its repetition, the Constitution of the United States, which recognizes and preserves the autonomy and independence of the States—independence in their legislative and independence in their judicial departments. Supervision over either the legislative or the judicial action of the States is in no case permissible except as to matters by the Constitution specifically authorized or delegated to the United States. Any interference with either, except as thus permitted, is an invasion of the authority of the State and, to that extent, a denial of its independence."

The fallacy underlying the rule declared in *Swift v. Tyson* is made clear by Mr. Justice Holmes. The doctrine rests upon the assumption that there is "a transcendental body of law outside of any particular State but obligatory within it unless and until changed by statute," that federal courts have the power to use their judgment as to what the rules of common law are; and that in the federal courts "the parties are entitled to an independent judgment on matters of general law":

"[B]ut law in the sense in which courts speak of it today does not exist without some definite authority behind it. The common law so far as it is enforced in a State, whether called common law or not, is not the common law

304 U.S. 64 (1938).

generally but the law of that State existing by the authority of that State . . . , and if that be so, the voice adopted by the State as its own (whether it be of its Legislature or of its Supreme Court) should utter the last word."

Thus the doctrine of *Swift v. Tyson* is, as Mr. Justice Holmes said, "an unconstitutional assumption of powers by courts of the United States which no lapse of time or respectable array of opinion should make us hesitate to correct."

CHAPTER 15

Liberal Constitutionalism

Foundations

73

As the Supreme Court abandoned its strict scrutiny of state and federal laws affecting property rights and of federal laws that seemed to invade state rights, it paid closer attention to laws affecting noneconomic civil liberties. As early as 1925 the Court had concluded in *Gitlow v. N.Y.*, 268 U.S. 652, that the same right of free speech that the Bill of Rights protected against federal infringement was also protected against state infringement by the Fourteenth Amendment. This was a clear repudiation of the position the Court had taken in *Hurtado v. California*, 110 U.S. 516 (1884), that no liberty protected by the Bill of Rights could be among those protected by the Due Process Clause of the Fourteenth Amendment. It could also be interpreted as an advance from the position the Court had taken in *Twining v. New Jersey*, 211 U.S. 78, in 1908. In that case, the Court had said that the Fourteenth Amendment had nothing to do with the Bill of Rights, but in itself protected whatever was fundamental to liberty.

In *Whitney v. California*, the Court upheld the conviction of Charlotte Anita Whitney for helping to found the Communist Labor party, an organization advocating the violent overthrow of the government. The majority of justices applied the Bad Tendency Test. Brandeis, joined by Holmes, concurred in the result, but urged application of the Clear and Present Danger Test in an opinion that eloquently presented liberal constitutionalism's view of freedom of expression.

Brandeis, Concurring Opinion in *Whitney v. California* (1927)

MR. JUSTICE Brandeis, concurring. . . .
[A]lthough the rights of free speech and assembly are fundamental, they

274 U.S. 357, 372 (1927) (Brandeis, concurring).

are not in their nature absolute. Their exercise is subject to restriction. . . . That the necessity which is essential to a valid restriction does not exist unless speech would produce, or is intended to produce, a clear and imminent danger of some substantive evil which the State constitutionally may seek to prevent has been settled. . . .

This Court has not yet fixed the standard by which to determine when a danger shall be deemed clear; how remote the danger may be and yet be deemed present; and what degree of evil shall be deemed sufficiently substantial to justify resort to abridgement of free speech and assembly as the means of protection. To reach sound conclusions on these matters, we must bear in mind why a State is, ordinarily, denied the power to prohibit dissemination of social, economic and political doctrine which a vast majority of its citizens believes to be false and fraught with evil consequence.

Those who won our independence believed that the final end of the State was to make men free to develop their faculties; and that in its government the deliberative forces should prevail over the arbitrary. They valued liberty both as an end and as a means. They believed liberty to be the secret of happiness and courage to be the secret of liberty. They believed that freedom to think as you will and to speak as you think are means indispensable to the discovery and spread of political truth; that without free speech and assembly discussion would be futile; that with them, discussion affords ordinarily adequate protection against the dissemination of noxious doctrine; that the greatest menace to freedom is an inert people; that public discussion is a political duty; and that this should be a fundamental principle of the American government. They recognized the risks to which all human institutions are subject. But they knew that order cannot be secured merely through fear of punishment for its infraction; that it is hazardous to discourage thought, hope and imagination; that fear breeds repression; that repression breeds hate; that hate menaces stable government; that the path of safety lies in the opportunity to discuss freely supposed grievances and proposed remedies; and that the fitting remedy for evil counsels is good ones. Believing in the power of reason as applied through public discussion, they eschewed silence coerced by law—the argument of force in its worst form. Recognizing the occasional tyrannies of governing majorities, they amended the Constitution so that free speech and assembly should be guaranteed.

Fear of serious injury cannot alone justify suppression of free speech and assembly. Men feared witches and burnt women. It is the function of speech to free men from the bondage of irrational fears. To justify suppression of free speech there must be reasonable ground to fear that serious evil will result if free speech is practiced. There must be a reasonable ground to believe that the danger apprehended is imminent. There must be reasonable ground to believe that the evil to be prevented is a serious one. Every denunciation of existing law tends in some measure to increase the probability that there will be violation of it. . . . But even advocacy of violation, however reprehensible morally, is not a justification for denying free speech where the advocacy falls short of incitement and there is nothing to indicate that advocacy would be immediately acted on. The wide difference between advocacy and incitement, between preparation and attempt, between assembling and conspiracy, must be borne in mind. In order to support a finding of a clear and present danger it must be shown either that immediate serious violence was to be expected or was advocated, or that the past conduct furnished reason to believe that such advocacy was then contemplated.

Those who won our independence by revolution were not cowards. They did not fear political change. They did not exalt order at the cost of liberty. To courageous, self-reliant men, with confidence in the power of free and fearless reasoning applied through the processes of popular government, no danger flowing from speech can be deemed clear and present, unless the incidence of the evil apprehended is so imminent that it may befall before there is an opportunity for full discussion. If there be time to expose through discussion the falsehood and fallacies, to avert the evil by processes of education, the remedy to be applied is more speech, not enforced silence. . . .

Whenever the fundamental rights of free speech and assembly are alleged to have been invaded, it must remain open to a defendant to present the issue whether there actually did exist at the time a clear danger; whether the danger, if any, was imminent; and whether the evil apprehended was one so substantial as to justify the stringent restriction interposed by the legislature.

74 ❧

By the early 1930s, the Court was beginning to fulfill the promise of *Gitlow*. In *Near v. Minnesota*, it overturned the law under which the state suppressed the muckraking Near's antiracketeering, antilabor, and antisemitic *Saturday Press*. The opinion suggested that all laws imposing prior restraint on political expression were unconstitutional.

Near v. Minnesota (1931)

M R . C H I E F Justice Hughes delivered the opinion of the Court. . . .

. . . It is no longer open to doubt that the liberty of the press, and of speech, is within the liberty safeguarded by the due process clause of the Fourteenth Amendment from invasion by state action. It was found impossible to conclude that this essential personal liberty of the citizen was left unprotected by the general guaranty of fundamental rights of person and property. . . .

If we cut through mere details of procedure, the operation and effect of the statute in substance is that public authorities may bring the owner or publisher of a newspaper or periodical before a judge upon a charge of conducting a business of publishing scandalous and defamatory matter—in particular that the matter consists of charges against public officers of official dereliction—and unless the owner or publisher is able and disposed to bring competent evidence to satisfy the judge that the charges are true and are published with good motives and for justifiable ends, his newspaper or periodical is suppressed and further publication is made punishable as a contempt. This is of the essence of censorship.

The question is whether a statute authorizing such proceedings in restraint of publication is consistent with the conception of the liberty of the press as historically conceived and guaranteed. In determining the extent of the constitutional protection, it has been generally, if not universally, considered that it is the chief purpose of the guaranty to prevent previous restraints upon publication. . . .

The fact that for approximately one hundred and fifty years there has been almost an entire absence of attempts to impose previous restraints upon publications relating to the malfeasance of public officers is significant of the deep-seated conviction that such restraints would violate constitutional right. Public officers, whose character and conduct remain open to debate and free discussion in the press, find their remedies for false accusations in actions under libel laws providing for redress and punishment, and not in proceedings to restrain the publication of newspapers and periodicals. The general principle that the constitutional guaranty of the liberty of the press gives immunity from previous restraints has been approved in many decisions under the provisions of state constitutions.

The importance of this immunity has not lessened. . . . [T]he administration of government has become more complex, the opportunities for malfeasance and corruption have multiplied, crime has grown to most serious proportions, and the danger of its protection by unfaithful officials and of the impairment of the fundamental security of life and property by criminal alliances and official neglect, emphasizes the primary need of a vigilant and courageous press, especially in great cities. The fact that the liberty of the press may be abused by miscreant purveyors of scandal does not make any the less necessary the immunity of the press from previous restraint in dealing with official misconduct. Subsequent punishment for such abuses as may exist is the appropriate remedy, consistent with constitutional privilege.

75 ∾

Having firmly espoused a position of judicial restraint in cases involving federalism and property rights, the Court found it necessary to present a rationale for greater activism in cases involving noneconomic liberties. It did so in the famous Footnote Number 4 of *U.S. v. Carolene Products Co.* The case involved the constitutionality of a federal ban on certain milk products from interstate commerce. Knowing that a state-rights argument would fail, the company argued that the ban deprived it of liberty without due process of law. The Court responded that any law that was reasonably related to the public welfare met the standard of due process. But in a footnote to his opinion for the Court, Justice Stone indicated that certain types of laws and government actions might be subject to stricter scrutiny. Stone's statement provided liberal constitutionalism with a foundation for judicial activism in the protection of civil liberties and equal rights. The liberties he identified as deserving active judicial protection are sometimes called the "preferred freedoms."

The Carolene Products Footnote (1938)

[4]THERE may be narrower scope for operation of the presumption of constitutionality when legislation appears on its face to be within a specific prohibition of the Constitution, such as those of the first ten amendments, which are deemed equally specific when held to be embraced within the Fourteenth. . . .

It is unnecessary to consider now whether legislation which restricts those political processes which can ordinarily be expected to bring about repeal of undesirable legislation, is to be subjected to more exacting judicial scrutiny under the general prohibitions of the Fourteenth Amendment than are most other types of legislation. . . .

Nor need we inquire whether similar considerations enter into the review of statutes directed at particular religions, . . . or national . . . or racial minorities, . . . [or] whether prejudice against discrete and insular minorities may be a special condition, which tends seriously to curtail the operation of those political processes ordinarily to be relied upon to protect minorities, and which may call for a correspondingly more searching judicial inquiry.

304 U.S. 144, at 152 (1938).

76 ♋

In *Palko v. Connecticut,* the Court clarified the relationship between the Bill of Rights and the Fourteenth Amendment. Connecticut law permitted the state to appeal judgments of trial courts in criminal cases. Palko was convicted of second-degree murder and sentenced to life in prison. But after a state appeals court ordered a new trial, he was convicted of murder in the first degree and sentenced to death.

Had the federal government instituted this second trial, it would have violated the Fifth Amendment, which says no person can be put in jeopardy twice for the same offense. Palko's lawyers argued that the Due Process Clause of the Fourteenth Amendment incorporated all the provisions of the Bill of Rights and applied them to the states. The justices disagreed. Only principles fundamental to the American heritage of liberty were "absorbed" into the Fourteenth Amendment—a doctrine that became known as "selective incorporation."

Palko v. Connecticut (1937)

MR. JUSTICE Cardozo delivered the opinion of the Court.

A statute of Connecticut permitting appeals in criminal cases to be taken by the state is challenged by appellant as an infringement of the Fourteenth Amendment of the Constitution of the United States. Whether the challenge should be upheld is now to be determined. . . .

. . . [I]n appellant's view the Fourteenth Amendment is to be taken as embodying the prohibitions of the Fifth. His thesis is even broader. Whatever would be a violation of the original bill of rights (Amendments 1 to 8) if done by the federal government is now equally unlawful by force of the Fourteenth Amendment if done by a state. There is no such general rule.

The Fifth Amendment provides, among other things, that no person shall be held to answer for a capital or otherwise infamous crime unless on presentment or indictment of a grand jury. This court has held that, in prosecutions by a state, presentment or indictment by a grand jury may give way to informations at the instance of a public officer. . . . The Fifth Amendment provides also that no person shall be compelled in any criminal case to be a witness against himself. This court has said that, in prosecutions by a state, the exemption will fail if the state elects to end it. . . . The Sixth Amendment calls for a jury trial in criminal cases and the Seventh for a jury trial in civil cases at common law where the value in controversy shall exceed twenty dollars. This court has ruled that consistently with those amendments trial by jury may be modified by a state or abolished altogether. . . .

302 U.S. 319 (1937).

On the other hand, the due process clause of the Fourteenth Amendment may make it unlawful for a state to abridge by its statutes the freedom of speech which the First Amendment safeguards against encroachment by the Congress . . . or the like freedom of the press . . . , or the free exercise of religion . . . , or the right of peaceable assembly, without which speech would be unduly trammeled . . . , or the right of one accused of crime to the benefit of counsel. . . . In these and other situations immunities that are valid as against the federal government by force of the specific pledges of particular amendments have been found to be implicit in the concept of ordered liberty, and thus, through the Fourteenth Amendment, become valid as against the states.

The line of division may seem to be wavering and broken if there is a hasty catalogue of the cases on the one side and the other. Reflection and analysis will induce a different view. There emerges the perception of a rationalizing principle which gives to discrete instances a proper order and coherence. The right to trial by jury and the immunity from prosecution except as the result of an indictment may have value and importance. Even so, they are not of the very essence of a scheme of ordered liberty. To abolish them is not to violate a "principle of justice so rooted in the traditions and conscience of our people as to be ranked as fundamental." . . . Few would be so narrow or provincial as to maintain that a fair and enlightened system of justice would be impossible without them. What is true of jury trials and indictments is true also, as the cases show, of the immunity from compulsory self-incrimination. . . .

We reach a different plane of social and moral values when we pass to the privileges and immunities that have been taken over from the earlier articles of the federal bill of rights and brought within the Fourteenth Amendment by a process of absorption. These in their origin were effective against the federal government alone. If the Fourteenth Amendment has absorbed them, the process of absorption has had its source in the belief that neither liberty nor justice would exist if they were sacrificed. . . . This is true, for illustration, of freedom of thought and speech. Of that freedom one may say that it is the matrix, the indispensable condition, of nearly every other form of freedom. . . .

Our survey of the cases serves, we think, to justify the statement that the dividing line between them, if not unfaltering throughout its course, has been true for the most part to a unifying principle. On which side of the line the case made out by the appellant has appropriate location must be the next inquiry and the final one. Is that kind of double jeopardy to which the statute has subjected him a hardship so acute and shocking that our polity will not endure it? Does it violate those "fundamental principles of liberty and justice which lie at the base of all our civil and political institutions?" . . . The answer surely must be "no."

77 ୬

The Supreme Court revisited the incorporation issue in *Adamson v. California* in 1947. The case involved the constitutionality of California's trial rules, which permitted the prosecutor to argue to the jury that a defendant's failure to testify on his or her own behalf suggested his or her guilt. Federal prosecutors were forbidden from making such comments by the Fifth Amendment, which prohibited the federal government from forcing defendants to testify against themselves. Like Palko's lawyers, Adamson's argued that the Fourteenth Amendment incorporated all the provisions of the Bill of Rights. Once again, the majority of the justices adhered to the idea of selective incorporation. Justice Felix Frankfurter, who believed strongly in judicial restraint, urged the Court to maintain the old *Twining* rule that the Fourteenth Amendment protected fundamental liberties independently of the Bill of Rights. Justice Hugo Black, joined by Justice William O. Douglas, dissented. They argued that the framers had intended the Fourteenth Amendment to apply all the provisions of the Bill of Rights to the states—the doctrine that became known as "total incorporation." Two more justices went even further than Black and Douglas, arguing for "total incorporation plus."

Adamson v. California (1947)

M R . J U S T I C E Reed delivered the opinion of the Court. . . .

Appellant . . . contends that . . . the privilege against self-incrimination . . . , to its full scope under the Fifth Amendment, inheres in the right to a fair trial. A right to a fair trial is a right admittedly protected by the due process clause of the Fourteenth Amendment. Therefore, appellant argues, the due process clause of the Fourteenth Amendment protects his privilege against self-incrimination. The due process clause of the Fourteenth Amendment, however, does not draw all the rights of the federal Bill of Rights under its protection. That contention was made and rejected in *Palko v. Connecticut.* . . . *Palko* held that such provisions of the Bill of Rights as were "implicit in the concept of ordered liberty," . . . became secure from state interference by the clause. But it held nothing more. . . .

. . . Therefore, we must examine the effect of the California law applied in this trial to see whether the comment on failure to testify violates the protection against state action that the due process clause does grant to an accused. The due process clause forbids compulsion to testify by fear of hurt, torture or exhaustion. It forbids any other type of coercion that falls within the scope of due process. California follows Anglo-American legal tradition in excusing

332 U.S. 46 (1947).

defendants in criminal prosecutions from compulsory testimony. . . . So our inquiry is directed, not at the broad question of the constitutionality of compulsory testimony from the accused under the due process clause, but to the constitutionality of the provision of the California law that permits comment upon his failure to testify. . . .

. . . We are of the view . . . that a state may control such a situation in accordance with its own ideas of the most efficient administration of criminal justice. . . .

Mr. Justice Frankfurter, concurring. . . .

. . . Those reading the English language with the meaning which it ordinarily conveys, those conversant with the political and legal history of the concept of due process, those sensitive to the relations of the States to the central government as well as the relation of some of the provisions of the Bill of Rights to the process of justice, would hardly recognize the Fourteenth Amendment as a cover for the various explicit provisions of the first eight Amendments. Some of these are enduring reflections of experience with human nature, while some express the restricted views of Eighteenth-Century England regarding the best methods for the ascertainment of facts. The notion that the Fourteenth Amendment was a covert way of imposing upon the States all the rules which it seemed important to Eighteenth Century statesmen to write into the Federal Amendments, was rejected by judges who were themselves witnesses of the process by which the Fourteenth Amendment became part of the Constitution. . . .

. . . [T]he suggestion that the Fourteenth Amendment incorporates the first eight Amendments as such is not unambiguously urged. . . . [T]here is suggested merely a selective incorporation of the first eight Amendments into the Fourteenth Amendment. Some are in and some are out, but we are left in the dark as to which are in and which are out. Nor are we given the calculus for determining which go in and which stay out. If the basis of selection is merely that those provisions of the first eight Amendments are incorporated which commend themselves to individual justices as indispensable to the dignity and happiness of a free man, we are thrown back to a merely subjective test. The protection against unreasonable search and seizure might have primacy for one judge, while trial by a jury of 12 for every claim above $20 might appear to another as an ultimate need in a free society. In the history of thought "natural law" has a much longer and much better founded meaning and justification than such subjective selection of the first eight Amendments for incorporation into the Fourteenth. . . .

. . . Judicial review of [the Due Process Clause] . . . inescapably imposes upon this Court an exercise of judgment upon the whole course of the proceedings in order to ascertain whether they offend those canons of decency and fairness which express the notions of justice of English-speaking peoples even toward those charged with the most heinous offenses. These standards of justice are not authoritatively formulated anywhere as though they were prescriptions in a pharmacopoeia. But neither does the application of the Due Process Clause imply that judges are wholly at large. The judicial judgment in applying the Due Process Clause must move within the limits of accepted notions of justice and is not to be based upon the idiosyncracies of a merely personal judgment.

Mr. Justice Black, dissenting. . . .

This decision reasserts a constitutional theory spelled out in *Twining* v. *New Jersey* . . . that this Court is endowed by the Constitution with boundless power under "natural law" periodically to expand and contract constitutional standards to conform to the Court's conception of what at a particular time constitutes "civilized decency" and "fundamental liberty and justice." Invoking this *Twining* rule, the Court concludes that although comment upon testimony in a federal court would violate the Fifth Amendment, identical comment in a state court does not violate today's fashion in civilized decency and fundamentals and is therefore not prohibited by the Federal Constitution as amended. . . .

My study of the historical events that culminated in the Fourteenth Amendment, and the expressions of those who sponsored and favored, as well as those who opposed its submission and passage, persuades me that one of the chief objects that the provisions of the Amendment's first section, separately, and as a whole, were intended to accomplish was to make the Bill of Rights, applicable to the states. . . .

In *Palko* v. *Connecticut,* . . . a case which involved former jeopardy only, this Court re-examined the path it had traveled in interpreting the Fourteenth Amendment since the *Twining* opinion was written. . . . [T]he Court in *Palko* . . . answered a contention that all eight applied with the more guarded statement . . . that "there is no such general rule." Implicit in this statement, and in the cases decided in the interim between *Twining* and *Palko* and since, is the understanding that some of the eight amendments do apply by their very terms. . . . In the *Twining* case fundamental liberties were things apart from the Bill of Rights. Now it appears that at least some of the provisions of the Bill of Rights in their very terms satisfy the Court as sound and meaningful expressions of fundamental liberty. . . .

I cannot consider the Bill of Rights to be an outworn 18th Century "strait jacket" as the *Twining* opinion did. Its provisions may be thought outdated abstractions by some. And it is true that they were designed to meet ancient evils. But they are the same kind of human evils that have emerged from century to century wherever excessive power is sought by the few at the expense of the many. In my judgment the people of no nation can lose their liberty so long as a Bill of Rights like ours survives and its basic purposes are conscientiously interpreted, enforced and respected so as to afford continuous protection against old, as well as new, devices and practices which might thwart those purposes. I fear to see the consequences of the Court's practice of substituting its own concepts of decency and fundamental justice for the language of the Bill of Rights as its point of departure in interpreting and enforcing that Bill of Rights. If the choice must be between the selective process of the *Palko* decision applying some of the Bill of Rights to the States, or the *Twining* rule applying none of them, I would choose the *Palko* selective process. But rather than accept either of these choices, I would follow what I believe was the original purpose of the Fourteenth Amendment—to extend to all the people of the nation the complete protection of the Bill of Rights. To hold that this Court can determine what, if any, provisions of the Bill of Rights will be enforced, and if so to what degree, is to frustrate the great design of a written Constitution. . . .

Mr. Justice Murphy, with whom Mr. Justice Rutledge concurs, dissenting.

While in substantial agreement with the views of Mr. Justice Black, I have one reservation and one addition to make.

I agree that the specific guarantees of the Bill of Rights should be carried over intact into the first section of the Fourteenth Amendment. But I am not prepared to say that the latter is entirely and necessarily limited by the Bill of Rights. Occasions may arise where a proceeding falls so far short of conforming to fundamental standards of procedure as to warrant constitutional condemnation in terms of a lack of due process despite the absence of a specific provision in the Bill of Rights.

Civil Liberties in World War II and the Cold War

78 ∾

With the world plunging into war, Americans placed a renewed emphasis on patriotism and loyalty. Many states required children to begin the school day by saluting the American flag while reciting the Pledge of Allegiance. (The salute was made often by standing at attention and extending the right arm, until the Nazis discredited that custom by requiring a similar salute to Adolf Hitler.) The requirement put Jehovah's Witnesses, a radical Christian sect that attracted adherents primarily among the poor, in a difficult position.

The Witnesses considered such salutes to be idolatry and thus forbidden; most would not permit their children to obey the rule. Already unpopular with more orthodox fundamentalist Christians, Jehovah's Witnesses were now identified as unpatriotic.

In 1940 the Supreme Court agreed that school authorities could expel children who refused to salute the flag in *Minersville School District v. Gobitis,* 319 U.S. 586. Justice Frankfurter, the champion of judicial restraint, wrote that requiring schoolchildren to salute the flag was a reasonable way to achieve the legitimate goal of promoting patriotism. Only Justice Stone disagreed.

Many took the Court's decision in the First Flag Salute Case to justify harsh measures against Jehovah's Witnesses. State legislatures passed new, tougher flag-salute laws. After Japan's surprise attack on Pearl Harbor, hundreds of Witnesses were assaulted and their meetinghouses burned. Shocked by such actions, the Court reconsidered the question in 1943. The law challenged in the Second Flag Salute Case not only expelled children who refused to salute the flag, but it treated children not attending school as delinquents and subjected their parents to fines and imprisonment. In a classic statement of civil libertarianism, the justices overruled their recent precedent, at the same time reiterating the rationale for active judicial protection of preferred freedoms.

West Virginia State Board of Education v. Barnette (The Second Flag Salute Case) (1943)

MR. JUSTICE Jackson delivered the opinion of the Court. . . .

This case calls upon us to reconsider a precedent decision, as the Court throughout its history often has been required to do. . . .

There is no doubt that, in connection with the pledges, the flag salute is a form of utterance. Symbolism is a primitive but effective way of communicating ideas. The use of an emblem or flag to symbolize some system, idea, institution, or personality, is a short cut from mind to mind. . . .

. . . Here it is the State that employs a flag as a symbol of adherence to government as presently organized. It requires the individual to communicate by word and sign his acceptance of the political ideas it thus bespeaks. Objection to this form of communication when coerced is an old one, well known to the framers of the Bill of Rights. . . .

. . . It is now a commonplace that censorship or suppression of expression of opinion is tolerated by our Constitution only when the expression presents a clear and present danger of action of a kind the State is empowered to prevent and punish. It would seem that involuntary affirmation could be commanded only on even more immediate and urgent grounds than silence. But here the power of compulsion is invoked without any allegation that remaining passive during a flag salute ritual creates a clear and present danger that would justify an effort even to muffle expression. . . .

Nor does the issue as we see it turn on one's possession of particular religious views or the sincerity with which they are held. While religion supplies appellees' motive for enduring the discomforts of making the issue in this case, many citizens who do not share these religious views hold such a compulsory rite to infringe constitutional liberty of the individual. It is not necessary to inquire whether nonconformist beliefs will exempt from the duty to salute unless we first find power to make the salute a legal duty.

The Gobitis decision, however, *assumed* . . . that power exists in the State to impose the flag salute discipline upon school children in general. The Court only examined and rejected a claim based on religious beliefs of immunity from an unquestioned general rule. The question which underlies the flag salute controversy is whether such a ceremony so touching matters of opinion and political attitude may be imposed upon the individual by official authority under powers committed to any political organization under our Constitution. . . .

The Gobitis opinion reasoned that this is a field "where courts possess no marked and certainly no controlling competence," that it is committed to the legislatures as well as the courts to guard cherished liberties and that it is constitutionally appropriate to "fight out the wise use of legislative authority in the forum of public opinion and before legislative assemblies rather than to transfer such a contest to the judicial arena," since all the "effective means of inducing political changes are left free." . . .

The very purpose of a Bill of Rights was to withdraw certain subjects from the vicissitudes of political controversy, to place them beyond the reach of majorities and officials and to establish them as legal principles to be applied by the courts. One's right to life, liberty, and property, to free speech, a free press, freedom of worship and assembly, and other fundamental rights may not be submitted to vote; they depend on the outcome of no elections.

In weighing arguments of the parties it is important to distinguish between the due process clause of the Fourteenth Amendment as an instrument for transmitting the principles of the First Amendment and those cases in which it is applied for its own sake. The test of legislation which collides with the Fourteenth Amendment, because it also collides with the principles of the First, is much more definite than the test when only the Fourteenth is involved. Much of the vagueness of the due process clause disappears when the specific prohibitions of the First become its standard. The right of a State to regulate, for example, a public utility may well include, so far as the due process test is concerned, power to impose all of the restrictions which a legislature may have a "rational basis" for adopting. But freedoms of speech and of press, of assembly, and of worship may not be infringed on such slender grounds. They are susceptible of restriction only to prevent grave and immediate danger to interests which the state may lawfully protect. . . .

National unity as an end which officials may foster by persuasion and example is not in question. The problem is whether under our Constitution compulsion as here employed is a permissible means for its achievement.

Struggles to coerce uniformity of sentiment in support of some end thought essential to their time and country have been waged by many good as well as by evil men. Nationalism is a relatively recent phenomenon but at other times and places the ends have been racial or territorial security, support of a dynasty or regime, and particular plans for saving souls. As first and moderate methods to attain unity have failed, those bent on its accomplishment must resort to an ever increasing severity. . . . Those who begin coercive elimination of dissent soon find themselves exterminating dissenters. Compulsory unification of opinion achieves only the unanimity of the graveyard.

It seems trite but necessary to say that the First Amendment to our Constitution was designed to avoid these ends by avoiding these beginnings. . . .

If there is any fixed star in our constitutional constellation, it is that no official, high or petty, can prescribe what shall be orthodox in politics, nationalism, religion, or other matters of opinion or force citizens to confess by word or act their faith therein. If there are any circumstances which permit an exception, they do not now occur to us.

We think the action of the local authorities in compelling the flag salute and pledge transcends constitutional limitations on their power and invades the sphere of intellect and spirit which it is the purpose of the First Amendment to our Constitution to reserve from all official control. . . .

Mr. Justice Frankfurter, dissenting:

One who belongs to the most vilified and persecuted minority in history is not likely to be insensible to the freedoms guaranteed by our Constitution. Were my purely personal attitude relevant I should wholeheartedly associate myself with the general libertarian views in the Court's opinion, representing as they do the thought and action of a lifetime. But as judges we are neither Jew nor Gentile, neither Catholic nor agnostic. We owe equal attachment to the Constitution and are equally bound by our judicial obligations whether we derive our citizenship from the earliest or the latest immigrants to these shores. As a member of this Court I am not justified in writing my private notions of policy into the Constitution, no matter how deeply I may cherish them or how mischievous I may deem their disregard. . . . The only opinion of our own even looking in that direction that is material is our opinion whether legislators could in reason have enacted such a law. In the light of all the circumstances, including the history of this question in this Court, it would require more daring than I possess to deny that reasonable legislators could have taken the action which is before us for review. Most unwillingly, therefore, I must differ from my brethren with regard to legislation like this. I cannot bring my mind to believe that the "liberty" secured by the Due Process Clause gives this Court authority to deny to the State of West Virginia the attainment of that which we all recognize as a legitimate legislative end, namely, the promotion of good citizenship, by employment of the means here chosen.

79 ∿

The West Coast of the United States had a long history of anti-Asian racism. Western congressional delegations had successfully secured legislation barring Chinese and Japanese immigration. But the federal courts had regularly ruled western state laws discriminating against Asians unconstitutional. The Japanese attack on Pearl Harbor exacerbated the hostile feelings. Responding to pressure from western politicians and military authorities, President Roosevelt authorized the expulsion not only of Japanese aliens but American citizens of Japanese descent from the coastal areas of the western states, on the grounds that they posed a threat to national security. The vast majority were relocated to desert camps, where they were kept under guard for years, until many moved to interior cities like Chicago.

In *Korematsu v. U.S.*, the Supreme Court held that laws making racial distinctions were subject to "the most rigid scrutiny"—language that in later decades would consistently lead the Court to hold such laws unconstitutional. But in *Korematsu* the Court held that the threat to national security justified the discrimination. Justice Robert H. Jackson, who had delivered the Court's opinion in the Second Flag Salute Case the previous year, dissented. Yet even he would not have enjoined the military from expelling the Japanese-Americans; he would only have refused to provide any judicial enforcement of such a policy.

Korematsu v. U.S. (1944)

MR. JUSTICE Black delivered the opinion of the Court. . . .

It should be noted, to begin with, that all legal restrictions which curtail the civil rights of a single racial group are immediately suspect. That is not to say that all such restrictions are unconstitutional. It is to say that courts must subject them to the most rigid scrutiny. Pressing public necessity may sometimes justify the existence of such restrictions; racial antagonism never can. . . .

323 U.S. 214 (1944).

. . . [W]e are unable to conclude that it was beyond the war power of Congress and the Executive to exclude those of Japanese ancestry from the West Coast war area at the time they did. True, exclusion from the area in which one's home is located is a far greater deprivation than constant confinement to the home from 8 P.M. to 6 A.M. Nothing short of apprehension by the proper military authorities of the gravest imminent danger to the public safety can constitutionally justify either. . . .

We uphold the exclusion order as of the time it was made and when the petitioner violated it. . . . In doing so, we are not unmindful of the hardships imposed by it upon a large group of American citizens. . . . But hardships are part of war, and war is an aggregation of hardships. All citizens alike, both in and out of uniform, feel the impact of war in greater or lesser measure. Citizenship has its responsibilities as well as its privileges, and in time of war the burden is always heavier. Compulsory exclusion of large groups of citizens from their homes, except under circumstances of direst emergency and peril, is inconsistent with our basic governmental institutions. But when under conditions of modern warfare our shores are threatened by hostile forces, the power to protect must be commensurate with the threatened danger. . . .

. . . Our task would be simple, our duty clear, were this a case involving the imprisonment of a loyal citizen in a concentration camp because of racial prejudice. . . . To cast this case into outlines of racial prejudice, without reference to the real military dangers which were presented, merely confuses the issue. Korematsu was not excluded from the Military Area because of hostility to him or his race. He *was* excluded because we are at war with the Japanese Empire, because the properly constituted military authorities feared an invasion of our West Coast and felt constrained to take proper security measures. . . . We cannot—by availing ourselves of the calm perspective of hindsight—now say that at that time these actions were unjustified. . . .

Mr. Justice Jackson, dissenting:

Korematsu was born on our soil, of parents born in Japan. The Constitution makes him a citizen of the United States by nativity and a citizen of California by residence. No claim is made that he is not loyal to this country. . . . Korematsu . . . has been convicted of an act not commonly a crime. It consists merely of being present in the state whereof he is a citizen, near the place where he was born, and where all his life he has lived. . . .

A citizen's presence in the locality . . . was made a crime only if his parents were of Japanese birth. . . . [H]ere is an attempt to make an otherwise innocent act a crime merely because this prisoner is the son of parents as to whom he had no choice, and belongs to a race from which there is no way to resign. . . .

... [I]t is said that if the military commander had reasonable military grounds for promulgating the orders, they are constitutional and become law, and the Court is required to enforce them. . . . I cannot subscribe to this doctrine. . . .

My duties as a justice as I see them do not require me to make a military judgment as to whether General DeWitt's evacuation and detention program was a reasonable military necessity. I do not suggest that the courts should have attempted to interfere with the Army in carrying out its task. But I do not think they may be asked to execute a military expedient that has no place in law under the Constitution. I would reverse the judgment and discharge the prisoner.

80 ∽

To the dismay of Americans, World War II was followed not by an era of peace and stability, but by the Cold War between the United States and its allies and the Communist world led by the Soviet Union. Communists, long subject to repression in the United States because of their radicalism, now were identified with America's international enemies as well. Identifying Communists as spies and traitors, extremist anticommunists began what historians now consider a witch-hunt for Americans who had once belonged to the Communist party or had cooperated with it in past political actions. Since the Communist party had followed a deliberate policy of cooperating with all groups opposed to fascism in the 1930s, trying to create what it called a "Popular Front," tens or even hundreds of thousands of Americans were vulnerable to charges of having been "soft" on communism.

Conservative business and political groups took advantage of the "Second Red Scare" to attack liberals, radicals, and labor unions. Liberal political and labor organizations, themselves recognizing communism's totalitarian nature, purged Communists from positions of leadership, further fueling the fire. Democratic President Harry S. Truman ordered loyalty investigations in the government. The Justice Department brought charges against the leaders of the Communist party under the Smith Act of 1940, which made it a crime to conspire to overthrow the government of the United States, to teach or advocate the overthrow of the government, or to establish any organization that taught or advocated doing so.

The indicted officials were convicted in a trial filled with questionable legal rulings and evidence of bias. Meanwhile, Republican Senator Joseph R. McCarthy created a furor by charging that the federal government was riddled with disloyal Communists and their sympathizers. The House Un-American Activities Committee opened investigations into supposed communist influence in Hollywood. Radicals were purged from college faculties and fired from jobs as schoolteachers.

The Supreme Court heard the Communist leaders' appeal of their convictions in this fevered environment. Claiming to apply the Clear and Present Danger Test, the Court found the law constitutional and sustained the convictions, despite the absence of evidence that the defendants did more than articulate communist ideas. Four justices joined in

Chief Justice Vinson's opinion, which formulated the test in a way that resembled the Bad Tendency Test more than it did Holmes's libertarian version. Two other justices sustained the convictions on narrower grounds, while Black and Douglas dissented.

The Justice Department interpreted the *Dennis* decision to authorize a full-scale assault on the Communist party, and it quickly brought indictments against the party's minor functionaries.

Dennis v. U.S. (1951)

M R . C H I E F Justice Vinson announced the judgment of the Court and an opinion in which Mr. Justice Reed, Mr. Justice Burton and Mr. Justice Minton join. . . .

The obvious purpose of the statute is to protect existing Government, not from change by peaceable, lawful and constitutional means, but from change by violence, revolution and terrorism. That it is within the *power* of the Congress to protect the Government of the United States from armed rebellion is a proposition which requires little discussion. . . . The question with which we are concerned here is not whether Congress has such *power*, but whether the *means* which it has employed conflict with the First and Fifth Amendments to the Constitution. . . .

The rule . . . is that where an offense is specified by a statute in nonspeech or nonpress terms, a conviction relying upon speech or press as evidence of violation may be sustained only when the speech or publication created a "clear and present danger" of attempting or accomplishing the prohibited crime. . . .

In this case we are squarely presented with the application of the "clear and present danger" test, and must decide what that phrase imports. . . . Overthrow of the Government by force and violence is certainly a substantial enough interest for the Government to limit speech. . . . If, then, this interest may be protected, the literal problem which is presented is what has been meant by the use of the phrase "clear and present danger" of the utterances bringing about the evil within the power of Congress to punish.

Obviously, the words cannot mean that before the Government may act, it must wait until the *putsch* is about to be executed, the plans have been laid and the signal is awaited. If Government is aware that a group aiming at its overthrow is attempting to indoctrinate its members and to commit them to a course whereby they will strike when the leaders feel the circumstances permit, action by the Government is required. . . . Certainly an attempt to overthrow the Government by force, even though doomed from the outset because of inadequate numbers or power of the revolutionists, is a sufficient

341 U.S. 494 (1951).

evil for Congress to prevent. . . . In the instant case the trial judge charged the jury that they could not convict unless they found that petitioners intended to overthrow the Government "as speedily as circumstances would permit." This does not mean, and could not properly mean, that they would not strike until there was certainty of success. What was meant was that the revolutionists would strike when they thought the time was ripe. We must therefore reject the contention that success or probability of success is the criterion. . . .

Chief Judge Learned Hand, writing for the majority below, interpreted the phrase as follows: "In each case [courts] must ask whether the gravity of the 'evil,' discounted by its improbability, justifies such invasion of free speech as is necessary to avoid the danger." . . . We adopt this statement of the rule. . . .

Likewise, we are in accord with the court below, which affirmed the trial court's finding that the requisite danger existed. . . . The formation by petitioners of such a highly organized conspiracy, with rigidly disciplined members subject to call when the leaders, these petitioners, felt that the time had come for action, coupled with the inflammable nature of world conditions, similar uprisings in other countries, and the touch-and-go nature of our relations with countries with whom petitioners were in the very least ideologically attuned, convince us that their convictions were justified on this score. . . .

. . . Petitioners intended to overthrow the Government of the United States as speedily as the circumstances would permit. Their conspiracy to organize the Communist Party and to teach and advocate the overthrow of the Government of the United States by force and violence created a "clear and present danger" of an attempt to overthrow the Government by force and violence. They were properly and constitutionally convicted for violation of the Smith Act.

The Warren Court and Civil Liberties

81 ℛ

In 1953 the Senate confirmed President Dwight D. Eisenhower's nomination of former California governor Earl Warren as chief justice. In that capacity, Warren presided over a remarkable burst of libertarian activism that continued beyond his tenure (which ended in 1969) to about 1973.

The Court's activism first became clear with its great desegregation decision, *Brown v. Board of Education*, in 1954 (Document 87 below). It quickly followed that decision with others protecting freedom of expression and association. In *Yates v. U.S.*, 354 U.S. 298 (1957), the Court overturned the convictions of the minor Communist party officials indicted after the *Dennis* decision. The justices ruled that conviction under the Smith Act required advocacy of *action* to overthrow the government followed by some immediate steps to prepare for that action, not merely advocacy of the government's overthrow in the abstract. By the late 1960s, after friction between the more conservative and the more liberal justices, the Court returned to Holmes's Clear and Present Danger Test. States could prosecute only the advocacy of imminent illegal action, the justices held. *Brandenburg v. Ohio* involved a Ku Klux Klansman convicted under a typical criminal syndicalism statute of advocating antiblack and antisemitic violence at a Klan rally. Like all such statutes, Ohio's law made it a crime to assemble with any group that advocated violence to accomplish economic or political reform. By overruling the act, the Court in effect nullified all such laws.

The Court's opinion, given below, did not go far enough for Justices Black and Douglas. Throughout their long tenure on the bench, they insisted that the First Amendment precluded *any* law that punished thought, speech, or association rather than illegal action, even if that speech presented an imminent danger of such action.

Brandenburg v. Ohio (1969)

P ER C U R I A M *

... [D]ecisions have fashioned the principle that the constitutional guarantees of free speech and free press do not permit a State to forbid or proscribe advocacy of the use of force or of law violation except where such advocacy is directed to inciting or producing imminent lawless action and is likely to incite or produce such action. As we said in Noto v. United States, ... "the mere abstract teaching ... of the moral propriety or even moral necessity for a resort to force and violence, is not the same as preparing a group for violent action and steeling it to such action." ... A statute which fails to draw this distinction impermissibly intrudes upon the freedoms guaranteed by the First and Fourteenth Amendments. ...

... In 1927, this Court sustained the constitutionality of California's Criminal Syndicalism Act, ... the text of which is quite similar to that of the laws of Ohio ... [in] Whitney v California. ... The Court upheld the statute on the ground that, without more, "advocating" violent means to effect political and economic change involves such danger to the security of the State that the State may outlaw it. ... But Whitney has been thoroughly discredited by later decisions. ...

... [W]e are here confronted with a statute which, by its own words and as applied, purports to punish mere advocacy and to forbid, on pain of criminal punishment, assembly with others merely to advocate the described type of

395 U.S. 444 (1969).

*A *per curiam* decision, order, or opinion is issued by the whole Court without attribution to particular justices.

action. Such a statute falls within the condemnation of the First and Fourteenth Amendments. The contrary teaching of Whitney v. California . . . cannot be supported, and that decision is therefore overruled.

82 ⌒

The Supreme Court's desegregation decisions, discussed in Chapter 16, helped to precipitate the great civil rights movement of the 1950s and 1960s. Among the high points of that movement were nonviolent civil and political-rights demonstrations in various Alabama cities from 1963 to 1965. Besides fighting the demonstrators with massive arrests, police violence, and extralegal intimidation, state and city officials utilized the civil courts. In *New York Times Co. v. Sullivan*, Alabama officials brought libel actions against four black clergymen who had placed an ad in the *Times* detailing events in Montgomery, the state's capital; the officials also sued the newspaper for carrying the ad. Pointing to several minor errors in the ads, the trial judge found them to be "false" and automatically "malicious." So instructed, the all-white jury imposed punitive damages of $500,000 (about $2.5 million in 1995 dollars) on each of the defendants in an obvious attempt to suppress both the protests and news coverage of them. Officials brought similar cases throughout Alabama. By the time the Supreme Court decided the Sullivan Case, the *Times* faced eleven suits totaling nearly six million dollars; CBS television faced suits seeking nearly $2 million.

Recognizing the impact such judgments would have on freedom of the press, the Court struck them down, establishing a stricter standard for winning libel actions against government officials. In later decisions, the Court extended the standard to "public figures," such as movie stars, business leaders, and athletes.

New York Times Co. v. Sullivan (1964)

M̲R. JUSTICE Brennan delivered the opinion of the Court. . . .

The general proposition that freedom of expression upon public questions is secured by the First Amendment has long been settled by our decisions. . . .

Thus we consider this case against the background of a profound national commitment to the principle that debate on public issues should be uninhibited, robust, and wide-open, and that it may well include vehement, caustic, and sometimes unpleasantly sharp attacks on government and public officials. . . . The present advertisement, as an expression of grievance and protest on one of the major public issues of our time, would seem clearly to

376 U.S. 254 (1964).

qualify for the constitutional protection. The question is whether it forfeits that protection by the falsity of some of its factual statements and by its alleged defamation of respondent.

Authoritative interpretations of the First Amendment guarantees have consistently refused to recognize an exception for any test of truth—whether administered by judges, juries, or administrative officials—and especially one that puts the burden of proving truth on the speaker. . . .

Injury to official reputation affords no more warrant for repressing speech that would otherwise be free than does factual error. . . . Criticism of their official conduct does not lose its constitutional protection merely because it is effective criticism and hence diminishes their official reputations.

If neither factual error nor defamatory content suffices to remove the constitutional shield from criticism of official conduct, the combination of the two elements is no less inadequate. This is the lesson to be drawn from the great controversy over the Sedition Act of 1798, . . . which first crystallized a national awareness of the central meaning of the First Amendment. . . .

Although the Sedition Act was never tested in this Court, the attack upon its validity has carried the day in the court of history. . . .

What a State may not constitutionally bring about by means of a criminal statute is likewise beyond the reach of its civil law of libel. The fear of damage awards under a rule such as that invoked by the Alabama courts here may be markedly more inhibiting than the fear of prosecution under a criminal statute. . . . Alabama, for example, has a criminal libel law . . . which allows as punishment upon conviction a fine not exceeding $500 and a prison sentence of six months. . . . Presumably a person charged with violation of this statute enjoys ordinary criminal-law safeguards such as the requirements of an indictment and of proof beyond a reasonable doubt. These safeguards are not available to the defendant in a civil action. The judgment awarded in this case—without the need for any proof of actual pecuniary loss—was one thousand times greater than the maximum fine provided by the Alabama criminal statute, and one hundred times greater than that provided by the Sedition Act. . . . [T]he pall of fear and timidity imposed upon those who would give voice to public criticism is an atmosphere in which the First Amendment freedoms cannot survive. Plainly the Alabama law of civil libel is "a form of regulation that creates hazards to protected freedoms markedly greater than those that attend reliance upon the criminal law." . . .

The state rule of law is not saved by its allowance of the defense of truth. . . .

A rule compelling the critic of official conduct to guarantee the truth of all his factual assertions—and to do so on pain of libel judgments virtually unlimited in amount—leads to "self-censorship." . . . Under such a rule, would-be critics of official conduct may be deterred from voicing their criticism, even though it is believed to be true and even though it is in fact true, because of doubt whether it can be proved in court or fear of the expense of having to do so. They tend to make only statements which "steer far wider of the unlawful zone." . . . The rule thus dampens the vigor and limits the variety of public debate. It is inconsistent with the First and Fourteenth Amendments.

The constitutional guarantees require, we think, a federal rule that prohibits a public official from recovering damages for a defamatory falsehood relating to his official conduct unless he proves that the statement was made with "actual malice"—that is, with knowledge that it was false or with reckless disregard of whether it was false or not.

Mr. Justice Black, with whom Mr. Justice Douglas joins, concurring.

I concur in reversing this half-million-dollar judgment against the New York Times Company and the four individual defendants. . . . I base my vote to reverse on the belief that the First and Fourteenth Amendments not merely "delimit" a State's power to award damages to "public officials against critics of their official conduct" but completely prohibit a State from exercising such a power. . . .

. . . [T]his technique for harassing and punishing a free press—now that it has been shown to be possible—is by no means limited to cases with racial overtones; it can be used in other fields where public feelings may make local as well as out-of-state newspapers easy prey for libel verdict seekers.

In my opinion the Federal Constitution has dealt with this deadly danger to the press in the only way possible without leaving the free press open to destruction—by granting the press an absolute immunity for criticism of the way public officials do their public duty.

83 ❧

In the 1940s and early 1950s, the Supreme Court had begun to wrestle with the problem of how to reconcile the principle of separation of church and state, enshrined in the First Amendment, with various activities that seemed to bring religion into the public schools. In *Everson v. Board of Education of Ewing Twp.*, 330 U.S. 1 (1947), the Supreme Court upheld programs reimbursing students for transportation costs to parochial schools. In *Zorach v. Clauson*, 343 U.S. 306 (1952), it permitted the release of students from classes to attend religious schools. Yet the decisions seemed muddled. In the first case the Court had said that the First Amendment was designed to build "a wall between Church and State" and then upheld a program that seemed to breach that wall. In the second, the Court seemed to contradict its earlier language, saying, "We are a religious people whose institutions presuppose a Supreme Being."

The civil rights movement made the Warren Court aware of the sensitivities of all minorities, and in the early 1960s it acted to limit the ways in which schools could reinforce the religious beliefs of the majority. In *Engel v. Vitale,* below, the Court ruled unconstitutional the nondenominational prayer that the New York State Board of Regents recommended for the opening of each school day: "Almighty God, we acknowledge our dependence upon Thee, and we beg Thy blessings upon us, our parents, our teachers and our Country." The following year it held religiously motivated Bible reading in the public schools unconstitutional, in *Abington School District v Schempp,* 374 U.S. 203 (1963). The decisions seemed to adopt the view that the First Amendment mandated strict separation between church and state—more like the "wall" the Court spoke of in *Everson* than the "accommodation" it suggested in *Zorach v. Clausen.*

Engel v. Vitale (1962)

MR. JUSTICE Black delivered the opinion of the Court. . . .

We think that by using its public school system to encourage recitation of the Regents' prayer, the State of New York has adopted a practice wholly inconsistent with the Establishment Clause. . . .

. . . [T]he constitutional prohibition against laws respecting an establishment of religion must at least mean that in this country it is no part of the business of government to compose official prayers for any group of the American people to recite as a part of a religious program carried on by government. . . .

By the time of the adoption of the Constitution, our history shows that there was a widespread awareness among many Americans of the dangers of a union of Church and State. These people knew, some of them from bitter personal experience, that one of the greatest dangers to the freedom of the individual to worship in his own way lay in the Government's placing its official stamp of approval upon one particular kind of prayer or one particular form of religious services. . . . The First Amendment was added to the Constitution to stand as a guarantee that neither the power nor the prestige of the Federal Government would be used to control, support or influence the kinds of prayer the American people can say. . . .

Under that Amendment's prohibition against governmental establishment of religion, as reinforced by the provisions of the Fourteenth Amendment, government in this country, be it state or federal, is without power to prescribe by law any particular form of prayer . . . in carrying on any program of governmentally sponsored religious activity.

370 U.S. 421 (1962).

There can be no doubt that New York's state prayer program officially establishes the religious beliefs embodied in the Regents' prayer. . . . Neither the fact that the prayer may be denominationally neutral nor the fact that its observance on the part of the students is voluntary can serve to free it from the limitations of the Establishment Clause. . . . The Establishment Clause . . . does not depend upon any showing of direct governmental compulsion and is violated by the enactment of laws which establish an official religion whether those laws operate directly to coerce nonobserving individuals or not. . . . The Establishment Clause thus stands as an expression of principle on the part of the Founders of our Constitution that religion is too personal, too sacred, too holy, to permit its "unhallowed perversion" by a civil magistrate.

84 ❧

Americans traditionally had considered pornography beyond the boundaries of freedom of expression. State and local officials had always suppressed offensive materials. The so-called Comstock laws, named after nineteenth-century antivice crusader Anthony Comstock, criminalized not only publications that we would find mild today but discussions of birth control and abortion. Many courts accepted the English rule of *Regina v. Hicklin*, defining as obscene any material that might incite susceptible people to improper behavior. However, the Supreme Court rejected that rule in 1957. In *Butler v. Michigan*, 352 U.S. 380 (1957), it overturned a state law that the Michigan courts construed to bar the sale of books "manifestly tending to corruption of the morals of youth." Justice Frankfurter denied that a state could "reduce the adult population of Michigan to reading only what is fit for children."

In the companion case of *Roth v U.S.*, the Court upheld the conviction of pornographers. Government could ban the sale of materials with no redeeming social value if their dominant theme was to appeal to prurient interests as judged by contemporary community standards. Douglas and Black dissented, as always arguing that the First Amendment barred any punishment for expression alone. Ten years later, the Court would come close to the Black-Douglas position, interpreting *Roth* to protect material with even the slimmest pretension to social value. One could be punished for distributing sexually explicit material only if it were "*utterly* without redeeming social value," the Court held in the Fanny Hill Case, *Memoirs v. Massachusetts*, 282 U.S. 413 (1966).

Roth v. U.S. (1957)

M R. J U S T I C E Brennan delivered the opinion of the court. . . .

. . . [T]his Court has always assumed the obscenity is not protected by the freedoms of speech and the press. . . . The protection given speech and press

354 U.S. 476 (1957).

was fashioned to assure unfettered interchange of ideas for the bringing about of political and social changes desired by the people. . . .

All ideas having even the slightest redeeming social importance—unorthodox ideas, controversial ideas, even ideas hateful to the prevailing climate of opinion—have the full protection of the guaranties, unless excludable because they encroach upon the limited area of more important interests. But implicit in the history of the First Amendment is the rejection of obscenity as utterly without redeeming social importance. . . .

However, sex and obscenity are not synonymous. Obscene material is material which deals with sex in a manner appealing to prurient interest. The portrayal of sex, e.g., in art, literature and scientific works, is not itself sufficient reason to deny material the constitutional protection of freedom of speech and press. . . .

The early leading standard of obscenity allowed material to be judged merely by the effect of an isolated excerpt upon particularly susceptible persons. Regina v. Hicklin (1868). . . . Some American courts adopted this standard but later decisions have rejected it and substituted this test: whether to the average person, applying contemporary community standards, the dominant theme of the material taken as a whole appeals to prurient interest. The Hicklin test, judging obscenity by the effect of isolated passages upon the most susceptible persons, might well encompass material legitimately treating with sex, and so it must be rejected as unconstitutionally restrictive of the freedoms of speech and press.

Mr. Justice Douglas, with whom Mr. Justice Black concurs, dissenting. . . .

The test of obscenity the Court endorses today gives the censor free range over a vast domain. . . .

The standard of what offends "the common conscience of the community" conflicts, in my judgment, with the command of the First Amendment that "Congress shall make no law . . . abridging the freedom of speech, or of the press." Certainly that standard would not be an acceptable one if religion, economics, politics or philosophy were involved. How does it become a constitutional standard when literature treating with sex is concerned?

Any test that turns on what is offensive to the community's standards is too loose, too capricious, too destructive of freedom of expression to be squared with the First Amendment. . . .

. . . The First Amendment, its prohibition in terms absolute, was designed to preclude courts as well as legislatures from weighing the values of speech against silence. The First Amendment puts free speech in the preferred position.

Freedom of expression can be suppressed if, and to the extent that, it is so closely brigaded with illegal action as to be an inseparable part of it. . . . As a people, we cannot afford to relax that standard.

85 ∽

The sexual revolution of the 1920s began to erode enforcement of Victorian-era laws punishing premarital sex, adultery, and the circulation of birth-control information and devices. The process was reinforced by a growing commitment to the right of privacy, which was recognized as a distinct legal concept only at the turn of the twentieth century. Nonetheless, such laws remained on the books in states like Connecticut, to be enforced by zealous officials or utilized by irate parents and spouses.

In *Griswold v. Connecticut,* the Supreme Court fashioned a fundamental right of privacy broad enough to encompass the right of married couples to secure advice about birth control. But the issue divided the Court. The majority of the justices insisted that privacy was implicitly included among the specific provisions of the Bill of Rights incorporated into the Fourteenth Amendment. Several justices went further, pointing to the Ninth Amendment, which states that the first eight amendments of the Bill of Rights should not be taken to preclude the existence of other, unspecified rights. The right to privacy was one of these, they argued, and could be applied against state infringement through the Fourteenth Amendment. Other justices agreed that Connecticut's ban on birth-control information violated the Due Process Clause of the Fourteenth Amendment but denied that the Fourteenth Amendment had anything to do with the Bill of Rights.

Remarkably, Justice Black, hitherto one of the most liberal members of the Court, dissented. He had said in *Adamson v. California* (Document 77) that the Fourteenth Amendment applied all the provisions of the Bill of Rights to the states, no more and no less, and he meant what he said. The Bill of Rights did not mention privacy and therefore the Fourteenth Amendment did not protect it. Many legal analysts agreed with Black that the decision amounted to a return to the idea of substantive due process of law—that courts could rule laws unconstitutional because their terms, rather than their mode of enforcement, struck judges as arbitrary and unreasonable.

Griswold v. Connecticut (1965)

MR. JUSTICE Douglas delivered the opinion of the Court. . . .

. . . We do not sit as a super legislature to determine the wisdom, need, and propriety of laws that touch economic problems, business affairs, or social conditions. This law, however, operates directly on an intimate relation of husband and wife and their physician's role in one aspect of that relation. . . .

In NAACP v. Alabama, . . . we protected the "freedom to associate and privacy in one's associations," noting that freedom of association was a peripheral First Amendment right. Disclosure of membership lists of a constitutionally valid association, we held, was invalid "as entailing the likelihood of a substantial restraint upon the exercise by petitioner's members of their right to freedom of association." . . . In other words, the First Amendment has a penumbra where privacy is protected from governmental intrusion. . . .

The . . . cases suggest that specific guarantees in the Bill of Rights have penumbras, formed by emanations from those guarantees that help give them life and substance. . . . Various guarantees create zones of privacy. The right of association contained in the penumbra of the First Amendment is one, as we have seen. The Third Amendment in its prohibition against the quartering of soldiers "in any house" in time of peace without the consent of the owner is another facet of that privacy. The Fourth Amendment explicitly affirms the "right of the people to be secure in their persons, houses, papers, and effects, against unreasonable searches and seizures." The Fifth Amendment in its Self-Incrimination Clause enables the citizen to create a zone of privacy which government may not force him to surrender to his detriment. The Ninth Amendment provides: "The enumeration in the Constitution, of certain rights, shall not be construed to deny or disparage others retained by the people." . . .

The present case, then, concerns a relationship lying within the zone of privacy created by several fundamental constitutional guarantees. And it concerns a law which, in forbidding the *use* of contraceptives rather than regulating their manufacture or sale, seeks to achieve its goals by means having a maximum destructive impact upon that relationship. Such a law cannot stand. . . . Would we allow the police to search the sacred precincts of marital bedrooms for telltale signs of the use of contraceptives? The very idea is repulsive to the notions of privacy surrounding the marriage relationship.

We deal with a right of privacy older than the Bill of Rights—older than our political parties, older than our school system. Marriage is a coming together for better or for worse, hopefully enduring, and intimate to the degree of being sacred. . . . [I]t is an association for as noble a purpose as any involved in our prior decisions.

Mr. Justice Goldberg, whom the Chief Justice and Mr. Justice Brennan join, concurring. . . .

. . . Although I have not accepted the view that "due process" as used in the Fourteenth Amendment incorporates all of the first eight Amendments . . . , I do agree that the concept of liberty protects those personal rights that are fundamental, and is not confined to the specific terms of the Bill of Rights. My conclusion that the concept of liberty is not so restricted and that it embraces the right of marital privacy though that right is not mentioned explicitly in the Constitution is supported both by numerous decisions of this Court, referred to in the Court's opinion, and by the language and history of the Ninth Amendment. . . .

The language and history of the Ninth Amendment reveal that the Framers of the Constitution believed that there are additional fundamental rights, protected from governmental infringement, which exist alongside those fundamental rights specifically mentioned. . . .

The Ninth Amendment reads, "The enumeration in the Constitution, of certain rights, shall not be construed to deny or disparage others retained by the people." . . . It was proffered to quiet expressed fears that a bill of specifically enumerated rights could not be sufficiently broad to cover all essential rights. . . .

Mr. Justice Black, with whom Mr. Justice Stewart joins, dissenting. . . .

. . . I do not to any extent whatever base my view that this Connecticut law is constitutional on a belief that the law is wise or that its policy is a good one. In order that there may be no room at all to doubt why I vote as I do, I feel constrained to add that the law is very bit as offensive to me as it is to my Brethren. . . .

The Court talks about a constitutional "right of privacy" as though there is some constitutional provision or provisions forbidding any law ever to be passed which might abridge the "privacy" of individuals. But there is not. There are, of course, guarantees in certain specific constitutional provisions which are designed in part to protect privacy at certain times and places with respect to certain activities. Such, for example, is the Fourth Amendment's guarantee against "unreasonable searches and seizures." But I think it belittles that Amendment to talk about it as though it protects nothing but "privacy." . . .

One of the most effective ways of diluting or expanding a constitutionally guaranteed right is to substitute for the crucial word or words of a constitutional guarantee another word or words more or less flexible and more or less restricted in meaning. . . . "Privacy" is a broad, abstract and ambiguous concept which can easily be shrunken in meaning but which can also, on the other hand, easily be interpreted as a constitutional ban against many things other than searches and seizures. . . . I get nowhere in this case by talk about a constitutional "right of privacy" as an emanation from one or more constitutional provisions. I like my privacy as well as the next one, but I am neverthe-less compelled to admit that government has a right to invade it unless pro-hibited by some specific constitutional provision. . . .

. . . [T]here is no provision of the Constitution which either expressly or impliedly vests power in this Court to sit as a supervisory agency over acts of duly constituted legislative bodies and set aside their laws because of the Court's belief that the legislative policies adopted are unreasonable, unwise, arbitrary, capricious or irrational. The adoption of such a loose, flexible, un-controlled standard for holding laws unconstitutional, if ever it is finally achieved, will amount to a great unconstitutional shift of power to the courts which I believe and am constrained to say will be bad for the courts and worse for the country.

86 ◠

Roe v. Wade was decided in 1973, four years after Chief Justice Earl Warren left the Court, but it may be considered the last great civil liberties decision of the Warren Court. Build-ing on the foundations laid by *Griswold v. Connecticut, Roe* ruled unconstitutional the laws banning abortion that had been on the statute books since the antivice crusades of the late nineteenth century. (Before that, abortion had been linked to infanticide; it was illegal only after the fetus had reached the point of "quickening"—the point when the first fetal movement could be felt.)

The decision reflected the great social revolution of the 1960s, which affected not only sexual mores but the role of women in American society. No longer relegated to the "sep-arate sphere" of homemaking and child rearing, more and more women demanded the right to control their own bodies. The *Griswold* decision had made birth control widely available. Many women came to view an unwanted pregnancy, disruptive of both career and family, as intolerable; to be forbidden by the government from ending one was even more unacceptable.

But the Court's decision overturning most of the antiabortion laws in the country proved extremely divisive. Many legal analysts agreed with the newly appointed Justice William H. Rehnquist, a conservative who charged that the Court had returned to the idea of substantive due process of law, overturning a statute simply because it did not comport with the justices' idea of right and wrong. Millions of Americans rejected the Court's definition of the point at which human life began; for them, overturning abor-tion laws permitted the slaughter of innocent human beings.

Roe v. Wade (1973)

MR. JUSTICE Blackmun delivered the opinion of the Court. . . .
   The Constitution does not explicitly mention any right of privacy. In a line

410 U.S. 113 (1973).

of decisions, . . . the Court has recognized that a right of personal privacy, or a guarantee of certain areas or zones of privacy, does exist under the Constitution. . . .

This right of privacy, whether it be founded in the Fourteenth Amendment's concept of personal liberty and restrictions upon state action, as we feel it is, or, as the District Court determined, in the Ninth Amendment's reservation of rights to the people, is broad enough to encompass a woman's decision whether or not to terminate her pregnancy. . . .

. . . [A]ppellant and some amici argue that the woman's right is absolute and that she is entitled to terminate her pregnancy at whatever time, in whatever way, and for whatever reason she alone chooses. With this we do not agree. . . . The Court's decisions recognizing a right of privacy also acknowledge that some state regulation in areas protected by that right is appropriate. . . . [A] State may properly assert important interests in safeguarding health, in maintaining medical standards, and in protecting potential life. At some point in pregnancy, these respective interests become sufficiently compelling to sustain regulation of the factors that govern the abortion decision. . . .

We, therefore, conclude that the right of personal privacy includes the abortion decision, but that this right is not unqualified and must be considered against important state interests in regulation. . . .

Where certain "fundamental rights" are involved, the Court has held that regulation limiting these rights may be justified only by a "compelling state interest" . . , and that legislative enactments must be narrowly drawn to express only the legitimate state interests at stake. . . .

The pregnant woman cannot be isolated in her privacy. She carries an embryo and, later, a fetus, if one accepts the medical definitions of the developing young in the human uterus. . . .

Texas urges that, apart from the Fourteenth Amendment, life begins at conception and is present throughout pregnancy, and that, therefore, the State has a compelling interest in protecting that life from and after conception. We need not resolve the difficult question of when life begins. When those trained in the respective disciplines of medicine, philosophy, and theology are unable to arrive at any consensus, the judiciary, at this point in the development of man's knowledge, is not in a position to speculate as to the answer. . . .

. . . [T]he unborn have never been recognized in the law as persons in the whole sense.

In view of all this, we do not agree that, by adopting one theory of life, Texas may override the rights of the pregnant woman that are at stake. We repeat, however, that the State does have an important and legitimate interest in preserving and protecting the health of the pregnant woman, whether she be a resident of the State or a nonresident who seeks medical consultation and treatment there, and that it has still *another* important and legitimate interest in protecting the potentiality of human life. These interests are separate and distinct. Each grows in substantiality as the woman approaches term and, at a point during pregnancy, each becomes "compelling."

With respect to the State's important and legitimate interest in the health of the mother, the "compelling" point, in the light of present medical knowledge, is at approximately the end of the first trimester. This is so because of the now-established medical fact . . . that until the end of the first trimester mortality in abortion may be less than mortality in normal childbirth. It follows that, from and after this point, a State may regulate the abortion procedure to the extent that the regulation reasonably relates to the preservation and protection of maternal health. . . .

With respect to the State's important and legitimate interest in potential life, the "compelling" point is at viability. This is so because the fetus then presumably has the capability of meaningful life outside the mother's womb. State regulation protective of fetal life after viability thus has both logical and biological justifications. If the State is interested in protecting fetal life after viability, it may go so far as to proscribe abortion during that period, except when it is necessary to preserve the life or health of the mother. . . .

To summarize and to repeat:

1. A state criminal abortion statute of the current Texas type, that excepts from criminality only a *lifesaving* procedure on behalf of the mother, without regard to pregnancy stage and without recognition of the other interests involved, is violative of the Due Process Clause of the Fourteenth Amendment.

(a) For the stage prior to approximately the end of the first trimester, the abortion decision and its effectuation must be left to the medical judgment of the pregnant woman's attending physician.

(b) For the stage subsequent to approximately the end of the first trimester, the State, in promoting its interest in the health of the mother, may, if it chooses, regulate the abortion procedure in ways that are reasonably related to maternal health.

(c) For the stage subsequent to viability, the State in promoting its interest in the potentiality of human life may, if it chooses, regulate, and even proscribe, abortion except where it is necessary, in appropriate medical judgment, for the preservation of the life or health of the mother. . . .

Mr. Justice Rehnquist, dissenting. . . .

. . . I have difficulty in concluding, as the Court does, that the right of "privacy" is involved in this case. . . .

If the Court means by the term "privacy" no more than that the claim of a person to be free from unwanted state regulation of consensual transactions may be a form of "liberty" protected by the Fourteenth Amendment, there is no doubt that similar claims have been upheld in our earlier decisions on the basis of that liberty. I agree . . . that the "liberty," against deprivation of which without due process the Fourteenth Amendment protects, embraces more than the rights found in the Bill of Rights. But that liberty is not guaranteed absolutely against deprivation, but only against deprivation without due process of law. The test traditionally applied in the area of social and economic legislation is whether or not a law such as that challenged has a rational relation to a valid state objective. . . . But the Court's sweeping invalidation of any restrictions on abortion during the first trimester is impossible to justify under that standard, and the conscious weighing of competing factors that the Court's opinion apparently substitutes for the established test is far more appropriate to a legislative judgment than to a judicial one. . . .

While the Court's opinion quotes from the dissent of Mr. Justice Holmes in Lochner v. New York (1905), the result it reaches is more closely attuned to the majority opinion of Mr. Justice Peckham in that case. As in Lochner and similar cases applying substantive due process standards to economic and social welfare legislation, the adoption of the compelling state interest standard will inevitably require this Court to examine the legislative policies and pass on the wisdom of these policies in the very process of deciding whether a particular state interest put forward may or may not be "compelling." . . .

The fact that a majority of the States reflecting, after all, the majority sentiment in those States, have had restrictions on abortions for at least a century is a strong indication, it seems to me, that the asserted right to an abortion is not "so rooted in the traditions and conscience of our people as to be ranked as fundamental." . . .

C H A P T E R   1 6

Liberal Constitutionalism and Equality

87 ∿

Opposition to the pervasive racial injustice that characterized the United States had been growing slowly ever since the Progressive era. Even in the 1920s, liberals tried to combat the grossest manifestations of racism by supporting antilynching legislation and opposing the Ku Klux Klan. The Roosevelt administration tried to help African Americans during the New Deal, as did northern Democratic congressmen. Few pressed for racial equality, however. World War II, in part a war against Nazi racial theories in which hundreds of thousands of black Americans served, reshaped many Americans' attitudes towards race. By the 1950s, social forces were gathering that would attack the most obvious and offensive expression of American racism, legally mandated racial segregation in the South.

At the same time, the National Association for the Advancement of Colored People (NAACP), led by a group of capable and dedicated lawyers, attacked racial inequities via the courts, concentrating especially on the inferior educational facilities that southern states provided for black youth. Focusing on higher and professional education, the NAACP successfully challenged school segregation laws that failed to meet the Separate But Equal Test that the Court had established in *Plessy v. Ferguson* (Document 50). By 1950, the Supreme Court was demanding complete equality in higher education, a standard that was almost impossible for states with segregated facilities to meet. As southern states frantically worked to improve their black schools, the stage was set for a final legal assault on segregated education.

Brown v. Board of Education of Topeka was one of a group of cases from the South and from border areas of the North that the Court brought together to reassess *Plessy*. After the hesitation of some of the judges was overcome through negotiation and persuasion, the Court unanimously ruled that segregated schools were unconstitutional. It was probably the most momentous Court decision of the twentieth century, and perhaps in the history of the nation. After a rehearing to determine an appropriate remedy, the Court in *Brown II* instructed the district courts to supervise the process "with all deliberate speed," a choice of words that encouraged southern officials to obstruct, delay, and minimize the change.

Brown v. Board of Education I and II (1954, 1955)

Brown v. Board of Education of Topeka (*Brown I*)

MR. CHIEF Justice Warren delivered the opinion of the Court. . . .

The plaintiffs contend that segregated public schools are not "equal" and cannot be made "equal," and that hence they are deprived of the equal protection of the laws. . . .

Reargument was largely devoted to the circumstances surrounding the adoption of the Fourteenth Amendment in 1868. It covered exhaustively consideration of the Amendment in Congress, ratification by the states, then existing practices in racial segregation, and the views of proponents and opponents of the Amendment. This discussion and our own investigation convince us that, although these sources cast some light, it is not enough to resolve the problem with which we are faced. At best, they are inconclusive. . . .

. . . The doctrine of "separate but equal" did not make its appearance in this Court until 1896 in the case of Plessy v. Ferguson . . . , involving not education but transportation. American courts have since labored with the doctrine for over half a century. . . . In . . . recent cases, all on the graduate school level, inequality was found in that specific benefits enjoyed by white students were denied to Negro students of the same educational qualifications. . . . In none of these cases was it necessary to reexamine the doctrine to grant relief to the Negro plaintiff. . . .

. . . Here . . . there are findings below that the Negro and white schools involved have been equalized, or are being equalized, with respect to buildings, curricula, qualifications and salaries of teachers, and other "tangible" factors. Our decision, therefore, cannot turn on merely a comparison of these tangible factors in the Negro and white schools involved in each of the cases. We must look instead to the effect of segregation itself on public education.

In approaching this problem, we cannot turn the clock back to 1868 when the Amendment was adopted, or even to 1896 when Plessy v. Ferguson was written. We must consider public education in the light of its full development and its present place in American life throughout the Nation. Only in this way can it be determined if segregation in public schools deprives these plaintiffs of the equal protection of the laws.

Today, education is perhaps the most important function of state and local governments. Compulsory school attendance laws and the great expenditures for education both demonstrate our recognition of the importance of education to our democratic society. It is required in the performance of our most basic public responsibilities, even service in the armed forces. It is the very foundation of good citizenship. Today it is a principal instrument in awakening the child to cultural values, in preparing him for later professional training, and in helping him to adjust normally to his environment. In these days, it is doubtful that any child may reasonably be expected to succeed in life if he is denied the opportunity of an education. Such an opportunity, where the state has undertaken to provide it, is a right which must be made available to all on equal terms. . . .

In Sweatt v. Painter . . . , in finding that a segregated law school for Negroes could not provide them equal educational opportunities, this Court relied in large part on "those qualities which are incapable of objective measurement but which make for greatness in a law school." In McLaurin v. Oklahoma State Regents . . . , the Court, in requiring that a Negro admitted to a white graduate school be treated like all other students, again resorted to intangible considerations: ". . . his ability to study, to engage in discussions and exchange views with other students, and, in general, to learn his profession." Such considerations apply with added force to children in grade and high schools. To separate them from others of similar age and qualifications solely because of their race generates a feeling of inferiority as to their status in the community that may affect their hearts and minds in a way unlikely ever to be undone. . . .

We conclude that in the field of public education the doctrine of "separate but equal" has no place. Separate educational facilities are inherently unequal. Therefore, we hold that the plaintiffs and others similarly situated for whom the actions have been brought are, by reason of the segregation complained of, deprived of the equal protection of the laws guaranteed by the Fourteenth Amendment. . . .

Because these are class actions, because of the wide applicability of this decision, and because of the great variety of local conditions, the formulation of decrees in these cases presents problems of considerable complexity. . . . In order that we may have the full assistance of the parties in formulating decrees, the cases will be restored to the docket, and the parties are requested to present further argument on Questions 4 and 5 previously propounded by the Court.*

Brown v. Board of Education of Topeka (Brown II)

MR. CHIEF Justice Warren delivered the opinion of the Court. . . .

Full implementation of these constitutional principles may require solution of varied local school problems. School authorities have the primary responsibility for elucidating, assessing, and solving these problems; courts will have to consider whether the action of school authorities constitutes good faith implementation of the governing constitutional principles. Because of their proximity to local conditions and the possible need for further hearings, the courts which originally heard these cases can best perform this judicial appraisal. . . .

In fashioning and effectuating the decrees, the courts will be guided by equitable principles. . . . Courts of equity may properly take into account the

---

*Questions 4 and 5 related to the appropriate remedies to end segregation.
349 U.S. 294 (1955).

public interest in the elimination of such obstacles in a systematic and effective manner. But it should go without saying that the vitality of these constitutional principles cannot be allowed to yield simply because of disagreement with them.

While giving weight to these public and private considerations, the courts will require that the defendants make a prompt and reasonable start toward full compliance with our May 17, 1954, ruling. Once such a start has been made, the courts may find that additional time is necessary to carry out the ruling in an effective manner. . . . During this period of transition, the courts will retain jurisdiction of these cases. . . .

. . . [T]he cases are remanded to the District Courts to take such proceedings and enter such orders and decrees consistent with this opinion as are necessary and proper to admit to public schools on a racially nondiscriminatory basis with all deliberate speed the parties to these cases.

88 ∾

Southern state officials, supported by most white southerners, bitterly resisted the Supreme Court's attack on state-mandated racial segregation. State legislatures and local governments put up numerous obstructions in a campaign they referred to as "massive resistance." Some governors vowed outright defiance of federal-court desegregation orders. The conflict came to a head in Little Rock, Arkansas, in 1957. The local school board had taken action to comply with a desegregation order issued by the federal district court, but Governor Orval Faubus whipped up emotional opposition. As the time for opening school with a token number of black students neared, Faubus ordered a suspension of the desegregation plan and sent in the state militia to prevent its enforcement. He claimed the authority as governor to reject the Supreme Court's interpretation of the Fourteenth Amendment and, especially, the responsibility as chief executive of a sovereign state to preserve order — although he himself had helped to foment the threat of violence. President Dwight D. Eisenhower responded by nationalizing the militia and ordering it to sustain the court order. The black children were admitted.

At the end of the school year, still faced with ongoing white hostility and the vehement denunciations of the governor and state legislature, the school board successfully petitioned the federal district court to permit the exclusion of the previously admitted black students and to delay the implementation of the desegregation order for more than two years. The Supreme Court's response in *Cooper v. Aaron* was individually signed by each of the justices, who not only ordered the desegregation plan to go forward, but denied the right of state or federal officials to refuse to obey Court orders because they disagreed with the Court's interpretation of the Constitution. The opinion was the most extreme claim of final authority to interpret the Constitution ever to come from the Supreme Court—a virtual declaration of judicial supremacy.

Cooper v. Aaron (1958)

O P I N I O N of the Court by The Chief Justice, Mr. Justice Black, Mr. Justice Frankfurter, Mr. Justice Douglas, Mr. Justice Burton, Mr. Justice Clark, Mr. Justice Harlan, Mr. Justice Brennan, and Mr. Justice Whittaker.

As this case reaches us it raises questions of the highest importance to the maintenance of our federal system of government. It necessarily involves a claim by the Governor and Legislature of a State that there is no duty on state officials to obey federal court orders resting on this Court's considered interpretation of the United States Constitution. Specifically it involves actions by the Governor and Legislature of Arkansas upon the premise that they are not bound by our holding in Brown v Board of Education. . . . We are urged to uphold a suspension of the Little Rock School Board's plan to do away with segregated public schools in Little Rock until state laws and efforts to upset and nullify our holding in Brown v Board of Education have been further challenged and tested in the courts. We reject these contentions. . . .

The constitutional rights of respondents are not to be sacrificed or yielded to the violence and disorder which have followed upon the actions of the Governor and Legislature. . . .

What has been said . . . is enough to dispose of the case. However, we should answer the premise of the actions of the Governor and Legislature that they are not bound by our holding in the Brown case. It is necessary only to recall some basic constitutional propositions which are settled doctrine.

Article 6 of the Constitution makes the Constitution the "supreme Law of the Land." In 1803, Chief Justice Marshall, speaking for a unanimous Court, referring to the Constitution as "the fundamental and paramount law of the nation," declared in the notable case of Marbury v Madison . . . that "It is emphatically the province and duty of the judicial department to say what the law is." This decision declared the basic principle that the federal judiciary is supreme in the exposition of the law of the Constitution, and that principle has ever since been respected by this Court and the Country as a permanent and indispensable feature of our constitutional system. It follows that the interpretation of the Fourteenth Amendment enunciated by this Court in the Brown Case is the supreme law of the land, and Art 6 of the Constitution makes it of binding effect on the States "any Thing in the Constitution or Laws of any State to the Contrary notwithstanding." Every state legislator and executive and judicial officer is solemnly committed by oath taken pursuant to Art 6, cl 3, "to support this Constitution." . . .

No state legislator or executive or judicial officer can war against the Constitution without violating his undertaking to support it. . . .

358 U.S. 1 (1957).

... The basic decision in Brown was unanimously reached by this Court only after the case had been briefed and twice argued and the issues had been given the most serious consideration. Since the first Brown opinion three new Justices have come to the Court. They are at one with the Justices still on the Court who participated in that basic decision as to its correctness, and that decision is now unanimously reaffirmed. The principles announced in that decision and the obedience of the States to them, according to the command of the Constitution, are indispensable for the protection of the freedoms guaranteed by our fundamental charter for all of us. Our constitutional ideal of equal justice under law is thus made a living truth.

89 ◯

Both encouraged by the Supreme Court's desegregation decisions and frustrated by the ability of white southerners to obstruct them, African Americans and their allies pressed for federal legislation to secure equality of civil and political rights. A new generation of civil rights leaders, including the Reverend Martin Luther King Jr., organized peaceful demonstrations and economic boycotts throughout the South, demanding an end to segregation, equal access to jobs, and the right to vote freely in elections. The demonstrations culminated in the 1963 March on Washington and in voting-rights demonstrations in Alabama in 1965.

Southern officials often reacted to the protests with violence, and they sometimes conspired with extremists to intimidate and even kill civil rights workers and their supporters. Shocked northerners joined African Americans to demand federal action. The result was the Civil Rights Act of 1964, followed by the Voting Rights Act of 1965.

The Civil and Voting Rights Acts (1964–1965)

The Civil Rights Act of 1964

*Title II—Injunctive Relief Against Discrimination in Places
of Public Accommodation*

Sec. 201.

(a) All persons shall be entitled to the full and equal enjoyment of the goods, services, facilities, privileges, advantages, and accommodations of any place of public accommodation, as defined in this section, without discrimination or segregation on the ground of race, color, religion, or national origin.

U.S. Statutes at Large, 78 (1964): 241.

(b) Each of the following establishments which serves the public is a place of public accommodation within the meaning of this title if its operations affect commerce, or if discrimination or segregation by it is supported by State action:

(1) any inn, hotel, motel, or other establishment which provides lodging to transient guests, other than an establishment located within a building which contains not more than five rooms for rent or hire and which is actually occupied by the proprietor of such establishment as his residence.

(2) any restaurant, cafeteria, lunchroom, lunch counter, soda fountain, or other facility principally engaged in selling food for consumption on the premises, including, but not limited to, any such facility located on the premises of any retail establishment; or any gasoline station;

(3) any motion picture house, theater, concert hall, sports arena, stadium or other place of exhibition or entertainment; and

(4) any establishment (A) (i) which is physically located within the premises of any establishment otherwise covered by this subsection, or (ii) within the premises of which is physically located any such covered establishment; and (B) which holds itself out as serving patrons of such covered establishment. . . .

(c) Discrimination or segregation by an establishment is supported by State action within the meaning of this title if such discrimination or segregation (1) is carried on under color of any law, statute, ordinance, or regulation; or (2) is carried on under color of any custom or usage required or enforced by officials of the State or political subdivision thereof. . . .

Title IV—Desegregation of Public Education . . .
Suits by the Attorney General

Sec 407. (a) Whenever the Attorney General receives a complaint in writing—

(1) signed by a parent or group of parents to the effect that his or their minor children, as members of a class of persons similarly situated, are being deprived by a school board of the equal protection of the laws, or

(2) signed by an individual, or his parent, to the effect that he has been denied admission to or not permitted to continue in attendance at a public college by reason of race, color, religion, or national origin,

and the Attorney General believes the complaint is meritorious and certifies that the signer or signers of such complaint are unable, in his judgment, to initiate and maintain appropriate legal proceedings for relief and that the institution of an action will materially further the orderly achievement of desegregation in public education, the Attorney General is authorized . . . to institute for or in the name of the United States a civil action in any appropriate district court of the United States against such parties and for such relief as may be appropriate, . . . provided that nothing herein shall empower any official or court of the United States to issue any order seeking to achieve a racial balance in any school by requiring the transportation of pupils or students from one school to another or one school district to another in order to achieve such racial balance . . . .

Title VI—Nondiscrimination in Federally Assisted Programs

Sec. 601. No person in the United States shall, on the ground of race, color, or national origin, be excluded from participation in, be denied the benefits of, or be subjected to discrimination under any program or activity receiving Federal financial assistance.

Sec. 602. Each Federal department and agency which is empowered to extend Federal financial assistance to any program or activity, by way of grant, loan, or contract . . . , is authorized and directed to effectuate the provisions of section 601 with respect to such program or activity by issuing rules, regulations, or orders of general applicability which shall be consistent with achievement of the objectives of the statute authorizing the financial assistance in connection with which the action is taken. . . .

Title VII—Equal Employment Opportunity

DEFINITIONS

Sec. 701. For the purposes of this title . . .

(b) The term "employer" means a person engaged in an industry affecting commerce who has twenty-five or more employees for each working day in each of twenty or more calendar weeks in the current or preceding calendar year, and any agent of such a person. . . .

Sec. 703.

(a) It shall be an unlawful employment practice for an employer—

(1) to fail or refuse to hire or to discharge any individual, or otherwise to discriminate against any individual with respect to his compensation, terms, conditions, or privileges of employment, because of such individual's race, color, religion, sex, or national origin; or

(2) to limit, segregate, or classify his employees in any way which would deprive or tend to deprive any individual of employment opportunities

or otherwise adversely affect his status as an employee, because of such individual's race, color, religion, sex, or national origin.

(b) It shall be an unlawful employment practice for an employment agency to fail or refuse to refer for employment, or otherwise to discriminate against, any individual because of his race, color, religion, sex, or national origin, or to classify or refer for employment any individual on the basis of his race, color, religion, sex, or national origin.

(c) It shall be an unlawful employment practice for a labor organization—

(1) to exclude or to expel from its membership, or to classify or discriminate against, any individual because of his race, color, religion, sex, or national origin;

(2) to limit, segregate, or classify its membership, or to classify or fail or refuse to refer for employment any individual, in any way which would deprive or tend to deprive any individual of employment opportunities, or would limit such employment opportunities or otherwise adversely affect his status as an employee or as an applicant for employment, because of such individual's race, color, religion, sex, or national origin; or

(3) to cause or attempt to cause an employer to discriminate against an individual in violation of this section.

The Voting Rights Act of 1965

Be it enacted by the Senate and House of Representatives of the United States of America in Congress assembled, That this Act shall be known as the "Voting Rights Act of 1965".

Sec. 2. No voting qualification or prerequisite to voting, or standard, practice, or procedure shall be imposed or applied by any State or political subdivision to deny or abridge the right of any citizen of the United States to vote on account of race or color.

Sec. 3. (a) Whenever the Attorney General institutes a proceeding under any statute to enforce the guarantees of the fifteenth amendment in any State or political subdivision the court shall authorize the appointment of Federal examiners by the United States Civil Service Commission . . . to serve for such period of time and for such political subdivisions as the court shall determine is appropriate to enforce the guarantees of the fifteenth amendment. . . .

(b) If in a proceeding instituted by the Attorney General under any statute

U.S. Statutes at Large, 79 (1965): 437.

to enforce the guarantees of the fifteenth amendment in any State or political subdivision the court finds that a test or device has been used for the purpose or with the effect of denying or abridging the right of any citizen of the United States to vote on account of race or color, it shall suspend the use of tests and devices in such State or political subdivisions as the court shall determine is appropriate and for such period as it deems necessary. . . .

Sec. 4.   (a) To assure that the right of citizens of the United States to vote is not denied or abridged on account of race or color, no citizen shall be denied the right to vote in any Federal, State, or local election because of his failure to comply with any test or device in any State with respect to which the determinations have been made under subsection (b) or in any political subdivision with respect to which such determinations have been made as a separate unit, unless the United States District Court for the District of Columbia in an action for a declaratory judgment brought by such State or subdivision against the United States has determined that no such test or device has been used during the five years preceding the filing of the action for the purpose or with the effect of denying or abridging the right to vote on account of race or color. . . .

(e)(1) Congress hereby declares that to secure the rights under the fourteenth amendment of persons educated in American-flag schools in which the predominant classroom language was other than English, it is necessary to prohibit the States from conditioning the right to vote of such persons on ability to read, write, understand, or interpret any matter in the English language. . . .

Sec. 6. Whenever . . . the Attorney General certifies with respect to any political subdivision named in, or included within the scope of, determinations made under section 4(b) that (1) he has received complaints in writing from twenty or more residents of such political subdivision alleging that they have been denied the right to vote under color of law on account of race or color, and that he believes such complaints to be meritorious, or (2) that in his judgment (considering, among other factors, whether the ratio of nonwhite persons to white persons registered to vote within such subdivision appears to him to be reasonably attributable to violations of the fifteenth amendment or whether substantial evidence exists that bona fide efforts are being made within such subdivision to comply with the fifteenth amendment), the appointment of examiners is otherwise necessary to enforce the guarantees of the fifteenth amendment, the Civil Service Commission shall appoint as many examiners for such subdivision as it may deem appropriate to prepare and maintain lists of persons eligible to vote in Federal, State, and local elections. . . .

(b) Any person whom the examiner finds, in accordance with instructions received under section 9(b), to have the qualifications prescribed by State law not inconsistent with the Constitution and laws of the United States shall promptly be placed on a list of eligible voters. . . .

Sec. 10.   (a) The Congress finds that the requirement of the payment of a poll tax as a precondition to voting (i) precludes persons of limited means from voting or imposes unreasonable financial hardship upon such persons as a precondition to their exercise of the franchise, (ii) does not bear a reasonable relationship to any legitimate State interest in the conduct of elections, and (iii) in some areas has the purpose or effect of denying persons the right to vote because of race or color. Upon the basis of these findings, Congress declares that the constitutional right of citizens to vote is denied or abridged in some areas by the requirement of the payment of a poll tax as a precondition to voting.

(b) In the exercise of the powers of Congress under section 5 of the fourteenth amendment and section 2 of the fifteenth amendment, the Attorney General is authorized and directed to institute forthwith in the name of the United States . . . actions, including actions against States or political subdivisions, for declaratory judgment or injunctive relief against the enforcement of any requirement of the payment of a poll tax as a precondition to voting.

90 ∾

The civil rights movement helped reawaken the women's rights movement. Revitalized feminists demanded equal employment opportunities, an end to double standards of morality, and complete control over their own bodies. Congress began to respond by outlawing sexual discrimination in employment in the Civil Rights Act of 1964 (Document 89). In 1972 it proposed the Equal Rights Amendment (ERA) to the Constitution. The amendment read, "Equality of rights under the law shall not be denied or abridged by the United States or any State on account of sex." Ratification of the ERA would have required strict judicial scrutiny of government actions and laws that made sexual classifications, as with those that classified by race. Although Congress extended the deadline for ratification, conservatives in several states managed to stave it off.

Despite the defeat of the ERA, the Supreme Court responded favorably to the goals of the women's rights movement. In *Reed v. Reed* (1971) the Court ruled that the states could not "irrationally" discriminate against women, defining as irrational a preference for men over women as executors of wills, a bias that reflected long-standing legal custom. In *Craig v. Boren* the justices held that *Reed* established a level of scrutiny that demanded more than mere rationality of laws making sexual classifications. But they did not require that such laws serve "compelling" state interests, as they did of laws making racial classifications. A "substantial" state interest was enough. Ironically, the vehicle for this change was an Oklahoma law that discriminated against young men by setting a higher minimum beer-drinking age for them than for young women. As justification, the state showed that young men were ten times more likely than women to be arrested for drunken driving.

Craig v. Boren (1976)

MR. JUSTICE Brennan delivered the opinion of the Court. . . .

Reed emphasized that statutory classifications that distinguish between males and females are "subject to scrutiny under the Equal Protection Clause." To withstand constitutional challenge, previous cases establish that classifications by gender must serve important governmental objections and must be substantially related to achievement of those objectives. . . .

Reed v. Reed has also provided the underpinning for decisions that have invalidated statutes employing gender as an inaccurate proxy for other, more germane bases of classification. Hence, "archaic and overbroad" generalizations could not justify use of a gender line in determining eligibility for certain government entitlements. . . . Similarly, increasingly outdated misconceptions concerning the role of females in the home rather than in the "marketplace and world of ideas" were rejected. . . . In light of the weak congruence between gender and the characteristic or trait that gender purported to represent, it was necessary that the legislature choose either to realign their substantive laws in a gender-neutral fashion, or to adopt procedures for identifying those instances where the sex-centered generalization actually comported with fact. . . .

Clearly, the protection of public health and safety represents an important function of state and local governments. However, appellee's statistics in our view cannot support the conclusion that the gender-based distinction closely serves to achieve that objective and therefore the distinction cannot under *Reed* withstand equal protection challenge. . . . [W]hen it is further recognized that Oklahoma's statute prohibits only the selling of 3.2% beer to young males and not their drinking the beverage once acquired (even after purchase by their 18–20-year-old female companions), the relationship between gender and traffic safety becomes far too tenuous to satisfy *Reed*'s requirement that the gender-based difference be substantially related to achievement of the statutory objective.

91 ❧

In the 1914 case of *Weeks v. U.S.*, the Supreme Court ruled that evidence seized in violation of the Fourth Amendment could not be used against defendants in the federal courts. The Court applied the so-called Exclusionary Rule to confessions secured in vio-

429 U.S. 190 (1976).

lation of the Fifth Amendment as well. When the justices ruled in the 1930s and 1940s that the Fourteenth Amendment applied the key provisions of the Fourth and Fifth Amendments to the states, the question arose whether it also applied the Exclusionary Rule. In *Wolf v. Colorado,* 338 U.S. 25 (1949), the Court ruled that it did not.

Civil libertarians severely criticized the *Wolf* decision, and in 1961 the Warren Court reconsidered the issue. By this time, the Court had become deeply sensitive to the effects of prejudice against minority groups by law-enforcement agencies, and it began to expand the rights of defendants in criminal cases to combat them. In *Mapp v. Ohio,* the police broke into the defendant's home to search for a fugitive and for gambling equipment, but they were never able to produce the search warrant they claimed to have secured. Instead of the fugitive or the gambling paraphernalia, the police found obscene books and pictures, and Mapp was convicted of possessing them.

Although the majority of the justices took the position that the Fourteenth Amendment incorporated the search and seizure provisions of the Fourth Amendment and applied them to the states, Justices Harlan, Frankfurter, and Whittaker continued to insist, as Frankfurter had in *Adamson v. California* (Document 77), that the Fourteenth Amendment operated on the states independently of the Bill of Rights. They insisted that principles of federalism should limit Supreme Court interference with state legal procedures.

Mapp v. Ohio (1961)

MR. JUSTICE Clark delivered the opinion of the Court. . . .

. . . Today we once again examine Wolf's constitutional documentation of the right to privacy free from unreasonable state intrusion, and, after its dozen years on our books, are led by it to close the only courtroom door remaining open to evidence secured by official lawlessness in flagrant abuse of that basic right, reserved to all persons as a specific guarantee against that very same unlawful conduct. We hold that all evidence obtained by searches and seizures in violation of the Constitution is, by that same authority, inadmissible in a state court. . . .

. . . [O]ur holding that the exclusionary rule is an essential part of both the Fourth and Fourteenth Amendments is not only the logical dictate of prior cases, but it also makes very good sense. . . . Presently, a federal prosecutor may make no use of evidence illegally seized, but a State's attorney across the street may, although he supposedly is operating under the enforceable prohibitions of the same Amendment. Thus the State, by admitting evidence unlawfully seized, serves to encourage disobedience to the Federal Constitution which it is bound to uphold. . . . In nonexclusionary States, federal officers, being human, were by it invited to and did, as our cases indicate, step across

367 U.S. 643 (1961).

the street to the State's attorney with their unconstitutionally seized evidence. Prosecution on the basis of that evidence was then had in a state court in utter disregard of the enforceable Fourth Amendment. . . .

There are those who say, as did Justice (then Judge) Cardozo, that under our constitutional exclusionary doctrine "[t]he criminal is to go free because the constable has blundered." . . . The criminal goes free, if he must, but it is the law that sets him free. Nothing can destroy a government more quickly than its failure to observe its own laws, or worse, its disregard of the charter of its own existence. . . .

The ignoble shortcut to conviction left open to the State tends to destroy the entire system of constitutional restraints on which the liberties of the people rest. Having once recognized that the right to privacy embodied in the Fourth Amendment is enforceable against the States, and that the right to be secure against rude invasions of privacy by state officers is, therefore, constitutional in origin, we can no longer permit that right to remain an empty promise. . . .

Mr. Justice Harlan, whom Mr. Justice Frankfurter and Mr. Justice Whittaker join, dissenting. . . .

At the heart of the majority's opinion in this case is the following syllogism: (1) the rule excluding in federal criminal trials evidence which is the product of an illegal search and seizure is "part and parcel" of the Fourth Amendment; (2) Wolf held that the "privacy" assured against federal action by the Fourth Amendment is also protected against state action by the Fourteenth Amendment; and (3) it is therefore "logically and constitutionally necessary" that the Weeks exclusionary rule should also be enforced against the States.

This reasoning ultimately rests on the unsound premise that because Wolf carried into the States, as part of "the concept of ordered liberty" embodied in the Fourteenth Amendment, the principle of "privacy" underlying the Fourth Amendment . . . , it must follow that whatever configurations of the Fourth Amendment have been developed in the particularizing federal precedents are likewise to be deemed a part of "ordered liberty," and as such are enforceable against the States. For me, this does not follow at all.

It cannot be too much emphasized that what was recognized in Wolf was not that the Fourth Amendment *as such* is enforceable against the States as a facet of due process, . . . but the principle of privacy "which is at the core of the Fourth Amendment." . . . It would not be proper to expect or impose any precise equivalence, either as regards the scope of the right or the means of its implementation, between the requirements of the Fourth and Fourteenth Amendments. . . .

. . . Our role in promulgating the Weeks rule and its extensions . . . was quite a different one than it is here. There, in implementing the Fourth Amendment, we occupied the position of a tribunal having the ultimate responsibility for developing the standards and procedures of judicial administration within the judicial system over which it presides. Here we review state procedures whose measure is to be taken not against the specific substantive commands of the Fourth Amendment but under the flexible contours of the Due Process Clause. I do not believe that the Fourteenth Amendment empowers this Court to mould state remedies effectuating the right to freedom from "arbitrary intrusion by the police" to suit its own notions of how things should be done.

92 ∾

The Warren Court's decisions in *Escobedo v. Illinois,* 378 U.S. 438 (1964), and *Miranda v. Arizona* were among its most controversial. Inducing suspects to confess was the central tool of law enforcement at the time. But the Court's struggle against discrimination during the civil rights movement made many of the justices aware that suspicion of criminal activity fell disproportionately upon members of minority groups. The justices realized that educated, more affluent suspects would demand their rights, whereas poorly educated, disadvantaged suspects would be unaware of them. Consequently, in *Escobedo* the Court ruled that suspects in criminal cases have the right to the presence of their lawyers while being interrogated and also must be told that they have the right to remain silent.

In *Miranda v. Arizona,* the defendant confessed after two hours of questioning, never having been told that he had the right to remain silent and to request an attorney. In overturning Miranda's conviction, the Court defined the rights that suspects had in the law-enforcement process, and it required the police to inform suspects about them.

Most law-enforcement agencies and many ordinary Americans reacted with outrage, charging that the decision would make conviction of lawbreakers nearly impossible. However, the critics' worst expectations did not come to pass, and giving the so-called Miranda warnings is now an accepted element of criminal procedure.

Miranda v. Arizona (1966)

MR. CHIEF Justice Warren delivered the opinion of the Court. . . .

. . . In these cases,* we might not find the defendants' statements to have been involuntary in traditional terms. . . . [But] in each of the cases, the defendant was thrust into an unfamiliar atmosphere and run through menacing

384 U.S. 436 (1966).
*Miranda was one of four similar cases decided together.

police interrogation procedures. . . . To be sure, the records do not evince overt physical coercion or patent psychological ploys. The fact remains that in none of these cases did the officers undertake to afford appropriate safeguards at the outset of the interrogation to insure that the statements were truly the product of free choice.

It is obvious that such an interrogation environment is created for no purpose other than to subjugate the individual to the will of his examiner. This atmosphere carries its own badge of intimidation. To be sure, this is not physical intimidation, but it is equally destructive of human dignity. The current practice of incommunicado interrogation is at odds with one of our Nation's most cherished principles—that the individual may not be compelled to incriminate himself. Unless adequate protective devices are employed to dispel the compulsion inherent in custodial surroundings, no statement obtained from the defendant can truly be the product of his free choice. . . .

. . . [W]e hold that when an individual is taken into custody or otherwise deprived of his freedom by the authorities in any significant way and is subjected to questioning, the privilege against self-incrimination is jeopardized. Procedural safeguards must be employed to protect the privilege, and unless other fully effective means are adopted to notify the person of his right of silence and to assure that the exercise of the right will be scrupulously honored, the following measures are required. He must be warned prior to any questioning that he has the right to remain silent, that anything he says can be used against him in a court of law, that he has the right to the presence of an attorney, and that if he cannot afford an attorney one will be appointed for him prior to any questioning if he so desires. Opportunity to exercise these rights must be afforded to him throughout the interrogation. After such warnings have been given, and such opportunity afforded him, the individual may knowingly and intelligently waive these rights and agree to answer questions or make a statement. . . .

A recurrent argument made in these cases is that society's need for interrogation outweighs the privilege. This argument is not unfamiliar to this Court. . . . As Mr. Justice Brandeis once observed:

"Decency, security and liberty alike demand that government officials shall be subjected to the same rules of conduct that are commands to the citizen. . . . Crime is contagious. If the Government becomes a lawbreaker, it breeds contempt for law; it invites every man to become a law unto himself; it invites anarchy. To declare that in the administration of the criminal law the end justifies the means . . . would bring terrible retribution. Against that pernicious doctrine this Court should resolutely set its face." Olmstead v United States . . . (dissenting opinion).

CHAPTER 17

Curbing Presidential Power

93

The powers of the executive branch of the federal government had been growing steadily since the Progressive era, when Congress began delegating broad authority to promulgate and enforce regulations to a number of executive agencies. The power and prestige of the president, as head of the executive branch, grew apace, especially under the dynamic Theodore Roosevelt during the Progressive era and under Franklin Delano Roosevelt during the New Deal. To the president's authority as chief executive was added prominence as representative of the nation and commander-in-chief of the armed forces during the First and Second World Wars. In *U.S. v. Curtiss-Wright Export Corp.*, 299 U.S. 304 (1936), the Supreme Court declared the primacy of the executive branch in foreign affairs, recognizing the president's broad, inherent powers in that sphere.

In 1951, without securing a declaration of war from Congress, President Harry S. Truman ordered American armed forces to participate in a United Nations "police action" to counteract North Korea's invasion of South Korea. Truman insisted that the United States was bound by the U.N. charter to join the operation in Korea.

In 1952 Truman faced the imminent outbreak of a nationwide strike in the steel industry that would cripple American war production. Truman eschewed using provisions of the Taft-Hartley Act of 1947, which authorized sixty-day injunctions of strikes in emergencies, but which he and the labor movement had bitterly opposed. While considering the Taft-Hartley Act, Congress had rejected a proposal authorizing the president to seize private businesses under such circumstances. Nonetheless, Truman seized the steel mills and ordered their continued operation, claiming inherent presidential authority to protect national security. The steel executives sued to regain control of the mills.

Despite their general sympathy for a strong presidency, the majority of the justices repudiated an action that appeared to put the president above the law.

Youngstown Sheet & Tube Co. v. Sawyer (1952)

MR. JUSTICE Black delivered the opinion of the Court. . . .

The President's power, if any, to issue the order must stem either from an act of Congress or from the Constitution itself. There is no statute that expressly authorizes the President to take possession of property as he did here. . . .

Moreover, the use of the seizure technique to solve labor disputes in order to prevent work stoppages was not only unauthorized by any congressional enactment; prior to this controversy, Congress had refused to adopt that method of settling labor disputes. . . . The contention is that presidential power should be implied from the aggregate of his powers under the Constitution. Particular reliance is placed on provisions in Article II which say that "The executive Power shall be vested in a President . . ."; that "he shall take Care that the Laws be faithfully executed"; and that he "shall be Commander in Chief of the Army and Navy of the United States."

The order cannot properly be sustained as an exercise of the President's military power as Commander in Chief of the Armed Forces. . . . [W]e cannot with faithfulness to our constitutional system hold that the Commander in Chief of the Armed Forces has the ultimate power as such to take possession of private property in order to keep labor disputes from stopping production. This is a job for the Nation's lawmakers, not for its military authorities.

Nor can the seizure order be sustained because of the several constitutional provisions that grant executive power to the President. In the framework of our Constitution, the President's power to see that the laws are faithfully executed refutes the idea that he is to be a lawmaker. The Constitution limits his functions in the lawmaking process to the recommending of laws he thinks wise and the vetoing of laws he thinks bad. . . .

The Founders of this Nation entrusted the lawmaking power to the Congress alone in both good and bad times. It would do no good to recall the historical events, the fears of power and the hopes for freedom that lay behind their choice. Such a review would but confirm our holding that this seizure order cannot stand.

94 ❧

The power of the presidency continued to grow in the decades following the New Deal. By the 1970s President Richard M. Nixon was claiming extensive authority to refuse to spend funds allocated by Congress, to shield executive activities from congressional in-

343 U.S. 579 (1952).

quiry, and to authorize otherwise illegal activity if necessary to protect national security. Informally, Nixon utilized his executive powers to intimidate political enemies and ultimately to engage in illegal operations against them.

In the Pentagon Papers Case, an employee of a private national-security "think tank" sent leading newspapers copies of a classified report showing that previous administrations had consciously misled Congress and the public about the course of the Vietnam War. The Nixon administration sought an injunction to prevent the report's publication, arguing not only that it would damage national security but that the courts must accept the president's judgment on such matters.

Forbidding the government from putting prior restraints on publication had long been considered the heart of freedom of the press. In fact, at the time of the American Revolution, conservatives had considered freedom of the press to consist of nothing more than a ban on prior restraint, with the government free to punish illicit publication *after* it occurred. Thus the administration's petition for an injunction seemed a clear violation of the First Amendment to many observers. In a brief order, the majority of the justices refused to sustain an injunction, but most did not rule out prior restraint of publication under certain circumstances.

The Pentagon Papers Case
(*New York Times Co. v. U.S.*) (1971)

PER CURIAM . . .

. . . "Any system of prior restraints of expression comes to this Court bearing a heavy presumption against its constitutional validity." . . . The Government "thus carries a heavy burden of showing justification for the imposition of such a restraint." . . . The District Court for the Southern District of New York in the New York Times case and the District Court for the District of Columbia and the Court of Appeals for the District of Columbia Circuit in the Washington Post case held that the Government had not met that burden. We agree. . . .

Separate Opinions

Mr. Justice Black, with whom Mr. Justice Douglas joins, concurring. . . .

. . . [W]e are asked to hold that despite the First Amendment's emphatic command, the Executive Branch, the Congress, and the Judiciary can make laws enjoining publication of current news and abridging freedom of the press in the name of "national security." The Government does not even attempt to rely on any act of Congress. Instead it makes the bold and dangerously far-reaching contention that the courts should take it upon themselves

403 U.S. 713 (1971).

to "make" a law abridging freedom of the press in the name of equity, presidential power, and national security, even when the representatives of the people in Congress have adhered to the command of the First Amendment and refused to make such a law. . . . To find that the President has "inherent power" to halt the publication of news by resort to the courts would wipe out the First Amendment and destroy the fundamental liberty and security of the very people the Government hopes to make "secure." . . .

Mr. Justice Brennan, concurring. . . .

The error that has pervaded these cases from the outset was the granting of any injunctive relief whatsoever, interim or otherwise. The entire thrust of the Government's claim throughout these cases has been that publication of the material sought to be enjoined "could," or "might," or "may" prejudice the national interest in various ways. But the First Amendment tolerates absolutely no prior judicial restraints of the press predicated upon surmise or conjecture that untoward consequences may result. . . .

Mr. Justice Stewart, with whom Mr. Justice White joins, concurring. . . .

. . . [I]t is elementary that the successful conduct of international diplomacy and the maintenance of an effective national defense require both confidentiality and secrecy. . . . The responsibility must be where the power is. If the Constitution gives the Executive a large degree of unshared power in the conduct of foreign affairs and the maintenance of our national defense, then under the Constitution the Executive must have the largely unshared duty to determine and preserve the degree of internal security necessary to exercise that power successfully. It is an awesome responsibility, requiring judgment and wisdom of a high order. . . .

But in the cases before us we are asked neither to construe specific regulations nor to apply specific laws. We are asked, instead, to perform a function that the Constitution gave to the Executive, not the Judiciary. We are asked, quite simply, to prevent the publication by two newspapers of material that the Executive Branch insists should not, in the national interest, be published. I am convinced that the Executive is correct with respect to some of the documents involved. But I cannot say that disclosure of any of them will surely result in direct, immediate, and irreparable damage to our Nation or its people. That being so, there can under the First Amendment be but one judicial resolution of the issues before us. I join the judgments of the Court. . . .

Mr. Justice Marshall, concurring. . . .

The problem here is whether in these particular cases the Executive Branch has authority to invoke the equity jurisdiction of the courts to protect what it believes to be the national interest. . . . [I]n some situations it may be that under whatever inherent powers the Government may have, as well as the implicit authority derived from the President's mandate to conduct foreign affairs and to act as Commander in Chief, there is a basis for the invocation of the equity jurisdiction of this Court as an aid to prevent the publication of material damaging to "national security," however that term may be defined.

It would, however, be utterly inconsistent with the concept of separation of powers for this Court to use its power of contempt to prevent behavior that Congress has specifically declined to prohibit. . . . The Constitution provides that Congress shall make laws, the President execute laws, and courts interpret laws. Youngstown Sheet & Tube Co. v Sawyer. . . . It did not provide for government by injunction in which the courts and the Executive Branch can "make law" without regard to the action of Congress. . . .

. . . [I]t is clear that Congress has specifically rejected passing legislation that would have clearly given the President the power he seeks here and made the current activity of the newspapers unlawful. When Congress specifically declines to make conduct unlawful it is not for this Court to redecide those issues—to overrule Congress. . . .

Mr. Justice Harlan, with whom The Chief Justice and Mr. Justice Blackmun join, dissenting.

These cases forcefully call to mind the wise admonition of Mr. Justice Holmes, dissenting in Northern Securities Co. v. United States . . . :

"Great cases like hard cases make bad law. For great cases are called great, not by reason of their real importance in shaping the law of the future, but because of some accident of immediate overwhelming interest which appeals to the feelings and distorts the judgment." . . .

This frenzied train of events took place in the name of the presumption against prior restraints created by the First Amendment. Due regard for the extraordinarily important and difficult questions involved in these litigations should have led the Court to shun such a precipitate timetable. . . .

Forced as I am to reach the merits of these cases, I dissent from the opinion and judgments of the Court. . . .

In a speech on the floor of the House of Representatives, Chief Justice John Marshall, then a member of that body, stated:

"The President is the sole organ of the nation in its external relations, and its sole representative with foreign nations." . . .

From this constitutional primacy in the field of foreign affairs, it seems to me that certain conclusions necessarily follow. . . .

. . . I agree that, in performance of its duty to protect the values of the First Amendment against political pressures, the judiciary must review the initial Executive determination to the point of satisfying itself that the subject matter of the dispute does lie within the proper compass of the President's foreign relations power. . . . Moreover, the judiciary may properly insist that the determination that disclosure of the subject matter would irreparably impair the national security be made by the head of the Executive Department concerned . . . after actual personal consideration by that officer. . . .

But in my judgment the judiciary may not properly go beyond these two inquiries and redetermine for itself the probable impact of disclosure on the national security.

"[T]he very nature of executive decisions as to foreign policy is political, not judicial. Such decisions are wholly confided by our Constitution to the political departments of the government, Executive and Legislative. . . . They are decisions of a kind for which the Judiciary has neither aptitude, facilities nor responsibility. . . ."

95 ℘

In an effort to stop embarrassing leaks in the executive branch, presidential aides authorized illegal wiretapping and burglaries of those suspected of transmitting or receiving information. During the presidential election of 1972, some of the operatives used in the so-called Plumbers Operation broke into the headquarters of the Democratic National Committee at the Watergate apartment complex in Washington. When the burglary was discovered, the White House illegally tried to cover up its role in the activities.

As the Watergate Scandal grew, the Justice Department named a special prosecutor to investigate. However, when the prosecutor subpoenaed tape recordings of conversations between President Nixon and suspected conspirators, the president refused to comply, claiming an executive privilege to safeguard the privacy of executive-branch conversations. When the prosecutor refused an order to drop his request for the material, President Nixon ordered the attorney general to fire him. Both the attorney general and the deputy attorney general resigned rather than do so. In the ensuing firestorm of criticism, the president had to agree to the appointment of an independent prosecutor, who continued to seek the tapes. The White House continued to argue that the president had an inherent right, not subject to judicial review, to refuse to make conversations in the executive branch available if he believed they would damage the security of the United States. The consequence of accepting the argument would have been to shield possible illegal activity by the president and his staff.

The Supreme Court unanimously rejected Nixon's argument and ordered him to make the tapes available. Although the opinion recognized the existence of executive privilege and implied a good deal of deference to the president's exercise of it, it could not be utilized to obstruct a criminal investigation.

U.S. v. Nixon (1974)

MR. CHIEF Justice Burger delivered the opinion of the Court. . . .

. . . [W]e turn to the claim that the subpoena should be quashed because it demands "confidential conversations between a President and his close advisors that it would be inconsistent with the public interest to produce." . . . The first contention is a broad claim that the separation of powers doctrine precludes judicial review of a President's claim of privilege. The second contention is that if he does not prevail on the claim of absolute privilege, the court should hold as a matter of constitutional law that the privilege prevails over the subpoena *duces tecum.*

In the performance of assigned constitutional duties each branch of the Government must initially interpret the Constitution, and the interpretation of its powers by any branch is due great respect from the others. . . . Many decisions of this Court, however, have unequivocally reaffirmed the holding of *Marbury v. Madison* . . . , that "[i]t is emphatically the province and duty of the judicial department to say what the law is." . . .

No holding of the Court has defined the scope of judicial power specifically relating to the enforcement of a subpoena for confidential Presidential communications for use in a criminal prosecution, but other exercises of power by the Executive Branch and the Legislative Branch have been found invalid as in conflict with the Constitution. . . .

In support of his claim of absolute privilege, the President's counsel urges two grounds, one of which is peculiar to our system of separation of powers. The first ground is the valid need for protection of communications between high Government officials and those who advise and assist them in the performance of their manifold duties; the importance of this confidentiality is too plain to require further discussions. . . . Whatever the nature of the privilege of confidentiality of Presidential communications in the exercise of Art. II powers, the privilege can be said to derive from the supremacy of each branch within its own assigned area of constitutional duties. Certain powers and privileges flow from the nature of enumerated powers; the protection of the confidentiality of Presidential communications has similar constitutional underpinnings.

The second ground asserted by the President's counsel in support of the claim of absolute privilege rests on the doctrine of separation of powers. Here

418 U.S. 683 (1974).

it is argued that the independence of the Executive Branch within its own sphere . . . insulates a President from a judicial subpoena in an ongoing criminal prosecution, and thereby protects confidential Presidential communications.

However, neither the doctrine of separation of powers, nor the need for confidentiality of high-level communications, without more, can sustain an absolute, unqualified Presidential privilege of immunity from judicial process under all circumstances. The President's need for complete candor and objectivity from advisers calls for great deference from the courts. However, when the privilege depends solely on the broad, undifferentiated claim of public interest in the confidentiality of such conversations, a confrontation with other values arises. Absent a claim of need to protect military, diplomatic, or sensitive national security secrets, we find it difficult to accept the argument that even the very important interest in confidentiality of Presidential communications is significantly diminished by production of such material for *in camera* inspection with all the protection that a district court will be obliged to provide.

The impediment that an absolute, unqualified privilege would place in the way of the primary constitutional duty of the Judicial Branch to do justice in criminal prosecutions would plainly conflict with the function of the courts under Art. III. In designing the structure of our Government and dividing and allocating the sovereign power among three co-equal branches, the Framers of the Constitution sought to provide a comprehensive system, but the separate powers were not intended to operate with absolute independence. . . .

We conclude that when the ground for asserting privilege as to subpoenaed materials sought for use in a criminal trial is based only on the generalized interest in confidentiality, it cannot prevail over the fundamental demands of due process of law in the fair administration of criminal justice. The generalized assertion of privilege must yield to the demonstrated, specific need for evidence in a pending criminal trial.

96 ⌘

After conducting an investigation for nearly a year, in August 1974 the Judiciary Committee of the House of Representatives voted to report articles impeaching President Nixon of high crimes and misdemeanors. Throughout the investigation members of the committee debated whether government officials were liable to impeachment only for clearly criminal conduct, as President Nixon's lawyers argued, or also for serious abuse of power that did not violate specific laws. In the end, the committee took the second position, voting articles that specified both illegal activity and abuse of power. With the just-released Watergate tapes indicating that Nixon had knowingly participated in the cover-up, the president resigned before the House could vote on the articles.

House Judiciary Committee, Report of Impeachment Resolutions (1974)

T HE COMMITTEE on the Judiciary, to whom was referred the consideration of recommendations concerning the exercise of the constitutional power to impeach Richard M. Nixon, President of the United States, having considered the same, . . . recommends that the House exercise its constitutional power to impeach Richard M. Nixon, President of the United States, and that articles of impeachment be exhibited to the Senate as follows:

Resolution

. . . *Resolved,* That Richard M. Nixon, President of the United States, is impeached for high crimes and misdemeanors, and that the following articles of impeachment be exhibited to the Senate: . . .

Article I

In his conduct of the office of President of the United States, Richard M. Nixon, in violation of his constitutional oath faithfully to execute the office of President of the United States and, to the best of his ability, preserve, protect, and defend the Constitution of the United States, and in violation of his constitutional duty to take care that the laws be faithfully executed, has prevented, obstructed, and impeded the administration of justice, in that:

On June 17, 1972, and prior thereto, agents of the Committee for the Reelection of the President committed unlawful entry of the headquarters of the Democratic National Committee in Washington, District of Columbia, for the purpose of securing political intelligence. Subsequent thereto, Richard M. Nixon, using the powers of his high office, engaged personally and through his subordinates and agents, in a course of conduct or plan designed to delay, impede, and obstruct the investigation of such unlawful entry; to cover up, conceal and protect those responsible; and to conceal the existence and scope of other unlawful covert activities. . . .

Article II

Using the powers of the office of President of the United States, Richard M. Nixon, in violation of his constitutional oath faithfully to execute the office of

Impeachment of Richard M. Nixon, President of the United States, *House of Representatives Report No. 93-1305,* 93d Cong., 2d sess., 1–4.

President of the United States and, to the best of his ability, preserve, protect, and defend the Constitution of the United States, and in disregard of his constitutional duty to take care that the laws be faithfully executed, has repeatedly engaged in conduct violating the constitutional rights of citizens, impairing the due and proper administration of justice and the conduct of lawful inquiries, or contravening the laws governing agencies of the executive branch and the purposes of these agencies.

This conduct has included one or more of the following:

(1) He has, acting personally and through his subordinates and agents, endeavored to obtain from the Internal Revenue Service, in violation of the constitutional rights of citizens, confidential information contained in income tax returns for purposes not authorized by law, and to cause, in violation of the constitutional rights of citizens, income tax audits or other income tax investigations to be initiated or conducted in a discriminatory manner.

(2) He misused the Federal Bureau of Investigation, the Secret Service, and other executive personnel, in violation or disregard of the constitutional rights of citizens, by directing or authorizing such agencies or personnel to conduct or continue electronic surveillance or other investigations for purposes unrelated to national security, the enforcement of laws, or any other lawful function of his office. . . .

(3) He has, acting personally and through his subordinates and agents, in violation or disregard of the constitutional rights of citizens, authorized and permitted to be maintained a secret investigative unit within the office of the President, financed in part with money derived from campaign contributions, which unlawfully utilized the resources of the Central Intelligence Agency, engaged in covert and unlawful activities, and attempted to prejudice the constitutional right of an accused to a fair trial.

(4) He has failed to take care that the laws were faithfully executed by failing to act when he knew or had reason to know that his close subordinates endeavored to impede and frustrate lawful inquiries by duly constituted executive, judicial, and legislative entities concerning the unlawful entry into the headquarters of the Democratic National Committee, and the cover-up thereof, and concerning other unlawful activities. . . .

(5) In disregard of the rule of law, he knowingly misused the executive power by interfering with agencies of the executive branch, including the Federal Bureau of Investigation, the Criminal Division, and the Office of Watergate Special Prosecution Force, of the Department of Justice, and the Central Intelligence Agency, in violation of his duty to take care that the laws be faithfully executed. . . .

Article III

In his conduct of the office of President of the United States, Richard M. Nixon, contrary to his oath faithfully to execute the office of President of the United States and, to the best of his ability, preserve, protect, and defend the Constitution of the United States, and in violation of his constitutional duty to take care that the laws be faithfully executed, has failed without lawful cause or excuse to produce papers and things as directed by duly authorized subpoenas issued by the Committee on the Judiciary of the House of Representatives. . . . In refusing to produce these papers and things, Richard M. Nixon, substituting his judgment as to what materials were necessary for the inquiry, interposed the powers of the Presidency against the lawful subpoenas of the House of Representatives, thereby assuming to himself functions and judgments necessary to the exercise of the sole power of impeachment vested by the Constitution in the House of Representatives.

In all of this, Richard M. Nixon has acted in a manner contrary to his trust as President and subversive of constitutional government, to the great prejudice of the cause of law and justice, and to the manifest injury of the people of the United States.

Wherefore Richard M. Nixon, by such conduct, warrants impeachment and trial, and removal from office.

C H A P T E R   1 8

The Revival of Constitutional Conservatism

97

A reaction against liberalism could already be detected in the late 1960s, as President Nixon orchestrated attacks on opponents of his Vietnam War policies and on liberal intellectuals in general. The backlash gathered force in the 1970s, as economic stagnation led many middle-class Americans to resent programs that redistributed wealth from the more affluent to the disadvantaged and that redistributed power and privileges from white men to women and to members of minority groups. Beginning with the elections of 1978, voters began to force rollbacks in state taxes and to impose caps on increases. State and federal welfare programs came under increasing attack. Calls grew for a reduction in the size and role of the federal government and for a transfer of many of its responsibilities to states and localities. In 1980 Americans elected the most conservative president since Herbert Hoover, Ronald W. Reagan.

The Reagan administration slashed federal taxes while dramatically increasing military spending. The pressure helped force the collapse of international communism and the Soviet Union, the United States's main rival for global leadership, but it created a huge national debt that made it impossible to fund domestic federal programs at current levels. In his first inaugural address, President Reagan expressed his attitude towards active government, the general-welfare state, and federalism in language that, despite its simplicity, embodied a clear and coherent attack on liberal constitutionalism.

Ronald Reagan, First Inaugural Address (1981)

THE ECONOMIC ills we suffer have come upon us over several decades. They will not go away in days, weeks, or months, but they will go away. They will go away because we as Americans have the capacity now, as

Papers of the Presidents of the United States: Ronald Reagan, 1981 (Washington, D.C.: Government Printing Office, 1982), 1–4.

we've had in the past, to do whatever needs to be done to preserve this last and greatest bastion of freedom.

In this present crisis, government is not the solution to our problem; government is the problem. From time to time we've been tempted to believe that society has become too complex to be managed by self-rule, that government by an elite group is superior to government for, by, and of the people. Well, if no one among us is capable of governing himself, then who among us has the capacity to govern someone else? All of us together, in and out of government, must bear the burden. The solutions we seek must be equitable, with no one group singled out to pay a higher price. . . .

So, as we begin, let us take inventory. We are a nation that has a government—not the other way around. And this makes us special among the nations of the earth. Our government has no power except that granted it by the people. It is time to check and reverse the growth of government, which shows signs of having grown beyond the consent of the governed.

It is my intention to curb the size and influence of the federal establishment and to demand recognition of the distinction between the powers granted to the federal government and those reserved to the states or to the people. All of us need to be reminded that the federal government did not create the states; the states created the federal government.

98 ∾

Conservatives attacked judicial activism and the idea of a "living Constitution" that permitted the courts to interpret constitutional provisions in light of evolving conceptions of their meaning. Conservatives called upon the Supreme Court to interpret the Constitution according to the "original intent" or "original understanding" of the framers. Among the leading critics of liberal constitutionalism was President Reagan's attorney general, Edwin Meese III. The following address, presented to the Lawyer's Division of the conservative Federalist Society in 1985, was typical of those he delivered to audiences across the country.

Edwin Meese on "A Jurisprudence of Original Intention" (1985)

T O D A Y I would like to discuss further the meaning of constitutional fidelity. In particular, I would like to describe in more detail this administration's approach.

The Federalist Society, *The Great Debate: Interpreting Our Written Constitution* (Washington, D.C.: The Federalist Society, 1989), 31–41. Reprinted by permission of the Federalist Society.

Before doing so, I would like to make a few commonplace observations about the original document itself. It is easy to forget what a young country America really is. The bicentennial of our independence was just a few years ago, that of the Constitution still two years off. The period surrounding the creation of the Constitution is not a dark and mythical realm. The young America of the 1780's and 90's was a vibrant place, alive with pamphlets, newspapers and books chronicling and commenting upon the great issues of the day. We know how the Founding Fathers lived, and much of what they read, thought, and believed. The disputes and compromises of the Constitutional Convention were carefully recorded. The minutes of the Convention are a matter of public record. Several of the most important participants—including James Madison, the "father" of the Constitution—wrote comprehensive accounts of the convention. Others, Federalists and Anti-Federalists alike, committed their arguments for and against ratification, as well as their understandings of the Constitution, to paper, so that their ideas and conclusions could be widely circulated, read, and understood.

In short, the Constitution is not buried in the mists of time. We know a tremendous amount of the history of its genesis. . . .

With these thoughts in mind, I would like to discuss the administration's approach to constitutional interpretation. . . .

. . . The Constitution is not a legislative code bound to the time in which it was written. Neither, however, is it a mirror that simply reflects the thoughts and ideas of those who stand before it.

Our approach to constitutional interpretation begins with the document itself. The plain fact is, it exists. It is something that has been written down. . . .

We know that those who framed the Constitution chose their words carefully. They debated at great length the most minute points. The language they chose meant something. They proposed, they substituted, they edited, and they carefully revised. Their words were studied with equal care by state ratifying conventions. . . . [T]he Framers were not clairvoyants—they could not foresee every issue that would be submitted for judicial review. Nor could they predict how all foreseeable disputes would be resolved under the Constitution. But the point is, the meaning of the Constitution can be known.

What does this written Constitution mean? In places it is exactingly specific. Where it says that Presidents of the United States must be at least 35 years of age it means exactly that. (I have not heard of any claim that 35 means 30 or 25 or 20.) Where it specifies how the House and Senate are to be organized, it means what it says.

The Constitution also expresses particular principles. One is the right to be free of an unreasonable search or seizure. Another concerns religious liberty. Another is the right to equal protection of the laws.

Those who framed these principles meant something by them. And the meanings can be found. The Constitution itself is also an expression of certain general principles. These principles reflect the deepest purpose of the Constitution—that of establishing a political system through which Americans can best govern themselves consistent with the goal of securing liberty.

The text and structure of the Constitution is instructive. It contains very little in the way of specific political solutions. It speaks volumes on how problems should be approached, and by *whom*. For example, the first three articles set out clearly the scope and limits of three distinct branches of national government. The powers of each being carefully and specifically enumerated. In this scheme it is no accident to find the legislative branch described first, as the Framers had fought and sacrificed to secure the right of democratic self-governance. Naturally, this faith in republicanism was not unbounded, as the next two articles make clear.

Yet the Constitution remains a document of powers and principles. And its undergirding premise remains that democratic self government is subject only to the limits of certain constitutional principles. This respect for the political process was made explicit early on. When John Marshall upheld the Act of Congress chartering a national bank in *McCulloch* v. *Maryland*, . . . he wrote: "The Constitution [was] intended to endure for ages to come, and, consequently, to be adapted to the various crises of human affairs." But to use *McCulloch*, as some have tried, as support for the idea that the Constitution is a protean, changeable thing is to stand history on its head. Marshall was keeping faith with the original intention that Congress be free to elaborate and apply constitutional powers and principles. He was not saying that the Court must invent some new constitutional value in order to keep pace with the times. . . .

The approach this administration advocates is rooted in the text of the Constitution as illuminated by those who drafted, proposed, and ratified it. . . .

In the main, jurisprudence that seeks to be faithful to our Constitution—a Jurisprudence of Original Intention, as I have called it—is not difficult to describe. Where the language of the Constitution is specific, it must be obeyed. Where there is a demonstrable consensus among the framers and ratifiers as to a principle stated or implied by the Constitution, it should be followed. Where there is ambiguity as to the precise meaning or reach of a constitutional provision, it should be interpreted and applied in a manner so as to at least not contradict the text of the Constitution itself. . . .

There is a frank proclamation by some judges and commentators that what matters most about the Constitution is not its words but its so-called "spirit." These individuals focus less on the language of specific provisions than on what they describe as the "vision" or "concepts of human dignity" they find embodied in the Constitution. This approach to jurisprudence has led to some remarkable and tragic conclusions.

In the 1850's, the Supreme Court under Chief Justice Roger B. Taney read blacks out of the Constitution in order to invalidate Congress' attempt to limit the spread of slavery. The *Dred Scott* decision, famously described as a judicial "self-inflicted wound," helped bring on the Civil War. There is a lesson in this history. There is danger in seeing the Constitution as an empty vessel into which each generation may pour its passion and prejudice.

Our own time has its own fashions and passions. In recent decades many have come to view the Constitution—more accurately, part of the Constitution, provisions of the Bill of Rights and the Fourteenth Amendment—as a charter for judicial activism on behalf of various constituencies. Those who hold this view often have lacked demonstrable textual or historical support for their conclusions. Instead they have "grounded" their rulings in appeals to social theories, to moral philosophies or personal notions of human dignity, or to "penumbras," somehow emanating ghostlike from various provisions—identified and not identified—in the Bill of Rights. . . .

Any true approach to constitutional interpretation must respect the document in all its parts and be faithful to the Constitution in its entirety. What must be remembered in the current debate is that interpretation does not imply results. The Framers were not trying to anticipate every answer. They were trying to create a tripartite national government, within a federal system, that would have the flexibility to adapt to face new exigencies—as it did, for example, in chartering a national bank. Their great interest was in the distribution of power and responsibility in order to secure the great goal of liberty for all.

A jurisprudence that seeks fidelity to the Constitution—a Jurisprudence of Original Intention—is not a jurisprudence of political results. It is very much concerned with process, and it is a jurisprudence that in our day seeks to depoliticize the law. The great genius of the constitutional blueprint is found in its creation and respect for spheres of authority and the limits it place[s] on governmental power. In this scheme the Framers did not see the courts as the exclusive custodians of the Constitution. Indeed, because the document posits so few conclusions it leaves to the more political branches the matter of adapting and vivifying its principles in each generation. It also leaves to the people of the states, in the 10th amendment, those responsibilities and rights not committed to federal care. The power to declare acts of Congress and laws of the states null and void is truly awesome. This power must be used when the Constitution clearly speaks. It should not be used when the Constitution does not. . . .

In summary, I would emphasize that what is at issue here is not an agenda of issues or a menu of results. At issue is a way of government. A jurisprudence based on first principles is neither conservative nor liberal, neither right nor left. It is a jurisprudence that cares about committing and limiting to each organ of government the proper ambit of its responsibilities. It is a jurisprudence faithful to our Constitution.

By the same token, an activist jurisprudence, one which anchors the Constitution only in the consciences of jurists, is a chameleon jurisprudence, changing color and form in each era. The same activism hailed today may threaten the capacity for decision through democratic consensus tomorrow, as it has in many yesterdays. Ultimately, as the early democrats wrote into the Massachusetts state constitution, the best defense of our liberties is a government of laws and not men.

99 ⌒

Faced with a growing deficit, Congress ended programs by which it had shared revenue with the states, but it continued to require state agencies to meet federal standards in policing the environment, providing welfare, and other areas. It imposed costly environmental rules on state and local sewage and waste disposal systems. Congress also expanded the coverage of the Fair Labor Standards Act, which governed minimum wages, maximum hours, and other aspects of employer-employee relations, to include state and local government workers. The requirement to remedy racial and sexual discrimination in schools and in government employment also created new expenses, as did adhering to federal laws barring age discrimination. Faced with an electorate that doggedly resisted tax increases, state and local officials bitterly resented these costly "federal mandates." They joined the chorus of those calling for a reduction in the size and scope of the federal government and the return of authority to the states.

In 1976 the National League of Cities persuaded the Supreme Court to rule unconstitutional the extension of the Fair Labor Standards Act to state and local government employees (*see National League of Cities v. Usery*, Document 107). But in 1985 the Court reversed its decision (see *Garcia v. San Antonio Metropolitan Transportation Authority*, Document 108). Governors, mayors, and state legislators then turned to Congress for relief. By 1990, fifteen state legislatures had passed a resolution, framed by the Council of State Governments, calling for constitutional amendments to revitalize state rights.

Council of State Governments, Resolution on Restoring Balance in the Federal System (1989)

Restoring Balance in the Federal System

1) Whereas, there has been a significant increase in recent decades of federal preemption of state and local authority, crossover grant-in-aid sanctions, and intrusions into state and local revenue-raising abilities; and

Intergovernmental Affairs Committee of the Council of State Governments, *Resolution to the CSG Executive Committee on Restoring Balance in the Federal System* (Adopted by the CSG Executive Committee, September 23, 1989) (Council of State Governments, P.O. Box 11910, Lexington, KY 40578; Washington Office, Hall of the States, 444 N. Capitol St., Washington, DC 20001).

2) Whereas, the federal government is promoting a lack of accountability in the federal system by mandating programs for which state and local governments must raise the revenue to pay the bills; and

3) Whereas, state and local governments have continuously modernized their fiscal, administrative, and governmental systems to respond to the needs of today's citizens, thereby making state and local governments centers of experimentation and innovation; and

4) Whereas, contrary to the constitutional design of our 200-year-old federal system, recent U.S. Supreme Court rulings have practically rendered the Tenth Amendment to the U.S. Constitution null and void by declaring that the states must look to the Congress, not to the courts, for protection against federal encroachments upon the reserved powers of the states; and

5) Whereas, the method of state-initiated amendment proposals under Article V of the U.S. Constitution that was established by our forefathers to help protect the states from unwarranted federal usurpation of their reserved powers has not worked because of its requirement of a Constitutional Convention; and

6) Whereas, the National Governor's Association, the U.S. Conference of Mayors, the National Association of Counties, the U.S. Advisory Commission on Intergovernmental Relations, affiliates of the Council of State Governments, and numerous other national organizations of state and local officials have expressed support for constitutional remedies to foster a more balanced approach to state-federal relations; . . .

10) Therefore, be it . . . resolved, that the Council of State Governments recommends the [following] two proposals for approval. . . .

A Concurrent Resolution

Whereas, the Tenth Amendment, part of the original Bill of Rights, reads as follows, "The powers not delegated to the United States by the Constitution, nor prohibited by it to the States, are reserved to the States respectively, or to the people"; and . . .

Whereas, the method of State-initiated amendment proposals under Article V of the U.S. Constitution that was established by our forefathers to help protect the states from unwarranted federal usurpation of their reserved powers has not worked because of its requirement of a Constitutional Convention; and

Whereas, . . . U.S. Supreme Court decisions invite further Federal preemption of State authority; now

Therefore, be it resolved by the State Legislature of _____ *that it is the* consensus of this body to affirm that the Tenth Amendment is a substantive limit on national power and should so be applied as a test by the Courts of the United States and of the several states in the cases coming before them where a question of the exercise of the federal authority is raised; and

Be it further resolved that consideration be given to modification of Article V of the Constitution to authorize specific, state-initiated amendments subject to Congressional veto.

CHAPTER 19

The Supreme Court and Conservative Constitutionalism

The Burger Court

100 ∞

The liberal activism of the Warren Court slowly waned after the conservative Warren E. Burger succeeded Earl Warren as chief justice. However, for the most part the Burger Court consolidated and rationalized the liberal decisions of the 1950s and 1960s rather than reversing them, especially at first. *Lemon v. Kurtzman* is a good example. In this case the Court analyzed its previous decisions applying the Establishment Clause of the First Amendment and discerned a three-pronged test for determining when government had gone too far in working with religious organizations or accommodating religious beliefs.

The case involved a Rhode Island law that supplemented the pay of educators teaching secular subjects in religious schools and a Pennsylvania law under which the state reimbursed religious schools for the entire cost of teaching secular subjects. The Court found that the programs created an "excessive entanglement" between church and state. The stress on excessive entanglement seemed to reflect a continued commitment to the idea that the First Amendment required strict separation of church and state rather than accommodation of religion by the state.

Lemon v. Kurtzman (1971)

M R . C H I E F Justice Burger delivered the opinion of the Court. . . .

In the absence of precisely stated constitutional prohibitions, we must draw lines with reference to the three main evils against which the Establish-

403 U.S. 602 (1971).

256

ment Clause was intended to afford protection: "sponsorship, financial support, and active involvement of the sovereign in religious activity." . . .

Every analysis in this area must begin with consideration of the cumulative criteria developed by the Court over many years. Three such tests may be gleaned from our cases. First, the statute must have a secular legislative purpose; second, its principal or primary effect must be one that neither advances nor inhibits religion . . . ; finally, the statute must not foster "an excessive government entanglement with religion." . . .

. . . [W]e conclude that the cumulative impact of the entire relationship arising under the statutes in each State involves excessive entanglement between government and religion. . . .

Our prior holdings do not call for total separation between church and state; total separation is not possible in an absolute sense. Some relationship between government and religious organizations is inevitable. . . . Fire inspections, building and zoning regulations, and state requirements under compulsory school-attendance laws are examples of necessary and permissible contacts. . . . [T]he line of separation, far from being a "wall," is a blurred, indistinct, and variable barrier depending on all the circumstances of a particular relationship. . . .

In order to determine whether the government entanglement with religion is excessive, we must examine the character and purposes of the institutions that are benefited, the nature of the aid that the State provides, and the resulting relationship between the government and the religious authority. . . . Here we find that both statutes foster an impermissible degree of entanglement.

101 ᴏᴡ

The Burger Court proved much less sensitive than the Warren Court to the discriminatory effects of poverty in the United States. In the crucial case of *San Antonio Independent School District v. Rodriguez,* parents in one of the poorest school districts challenged the way that Texas and most other states financed their public education systems. Texas supplemented every school district's local revenues with enough money to reach a minimal expenditure per student; each district could augment this amount through local taxes. Of course, wealthier districts could raise more extra money than poor ones, even with lower tax rates; thus the wealthier school districts maintained far superior schools.

The plaintiff's lawyers argued that the Texas system effectively discriminated against the poor. They urged the Court to consider wealth a "suspect classification" requiring special judicial scrutiny under the Equal Protection Clause of the Fourteenth Amendment, just like laws classifying by race, gender, religion, or ethnic origin. They argued further that education was a "fundamental right," which also would raise the level of scrutiny that the justices would apply to the law.

However, the majority of the justices rejected the arguments. Had they not, they would have opened huge new vistas for federal judicial intervention on behalf of the disadvantaged. Despite the Court's decision, many state courts have since found such educational financing systems to violate state constitutional provisions that guarantee a right to education.

The case also illustrates the terms in which the Burger Court analyzed cases involving civil rights and liberties. Laws affecting "fundamental liberties" required "strict scrutiny" to see whether they served "compelling" state interests. Laws that made "suspect classifications" required similar scrutiny. See *Roe v. Wade* (Document 86) and *Craig v. Boren* (Document 90) for similar terms of analysis. Finally, the opinion manifested the Court's growing concern with protecting state autonomy in the federal system.

San Antonio Independent School District v. Rodriguez (1973)

M R . J U S T I C E Powell delivered the opinion of the Court. . . .

[A]ppellees' suit asks this Court to extend its most exacting scrutiny to review a system that allegedly discriminates against a large, diverse, and amorphous class, unified only by the common factor of residence in districts that happen to have less taxable wealth than other districts. The system of alleged discrimination and the class it defines have none of the traditional indicia of suspectness: the class is not saddled with such disabilities, or subjected to such a history of purposeful unequal treatment, or relegated to such a position of political powerlessness as to command extraordinary protection from the majoritarian political process.

We thus conclude that the Texas system does not operate to the peculiar disadvantage of any suspect class. But in recognition of the fact that this Court has never heretofore held that wealth discrimination alone provides an adequate basis for invoking strict scrutiny, appellees have not relied solely on this contention. They also assert that the State's system impermissibly interferes with the exercise of a "fundamental" right and that accordingly the prior decisions of this Court require the application of the strict standard of judicial review. . . .

Nothing this Court holds today in any way detracts from our historic dedication to public education. We are in complete agreement with the conclusion of the three-judge panel below that "the grave significance of education both to the individual and to our society" cannot be doubted. But the importance of a service performed by the State does not determine whether it must

411 U.S. 1 (1973).

be regarded as fundamental for purposes of examination under the Equal Protection Clause. . . .

. . . [I]f the degree of judicial scrutiny of state legislation fluctuated depending on a majority's view of the importance of the interest affected, we would have gone "far toward making this Court a 'super-legislature.'" . . . We would, indeed, then be assuming a legislative role and one for which the Court lacks both authority and competence. . . .

. . . It is not the province of this Court to create substantive constitutional rights in the name of guaranteeing equal protection of the laws. Thus, the key to discovering whether education is "fundamental" is not to be found in comparisons of the relative societal significance of education as opposed to subsistence or housing. . . . Rather, the answer lies in assessing whether there is a right to education explicitly or implicitly guaranteed by the Constitution. . . .

Education, of course, is not among the rights afforded explicit protection under our Federal Constitution. Nor do we find any basis for saying it is implicitly so protected. . . .

It must be remembered, also, that every claim arising under the Equal Protection Clause has implications for the relationship between national and state power under our federal system. Questions of federalism are always inherent in the process of determining whether a State's laws are to be accorded the traditional presumption of constitutionality, or are to be subjected instead to rigorous judicial scrutiny. While "[t]he maintenance of the principles of federalism is a foremost consideration in interpreting any of the pertinent constitutional provisions under which this Court examines state action," it would be difficult to imagine a case having a greater potential impact on our federal system than the one now before us, in which we are urged to abrogate systems of financing public education presently in existence in virtually every State.

The foregoing considerations buttress our conclusion that Texas' system of public school finance is an inappropriate candidate for strict judicial scrutiny. . . .

. . . Because of differences in expenditure levels occasioned by disparities in property tax income, appellees claim that children in less affluent districts have been made the subject of invidious discrimination. The District Court found that the State had failed even "to establish a reasonable basis" for a system that results in different levels of per-pupil expenditure. We disagree. . . .

. . . While it is no doubt true that reliance on local property taxation for school revenues provides less freedom of choice with respect to expenditures for some districts than for others, the existence of "some inequality" in the manner in which the State's rationale is achieved is not alone a sufficent basis for striking down the entire system. . . .

. . . It has simply never been within the constitutional prerogative of this

Court to nullify statewide measures for financing public services merely because the burdens or benefits thereof fall unevenly depending upon the relative wealth of the political subdivisions in which citizens live.

In sum, to the extent that the Texas system of school financing results in unequal expenditures between children who happen to reside in different districts, we cannot say that such disparities are the product of a system that is so irrational as to be invidiously discriminatory. . . .

Mr. Justice Marshall, with whom Mr. Justice Douglas concurs, dissenting.

The Court today decides, in effect, that a State may constitutionally vary the quality of education which it offers its children in accordance with the amount of taxable wealth located in the school districts within which they reside. . . . The Court does this despite the absence of any substantial justification for a scheme which arbitrarily channels educational resources in accordance with the fortuity of the amount of taxable wealth within each district.

In my judgment, the right of every American to an equal start in life, so far as the provision of a state service as important as education is concerned, is far too vital to permit state discrimination on grounds as tenuous as those presented by this record. . . .

I . . . cannot accept the majority's labored efforts to demonstrate that fundamental interests, which call for strict scrutiny of the challenged classification, encompass only established rights which we are somehow bound to recognize from the text of the Constitution itself. . . .

. . . The task in every case should be to determine the extent to which constitutionally guaranteed rights are dependent on interests not mentioned in the Constitution. . . . Only if we closely protect the related interests from state discrimination do we ultimately ensure the integrity of the constitutional guarantee itself. . . .

. . . [T]he relationship between education and the social and political interests enshrined within the Constitution, compel us to recognize the fundamentality of education and to scrutinize with appropriate care the bases for state discrimination affecting equality of educational opportunity in Texas' school districts—a conclusion which is only strengthened when we consider the character of the classification in this case. . . .

. . . [D]iscrimination on the basis of group wealth in this case likewise calls for careful judicial scrutiny. . . . [I]t must be recognized that while local district wealth may serve other interests, it bears no relationship whatsoever to the interest of Texas school children in the educational opportunity afforded them by the State of Texas. Given the importance of that interest, we must be particularly sensitive to the invidious characteristics of any form of discrimination that is not clearly intended to serve it, as opposed to some other distinct state interest. . . .

The only justification offered by appellants to sustain the discrimination in educational opportunity caused by the Texas financing scheme is local educational control. Presented with this justification, the District Court concluded that "[n]ot only are defendants unable to demonstrate compelling state interests for their classifications based upon wealth, they fail even to establish a reasonable basis for these classifications." . . . I must agree with this conclusion.

. . . [O]n this record, it is apparent that the State's purported concern with local control is offered primarily as an excuse rather than as a justification for interdistrict inequality. . . .

In my judgment, any substantial degree of scrutiny of the operation of the Texas financing scheme reveals that the State has selected means wholly inappropriate to secure its purported interest in assuring its school districts local fiscal control.

102 ❧

The Burger Court proved most hostile to the libertarianism of the Warren Court in the area of criminal procedure. Its decisions made clear that the majority of the justices were less sensitive to the ways in which the criminal-justice system discriminated against the poor, the uneducated, and members of various minority groups. In *Furman v. Georgia,* 408 U.S. 238 (1972), the Court—still manifesting its Warren-era activism—ruled most states' death-penalty procedures unconstitutional. Some of the justices held that capital punishment was inconsistent with society's evolving idea of what was "cruel and unusual" and therefore violated the Eighth Amendment. Others found that the sentencing process permitted too random a pattern of decisions, and that this very randomness made the death penalty "cruel and unusual." Still others pointed to the overrepresentation of African Americans among those sentenced to death, which suggested a violation of the Fourteenth Amendment's Equal Protection Clause.

In the aftermath of the *Furman* decision, states rushed to enact sentencing regulations that would guard against the randomness condemned by several of the justices. In *Gregg v. Georgia,* the Court considered the new statutes and sustained them, now ruling explicitly that capital punishment itself was *not* inherently a violation of the Eighth Amendment. Dissents by Justices William J. Brennan and Thurgood Marshall indicated clearly that these two members of the old Warren Court majority were now isolated on criminal-procedure issues.

Gregg v. Georgia (1976)

J U D G E M E N T of the Court, and opinion of Mr. Justice Stewart, Mr. Justice Powell, and Mr. Justice Stevens. . . .

. . . We now consider specifically whether the sentence of death for the

428 U.S. 153 (1976).

crime of murder is a per se violation of the Eighth and Fourteenth Amendments to the Constitution. . . . [H]istory and precedent strongly support a negative answer to this question. . . .

It is apparent from the text of the Constitution itself that the existence of capital punishment was accepted by the Framers. . . .

For nearly two centuries, this Court, repeatedly and often expressly, has recognized that capital punishment is not invalid per se. . . .

Four years ago, the petitioners in Furman and its companion cases predicated their argument primarily upon the asserted proposition that standards of decency had evolved to the point where capital punishment no longer could be tolerated. . . .

The petitioners in the capital cases before the Court today renew the "standards of decency" argument, but developments during the four years since Furman have undercut substantially the assumptions upon which their argument rested. Despite the continuing debate, dating back to the 19th century, over the morality and utility of capital punishment, it is now evident that a large proportion of American society continues to regard it as an appropriate and necessary criminal sanction. . . .

. . . [H]owever, the Eighth Amendment demands more than that a challenged punishment be acceptable to contemporary society. The Court also must ask whether it comports with the basic concept of human dignity at the core of the Amendment. . . .

The death penalty is said to serve two principal social purposes: retribution and deterrence of capital crimes by prospective offenders.

In part, capital punishment is an expression of society's moral outrage at particularly offensive conduct. This function may be unappealing to many, but it is essential in an ordered society that asks its citizens to rely on legal processes rather than self-help to vindicate their wrongs. . . . "Retribution is no longer the dominant objective of the criminal law," . . . but neither is it a forbidden objective nor one inconsistent with our respect for the dignity of men. . . .

Statistical attempts to evaluate the worth of the death penalty as a deterrent to crimes by potential offenders have occasioned a great deal of debate. The results simply have been inconclusive. . . .

In sum, we cannot say that the judgment of the Georgia legislature that capital punishment may be necessary in some cases is clearly wrong. Considerations of federalism, as well as respect for the ability of a legislature to evaluate, in terms of its particular state the moral consensus concerning the death penalty and its social utility as a sanction, require us to conclude, in the absence of more convincing evidence, that the infliction of death as a punishment for murder is not without justification and thus is not unconstitutionally severe. . . .

While Furman did not hold that the infliction of the death penalty per se violates the Constitution's ban on cruel and unusual punishments, it did recognize that the penalty of death is different in kind from any other punishment imposed under our system of criminal justice. Because of the uniqueness of the death penalty, Furman held that it could not be imposed under sentencing procedures that created a substantial risk that it would be inflicted in an arbitrary and capricious manner. . . .

Furman mandates that where discretion is afforded a sentencing body on a matter so grave as the determination of whether a human life should be taken or spared, that discretion must be suitably directed and limited so as to minimize the risk of wholly arbitrary and capricious action. . . .

. . . [T]he concerns expressed in Furman that the penalty of death not be imposed in an arbitrary or capricious manner can be met by a carefully drafted statute that ensures that the sentencing authority is given adequate information and guidance. As a general proposition these concerns are best met by a system that provides for a bifurcated proceeding at which the sentencing authority is apprised of the information relevant to the imposition of sentence and provided with standards to guide its use of the information. . . .

Mr. Justice Brennan, dissenting. . . .

. . . My opinion in Furman v. Georgia concluded that our civilization and the law had progressed to this point and that therefore the punishment of death, for whatever crime and under all circumstances, is "cruel and unusual" in violation of the Eighth and Fourteenth Amendments of the Constitution. . . . [I]nherent in the Clause is the primary moral principle that the State, even as it punishes, must treat its citizens in a manner consistent with their intrinsic worth as human beings—a punishment must not be so severe as to be degrading to human dignity. . . .

The fatal constitutional infirmity in the punishment of death is that it treats "members of the human race as nonhumans, as objects to be toyed with and discarded. [It is] thus inconsistent with the fundamental premise of the Clause that even the vilest criminal remains a human being possessed of common human dignity."

103 ∾

As conservative constitutionalism revived in the 1970s and 1980s, the Exclusionary Rule (see Document 91) came under increasing attack. Calling for its entire elimination, conservatives urged at least a broad exception to it where police investigators made "honest mistakes" of judgment. After all, they argued, the rule's chief purpose was to deter police wrongdoing, and it could not serve this function in cases where law-enforcement officers honestly thought they had complied with constitutional requirements. Indicating its diminishing concern for the protection of the rights of criminal suspects, the Burger Court in *U.S. v. Leon* created a "good-faith exception" in cases where judges mistakenly issued improper search warrants; such cases did not involve police misconduct. *U.S. v. Leon* was typical of criminal-procedure cases in which the Burger Court widened the circumstances in which improperly secured evidence or confessions could be used against defendants in court.

U.S. v. Leon (1984)

M R . J U S T I C E White* delivered the opinion of the Court. . . .

The substantial social costs exacted by the exclusionary rule for the vindication of Fourth Amendment rights have long been a source of concern. "Our cases have consistently recognized that unbending application of the exclusionary sanction to enforce ideals of government rectitude would impede unacceptably the truth-finding functions of judge and jury." . . . An objectionable collateral consequence of this interference with the criminal justice system's truth-finding function is that some guilty defendants may go free or receive reduced sentences as a result of favorable plea bargains. Particularly when law enforcement officers have acted in objective good faith or their transgressions have been minor, the magnitude of the benefit conferred on such guilty defendants offends basic concepts of the criminal justice system. . . .

. . . To the extent that proponents of exclusion rely on its behavioral effects on judges and magistrates in these areas, their reliance is misplaced. First, the exclusionary rule is designed to deter police misconduct rather than to punish the errors of judges and magistrates. Second, there exists no evidence suggesting that judges and magistrates are inclined to ignore or subvert the Fourth Amendment or that lawlessness among these actors requires application of the extreme sanction of exclusion.

Third, and most important, we discern no basis, and are offered none, for believing that exclusion of evidence seized pursuant to a warrant will have a significant deterrent effect on the issuing judge or magistrate. Many of the factors that indicate that the exclusionary rule cannot provide an effective "special" or "general" deterrent for individual offending law enforcement officers apply as well to judges or magistrates. And, to the extent that the rule is thought to operate as a "systemic" deterrent on a wider audience, it clearly can have no such effect on individuals empowered to issue search warrants.

468 U.S. 897 (1984).

*In October of 1980, the Supreme Court Reports ceased referring to the members of the Court as "Mr. Justice," turning to "Justice" as a gender-neutral term of respect.

Judges and magistrates are not adjuncts to the law enforcement team; as neutral judicial officers, they have no stake in the outcome of particular criminal prosecutions. The threat of exclusion thus cannot be expected significantly to deter them. . . .

We have frequently questioned whether the exclusionary rule can have any deterrent effect when the offending officers acted in the objectively reasonable belief that their conduct did not violate the Fourth Amendment. "No empirical researcher, proponent or opponent of the rule, has yet been able to establish with any assurance whether the rule has a deterrent effect." . . . But even assuming that the rule effectively deters some police misconduct and provides incentives for the law enforcement profession as a whole to conduct itself in accord with the Fourth Amendment, it cannot be expected, and should not be applied, to deter objectively reasonable law enforcement activity. . . .

This is particularly true, we believe, when an officer acting with objective good faith has obtained a search warrant from a judge or magistrate and acted within its scope. In most such cases, there is no police illegality and thus nothing to deter. . . .

We conclude that the marginal or nonexistent benefits produced by suppressing evidence obtained in objectively reasonable reliance on a subsequently invalidated search warrant cannot justify the substantial costs of exclusion.

104 ∽

The Burger Court was less sensitive than the Warren Court to the effects of racial discrimination in American life. More concerned than the Warren Court about consistency and rationality in its decisions, the Burger Court had trouble reconciling affirmative-action programs designed to help minority groups with the commitment to a color-blind Constitution that seemed to lie at the heart of the Court's Fourteenth Amendment jurisprudence. At the same time, the justices were aware that such preferences for members of minorities were coming under increasing political attack from resurgent conservatives.

The problem came to a head in the *Bakke* case, which involved the affirmative-action program established by the medical school of the University of California at Davis. The program set aside a fixed number of places for members of specified minority groups. The Court divided badly. Four conservative justices said that the Civil Rights Act of 1964 forbade the exclusion of *any* individual from an educational institution on racial grounds. Four more-liberal justices argued that a "benign" discrimination need not be subjected to the Court's strictest scrutiny, but merely to "heightened" scrutiny. Such a law could be sustained if it served important state interests and did not unduly burden those least represented in the political process—usually members of minority groups. This allowed Justice Lewis F. Powell, the swing vote, to fashion the following Court opinion, which sustained affirmative action to promote diversity but precluded the use of rigid quotas.

Regents of University of California v. Bakke (1978)

MR. JUSTICE Powell announced the judgment of the Court. . . .

Petitioner does not deny that decisions based on race or ethnic origin by faculties and administrations of state universities are reviewable under the Fourteenth Amendment. . . . For his part, respondent does not argue that all racial or ethnic classifications are per se invalid. . . . The parties do disagree as to the level of judicial scrutiny to be applied to the special admissions program. Petitioner argues that the court below erred in applying strict scrutiny, as this inexact term has been applied in our cases. That level of review, petitioner asserts, should be reserved for classifications that disadvantage "discrete and insular minorities." . . . Respondent, on the other hand, contends that the California court correctly rejected the notion that the degree of judicial scrutiny accorded a particular racial or ethnic classification hinges upon membership in a discrete and insular minority and duly recognized that the "rights established [by the Fourteenth Amendment] are personal rights." . . .

This semantic distinction is beside the point; The special admissions program is undeniably a classification based on race and ethnic background. . . .

The guarantees of the Fourteenth Amendment extend to all persons. Its language is explicit: "No State shall . . . deny to any person within its jurisdiction the equal protection of the laws." It is settled beyond question that the "rights created by the first section of the Fourteenth Amendment are, by its terms, guraranteed to the individual. The rights established are personal rights." . . . The guarantee of equal protection cannot mean one thing when applied to one individual and something else when applied to a person of another color. If both are not accorded the same protection, then it is not equal. . . .

. . . Racial and ethnic distinctions of any sort are inherently suspect and thus call for the most exacting judicial examination. . . .

. . . Because the landmark decisions in this area arose in response to the continued exclusion of Negroes from the mainstream of American society, they could be characterized as involving discrimination by the "majority" white race against the Negro minority. But they need not be read as depending upon that characterization for their results. It suffices to say that "[o]ver the years, this Court has consistently repudiated '[d]istinctions between citizens solely because of their ancestry' as being 'odious to a free people whose institutions are founded upon the doctrine of equality.'" . . .

438 U.S. 265 (1978).

Petitioner urges us to adopt for the first time a more restrictive view of the Equal Protection Clause and hold that discrimination against members of the white "majority" cannot be suspect if its purpose can be characterized as "benign." The clock of our liberties, however, cannot be turned back to 1868. . . . It is far too late to argue that the guarantee of equal protection to *all* persons permits the recognition of special wards entitled to a degree of protection greater than that accorded others. . . .

We have held that in "order to justify the use of a suspect classification, a State must show that its purpose or interest is both constitutionally permissible and substantial, and that its use of the classification is 'necessary . . . to the accomplishment' of its purpose or the safeguarding of its interest." . . .

If petitioner's purpose is to assure within its student body some specified percentage of a particular group merely because of its race or ethnic origin, such a preferential purpose must be rejected not as insubstantial but as facially invalid. Preferring members of any one group for no reason other than race or ethnic origin is discrimination for its own sake. This the Constitution forbids. . . .

The State certainly has a legitimate and substantial interest in ameliorating, or eliminating where feasible, the disabling effects of identified discrimination. . . .

We have never approved a classification that aids persons perceived as members of relatively victimized groups at the expense of other innocent individuals in the absence of judicial, legislative, or administrative findings of constitutional or statutory violations. . . . After such findings have been made, the governmental interest in preferring members of the injured groups at the expense of others is substantial, since the legal rights of the victims must be vindicated. . . . Without such findings of constitutional or statutory violations, it cannot be said that the government has any greater interest in helping one individual than in refraining from harming another. . . .

Petitioner does not purport to have made, and is in no position to make, such findings. . . .

Hence, the purpose of helping certain groups whom the faculty of the Davis Medical School perceived as victims of "societal discrimination" does not justify a classification that imposes disadvantages upon persons like respondent, who bear no responsibility for whatever harm the beneficiaries of the special admissions program are thought to have suffered. . . .

The fourth goal asserted by petitioner is the attainment of a diverse student body. This clearly is a constitutionally permissible goal for an institution of higher education. . . .

The atmosphere of "speculation, experiment and creation"—so essential to the quality of higher education—is widely believed to be promoted by a diverse student body. . . .

Thus, in arguing that its universities must be accorded the right to select those students who will contribute the most to the "robust exchange of ideas," petitioner invokes a countervailing constitutional interest, that of the First Amendment. In this light, petitioner must be viewed as seeking to achieve a goal that is of paramount importance in the fulfillment of its mission. . . .

It may be assumed that the reservation of a specified number of seats in each class for individuals from the preferred ethnic groups would contribute to the attainment of considerable ethnic diversity in the student body. But petitioner's argument that this is the only effective means of serving the interest of diversity is seriously flawed. . . .

The experience of other university admissions programs, which take race into account in achieving the educational diversity valued by the First Amendment, demonstrates that the assignment of a fixed number of places to a minority group is not a necessary means toward that end. . . .

In such an admissions program, race or ethnic background may be deemed a "plus" in a particular applicant's file, yet it does not insulate the individual from comparison with all other candidates for the available seats. . . .

The fatal flaw in petitioner's preferential program is its disregard of individual rights as guaranteed by the Fourteenth Amendment. . . . Such rights are not absolute. But when a State's distribution of benefits or imposition of burdens hinges on ancestry or the color of a person's skin, . . . that individual is entitled to a demonstration that the challenged classification is necessary to promote a substantial state interest. Petitioner has failed to carry this burden. For this reason, that portion of the California court's judgment holding petitioner's special admissions program invalid under the Fourteenth Amendment must be affirmed.

In enjoining petitioner from ever considering the race of any applicant, however, the courts below failed to recognize that the State has a substantial interest that legitimately may be served by a properly devised admissions program involving the competitive consideration of race and ethnic origin. For this reason, so much of the California court's judgment as enjoins petitioner from any consideration of the race of any applicant must be reversed.

105 ∾

Conservative jurisprudents vigorously criticized the Warren Court's freedom-of-religion decisions and the so-called *Lemon* Test that rationalized them (see Document 100). Because it was being applied to maintain strict separation of church and state, conservatives complained that the *Lemon* Test was hostile to religion, and they urged the Court to repudiate it. They insisted that the Revolutionary generation had been committed to spiritual values. The founders had understood freedom of religion to mean no special preference for any sect but sympathy for all; they had not intended the First Amendment to erect a "wall" between church and state. Rather, the amendment should be read to accommodate the fact that Americans are a religious, mostly Christian people.

The decision in *Lynch v. Donnelly* made clear that by the 1980s the "accommodationist" view was making headway among the justices. The case involved a challenge to a traditional Christmas display, including a nativity scene, or "crèche," placed in a park in the shopping district of Pawtucket, Rhode Island. Such a display was plainly a reference to, and endorsement of, Christianity, the plaintiffs insisted. Rejecting the argument, the conservative majority on the Court devalued the *Lemon* Test, stating it was just one of many approaches the Court had used to analyze First Amendment cases. Yet at the same time, the analysis seemed to fit within the *Lemon* framework. Instead of explicitly repudiating the *Lemon* Test, the Court seemed to reinterpret its excessive-entanglement prong to permit far more accommodation of religion than would have been tolerated under a strict-separation standard.

In the following decade, justices often expressed unhappiness with the *Lemon* Test, but the Court never explicitly repudiated it, leaving the status of the test unclear.

Lynch v. Donnelly (1984)

CHIEF JUSTICE Burger delivered the opinion of the Court. . . .

. . . In every Establishment Clause case, we must reconcile the inescapable tension between the objective of preventing unnecessary intrusion of either the church or the state upon the other, and the reality that, as the Court has so often noted, total separation of the two is not possible. . . .

There is an unbroken history of official acknowledgment by all three branches of government of the role of religion in American life from at least 1789. Seldom in our opinions was this more affirmatively expressed than in Justice Douglas' opinion for the Court validating a program allowing release of school students from classes to attend off-campus religious exercises. Rejecting a claim that the program violated the Establishment Clause, the Court asserted pointedly:

> "We are a religious people whose institutions presuppose a Supreme Being." Zorach v. Clauson. . . .

This history may help explain why the Court consistently has declined to take a rigid, absolutist view of the Establishment Clause. . . .

Rather than mechanically invalidating all governmental conduct or statutes that confer benefits or give special recognition to religion in general or to one faith—as an absolutist approach would dictate—the Court has scrutinized challenged legislation or official conduct to determine whether, in reality, it establishes a religion or religious faith, or tends to do so. . . .

465 U.S. 668 (1984).

In each case, the inquiry calls for line-drawing; no fixed, per se rule can be framed. . . .

In the line-drawing process we have often found it useful to inquire whether the challenged law or conduct has a secular purpose, whether its principal or primary effect is to advance or inhibit religion, and whether it creates an excessive entanglement of government with religion. But, we have repeatedly emphasized our unwillingness to be confined to any single test or criterion in this sensitive area. . . .

In this case, the focus of our inquiry must be on the crèche in the context of the Christmas season. . . .

The narrow question is whether there is a secular purpose for Pawtucket's display of the crèche. The display is sponsored by the city to celebrate the Holiday and to depict the origins of that Holiday. These are legitimate secular purposes. . . .

We are unable to discern a greater aid to religion deriving from inclusion of the crèche than from [the] benefits and endorsements previously held not violative of the Establishment Clause. What was said about the legislative prayers . . . and implied about the Sunday Closing Laws . . . is true of the city's inclusion of the crèche: its "reason or effect merely happens to coincide or harmonize with the tenets of some . . . religions."

. . . [O]ur precedents plainly contemplate that on occasion some advance-ment of religion will result from governmental action. The Court has made it abundantly clear, however, that "not every law that confers an 'indirect,' 're-mote,' or 'incidental' benefit upon [religion] is, for that reason alone, consti-tutionally invalid." . . .

Entanglement is a question of kind and degree. . . . There is no evidence of contact with church authorities concerning the content or design of the ex-hibit prior to or since Pawtucket's purchase of the crèche. No expenditures for maintenance of the crèche have been necessary. . . . There is nothing here, of course, like the "comprehensive, discriminating, and continu-ing state surveillance" or the "enduring entanglement" present in Lemon. . . .

We are satisfied that the city has a secular purpose for including the crèche, that the city has not impermissibly advanced religion, and that including the crèche does not create excessive entanglement between religion and govern-ment.

106 ~

With its decisions in *U.S. v. Darby* (1941) and *Wickard v. Filburn* (1942) (see Documents 70 and 71), the Supreme Court seemed to have abandoned state rights as a significant re-striction on federal action. The effort to use state-rights arguments to resist the Supreme

Court's desegregation decisions and to oppose congressional civil rights legislation strengthened most Americans' commitment to nationalist ideas of federalism. Congress became less and less likely even to articulate an interstate-commerce justification for its legislation, simply assuming that any federal regulation would be sustained against a state rights–based challenge. At the same time, federal district and circuit courts became more and more aggressive in interfering with state court proceedings when they seemed to impair civil liberties and civil rights.

The civil rights conflict made federal judges acutely aware of how state courts could be used to suppress those who deviated from majority norms, and how difficult and expensive it was to appeal such decisions through the state court system and finally to the Supreme Court. Moreover, civil libertarians recognized that the Supreme Court's docket was too full to permit it to review all the state court decisions that upheld state actions of doubtful constitutionality. When the Court agreed in *Dombrowski v. Pfister*, 380 U.S. 499 (1965), that the lower federal courts could prohibit the enforcement of state laws that they believed unconstitutional, civil libertarians took full advantage. They went directly to federal courts to prevent enforcement of state legislation, and federal judges regularly obliged by enjoining it, sometimes halting state court proceedings after they had begun. In effect, the federal courts had assumed a direct supervisory power over state courts.

In *Younger v. Harris*, the Court rejected such direct federal supervision of state authorities, depriving civil libertarians of a potent tool for the protection of rights. The federal courts could intervene only when the state proceedings were designed to harass the defendants. In the following decades, the Burger and Rehnquist Courts would progressively narrow the power of the federal courts to intervene in state court proceedings, especially in ordinary criminal cases (where the conservative justices showed slight concern for the rights of the accused anyway), until intervention in such cases became almost impossible.

Of particular importance was the language of Justice Hugo Black's opinion for the Court in *Younger v. Harris*. Black's opinion was a paean to "Our Federalism"—the most passionate defense of state autonomy since the New Deal revolution in constitutional interpretation. It signaled a renewed concern among the justices for maintaining a separate sphere for state authority.

Younger v. Harris (1971)

M R . J U S T I C E Black delivered the opinion of the Court....

Since the beginning of this country's history Congress has, subject to few exceptions, manifested a desire to permit state courts to try state cases free from interference by federal courts....

The precise reasons for this longstanding public policy against federal court interference with state court proceedings have never been specifically identified but the primary sources of the policy are plain. One is the basic doctrine of equity jurisprudence that courts of equity should not act, and particularly should not act to restrain a criminal prosecution, when the mov-

401 U.S. 37 (1971).

ing party has an adequate remedy at law and will not suffer irreparable injury if denied equitable relief. . . . This underlying reason for restraining courts of equity from interfering with criminal prosecutions is reinforced by an even more vital consideration, the notion of "comity," that is, a proper respect for state functions, a recognition of the fact that the entire country is made up of a Union of separate state governments, and a continuance of the belief that the National Government will fare best if the States and their institutions are left free to perform their separate functions in their separate ways. This, perhaps for lack of a better and clearer way to describe it, is referred to by many as "Our Federalism," and one familiar with the profound debates that ushered our Federal Constitution into existence is bound to respect those who remain loyal to the ideals and dreams of "Our Federalism." The concept does not mean blind deference to "States' Rights" any more than it means centralization of control over every important issue in our National Government and its courts. The Framers rejected both these courses. What the concept does represent is a system in which there is sensitivity to the legitimate interests of both State and National Governments, and in which the National Government, anxious though it may be to vindicate and protect federal rights and federal interests, always endeavors to do so in ways that will not unduly interfere with the legitimate activities of the States. It should never be forgotten that this slogan, "Our Federalism," born in the early struggling days of our Union of States, occupies a highly important place in our Nation's history and its future.

107 ⌒⌒

In 1974, responding to the demands of labor unions representing state, county, and municipal workers, Congress extended the coverage of the minimum-wage and maximum-hours provisions of the Fair Labor Standards Act to the employees of state and local governments. Faced with rising costs in a declining economy, state and local officials complained bitterly about federal interference (see Document 99). Their complaints resonated with growing calls from conservatives for renewed attention to state rights and decentralization of governmental power. The National League of Cities, representing municipal officials, challenged the constitutionality of the amendment, saying that it went to the heart of state sovereignty by implying complete subordination of state and local government to federal authority. The league sued despite the fact that the Court had upheld the application of other provisions of the Fair Labor Standards Act to the states in *Maryland v. Wirz*, 392 U.S. 183 (1968).

In a decision that astounded informed observers, the majority of the justices agreed with the plaintiffs, overruling *Maryland v. Wirz*. For the first time since the New Deal, the Court overturned federal legislation for invading state rights. Although the Court could not bring itself explicitly to say that the Tenth Amendment limited expressly delegated federal power, it quoted—out of context—language from other cases that appeared to do so. The decision was patently inconsistent with *U.S. v. Darby*'s conclusion that the Tenth Amendment was "but a truism that all is retained which has not been surrendered" (see Document 70).

National League of Cities v. Usery (1976)

$\mathbf{M}$ R . J U S T I C E Rehnquist delivered the opinion of the Court. . . .

It is established beyond peradventure that the Commerce Clause of Art. I of the Constitution is a grant of plenary authority to Congress. . . .

Appellants in no way challenge these decisions establishing the breadth of authority granted Congress under the commerce power. Their contention, on the contrary, is that when Congress seeks to regulate directly the activities of States as public employers, it transgresses an affirmative limitation on the exercise of its power akin to other commerce power affirmative limitations contained in the Constitution. Congressional enactments which may be fully within the grant of legislative authority contained in the Commerce Clause may nonetheless be invalid because [they are] found to offend against the right to trial by jury contained in the Sixth Amendment, or the Due Process Clause of the Fifth Amendment. . . . Appellants' essential contention is that the 1974 amendments to the Act, while undoubtedly within the scope of the Commerce Clause, encounter a similar constitutional barrier because they are to be applied directly to the States and subdivisions of States as employers.

This Court has never doubted that there are limits upon the power of Congress to override state sovereignty, even when exercising its otherwise plenary powers to tax or to regulate commerce. . . . In Fry [v. U.S.] . . . , the Court recognized that an express declaration of this limitation is found in the Tenth Amendment:

> "While the Tenth Amendment has been characterized as a 'truism,' stating merely that 'all is retained which has not been surrendered,' United States v. Darby, . . . it is not without significance. The Amendment expressly declares the constitutional policy that Congress may not exercise power in a fashion that impairs the States' integrity or their ability to function effectively in a federal system." . . .

The expressions in these more recent cases trace back to earlier decisions of this Court recognizing the essential role of the States in our federal system of

426 U.S. 833 (1976).

government. Mr. Chief Justice Chase, perhaps because of the particular time at which he occupied that office, had occasion more than once to speak for the Court on this point. In Texas v. White, . . . he declared that "[t]he Constitution, in all its provisions, looks to an indestructible Union, composed of indestructible States." In Lane County v. Oregon, . . . his opinon for the Court said:

"Both the States and the United States existed before the Constitution. . . . [I]n many articles of the Constitution the necessary existence of the States, and, within their proper spheres, the independent authority of the States, is distinctly recognized.". . . .

One undoubted attribute of state sovereignty is the States' power to determine the wages which shall be paid to those whom they employ in order to carry out their governmental functions, what hours those persons will work, and what compensation will be provided where these employees may be called upon to work overtime. The question we must resolve here, then, is whether these determinations are " 'functions essential to separate and independent existence,'". . . .

Judged solely in terms of increased costs in dollars, these allegations show a significant impact on the functioning of the governmental bodies involved. . . .

Quite apart from the substantial costs imposed upon the States and their political subdivisions, the Act displaces state policies regarding the manner in which they will structure delivery of those governmental services which their citizens require. . . . [I]t cannot be gainsaid that the federal requirement directly supplants the considered policy choices of the States' elected officials and administrators as to how they wish to structure pay scales in state employment. . . . The only "discretion" left to them under the Act is either to attempt to increase their revenue to meet the additional financial burden imposed upon them by paying congressionally prescribed wages to their existing complement of employees, or to reduce that complement to a number which can be paid the federal minimum wage without increasing revenue. . . .

Our examination of the effect of the 1974 amendments, as sought to be extended to the States and their political subdivisions, satisfies us that both the minimum wage and the maximum hour provisions will impermissibly interfere with the integral governmental functions of these bodies. . . . If Congress may withdraw from the States the authority to make those fundamental employment decisions upon which their systems for performance of these functions must rest, we think there would be little left of the States' " 'separate and independent existence.'" . . .

Mr. Justice Blackmun, concurring. . . .

. . . Although I am not untroubled by certain possible implications of the Court's opinion—some of them suggested by the dissents—I do not read the opinion so despairingly as does my Brother Brennan. . . . I may misinterpret the Court's opinion, but it seems to me that it adopts a balancing approach, and does not outlaw federal power in areas such as environmental protection, where the federal interest is demonstrably greater and where state facility compliance with imposed federal standards would be essential. . . .

Mr. Justice Brennan, with whom Mr. Justice White and Mr. Justice Marshall join, dissenting. . . .

The reliance of my Brethren upon the Tenth Amendment as "an express declaration of [a state sovereignty] limitation," . . . not only suggests that they overrule governing decisions of this Court that address this question but must astound scholars of the Constitution. For not only early decisions, Gibbons v. Ogden . . . ; McCulloch v. Maryland . . . ; and Martin v. Hunter's Lessee . . . , hold that nothing in the Tenth Amendment constitutes a limitation on congressional exercise of powers delegated by the Constitution to Congress. . . . Rather, as the Tenth Amendment's significance was more recently summarized:

> "The amendment states but a truism that all is retained which has not been surrendered. . . .
>
> "From the beginning and for many years the amendment has been construed as not depriving the national government of authority to resort to all means for the exercise of a granted power which are appropriate and plainly adapted to the permitted end." United States v. Darby. . . .

Today's repudiation of this unbroken line of precedents that firmly reject my Brethren's ill-conceived abstraction can only be regarded as a transparent cover for invalidating a congressional judgment with which they disagree. The only analysis even remotely resembling that adopted today is found in a line of opinions dealing with the Commerce Clause and the Tenth Amendment that ultimately provoked a constitutional crisis for the Court in the 1930's. . . .

I cannot recall another instance in the Court's history when the reasoning of so many decisions covering so long a span of time has been discarded in such a roughshod manner. . . .

My Brethren do more than turn aside longstanding constitutional jurisprudence that emphatically rejects today's conclusion. More alarming is the startling restructuring of our federal system, and the role they create therein for the federal judiciary. This Court is simply not at liberty to erect a mirror of its own conception of a desirable governmental structure. . . . It bears repeating "that effective restraints on . . . exercise [of the commerce power] must proceed from political rather than from judicial processes." . . .

Judicial restraint in this area merely recognizes that the political branches of our Government are structured to protect the interests of the States, as well as the Nation as a whole, and that the States are fully able to protect their own interests in the premises. Congress is constituted of representatives in both the Senate and House elected from the States. . . .

We are left then with a catastrophic judicial body blow at Congress' power under the Commerce Clause. . . . [T]here is an ominous portent of disruption of our constitutional structure implicit in today's mischievous decision.

108 ♫

The Supreme Court's decision in *National League of Cities v. Usery* (Document 107) led to a flood of state-rights challenges to federal legislation. Plaintiffs attacked the application to the states of laws forbidding age discrimination. They sought to enjoin laws that made federal financial support for state programs conditional on meeting various requirements; tried to overturn laws that required state officials to enforce federal environmental standards; attempted to nullify federal airport safety regulations, since airports were run by state and local authorities. Federal judges enjoined the enforcement of federal laws requiring companies to meet environmental and other standards, on the grounds that these subjects were within state jurisdiction. State and local agencies claimed that the *National League of Cities* decision exempted *all* of their workers from federal labor and safety regulations—including bus drivers and all other transportation employees, sanitation workers, teachers, social workers, and so on—approximately 15 percent of the entire workforce of the United States.

Although several conservative justices endorsed a full revival of state-rights constitutionalism, the majority rejected efforts to restrict federal authority. In doing so, the Court repeatedly attempted to define the point at which a federal law went too far in regulating state activities. In *Garcia v. San Antonio Metropolitan Transit Authority,* Justice Blackmun, who had with some hesitation concurred in the Court's earlier decision, finally gave up. The case involved San Antonio's claim that its transportation workers were not entitled to the protections of the Fair Labor Standards Act. A sharply divided Court overruled the troublesome precedent, with the dissenters vowing to revive it. In *New York v. U.S.,* 112 Supreme Court Reporter 2408 (1992), the Court returned to the state-rights approach of the National League of Cities Case, without overruling *Garcia,* however, and over the powerful dissent of four justices. Thus, the Court remains bitterly divided over the basic nature of the federal system.

Garcia v. San Antonio Metropolitan Transportation Authority (1985)

J U S T I C E Blackmun delivered the opinion of the Court.

We revisit in these cases an issue raised in National League of Cities v. Usery. . . . In that litigation, this Court, by a sharply divided vote, ruled that the Commerce Clause does not empower Congress to enforce the minimum-wage and overtime provisions of the Fair Labor Standards Act (FLSA) against the States "in areas of traditional governmental functions." . . . Although National League of Cities supplied some examples of "traditional governmental functions," it did not offer a general explanation of how a "traditional" function is to be distinguished from a "nontraditional" one. Since then, federal and state courts have struggled with the task, thus imposed, of identifying a traditional function for purposes of state immunity under the Commerce Clause. . . .

Our examination of this "function" standard applied in these and other cases over the last eight years now persuades us that the attempt to draw the boundaries of state regulatory immunity in terms of "traditional governmental function" is not only unworkable but is also inconsistent with established principles of federalism and, indeed, with those very federalism principles on which National League of Cities purported to rest. That case, accordingly, is overruled.

Justice Powell, with whom the Chief Justice, Justice Rehnquist, and Justice O'Connor join, dissenting. . . .

. . . There are, of course, numerous examples over the history of this Court in which prior decisions have been reconsidered and overruled. There have been few cases, however, in which the principle of stare decisis and the rationale of recent decisions were ignored as abruptly as we now witness. . . .

Whatever effect the Court's decision may have in weakening the application of stare decisis, it is likely to be less important than what the Court has done to the Constitution itself. A unique feature of the United States is the *federal* system of government guaranteed by the Constitution and implicit in the very name of our country. Despite some genuflecting in the Court's opinion to the concept of federalism, today's decision effectively reduces the Tenth Amendment to meaningless rhetoric when Congress acts pursuant to the Commerce Clause. . . .

469 U.S. 528 (1985).

... The Court today propounds a view of federalism that pays only lip service to the role of the States. ... Indeed, the Court barely acknowledges that the Tenth Amendment exists. That Amendment states explicitly that "[t]he powers not delegated to the United States ... are reserved to the States." ... The Court recasts this language to say that the States retain their sovereign powers "only to the extent that the Constitution has not divested them of their original powers and transferred those powers to the Federal Government." This rephrasing is not a distinction without a difference; rather, it reflects the Court's unprecedented view that Congress is free under the Commerce Clause to assume a State's traditional sovereign power, and to do so without judicial review of its action. Indeed, the Court's view of federalism appears to relegate the States to precisely the trivial role that opponents of the Constitution feared they would occupy.

109 ❧

Although a strong executive had been a component of American liberalism since the Progressive era, the excesses of the Nixon presidency undermined that commitment. At the same time, conservatives became more sympathetic to executive power once they gained control of the White House under Nixon, Ford, and especially the extremely conservative Ronald Reagan. With Republican presidents locked in combat with the more liberal and Democratic Congress, conservative jurisprudents revived arguments for a stricter separation of powers that would make the executive more independent of legislative and judicial control.

The Burger Court reflected this movement. Even in *United States v. Nixon* (1974) (Document 95), in which it ordered President Nixon to surrender the Watergate tapes, the Court indicated its general deference to the president's right to keep communications within the executive branch confidential. In *Buckley v. Valeo*, 424 U.S. 1 (1976), the Court overturned a law authorizing Congress to name a majority of the members of a new commission to supervise federal elections, on the grounds that it violated the president's right to make such appointments. In *Immigration and Naturalization Service v. Chadha*, 462 U.S. 919 (1983), the Court ruled "legislative vetoes" unconstitutional. This was a procedure, established in the wake of President Nixon's abuses of power, by which Congress authorized executive agencies to make rulings or propose regulations, subject to congressional reversal upon the vote of one or both Houses. The Court ruled, among other things, that this procedure unconstitutionally deprived the president of his right to veto legislation.

Bowsher v. Synar overturned a key provision of the Balanced Budget Act of 1985. The law provided that if Congress could not agree on how to cut the federal budget to progressively reduce the annual deficit, then the comptroller general, an independent government official appointed and removable by Congress rather than the president, would order across-the-board cuts. The Court ruled that this arrangement violated the principle of separation of powers. These decisions suggested that the Court was growing progressively more hostile to all congressional efforts to limit executive discretion.

Bowsher v. Synar (1986)

C H I E F   J U S T I C E Burger delivered the opinion of the Court.

The question presented by these appeals is whether the assignment by Congress to the Comptroller General of the United States of certain functions under the Balanced Budget and Emergency Deficit Control Act of 1985 violates the doctrine of separation of powers. . . .

We noted recently that "[t]he Constitution sought to divide the delegated powers of the new Federal Government into three defined categories, Legislative, Executive, and Judicial." *INS v. Chadha.* . . .

The Constitution does not contemplate an active role for Congress in the supervision of officers charged with the execution of the laws it enacts. The President appoints "Officers of the United States" with the "Advice and Consent of the Senate. . . ." Article II, § 2. Once the appointment has been made and confirmed, however, the Constitution explicitly provides for removal of Officers of the United States by Congress only upon impeachment by the House of Representatives and conviction by the Senate. . . .

. . . Congress cannot reserve for itself the power of removal of an officer charged with the execution of the laws except by impeachment. To permit the execution of the laws to be vested in an officer answerable only to Congress would, in practical terms, reserve in Congress control over the execution of the laws. . . .

Our decision in *INS v. Chadha* . . . supports this conclusion. In *Chadha,* we struck down a one house "legislative veto" provision by which each House of Congress retained the power to reverse a decision Congress had expressly authorized the Attorney General to make. . . . To permit an officer controlled by Congress to execute the laws would be, in essence, to permit a congressional veto. Congress could simply remove, or threaten to remove, an officer for executing the laws in any fashion found to be unsatisfactory to Congress. This kind of congressional control over the execution of the laws, *Chadha* makes clear, is constitutionally impermissible.

The Rehnquist Court

110 ∾

In general, the Burger Court responded to conservative calls for a strict conception of separation of powers that exalted presidential authority. With the growing strength of conservatives on the Court, most observers expected this trend to continue. Among the

478 U.S. 417 (1986).

right wing's chief targets was the provision of the 1978 Ethics in Government Act, which authorized the judiciary to appoint independent prosecutors to investigate wrongdoing in the executive branch and forbade their removal except for "good cause." When the Reagan administration came under investigation for criminal conduct associated with the illicit sale of embargoed weapons to Iran and the diversion of the resulting funds to support anticommunist guerrillas in Central America, conservatives redoubled their attacks. They argued that the law violated the clause of the Constitution giving the president the power to appoint principal officers of the government, that it unconstitutionally limited the president's power of removal, and that it encroached on the principle of separation of powers by giving judges the power to appoint officers in the executive branch.

The Court received the opportunity to weigh these arguments in *Morrison v. Olson,* which challenged a special prosecutor's investigation of corruption in the Environmental Protection Agency. To the surprise of many observers, the Court sustained the law. Not only did it hold the prosecutor to be an "inferior officer," whose appointment Congress could vest where it pleased, but the Court also endorsed a flexible understanding of separation of powers.

Morrison v. Olson (1988)

CHIEF JUSTICE Rehnquist delivered the opinion of the Court. . . .

We now turn to consider whether the Act is invalid under the constitutional principle of separation of powers. Two related issues must be addressed: The first is whether the provision of the Act restricting the Attorney General's power to remove the independent counsel to only those instances in which he can show "good cause," taken by itself, impermissibly interferes with the President's exercise of his constitutionally appointed functions. The second is whether, taken as a whole, the Act violates the separation of powers by reducing the President's ability to control the prosecutorial powers wielded by the independent counsel.

Two Terms ago we had occasion to consider whether it was consistent with the separation of powers for Congress to pass a statute that authorized a Government official who is removable only by Congress to participate in what we found to be "executive powers." We held in *Bowsher* [v. *Synar*] that "Congress cannot reserve for itself the power of removal of an officer charged with the execution of the laws except by impeachment." . . . A primary antecedent for this ruling was our 1926 decision in *Myers v. United States.* . . .

Unlike both *Bowsher* and *Myers,* this case does not involve an attempt by Congress itself to gain a role in the removal of executive officials other than its established powers of impeachment and conviction. The Act instead puts the removal power squarely in the hands of the Executive Branch; an inde-

487 U.S. 684 (1988).

pendent counsel may be removed from office, "only by the personal action of the Attorney General, and only for good cause." . . . There is no requirement of congressional approval of the Attorney General's removal decision. . . .

. . . The analysis contained in our removal cases is designed not to define rigid categories of those officials who may or may not be removed at will by the President, but to ensure that Congress does not interfere with the President's exercise of the "executive power" and his constitutionally appointed duty to "take care that the laws be faithfully executed" under Article II. . . . [T]he real question is whether the removal restrictions are of such a nature that they impede the President's ability to perform his constitutional duty, and the functions of the officials in question must be analyzed in that light.

Considering for the moment the "good cause" removal provision in isolation from the other parts of the Act at issue in this case, we cannot say that the imposition of a "good cause" standard for removal by itself unduly trammels on executive authority. . . .

The final question to be addressed is whether the Act, taken as a whole, violates the principle of separation of powers by unduly interfering with the role of the Executive Branch. Time and again we have reaffirmed the importance in our constitutional scheme of the separation of governmental powers into the three coordinate branches. . . . We have not hesitated to invalidate provisions of law which violate this principle. . . . On the other hand, we have never held that the Constitution requires that the three branches of Government "operate with absolute independence." . . .

. . . [T]his case does not involve an attempt by Congress to increase its own powers at the expense of the Executive Branch. . . . Unlike some of our previous cases, most recently *Bowsher v. Synar,* this case simply does not pose a "dange[r] of congressional usurpation of Executive Branch functions." . . . Indeed, with the exception of the power of impeachment—which applies to all officers of the United States—Congress retained for itself no powers of control or supervision over an independent counsel. . . .

Similarly, we do not think that the Act works any *judicial* usurpation of properly executive functions. As should be apparent from our discussion of the Appointments Clause above, the power to appoint inferior officers such as independent counsel is not in itself an "executive" function in the constitutional sense, at least when Congress has exercised its power to vest the appointment of an inferior office in the "courts of Law." . . .

Finally, we do not think that the Act "impermissibly undermine[s]" the powers of the Executive Branch . . . or "disrupts the proper balance between the coordinate branches [by] prevent[ing] the Executive Branch from accomplishing its constitutionally assigned functions." . . . It is undeniable that the Act reduces the amount of control or supervision that the Attorney General and, through him, the President exercises over the investigation and prosecution of a certain class of alleged criminal activity. . . . Nonetheless, the Act does give the Attorney General several means of supervising or controlling the prosecutorial powers that may be wielded by an independent counsel. Most importantly, the Attorney General retains the power to remove the counsel for "good cause," a power that we have already concluded provides the Executive with substantial ability to ensure that the laws are "faithfully executed" by an independent counsel. . . . Notwithstanding the fact that the counsel is to some degree "independent" and free from executive supervision to a greater extent than other federal prosecutors, in our view these features of the Act give the Executive Branch sufficient control over the independent counsel to ensure that the President is able to perform his constitutionally assigned duties.

111 ∿

In the 1980s conservatives ever more vigorously attacked affirmative action to remedy the effects of past racial, ethnic, and sexual discrimination. They insisted that the Equal Protection Clause of the Fourteenth Amendment forbade government from establishing a preference for either sex, or for one racial or ethnic group over another, even to redress past inequities. They condemned such "group remedies," which harmed innocent persons while favoring members of minority groups who were not required to show that they themselves had suffered discrimination. All such remedies should be individual, argued the conservatives, and limited to those actually damaged.

Despite its overall conservatism, the Burger Court had generally continued the Warren Court's assault on segregation and had supported congressional and executive initiatives to combat discrimination, including the requirement of affirmative action to promote diversity. (See *Regents of University of California v. Bakke,* Document 104.) However, by the time William H. Rehnquist became chief justice in 1986, a change was apparent. More and more of the justices argued that *any* law making a racial classification must undergo strict scrutiny and meet the Compelling State Interest Test no matter how benign its purpose.

In *Richmond v. J. A. Croson Co.,* the Court evaluated the constitutionality of "minority set-asides" established by the city of Richmond, Virginia, after its African-American majority gained political power. These were regulations requiring that a certain proportion of government business be reserved for minority contractors, including not only African Americans but Hispanics, women, Asian Americans, Native Americans, and even Inuits. The Court ruled that such regulations were unconstitutional unless the state or local government could demonstrate that they remedied specific past discrimination.

The decision put at risk all affirmative-action programs where such discrimination had not been proven—a serious problem for programs voluntarily instituted to increase minority participation in business, education, or employment. However, only the arch-conservative Justice Antonin Scalia insisted that racial preferences were unconstitutional even to remedy past discrimination.

Although the Court indicated in *Croson* that Congress had greater latitude than the states to use quotas to aid members of minority groups, in 1995 it ruled similar federal programs unconstitutional in *Adarand v. Pena,* 115 Supreme Court Reporter 2097.

Richmond v. J. A. Croson Co. (1989)

J U S T I C E O'Connor announced the judgment of the Court. . . .

There was no direct evidence of race discrimination on the part of the city in letting contracts or any evidence that the city's prime contractors had discriminated against minority-owned subcontractors. . . .

. . . [A] state or local subdivision (if delegated the authority from the State) has the authority to eradicate the effects of private discrimination within its own legislative jurisdiction. This authority must, of course, be exercised within the constraints of § 1 of the Fourteenth Amendment. . . .

Thus, if the city could show that it had essentially become a "passive participant" in a system of racial exclusion practiced by elements of the local construction industry, we think it clear that the city could take affirmative steps to dismantle such a system. It is beyond dispute that any public entity, state or federal, has a compelling interest in assuring that public dollars, drawn from the tax contributions of all citizens, do not serve to finance the evil of private prejudice. . . .

Absent searching judicial inquiry into the justification for such race-based measures, there is simply no way of determining what classifications are "benign" or "remedial" and what classifications are in fact motivated by illegitimate notions of racial inferiority or simple racial politics. Indeed, the purpose of strict scrutiny is to "smoke out" illegitimate uses of race by assuring that the legislative body is pursuing a goal important enough to warrant use of a highly suspect tool. The test also ensures that the means chosen "fit" this compelling goal so closely that there is little or no possibility that the motive for the classification was illegitimate racial prejudice or stereotype. . . .

Appellant argues that it is attempting to remedy various forms of past discrimination that are alleged to be responsible for the small number of minority businesses in the local contracting industry. Among these the city cites the exclusion of blacks from skilled construction trade unions and training programs. This past discrimination has prevented them "from following the traditional path from laborer to entrepreneur." . . .

488 U.S. 469 (1989).

While there is no doubt that the sorry history of both private and public discrimination in this country has contributed to a lack of opportunities for black entrepreneurs, this observation, standing alone, cannot justify a rigid racial quota in the awarding of public contracts in Richmond, Virginia. . . . [A]n amorphous claim that there has been past discrimination in a particular industry cannot justify the use of an unyielding racial quota.

It is sheer speculation how many minority firms there would be in Richmond absent past societal discrimination. . . . Defining these sorts of injuries as "identified discrimination" would give local governments license to create a patchwork of racial preferences based on statistical generalizations about any particular field of endeavor. . . .

In sum, none of the evidence presented by the city points to any identified discrimination in the Richmond construction industry. We, therefore, hold that the city has failed to demonstrate a compelling interest in apportioning public contracting opportunities on the basis of race. To accept Richmond's claim that past societal discrimination alone can serve as the basis for rigid racial preferences would be to open the door to competing claims for "remedial relief" for every disadvantaged group. The dream of a Nation of equal citizens in a society where race is irrelevant to personal opportunity and achievement would be lost in a mosaic of shifting preferences based on inherently unmeasurable claims of past wrongs. . . . We think such a result would be contrary to both the letter and spirit of a constitutional provision whose central command is equality.

112 ∾

Of all the Supreme Court decisions of the libertarian era, the decision in the abortion case of *Roe v. Wade* (Document 86) was the most bitterly criticized. It was attacked by the Roman Catholic church, fundamentalist Christians, orthodox Jews, and all who saw the decision as undermining the centrality of the family in American life. As early as the mid-1970s, Congress responded by passing legislation designed to limit *Roe*'s effect, especially barring federal reimbursement for the procedure in a variety of contexts, including payment for abortions for poor people receiving Medicaid. Although the Supreme Court sustained the constitutionality of such legislation, until the mid-1980s it consistently overturned state laws placing any general restrictions on abortions.

But as the conservative Reagan administration nominated only firm opponents of *Roe* to the federal judiciary, support for it began to wane. Chief Justice Rehnquist consistently called for its reversal. He was joined by more and more allies. When another Republican, George Bush, succeeded Reagan, it seemed that *Roe v. Wade*'s days were numbered. In 1989 Chief Justice Rehnquist finally secured a majority to sustain a Missouri statute placing a variety of significant obstacles in the way of abortions, in *Webster v. Reproductive Health Services*, 492 U.S. 490 (1989).

The opportunity to reverse *Roe* came in 1992 with *Planned Parenthood v. Casey*. The case involved a number of Pennsylvania regulations similar to the ones already sustained in *Webster;* the only reason to hear an appeal of the lower-court decision sustaining the laws seemed to be to finally overrule *Roe* itself. To the surprise of observers, however, President Bush's recent appointee, Justice David H. Souter, and two other conservative justices joined the remaining moderates on the Court to reaffirm *Roe's* central holding that women had a right to abort pregnancies before the fetus reached the point of viability outside the womb. States could not place an "undue burden" on the exercise of that right. In reaching the decision, the newly formed centrist bloc stressed the importance of *stare decisis,* the principle that courts should not lightly overturn precedent. However, the justices also held that states could regulate various aspects of abortions, and they rejected *Roe's* trimester-based formula as too rigid. Using the new Undue Burden Test, the majority upheld most of the regulations but ruled unconstitutional one requiring a woman to report a failure to notify her spouse, saying it gave the spouse a virtual veto over the procedure.

In the course of their remarkable opinion, much but not all of which was joined by a majority of the justices, the moderate bloc adopted the view that the Fourteenth Amendment protected rights independently of the Bill of Rights, discussed the nature of *stare decisis,* and put the controversy over *Roe v. Wade* in a historical context that went to the heart of the Supreme Court's role in the American constitutional system.

Chief Justice Rehnquist filed a vigorous dissent, advocating the complete reversal of *Roe.*

Planned Parenthood v. Casey (1992)

J U S T I C E O'Connor, Justice Kennedy, and Justice Souter announced the judgment of the Court and delivered the opinion of the Court. . . .

After considering the fundamental constitutional questions resolved by Roe, principles of institutional integrity, and the rule of stare decisis, we are led to conclude this: the essential holding of Roe v. Wade should be retained and once again reaffirmed.

. . . As the second Justice Harlan recognized:

"[T]he full scope of the liberty guaranteed by the Due Process Clause cannot be found in or limited by the precise terms of the specific guarantees elsewhere provided in the Constitution. This 'liberty' is not a series of isolated points pricked out in terms of the taking of property; the freedom of speech, press, and religion; the right to keep and bear arms; the freedom from unreasonable searches and

114 Supreme Court Reporter 909 (1994).

seizures; and so on. It is a rational continuum which, broadly speaking, includes a freedom from all substantial arbitrary impositions and purposeless restraints, . . . and which also recognizes, what a reasonable and sensitive judgment must, that certain interests require particularly careful scrutiny of the state needs asserted to justify their abridgment." . . .

The inescapable fact is that adjudication of substantive due process claims may call upon the Court in interpreting the Constitution to exercise that same capacity which by tradition courts always have exercised: reasoned judgment. Its boundaries are not susceptible of expression as a simple rule. That does not mean we are free to invalidate state policy choices with which we disagree; yet neither does it permit us to shrink from the duties of our office. . . .

Men and women of good conscience can disagree, and we suppose some always shall disagree, about the profound moral and spiritual implications of terminating a pregnancy, even in its earliest stage. Some of us as individuals find abortion offensive to our most basic principles of morality, but that cannot control our decision. Our obligation is to define the liberty of all, not to mandate our own moral code. The underlying constitutional issue is whether the State can resolve these philosophic questions in such a definitive way that a woman lacks all choice in the matter, except perhaps in those rare circumstances in which the pregnancy is itself a danger to her own life or health, or is the result of rape or incest. . . .

Our law affords constitutional protection to personal decisions relating to marriage, procreation, contraception, family relationships, child rearing, and education. . . . Our cases recognize "the right of the *individual,* married or single, to be free from unwarranted governmental intrusion into matters so fundamentally affecting a person as the decision whether to bear or beget a child." . . . At the heart of liberty is the right to define one's own concept of existence, of meaning, of the universe, and of the mystery of human life. Beliefs about these matters could not define the attributes of personhood were they formed under compulsion of the State. . . .

While we appreciate the weight of the arguments made on behalf of the State in the case before us, arguments which in their ultimate formulation conclude that Roe should be overruled, the reservations any of us may have in reaffirming the central holding of Roe are outweighed by the explication of individual liberty we have given combined with the force of stare decisis. We turn now to that doctrine. . . .

. . . [I]t is common wisdom that the rule of stare decisis is not an "inexorable command," and certainly it is not such in every constitutional case. . . . Rather, when this Court reexamines a prior holding, its judgment is customarily informed by a series of prudential and pragmatic considerations designed to test the consistency of overruling a prior decision with the ideal of the rule of law, and to gauge the respective costs of reaffirming and overruling a prior case. . . .

So in this case we may inquire whether Roe's central rule has been found unworkable; whether the rule's limitation on state power could be removed without serious inequity to those who have relied upon it or significant damage to the stability of the society governed by the rule in question; whether the law's growth in the intervening years has left Roe's central rule a doctrinal anachronism discounted by society; and whether Roe's premises of fact have so far changed in the ensuing two decades as to render its central holding somehow irrelevant or unjustifiable in dealing with the issue it addressed.

Although Roe has engendered opposition, it has in no sense proven "unworkable," . . . representing as it does a simple limitation beyond which a state law is unenforceable. . . .

The inquiry into reliance counts the cost of a rule's repudiation as it would fall on those who have relied reasonably on the rule's continued application. . . .

. . . [F]or two decades of economic and social developments, people have organized intimate relationships and made choices that define their views of themselves and their places in society, in reliance on the availability of abortion in the event that contraception should fail. The ability of women to participate equally in the economic and social life of the Nation has been facilitated by their ability to control their reproductive lives. . . .

No evolution of legal principle has left Roe's doctrinal footings weaker than they were in 1973. No development of constitutional law since the case was decided has implicitly or explicitly left Roe behind as a mere survivor of obsolete constitutional thinking. . . .

In a less significant case, stare decisis analysis could, and would, stop at the point we have reached. But the sustained and widespread debate Roe has provoked calls for some comparison between that case and others of comparable dimension that have responded to national controversies and taken on the impress of the controversies addressed. Only two such decisional lines from the past century present themselves for examination, and in each instance the result reached by the Court accorded with the principles we apply today.

The first example is that line of cases identified with Lochner v New York, . . . which imposed substantive limitations on legislation limiting economic autonomy in favor of health and welfare regulation, adopting, in Justice Holmes' view, the theory of laissez-faire. . . . Fourteen years later, West Coast Hotel Co. v Parrish . . . signalled the demise of Lochner by overruling Adkins. In the meantime, the Depression had come and, with it, the lesson that seemed unmistakable to most people by 1937, that the interpretation of contractual freedom protected in Adkins rested on fundamentally false factual assumptions about the capacity of a relatively unregulated market to satisfy minimal levels of human welfare. . . .

The second comparison that 20th century history invites is with the cases employing the separate-but-equal rule for applying the Fourteenth Amendment's equal protection guarantee. They began with Plessy v. Ferguson, . . . holding that legislatively mandated racial segregation in public transportation works no denial of equal protection, rejecting the argument that racial separation enforced by the legal machinery of American society treats the black race as inferior. The Plessy Court considered "the underlying fallacy of the plaintiff's argument to consist in the assumption that the enforced separation of the two races stamps the colored race with a badge of inferiority. . . . [T]his understanding of the facts and the rule it was stated to justify were repudiated in Brown v. Board of Education. . . .

The Court in Brown [observed] that whatever may have been the understanding in Plessy's time of the power of segregation to stigmatize those who were segregated with a "badge of inferiority," it was clear by 1954 that legally sanctioned segregation had just such an effect. . . .

West Coast Hotel and Brown each rested on facts, or an understanding of facts, changed from those which furnished the claimed justifications for the earlier constitutional resolutions. Each case was comprehensible as the Court's response to facts that the country could understand, or had come to understand already, but which the Court of an earlier day, as its own declarations disclosed, had not been able to perceive. As the decisions were thus comprehensible they were also defensible, not merely as the victories of one doctrinal school over another by dint of numbers (victories though they were), but as applications of constitutional principle to facts as they had not been seen by the Court before. . . .

Because the case before us presents no such occasion it could be seen as no such response. Because neither the factual underpinnings of Roe's central holding nor our understanding of it has changed (and because no other indication of weakened precedent has been shown) the Court could not pretend to be reexamining the prior law with any justification beyond a present doctrinal disposition to come out differently from the Court of 1973. To overrule prior law for no other reason than that would run counter to the view repeated in our cases, that a decision to overrule should rest on some special reason over and above the belief that a prior case was wrongly decided. . . .

... [O]verruling Roe's central holding would not only reach an unjustifiable result under principles of stare decisis, but would seriously weaken the Court's capacity to exercise the judicial power and to function as the Supreme Court of a Nation dedicated to the rule of law. ...

... [T]he Court's legitimacy depends on making legally principled decisions under circumstances in which their principled character is sufficiently plausible to be accepted by the Nation. ...

... There is ... a point beyond which frequent overruling would overtax the country's belief in the Court's good faith. ... There is a limit to the amount of error that can plausibly be imputed to prior courts. If that limit should be exceeded, disturbance of prior rulings would be taken as evidence that justifiable reexamination of principle had given way to drives for particular results in the short term. ...

... Where, in the performance of its judicial duties, the Court decides a case in such a way as to resolve the sort of intensely divisive controversy reflected in Roe and those rare, comparable cases, its decision has a dimension that the resolution of the normal case does not carry. It is the dimension present whenever the Court's interpretation of the Constitution calls the contending sides of a national controversy to end their national division by accepting a common mandate rooted in the Constitution.

The Court is not asked to do this very often, having thus addressed the Nation only twice in our lifetime, the decisions of Brown and Roe. But when the Court does act in this way, its decision requires an equally rare precedential force to counter the inevitable efforts to overturn it and to thwart its implementation. ... [W]hatever the premises of opposition may be, only the most convincing justification under accepted standards of precedent could suffice to demonstrate that a later decision overruling the first was anything but a surrender to political pressure, and an unjustified repudiation of the principle on which the Court staked its authority in the first instance. ...

The Court's duty in the present case is clear. In 1973, it confronted the already-divisive issue of governmental power to limit personal choice to undergo abortion, for which it provided a new resolution based on the due process guaranteed by the Fourteenth Amendment. Whether or not a new social consensus is developing on that issue, its divisiveness is no less today than in 1973, and pressure to overrule the decision, like pressure to retain it, has grown only more intense. A decision to overrule Roe's essential holding under the existing circumstances would address error, if error there was, at the cost of both profound and unnecessary damage to the Court's legitimacy, and to the Nation's commitment to the rule of law. ...

... We conclude that the basic decision in Roe was based on a constitutional analysis which we cannot now repudiate. The woman's liberty is not so unlimited, however, that from the outset the State cannot show its concern for the life of the unborn, and at a later point in fetal development the State's interest in life has sufficient force so that the right of the woman to terminate the pregnancy can be restricted. . . .

We conclude the line should be drawn at viability, so that before that time the woman has a right to choose to terminate her pregnancy. . . .

. . . [T]he concept of viability, as we noted in Roe, is the time at which there is a realistic possibility of maintaining and nourishing a life outside the womb, so that the independent existence of the second life can in reason and all fairness be the object of state protection that now overrides the rights of the woman. . . .

Yet it must be remembered that Roe v. Wade speaks with clarity in establishing not only the woman's liberty but also the State's "important and legitimate interest in potential life." . . .

Roe established a trimester framework to govern abortion regulations. Under this elaborate but rigid construct, almost no regulation at all is permitted during the first trimester of pregnancy; regulations designed to protect the woman's health, but not to further the State's interest in potential life, are permitted during the second trimester; and during the third trimester, when the fetus is viable, prohibitions are permitted provided the life or health of the mother is not at stake. . . .

. . . We do not agree, however, that the trimester approach is necessary to accomplish this objective. . . .

. . . Even in the earliest stages of pregnancy, the State may enact rules and regulations designed to encourage her to know that there are philosophic and social arguments of great weight that can be brought to bear in favor of continuing the pregnancy to full term. . . . It follows that States are free to enact laws to provide a reasonable framework for a woman to make a decision that has such profound and lasting meaning. . . .

The very notion that the State has a substantial interest in potential life leads to the conclusion that not all regulations must be deemed unwarranted. Not all burdens on the right to decide whether to terminate a pregnancy will be undue. In our view, the undue burden standard is the appropriate means of reconciling the State's interest with the woman's constitutionally protected liberty. . . .

A finding of an undue burden is a shorthand for the conclusion that a state regulation has the purpose or effect of placing a substantial obstacle in the path of a woman seeking an abortion of a nonviable fetus. A statute with this purpose is invalid. . . .

Some guiding principles should emerge. What is at stake is the woman's right to make the ultimate decision, not a right to be insulated from all others in doing so. Regulations which do no more than create a structural mechanism by which the State, or the parent or guardian of a minor, may express profound respect for the life of the unborn are permitted, if they are not a substantial obstacle to the woman's exercise of the right to choose. . . .

Chief Justice Rehnquist, with whom Justice White, Justice Scalia, and Justice Thomas join, concurring in the judgment in part and dissenting in part.

. . . Unfortunately for those who must apply this Court's decisions, the re-examination undertaken today leaves the Court no less divided than beforehand. Although they reject the trimester framework that formed the underpinning of Roe, Justices O'Connor, Kennedy, and Souter adopt a revised undue burden standard to analyze the challenged regulations. We conclude, however, that such an outcome is an unjustified constitutional compromise, one which leaves the Court in a position to closely scrutinize all types of abortion regulations despite the fact that it lacks the power to do so under the Constitution. . . .

We have held that a liberty interest protected under the Due Process Clause of the Fourteenth Amendment will be deemed fundamental if it is "implicit in the concept of ordered liberty." Palko v Connecticut. . . .

In Roe v. Wade, the Court recognized a "guarantee of personal privacy" which "is broad enough to encompass a woman's decision whether or not to terminate her pregnancy." . . . We are now of the view that, in terming this right fundamental, the Court in Roe read the earlier opinions upon which it based its decision much too broadly. . . .

. . . At the time of the adoption of the Fourteenth Amendment, statutory prohibitions or restrictions on abortion were commonplace; in 1868, at least 28 of the then-37 States and 8 Territories had statutes banning or limiting abortion. . . . By the turn of the century virtually every State had a law prohibiting or restricting abortion on its books. By the middle of the present century, a liberalization trend had set in. But 21 of the restrictive abortion laws in effect in 1868 were still in effect in 1973 when Roe was decided, and an overwhelming majority of the States prohibited abortion unless necessary to preserve the life or health of the mother. . . . On this record, it can scarcely be said that any deeply rooted tradition of relatively unrestricted abortion in our history supported the classification of the right to abortion as "fundamental" under the Due Process Clause of the Fourteenth Amendment.

We think, . . . both in view of . . . history and of our decided cases dealing with substantive liberty under the Due Process Clause, that the Court was mistaken in Roe when it classified a woman's decision to terminate her pregnancy as a "fundamental right" that could be abridged only in a manner which withstood "strict scrutiny." . . .

The joint opinion of Justices O'Connor, Kennedy, and Souter cannot bring itself to say that Roe was correct as an original matter, but the authors are of the view that "the immediate question is not the soundness of Roe's resolution of the issue, but the precedential force that must be accorded to its holding." . . .

In our view, authentic principles of stare decisis do not require that any portion of the reasoning in Roe be kept intact. "Stare decisis is not . . . a universal, inexorable command," especially in cases involving the interpretation of the Federal Constitution. . . . Erroneous decisions in such constitutional cases are uniquely durable, because correction through legislative action, save for constitutional amendment, is impossible. It is therefore our duty to reconsider constitutional interpretations that "depar[t] from a proper understanding" of the Constitution. . . .

. . . And surely there is no requirement, in considering whether to depart from stare decisis in a constitutional case, that a decision be more wrong now than it was at the time it was rendered. If that were true, the most outlandish constitutional decision could survive forever, based simply on the fact that it was no more outlandish later than it was when originally rendered. . . .

The joint opinion . . . turns to what can only be described as an unconventional—and unconvincing—notion of reliance, a view based on the surmise that the availability of abortion since Roe has led to "two decades of economic and social developments" that would be undercut if the error of Roe were recognized. . . . The joint opinion's assertion of this fact is undeveloped and totally conclusory. . . .

In the end, having failed to put forth any evidence to prove any true reliance, the joint opinion's argument is based solely on generalized assertions about the national psyche. . . . The "separate but equal" doctrine lasted 58 years after Plessy, and Lochner's protection of contractual freedom lasted 32 years. However, the simple fact that a generation or more had grown used to these major decisions did not prevent the Court from correcting its errors in those cases, nor should it prevent us from correctly interpreting the Constitution here. . . .

We have stated above our belief that the Constitution does not subject state abortion regulations to heightened scrutiny. Accordingly, we think that the correct analysis is that set forth by the plurality opinion in Webster. A woman's interest in having an abortion is a form of liberty protected by the

Due Process Clause, but States may regulate abortion procedures in ways rationally related to a legitimate state interest.

113 ❧

In the 1970s and 1980s, conservative constitutional commentators began to argue forcefully that many government regulations unconscionably deprived owners of the value of their property. With the doctrine of substantive due process of law discredited, jurisprudents turned to the Takings Clause of the Fifth Amendment (see the appendix, page A-11). Government, they insisted, either must compensate property owners for the loss they suffered through the enforcement of such regulations, or laws entailing such uncompensated "takings" should be ruled unconstitutional.

Decisions in a few cases in the 1980s suggested that the Supreme Court was receptive to this argument. The decision in *Pennel v. City of San Jose*, 485 U.S. 1 (1987), however, seemed to check the trend, as the Court rejected the proposition that rent-control laws constituted an uncompensated "taking" in violation of the Fifth Amendment. But in *Dolan v. City of Tigard,* the Court endorsed the general takings argument. In this case, city officials had granted Dolan's request for an exemption from a water and sewer regulation, but only on condition that Dolan turn over a portion of her land along a riverside park for use as a bicycle path. This constituted a forbidden taking, the Court ruled.

The decision had dramatic implications. It drew into question the common practice of making zoning changes and exemptions conditional on the dedication of a portion of the petitioner's land to public use. Even more vulnerable to constitutional challenge were environmental regulations that limited landowners' ability to improve their property.

Dolan v. City of Tigard (1994)

[**M**R. CHIEF Justice Rehnquist delivered the opinion of the Court. . . .]
. . . The Takings Clause of the Fifth Amendment of the United States Constitution, made applicable to the States through the Fourteenth Amendment, provides: "[N]or shall private property be taken for public use, without just compensation." One of the principal purposes of the Takings Clause is "to bar Government from forcing some people alone to bear public burdens which, in all fairness and justice, should be borne by the public as a whole." . . . Without question, had the city simply required petitioner to dedicate a strip of land along Fanno Creek for public use, rather than conditioning the grant of her permit to redevelop her property on such a dedication, a

114 Supreme Court Reporter 2309 (1994).

taking would have occurred. Such public access would deprive petitioner of the right to exclude others, "one of the most essential sticks in the bundle of rights that are commonly characterized as property." . . .

On the other side of the ledger, the authority of state and local governments to engage in land use planning has been sustained against constitutional challenge as long ago as our decision in Euclid v. Ambler Realty Co., (1926). . . .

Undoubtedly, the prevention of flooding along Fanno Creek and the reduction of traffic congestion in the central business district qualify as the type of legitimate public purposes we have upheld. . . .

The same may be said for the city's attempt to reduce traffic congestion by providing for alternative means of transportation. . . .

The second part of our analysis requires us to determine whether the degree of the exactions demanded by the city's permit conditions bear the required relationship to the projected impact of petitioner's proposed development. . . .

. . . We think a term such as "rough proportionality" best encapsulates what we hold to be the requirement of the Fifth Amendment. No precise mathematical calculation is required, but the city must make some sort of individualized determination that the required dedication is related both in nature and extent to the impact of the proposed development. . . .

We see no reason why the Takings Clause of the Fifth Amendment, as much a part of the Bill of Rights as the First Amendment or Fourth Amendment, should be relegated to the status of a poor relation. . . .

We conclude that the findings upon which the city relies do not show the required reasonable relationship between the floodplain easement and the petitioner's proposed new building.

With respect to the pedestrian/bicycle pathway, we have no doubt that the city was correct in finding that the larger retail sales facility proposed by petitioner will increase traffic on the streets of the central business district. . . . But on the record before us, the city has not met its burden of demonstrating that the additional number of vehicle and bicycle trips generated by the petitioner's development reasonably relate to the city's requirement for a dedication of the pedestrian/bicycle pathway easement. The city simply found that the creation of the pathway "could offset some of the traffic demand . . . and lessen the increase in traffic congestion." . . .

[Justice Stevens, with whom Justice Blackmun and Justice Ginsburg join, dissenting.]

. . . [T]he Court's description of the doctrinal underpinnings of its decision, the phrasing of its fledging test of "rough proportionality," and the application of that test to this case run contrary to the traditional treatment of these cases and break considerable and unpropitious new ground. . . .

The Court has made a serious error by abandoning the traditional presumption of constitutionality and imposing a novel burden of proof on a city implementing an admittedly valid comprehensive land use plan. Even more consequential than its incorrect disposition of this case, however, is the Court's resurrection of a species of substantive due process analysis that it firmly rejected decades ago. . . .

In our changing world one thing is certain: uncertainty will characterize predictions about the impact of new urban developments on the risks of flood, earthquakes, traffic congestion, or environmental harms. When there is doubt concerning the magnitude of those impacts, the public interest in averting them must outweigh the private interest of the commercial entrepreneur.

114 ᕲ

Having moved towards reviving judicial protection of property rights in *Dolan v. City of Tigard,* the Rehnquist Court moved towards a return to state-rights constitutionalism as well. In *U.S. v. Lopez,* a narrow majority of the Court overturned the Gun-Free School Zone Act, Section 922(q) of the U.S. criminal code, passed in 1990. Enacted in response to growing worries about violence in the classroom, the law made it a crime to possess a firearm within one thousand feet of a school. The Court ruled that Congress could regulate noncommercial activities only if they "substantially" affected interstate or foreign commerce, a potentially significant narrowing of the range of federal authority. That clearly subjected federal police power–type regulations to a new, higher level of judicial scrutiny.

U.S. v. Lopez (1995)

CHIEF JUSTICE Rehnquist delivered the opinion of the Court. . . .

We start with first principles. The Constitution creates a Federal Government of enumerated powers. . . . As James Madison wrote, "the powers delegated by the proposed Constitution to the federal government are few and defined. Those which are to remain in the State governments are numerous and indefinite." The Federalist No. 45. . . .

115 Supreme Court Reporter 1624 (1995).

Jones & Laughlin Steel, Darby, and Wickard ushered in an era of Commerce Clause jurisprudence that greatly expanded the previously defined authority of Congress under that Clause. In part, this was a recognition of the great changes that had occurred in the way business was carried on in this country. Enterprises that had once been local or at most regional in nature had become national in scope. But the doctrinal change also reflected a view that earlier Commerce Clause cases artificially had constrained the authority of Congress to regulate interstate commerce.

But even these modern-era precedents which have expanded congressional power under the Commerce Clause confirm that this power is subject to outer limits. . . .

Consistent with this structure, we have identified three broad categories of activity that Congress may regulate under its commerce power. . . . First, Congress may regulate the use of the channels of interstate commerce. . . . Second, Congress is empowered to regulate and protect the instrumentalities of interstate commerce, or persons or things in interstate commerce, even though the threat may come only from intrastate activities. . . . Finally, Congress' commerce authority includes the power to regulate those activities having a substantial relation to interstate commerce, . . . i.e., those activities that substantially affect interstate commerce. . . .

Within this final category, admittedly, our case law has not been clear whether an activity must "affect" or "substantially affect" interstate commerce in order to be within Congress' power to regulate it under the Commerce Clause. . . . We conclude, consistent with the great weight of our case law, that the proper test requires an analysis of whether the regulated activity "substantially affects" interstate commerce.

We now turn to consider the power of Congress, in the light of this framework, to enact §922(q). The first two categories of authority may be quickly disposed of: §922(q) is not a regulation of the use of the channels of interstate commerce, nor is it an attempt to prohibit the interstate transportation of a commodity through the channels of commerce; nor can §922(q) be justified as a regulation by which Congress has sought to protect an instrumentality of interstate commerce or a thing in interstate commerce. Thus, if § 922(q) is to be sustained, it must be under the third category as a regulation of an activity that substantially affects interstate commerce. . . .

Even Wickard, which is perhaps the most far reaching example of Commerce Clause authority over intrastate activity, involved economic activity in a way that the possession of a gun in a school zone does not. . . .

Section 922(q) is a criminal statute that by its terms has nothing to do with "commerce" or any sort of economic enterprise, however broadly one might define those terms. Section 922(q) is not an essential part of a larger regulation of economic activity, in which the regulatory scheme could be undercut unless the intrastate activity were regulated. It cannot, therefore, be sustained under our cases upholding regulations of activities that arise out of or are connected with a commercial transaction, which viewed in the aggregate, substantially affects interstate commerce. . . .

The Government's essential contention, in fine, is that we may determine here that §922(q) is valid because possession of a firearm in a local school zone does indeed substantially affect interstate commerce. . . . The Government argues that possession of a firearm in a school zone may result in violent crime and that violent crime can be expected to affect the functioning of the national economy in two ways. First, the costs of violent crime are substantial, and, through the mechanism of insurance, those costs are spread throughout the population. . . . Second, violent crime reduces the willingness of individuals to travel to areas within the country that are perceived to be unsafe. . . . The Government also argues that the presence of guns in schools poses a substantial threat to the educational process by threatening the learning environment. A handicapped educational process, in turn, will result in a less productive citizenry. That, in turn, would have an adverse effect on the Nation's economic well-being. As a result, the Government argues that Congress could rationally have concluded that § 922(q) substantially affects interstate commerce.

We pause to consider the implications of the Government's arguments. The Government admits, under its "costs of crime" reasoning, that Congress could regulate not only all violent crime, but all activities that might lead to violent crime, regardless of how tenuously they relate to interstate commerce. . . . Similarly, under the Government's "national productivity" reasoning, Congress could regulate any activity that it found was related to the economic productivity of individual citizens: family law (including marriage, divorce, and child custody), for example. Under the theories that the Government presents in support of §922(q), it is difficult to perceive any limitation on federal power, even in areas such as criminal law enforcement or education where States historically have been sovereign. Thus, if we were to accept the Government's arguments, we are hard-pressed to posit any activity by an individual that Congress is without power to regulate. . . .

To uphold the Government's contentions here, we would have to pile inference upon inference in a manner that would bid fair to convert congressional authority under the Commerce Clause to a general police power of the sort retained by the States. Admittedly, some of our prior cases have taken long steps down that road, giving great deference to congressional action. . . . The broad language in these opinions has suggested the possibility of additional expansion, but we decline here to proceed any further. To do so would require us to conclude that the Constitution's enumeration of powers does not presuppose something not enumerated, . . . and that there never will be a distinction between what is truly national and what is truly local. . . . This we are unwilling to do. . . .

Justice Souter, dissenting. . . .

It was not merely coincidental . . . that sea changes in the Court's conceptions of its authority under the Due Process and Commerce Clauses occurred virtually together, in 1937, with *West Coast Hotel Co. v. Parrish* . . . and *NLRB v. Jones & Laughlin Steel Corp.* . . .

In the years following these decisions, deference to legislative policy judgments on commercial regulation became the powerful theme under both the Due Process and Commerce Clauses, . . . and in due course that deference became articulate in the standard of rationality review. In due process litigation, the Court's statement of a rational basis test came quickly. . . . The parallel formulation of the Commerce Clause test came later. . . . [U]nder commerce, as under due process, adoption of rational basis review expressed the recognition that the Court had no sustainable basis for subjecting economic regulation as such to judicial policy judgments, and for the past half-century the Court has no more turned back in the direction of formalistic Commerce Clause review (as in deciding whether regulation of commerce was sufficiently direct) than it has inclined toward reasserting the substantive authority of Lochner due process. . . .

There is today . . . a backward glance at both the old pitfalls, as the Court treats deference under the rationality rule as subject to gradation according to the commercial or noncommercial nature of the immediate subject of the challenged regulation. . . . The distinction between what is patently commercial and what is not looks much like the old distinction between what directly affects commerce and what touches it only indirectly. . . . Thus, it seems fair to ask whether the step taken by the Court today does anything but portend a return to the untenable jurisprudence from which the Court extricated itself almost 60 years ago. The answer is not reassuring. . . .

. . . [T]oday's decision may be seen as only a misstep, its reasoning and its suggestions not quite in gear with the prevailing standard, but hardly an epochal case. I would not argue otherwise, but I would raise a caveat. Not every epochal case has come in epochal trappings. Jones & Laughlin did not reject the direct-indirect standard in so many words; it just said the relation of the regulated subject matter to commerce was direct enough. . . . But we know what happened.

115 ❧

By 1995, twenty-three states had passed laws imposing term limits on their own officers and on their congressional representatives. Opponents of term limits argued that the Constitution fixed the qualifications of representatives and senators and that they could be changed only by a constitutional amendment. In *Powell v. McCormack,* 395 U.S. 486 (1969), the Supreme Court had ruled that Congress could not impose requirements beyond those that the Constitution specified. However, proponents of term limits claimed that this did not prevent the states from doing so, since powers not delegated to Congress were reserved to the states or the people, as stated by the Tenth Amendment.

   U.S. Term Limits, Inc. v. Thornton made clear the fundamental division between those justices who adhered to the nationalist view of the federal system and those who espoused state rights. A narrow majority ruled that state-imposed term limits were unconstitutional, saying that the Constitution created a relationship between the people of the United States and Congress that was completely separate from the relationship between the people and the states. The majority held that the people of the United States, as a nation, created a national government. Undelegated powers were reserved, as the Tenth Amendment confirmed, either to the states or to the people *of the United States,* they insisted. In the case of changing the qualifications of legislators, the power was reserved to the people, not to the states, and could be exercised only through a constitutional amendment.

   The state-rights minority vigorously disagreed. The Constitution was created by the people *of the individual states,* they insisted. The Tenth Amendment reserved undelegated powers either to the states or to their inhabitants. If the people of the states authorized their state governments to impose term limits or other restrictions, the states had the power to do so.

U.S. Term Limits, Inc. v. Thornton (1995)

[**J** U S T I C E Stevens delivered the opinion of the Court. . . .]
   . . . [P]etitioners argue that whatever the constitutionality of additional qualifications for membership imposed by Congress, the historical and textual materials discussed in Powell do not support the conclusion that the

U.S. Term Limits, Inc. v. Thornton, 115 Supreme Court Reporter 1842 (1995).

Constitution prohibits additional qualifications imposed by states. In the absence of such a constitutional prohibition, petitioners argue, the Tenth Amendment and the principle of reserved powers require that states be allowed to add such qualifications. . . .

We disagree for two independent reasons. First, we conclude that the power to add qualifications is not within the "original powers" of the states, and thus is not reserved to the states by the Tenth Amendment. Second, even if states possessed some original power in this area, we conclude that the framers intended the Constitution to be the exclusive source of qualifications for members of Congress, and that the framers thereby "divested" states of any power to add qualifications. . . .

Contrary to petitioners' assertions, the power to add qualifications is not part of the original powers of sovereignty that the Tenth Amendment reserved to the states. Petitioners' Tenth Amendment argument misconceives the nature of the right at issue because that amendment could only "reserve" that which existed before. As Justice Story recognized, "the states can exercise no powers whatsoever which exclusively spring out of the existence of the national Government, which the Constitution does not delegate to them. . . . No state can say that it has reserved what it never possessed." . . .

With respect to setting qualifications for service in Congress, no such right existed before the Constitution was ratified. The contrary argument overlooks the revolutionary character of the government that the framers conceived. Prior to the adoption of the Constitution, the states had joined together under the Articles of Confederation. In that system, "the states retained most of their sovereignty, like independent nations bound together only by treaties." . . . After the Constitutional Convention convened, the framers were presented with, and eventually adopted a variation of, "a plan not merely to amend the Articles of Confederation but to create an entirely new national Government with a national executive, national judiciary, and a national legislature." In adopting that plan, the framers envisioned a uniform national system, rejecting the notion that the nation was a collection of states, and instead creating a direct link between the national Government and the people of the United States. . . . In that national Government, representatives owe primary allegiance not to the people of a state, but to the people of the nation. . . .

In short, as the framers recognized, electing representatives to the national legislature was a new right, arising from the Constitution itself. The Tenth Amendment thus provides no basis for concluding that the states possess reserved power to add qualifications to those that are fixed in the Constitution. Instead, any state power to set the qualifications for membership in Congress must derive not from the reserved powers of state sovereignty, but rather from the delegated powers of national sovereignty. In the absence of any constitutional delegation to the states of power to add qualifications to those enumerated in the Constitution, such a power does not exist. . . .

[T]he right to choose representatives belongs not to the states, but to the people. From the start, the framers recognized that the "great and radical vice" of the Articles of Confederation was "the principle of legislation for states or governments, in their corporate or collective capacities, and as contradistinguished from the individuals of whom they consist." The Federalist No. 15. Thus the framers, in perhaps their most important contribution, conceived of a Federal Government directly responsible to the people, possessed of direct power over the people, and chosen directly, not by states, but by the people. . . . Ours is a "government of the people, by the people, for the people." A. Lincoln, Gettysburg Address (1863). . . .

Permitting individual states to formulate diverse qualifications for their representatives would result in a patchwork of state qualifications, undermining the uniformity and the national character that the framers envisioned and sought to ensure. . . .

We are . . . firmly convinced that allowing the several states to adopt term limits for Congressional service would effect a fundamental change in the constitutional framework. Any such change must come not by legislation adopted either by Congress or by an individual state, but rather as have other important changes in the electoral process, through the amendment procedures set forth in Article V. The framers decided that the qualifications for service in the Congress of the United States be fixed in the Constitution and be uniform throughout the nation. That decision reflects the framers' understanding that members of Congress are chosen by separate constituencies but that they become, when elected, servants of the people of the United States. They are not merely delegates appointed by separate, sovereign states; they occupy offices that are integral and essential components of a single national Government. In the absence of a properly passed constitutional amendment, allowing individual states to craft their own qualifications for Congress would thus erode the structure envisioned by the framers. . . .

Justice Thomas, with whom the Chief Justice, Justice O'Connor, and Justice Scalia join, dissenting. . . .

. . . Nothing in the Constitution deprives the people of each state of the power to prescribe eligibility requirements for the candidates who seek to represent them in Congress. The Constitution is simply silent on this question. And where the Constitution is silent, it raises no bar to action by the states or the people. . . .

Our system of government rests on one overriding principle: all power stems from the consent of the people. To phrase the principle in this way, however, is to be imprecise about something important to the notion of "reserved" powers. The ultimate source of the Constitution's authority is the consent of the people of each individual state, not the consent of the undifferentiated people of the nation as a whole. . . .

When they adopted the Federal Constitution, of course, the people of each state surrendered some of their authority to the United States. . . . They affirmatively deprived their states of certain powers, and they affirmatively conferred certain powers upon the Federal Government. Because the people of the several states are the only true source of power, however, the Federal Government enjoys no authority beyond what the Constitution confers: the Federal Government's powers are limited and enumerated. . . .

These basic principles are enshrined in the Tenth Amendment, which declares that all powers neither delegated to the Federal Government nor prohibited to the states "are reserved to the states respectively, or to the people." With this careful last phrase, the amendment avoids taking any position on the division of power between the state governments and the people of the states: it is up to the people of each state to determine which "reserved" powers their state government may exercise. But the amendment does make clear that powers reside at the state level except where the Constitution removes them from that level. All powers that the Constitution neither delegates to the Federal Government nor prohibits to the states are controlled by the people of each state. . . .

The Constitution simply does not recognize any mechanism for action by the undifferentiated people of the Nation. . . .

The majority's essential logic is that the state governments could not "reserve" any powers that they did not control at the time the Constitution was drafted. But it was not the state governments that were doing the reserving. The Constitution derives its authority instead from the consent of the people of the states. Given the fundamental principle that all governmental powers stem from the people of the states, it would simply be incoherent to assert that the people of the states could not reserve any powers that they had not previously controlled.

Conservative Constitutionalism in Congress

116 ❧

During the congressional elections of 1994, most Republican candidates for the House of Representatives endorsed a "Contract With America," specifying a series of actions that they promised to take within the first one hundred days of achieving a majority in the

House. Several of the proposals called for reforms in House procedure, but others embodied conservative ideas about cutting government regulation of business, lowering taxes, reducing federal expenditures, and transferring governmental responsibilities to the states. When the House completed action on the last of the promised measures, Speaker of the House Newt Gingrich addressed the nation. Using language that embodied conservative concepts of society and government, he proposed jettisoning the general-welfare state and decentralizing government.

Newt Gingrich, Address to the Nation (1995)

Every night on every local news we see the human tragedies that have grown out of the current welfare state. . . .

We must start by recognizing the moral and economic failure of the current methods of government. In these last 100 days, we have begun to change those failed methods. . . .

[T]he Contract With America is only a beginning. It is the preliminary skirmish to the big battles yet to come. The big battles will deal with how we remake the Government of the United States. . . . New ideas, new ways and old fashioned common sense can improve Government while reducing its costs.

The purpose of all this change is not simply a better government. It is a better America. A truly compassionate government would replace the welfare state with opportunity, because the welfare system's greatest cost is the human cost to the poor. In the name of compassion, we have funded a system that is cruel and destroys families. Its failure is reflected by the violence, brutality, child abuse and drug addiction in every local TV news broadcast.

I believe we have to do a number of things to become an opportunity society. We must restore freedom by ending bureaucratic micromanagement here in Washington. As any good business leader will tell you, decisions should be made as closely as possible to the source of the problem. This country is too big and too diverse for Washington to have the knowledge to make the right decisions on local matters. We've got to return power back to you, to your families, your neighborhoods, your local and state governments.

117 ∾

Responding to pressure from state and local officials and reflecting conservative commitment to state rights, Congress passed an act designed to lift the financial burden that federal regulations imposed on state and local government. While the Senate wanted only to

New York Times, April 8, 1995, sec. A, p. 8.

express a general concern with the problem of unfunded mandates, the House sought to prevent their imposition. The result was an odd law that declared it a violation of the rules of the House and Senate to pass a bill imposing significant costs upon the states without appropriating money to offset the burden. A law or regulation exceeding the limit would be subject to a point of order, which the House Rules Committee might waive. The effect was to enable Congress to exceed the limit simply by voting down the point of order.

Despite the potential for evasion, the law marked a dramatic shift in federalism. Under its provisions, for example, Congress could not have amended the Fair Labor Standards Act as it did in 1974 (thereby precipitating *National League of Cities v. Usery*; see Document 107) without appropriating money to reimburse state and local governments for the cost of implementing the act.

The Unfunded Mandates Reform Act (1995)

Purposes

The purposes of this Act are—

(1) to strengthen the partnership between the Federal Government and State, local, and tribal governments;

(2) to end the imposition, in the absence of full consideration by Congress, of Federal mandates on State, local, and tribal governments without adequate Federal funding, in a manner that may displace other essential State, local, and tribal governmental priorities. . . .

Exclusions

This Act shall not apply to any provision in a bill, joint resolution, amendment, motion, or conference report before Congress and any provision in a proposed or final Federal regulation that—

(1) enforces constitutional rights of individuals;

(2) establishes or enforces any statutory rights that prohibit discrimination on the basis of race, color, religion, sex, national origin, age, handicap, or disability; . . .

(5) is necessary for the national security or the ratification or implementation of international treaty obligations;

(6) the President designates as emergency legislation and that the Congress so designates in statute: or

Congressional Record, 104th Congress, 1st sess., H3053-59 (March 13, 1995).

(7) relates to the old-age, survivors, and disability insurance program under title II of the Social Security Act. . . .

In general.—Title IV of the Congressional Budget and Impoundment Control Act of 1974 is amended by . . . adding at the end thereof the following new part:

"Part B—Federal Mandates

. . . "Sec. 425. Legislation Subject to Point of order.

"*(a) In General.*—It shall not be in order in the Senate or the House of Representatives to consider—

"(1) any bill or joint resolution that is reported by a committee unless the committee has published a statement of the Director [of the Congressional Budget Office] on the direct costs of Federal mandates . . . ; and

"(2) any bill, joint resolution, amendment, motion, or conference report that would increase the direct costs of Federal intergovernmental mandates by an amount that causes the thresholds specified in section 424(a)(1) [$50,000,000 adjusted annually for inflation] to be exceeded, unless—

"(A) the bill, joint resolution, amendment, motion, or conference report provides new budget authority or new entitlement authority in the House of Representatives or direct spending authority in the Senate for each fiscal year for such mandates included in the bill, joint resolution, amendment, motion, or conference report in an amount equal to or exceeding the direct costs of such mandate; or

"(B) the bill, joint resolution, amendment, motion, or conference report includes an authorization for appropriations in an amount equal to or exceeding the direct costs of such mandate. . . .

"Sec. 426. Provisions Relating to the House of Representatives

"*(a) Enforcement in the House of Representatives.*—It shall not be in order in the House of Representatives to consider a rule or order that waives the application of section 425. . . ."

118 ❧

As part of the Contract With America, House Republicans promised legislation that would incorporate into law the conservative view that the Takings Clause mandated compensation to property owners for losses suffered as the result of federal regulations. Assuming that the Supreme Court had accepted the conservatives' argument in *Dolan v.*

City of Tigard (Document 113), the House passed the Private Property Protection Act of 1995.*

The Private Property Protection Bill (1995)

Sec. 1. Short Title.

This Act may be cited as the "Private Property Protection Act of 1995"

Sec. 2. Federal Policy and Direction.

(a) General Policy.—It is the policy of the Federal Government that no law or agency action should limit the use of privately owned property so as to diminish its value.

(b) Application to Federal Agency Action.—Each Federal agency, officer, and employee should exercise Federal authority to ensure that agency action will not limit the use of privately owned property so as to diminish its value.

Sec. 3. Right to Compensation.

(a) In General.—The Federal Government shall compensate an owner of property whose use of any portion of that property has been limited by an agency action, under a specified regulatory law, that diminishes the fair market value of that portion by 20 percent or more. The amount of the compensation shall equal the diminution in value that resulted from the agency action. If the diminution in value of a portion of that property is greater than 50 percent, at the option of the owner, the Federal Government shall buy that portion of the property for its fair market value. . . .

Sec. 5. Exceptions.

(a) Prevention of Hazard to Health or Safety or Damage to Specific Property.—No compensation shall be made under this Act with respect to an agency action the primary purpose of which is to prevent an identifiable hazard to public health or safety.

---

*The bill had not become law as this sourcebook went to press.
Congressional Record, 104th Congress, 1st sess., H2629-30 (March 3, 1995).

Appendix

Constitution of the United States of America

PREAMBLE *← not law just statement*

We the people of the United States, in order to form a more perfect union, establish justice, insure domestic tranquillity, provide for the common defense, promote the general welfare, and secure the blessings of liberty to ourselves and our posterity, do ordain and establish this Constitution for the United States of America.

Article I *legislative*

Section 1. All legislative powers herein granted shall be vested in a Congress of the United States, which shall consist of a Senate and a House of Representatives.

Section 2. *executive* The House of Representatives shall be composed of members chosen every second year by the people of the several States, and the electors in each State shall have the qualifications requisite for electors of the most numerous branch of the State Legislature.

No person shall be a Representative who shall not have attained to the age of twenty-five years, and been seven years a citizen of the United States, and who shall not, when elected, be an inhabitant of that State in which he shall be chosen.

Representatives and direct taxes shall be apportioned among the several States which may be included within this Union, according to their respective numbers, which shall be determined by adding to the whole number of free persons, including those bound to service for a term of years and excluding Indians not taxed, three-fifths of all other persons. The actual enumeration shall be made within three years after the first meeting of the Congress of the United States, and within every subsequent term of ten years, in such manner as they shall by law direct. The number of Representatives shall not exceed one for every thirty thousand, but each State shall have at least one Representative; and until such enumeration shall be made, the State of New Hampshire shall be entitled to choose three, Massachusetts eight, Rhode Island and Providence Plantations one, Connecticut five, New York six, New Jersey four, Pennsylvania eight, Delaware one, Maryland six, Virginia ten, North Carolina five, South Carolina five, and Georgia three.

When vacancies happen in the representation from any State, the Executive authority thereof shall issue writs of election to fill such vacancies.

The House of Representatives shall choose their Speaker and other officers; and shall have the sole power of impeachment.

Section 3. The Senate of the United States shall be composed of two Senators from each State, chosen by the legislature thereof, for six years; and each Senator shall have one vote.

Immediately after they shall be assembled in consequence of the first election, they shall be divided as equally as may be into three classes. The seats of the Senators of the first class shall be vacated at the expiration of the second year, of the second class at the expiration of the fourth year, and of the third class at the expiration of the sixth year, so that one-third may be chosen every second year; and if vacancies happen by resignation or otherwise, during the recess of the legislature of any State, the Executive thereof may make temporary appointments until the next meeting of the legislature, which shall then fill such vacancies.

No person shall be a Senator who shall not have attained to the age of thirty years, and been nine years a citizen of the United States, and who shall not, when elected, be an inhabitant of that State for which he shall be chosen.

The Vice President of the United States shall be President of the Senate, but shall have no vote, unless they be equally divided.

The Senate shall choose their other officers, and also a President *pro tempore*, in the absence of the Vice President, or when he shall exercise the office of the President of the United States.

The Senate shall have the sole power to try all impeachments. When sitting for that purpose, they shall be on oath or affirmation. When the President of the United States is tried, the Chief Justice shall preside: and no person shall be convicted without the concurrence of two-thirds of the members present.

Judgment in cases of impeachment shall not extend further than to removal from the office, and disqualification to hold and enjoy any office of honor, trust or profit under the United States; but the party convicted shall nevertheless be liable and subject to indictment, trial, judgment and punishment, according to law.

Section 4.   The times, places and manner of holding elections for Senators and Representatives shall be prescribed in each State by the legislature thereof; but the Congress may at any time by law make or alter such regulations, except as to the places of choosing Senators.

The Congress shall assemble at least once in every year, and such meeting shall be on the first Monday in December, unless they shall by law appoint a different day.

Section 5.   Each house shall be the judge of the elections, returns and qualifications of its own members, and a majority of each shall constitute a quorum to do business; but a smaller number may adjourn from day to day, and may be authorized to compel the attendance of absent members, in such manner, and under such penalties, as each house may provide.

Each house may determine the rules of its proceedings, punish its members for disorderly behavior, and with the concurrence of two-thirds, expel a member.

Each house shall keep a journal of its proceedings, and from time to time publish the same, excepting such parts as may in their judgment require secrecy; and the yeas and nays of the members of either house on any question shall, at the desire of one-fifth of those present, be entered on the journal.

Neither house, during the session of Congress, shall, without the consent of the other, adjourn for more than three days, nor to any other place than that in which the two houses shall be sitting.

Section 6.   The Senators and Representatives shall receive a compensation for their services, to be ascertained by law and paid out of the treasury of the United States. They shall in all cases except treason, felony and breach of the peace, be privileged from arrest during their attendance at the session of their respective houses, and in going to and returning from the same; and for any speech or debate in either house, they shall not be questioned in any other place.

No Senator or Representative shall, during the time for which he was elected, be appointed to any civil office under the authority of the United States, which shall have been created, or the emoluments whereof shall have been increased, during such time; and no person holding any office under the United States shall be a member of either house during his continuance in office.

Section 7.   All bills for raising revenue shall originate in the House of Representatives; but the Senate may propose or concur with amendments as on other bills.

Every bill which shall have passed the House of Representatives and the Senate, shall, before it become a law, be presented to the President of the

United States; if he approve he shall sign it, but if not he shall return it with objections to that house in which it originated, who shall enter the objections at large on their journal, and proceed to reconsider it. If after such reconsideration two-thirds of that house shall agree to pass the bill, it shall be sent, together with the objections, to the other house, by which it shall likewise be reconsidered, and, if approved by two-thirds of that house, it shall become a law. But in all such cases the votes of both houses shall be determined by yeas and nays, and the names of the persons voting for and against the bill shall be entered on the journal of each house respectively. If any bill shall not be returned by the President within ten days (Sundays excepted) after it shall have been presented to him, the same shall be a law, in like manner as if he had signed it, unless the Congress by their adjournment prevent its return, in which case it shall not be a law.

Every order, resolution, or vote to which the concurrence of the Senate and House of Representatives may be necessary (except on a question of adjournment) shall be presented to the President of the United States; and before the same shall take effect, shall be approved by him, or being disapproved by him, shall be repassed by two-thirds of the Senate and House of Representatives, according to the rules and limitations prescribed in the case of a bill.

Section 8.   The Congress shall have power [*Powers of Congress*]
To lay and collect taxes, duties, imposts, and excises, to pay the debts and provide for the common defense and general welfare of the United States; but all duties, imposts and excises shall be uniform throughout the United States;

To borrow money on the credit of the United States;

To regulate commerce with foreign nations, and among the several States, and with the Indian tribes;

To establish an uniform rule of naturalization, and uniform laws on the subject of bankruptcies throughout the United States;

To coin money, regulate the value thereof, and of foreign coin, and fix the standard of weights and measures;

To provide for the punishment of counterfeiting the securities and current coin of the United States;

To establish post offices and post roads;

To promote the progress of science and useful arts by securing for limited times to authors and inventors the exclusive right to their respective writings and discoveries; — [*patents*]

To constitute tribunals inferior to the Supreme Court;

To define and punish piracies and felonies committed on the high seas and offenses against the law of nations;

To declare war, grant letters of marque and reprisal, and make rules concerning captures on land and water;

To raise and support armies, but no appropriation of money to that use shall be for a longer term than two years;

To provide and maintain a navy;

To make rules for the government and regulation of the land and naval forces;

To provide for calling forth the militia to execute the laws of the Union, suppress insurrections, and repel invasions;

To provide for organizing, arming, and disciplining the militia, and for governing such part of them as may be employed in the service of the United States, reserving to the States respectively the appointment of the officers, and the authority of training the militia according to the discipline prescribed by Congress;

To exercise exclusive legislation in all cases whatsoever, over such district (not exceeding ten miles square) as may, by cession of particular States, and the acceptance of Congress, become the seat of government of the United States, and to exercise like authority over all places purchased by the consent of the legislature of the State, in which the same shall be, for erection of forts, magazines, arsenals, dock-yards, and other needful buildings and

To make all laws which shall be necessary and proper for carrying into execution the foregoing powers, and all other powers vested by this Constitution in the government of the United States, or in any department or officer thereof.

Section 9. The migration or importation of such persons as any of the States now existing shall think proper to admit shall not be prohibited by the Congress prior to the year 1808; but a tax or duty may be imposed on such importation, not exceeding $10 for each person.

The privilege of the writ of habeas corpus shall not be suspended, unless when in cases of rebellion or invasion the public safety may require it.

No bill of attainder or ex post facto law shall be passed.

No capitation, or other direct, tax shall be laid, unless in proportion to the census or enumeration herein before directed to be taken.

No tax or duty shall be laid on articles exported from any State.

No preference shall be given by any regulation of commerce or revenue to the ports of one State over those of another; nor shall vessels bound to, or from, one State, be obliged to enter, clear, or pay duties in another.

No money shall be drawn from the treasury, but in consequence of appropriations made by law; and a regular statement and account of the receipts and expenditures of all public money shall be published from time to time.

No title of nobility shall be granted by the United States: and no person holding any office of profit or trust under them, shall, without the consent of the Congress, accept of any present, emolument, office, or title, of any kind whatever, from any king, prince, or foreign state.

Section 10.   No State shall enter into any treaty, alliance, or confederation; grant letters of marque and reprisal; coin money; emit bills of credit; make anything but gold and silver coin a tender in payment of debts; pass any bill of attainder, ex post facto law, or law impairing the obligation of contracts, or grant any title of nobility.

No State shall, without the consent of Congress, lay any imposts or duties on imports or exports, except what may be absolutely necessary for executing its inspection laws: and the net produce of all duties and imposts, laid by any State on imports or exports, shall be for the use of the treasury of the United States; and all such laws shall be subject to the revision and control of the Congress.

No State shall, without the consent of Congress, lay any duty of tonnage, keep troops or ships of war in time of peace, enter into any agreement or compact with another State, or with a foreign power, or engage in war, unless actually invaded, or in such imminent danger as will not admit of delay.

Article II

Section 1.   The executive power shall be vested in a President of the United States of America. He shall hold his office during the term of four years, and, together with the Vice President, chosen for the same term, be elected as follows:

Each state shall appoint, in such manner as the legislature thereof may direct, a number of electors, equal to the whole number of Senators and Representatives to which the State may be entitled in the Congress; but no Senator or Representative, or person holding an office of trust or profit under the United States, shall be appointed an elector.

The electors shall meet in their respective States, and vote by ballot for two persons, of whom one at least shall not be an inhabitant of the same State with themselves. And they shall make a list of all the persons voted for, and of the number of votes for each; which list they shall sign and certify, and transmit sealed to the seat of government of the United States, directed to the President of the Senate. The President of the Senate shall, in the presence of the Senate and the House of Representatives, open all the certificates, and the votes shall then be counted. The person having the greatest number of votes shall be the President, if such number be a majority of the whole number of electors appointed; and if there be more than one who have such majority, and have an equal number of votes, then the House of Representatives shall immediately choose by ballot one of them for President; and if no person have a majority, then from the five highest on the list said house shall in like manner choose the President. But in choosing the President the votes shall be taken by States, the representation from each State having one vote; a quorum for this purpose shall consist of a member or members from two-thirds of the States, and a majority of all the States shall be necessary to a choice. In every case, after the choice of the President, the person having the greatest number of votes of the electors shall be the Vice President. But if there should remain two or more who have equal votes, the Senate shall choose from them by ballot the Vice President.

The Congress may determine the time of choosing the electors and the day on which they shall give their votes; which day shall be the same throughout the United States.

No person except a natural-born citizen, or a citizen of the United States at the time of the adoption of this Constitution, shall be eligible to the office of President; neither shall any person be eligible to that office who shall not have attained to the age of thirty-five years, and been fourteen years a resident within the United States.

In case of the removal of the President from office or of his death, resignation, or inability to discharge the powers and duties of the said office, the same shall devolve on the Vice President, and the Congress may by law provide for the case of removal, death, resignation, or inability, both of the President and Vice President, declaring what officer shall then act as President, and such officer shall act accordingly, until the disability be removed, or a President shall be elected.

The President shall, at stated times, receive for his services a compensation, which shall neither be increased nor diminished during the period for which he shall have been elected, and he shall not receive within that period any other emolument from the United States, or any of them.

Before he enter on the execution of his office, he shall take the following oath or affirmation:—"I do solemnly swear (or affirm) that I will faithfully execute the office of the President of the United States, and will to the best of my ability preserve, protect and defend the Constitution of the United States."

Section 2.   The President shall be commander in chief of the army and navy of the United States, and of the militia of the several States, when called into the actual service of the United States; he may require the opinion, in writing, of the principal officer in each of the executive departments, upon any subject relating to the duties of their respective offices, and he shall have power to grant reprieves and pardons for offenses against the United States, except in cases of impeachment.

He shall have power, by and with the advice and consent of the Senate, to make treaties, provided two-thirds of the Senators present concur; and he shall nominate, and by and with the advice and consent of the Senate, shall appoint ambassadors, other public ministers and consuls, judges of the

Supreme Court, and all other officers of the United States, whose appointments are not herein otherwise provided for, and which shall be established by law; but Congress may by law vest the appointment of such inferior officers, as they think proper, in the President alone, in the courts of law, or in the heads of departments.

The President shall have power to fill up all vacancies that may happen during the recess of the Senate, by granting commissions which shall expire at the end of their next session.

Section 3.   He shall from time to time give to the Congress information of the state of the Union, and recommend to their consideration such measures as he shall judge necessary and expedient; he may, on extraordinary occasions, convene both houses, or either of them, and in case of disagreement between them, with respect to the time of adjournment, he may adjourn them to such time as he shall think proper; he shall receive ambassadors and other public ministers; he shall take care that the laws be faithfully executed, and shall commission all the officers of the United States.

Section 4.   The President, Vice President and all civil officers of the United States shall be removed from office on impeachment for, and on conviction of, treason, bribery, or other high crimes and misdemeanors.

Article III

Section 1.   The judicial power of the United States shall be vested in one Supreme Court, and in such inferior courts as the Congress may from time to time ordain and establish. The judges, both of the Supreme and inferior courts, shall hold their offices during good behavior, and shall, at stated times, receive for their services a compensation which shall not be diminished during their continuance in office.

Section 2.   The judicial power shall extend to all cases, in law and equity, arising under this Constitution, the laws of the United States, and treaties made, or which shall be made, under their authority—to all cases affecting ambassadors, other public ministers and consuls—to all cases of admiralty and maritime jurisdiction—to controversies to which the United States shall be a party—to controversies between two or more States—between a State and citizens of another State;—between citizens of different States—between citizens of the same State claiming lands under grants of different States, and between a State, or the citizens thereof, and foreign states, citizens or subjects.

In all cases affecting ambassadors, other public ministers and consuls, and those in which a State shall be party, the Supreme Court shall have original jurisdiction. In all the other cases before mentioned, the Supreme Court shall have appellate jurisdiction, both as to law and fact, with such exceptions, and under such regulations, as the Congress shall make.

The trial of all crimes, except in cases of impeachment, shall be by jury; and such trial shall be held in the State where said crimes shall have been committed; but when not committed within any State, the trial shall be at such place or places as the Congress may by law have directed.

Section 3.   Treason against the United States shall consist only in levying war against them, or in adhering to their enemies, giving them aid and comfort. No person shall be convicted of treason unless on the testimony of two witnesses to the same overt act, or on confession in open court.

The Congress shall have power to declare the punishment of treason, but no attainder of treason shall work corruption of blood, or forfeiture except during the life of the person attainted.

Article IV   *relations between States and federal gov*

Section 1.   Full faith and credit shall be given in each State to the public acts, records, and judicial proceedings of every other State. And the Congress may by general laws prescribe the manner in which such acts, records, and proceedings shall be proved, and the effect thereof.

Section 2.   The citizens of each State shall be entitled to all privileges and immunities of citizens in the several States.

A person charged in any State with treason, felony, or other crime, who shall flee from justice, and be found in another State, shall on demand of the executive authority of the State from which he fled, be delivered up, to be removed to the State having jurisdiction of the crime.

No person held to service or labor in one State, under the laws thereof, escaping into another, shall, in consequence of any law or regulation therein, be discharged from such service or labor, but shall be delivered up on claim of the party to whom such service or labor may be due.

Section 3.   New States may be admitted by the Congress into this Union; but no new State shall be formed or erected within the jurisdiction of any other State; nor any State be formed by the junction of two or more States, or parts of States, without the consent of the legislatures of the States concerned as well as of the Congress.

The Congress shall have power to dispose of and make all needful rules and regulations respecting the territory or other property belonging to the United States; and nothing in this Constitution shall be so construed as to prejudice any claims of the United States, or of any particular State.

Section 4. The United States shall guarantee to every State in this Union a republican form of government, and shall protect each of them against invasion; and on application of the legislature, or of the executive (when the legislature cannot be convened), against domestic violence.

Article V   — *Amendments article*

The Congress, whenever two-thirds of both houses shall deem it necessary, shall propose amendments to this Constitution, or, on the application of the legislatures of two-thirds of the several States, shall call a convention for proposing amendments, which, in either case, shall be valid to all intents and purposes, as part of this Constitution, when ratified by the legislatures of three-fourths of the several States, or by conventions in three-fourths thereof, as the one or the other mode of ratification may be proposed by the Congress; provided that no amendments which may be made prior to the year one thousand eight hundred and eight shall in any manner affect the first and fourth clauses in the ninth section of the first article; and that no State, without its consent, shall be deprived of its equal suffrage in the Senate.

Article VI

All debts contracted and engagements entered into, before the adoption of this Constitution, shall be as valid against the United States under this Constitution, as under the Confederation.

This Constitution, and the laws of the United States which shall be made in pursuance thereof; and all treaties made, or which shall be made, under the authority of the United States, shall be the supreme law of the land; and the judges in every State shall be bound thereby, anything in the Constitution or laws of any State to the contrary notwithstanding.

The Senators and Representatives before mentioned, and the members of the several State legislatures, and all executive and judicial officers, both of the United States and of the several States, shall be bound by oath or affirmation to support this Constitution; but no religious test shall ever be required as a qualification to any office or public trust under the United States.

Article VII

The ratification of the conventions of nine States shall be sufficient for the establishment of this Constitution between the States so ratifying the same.

Done in Convention by the unanimous consent of the States present, the seventeenth day of September in the year of our Lord one thousand seven hundred and eighty-seven and of the Independence of the United States of America the twelfth. In witness whereof we have hereunto subscribed our names.

Amendments to the Constitution

Article I*

Congress shall make no law respecting an establishment of religion, or prohibiting the free exercise thereof; or abridging the freedom of speech, or of the press; or the right of the people peaceably to assemble, and to petition the government for a redress of grievances.

Article II

A well-regulated militia being necessary to the security of a free State, the right of the people to keep and bear arms shall not be infringed.

Article III

No soldier shall, in time of peace, be quartered in any house without the consent of the owner, nor in time of war, but in a manner to be prescribed by law.

Article IV

The right of the people to be secure in their persons, houses, papers, and effects, against unreasonable searches and seizures, shall not be violated, and no warrants shall issue but upon probable cause, supported by oath or affirmation, and particularly describing the place to be searched, and the persons or things to be seized.

Article V

No person shall be held to answer for a capital, or otherwise infamous crime, unless on a presentment or indictment of a grand jury, except in cases arising in the land or naval forces, or in the militia, when in actual service in time of war or public danger; nor shall any person be subject for the same offense to be twice put in jeopardy of life or limb; nor shall be compelled in any criminal case to be a witness against himself, nor be deprived of life, liberty, or property, without due process of law; nor shall private property be taken for public use without just compensation.

Article VI

In all criminal prosecutions, the accused shall enjoy the right to a speedy and public trial, by an impartial jury of the State and district wherein the crime shall have been committed, which district shall have been previously ascertained

*The first ten Amendments (Bill of Rights) were adopted in 1791.

by law, and to be informed of the nature and cause of the accusation; to be confronted with the witnesses against him; to have compulsory process for obtaining witnesses in his favor, and to have the assistance of counsel for his defense.

Article VII

In suits at common law, where the value in controversy shall exceed twenty dollars, the right of trial by jury shall be preserved, and no fact tried by a jury shall be otherwise reexamined in any court of the United States, than according to the rules of the common law.

Article VIII

Excessive bail shall not be required, nor excessive fines imposed, nor cruel and unusual punishments inflicted.

Article IX

The enumeration in the Constitution, of certain rights, shall not be construed to deny or disparage others retained by the people.

Article X

The powers not delegated to the United States by the Constitution, nor prohibited by it to the States, are reserved to the States respectively, or to the people.

Article XI

[*Adopted 1798*]

The judicial power of the United States shall not be construed to extend to any suit in law or equity, commenced or prosecuted against one of the United States by citizens of another State, or by citizens or subjects of any foreign state.

Article XII

[*Adopted 1804*]

The electors shall meet in their respective States, and vote by ballot for President and Vice President, one of whom, at least, shall not be an inhabitant of the same State with themselves; they shall name in their ballots the person voted for as President, and in distinct ballots the person voted for as Vice President, and they shall make distinct lists of all persons voted for as President, and of all persons voted for as Vice President, and of the number of votes for each, which lists they shall sign and certify, and transmit sealed to the seat of government of the United States, directed to the President of the Senate—the President of the Senate shall, in the presence of the Senate and House of Representatives, open all the certificates and the votes shall then be counted—the person having the greatest number of votes for President shall be the President, if such number be a majority of the whole number of electors appointed; and if no person have such majority, then from the persons having the highest numbers not exceeding three on the list of those voted for as President, the House of Representatives shall choose immediately, by ballot, the President. But in choosing the President, the votes shall be taken by States, the representation from each State having one vote; a quorum for this purpose shall consist of a member or members from two-thirds of the States, and a majority of all the States shall be necessary to a choice. And if the House of Representatives shall not choose a President whenever the right of choice shall devolve upon them, before the fourth day of March next following, then the Vice President shall act as President, as in the case of the death or other constitutional disability of the President.

The person having the greatest number of votes as Vice President shall be the Vice President, if such a number be a majority of the whole number of electors appointed; and if no person have a majority, then from the two highest numbers on the list the Senate shall choose the Vice President; a quorum for the purpose shall consist of two-thirds of the whole number of Senators, and a majority of the whole number shall be necessary to a choice. But no person constitutionally ineligible to the office of President shall be eligible to that of Vice President of the United States.

Article XIII
[*Adopted 1865*]

Section 1.   Neither slavery nor involuntary servitude, except as a punishment for crime whereof the party shall have been duly convicted, shall exist within the United States, or any place subject to their jurisdiction.

Section 2.   Congress shall have power to enforce this article by appropriate legislation.

Article XIV
[*Adopted 1868*]

Section 1.   All persons born or naturalized in the United States, and subject to the jurisdiction thereof, are citizens of the United States and of the State wherein they reside. No State shall make or enforce any law which shall abridge the privileges or immunities of citizens of the United States; nor shall any State deprive any person of life, liberty, or property, without due process of law; nor deny to any person within its jurisdiction the equal protection of the laws.

Section 2.   Representatives shall be apportioned among the several States according to their respective numbers, counting the whole number of persons in each State, excluding Indians not taxed. But when the right to vote at any election for the choice of Electors for President and Vice President of the United States, Representatives in Congress, the executive and judicial officers of a State, or the members of the legislature thereof, is denied to any of the male inhabitants of such State, being twenty-one years of age and citizens of the United States, or in any way abridged, except for participation in rebellion, or other crime, the basis of representation therein shall be reduced in the proportion which the number of such male citizens shall bear to the whole number of male citizens twenty-one years of age in such State.

Section 3.   No person shall be a Senator or Representative in Congress or Elector of President and Vice President, or hold any office, civil or military, under the United States, or under any State, who, having previously taken an oath, as a member of Congress, or as an officer of the United States, or as a member of any State legislature, or as an executive or judicial officer of any State, to support the Constitution of the United States, shall have engaged in insurrection or rebellion against the same, or given aid and comfort to the enemies thereof. Congress may, by a vote of two-thirds of each house, remove such disability.

Section 4.   The validity of the public debt of the United States, authorized by law, including debts incurred for payment of pensions and bounties for services in suppressing insurrection or rebellion, shall not be questioned. But neither the United States nor any State shall assume or pay any debt or obligation incurred in aid of insurrection or rebellion against the United States, or any claim for the loss or emancipation of any slave; but all such debts, obligations, and claims shall be held illegal and void.

Section 5.   The Congress shall have the power to enforce, by appropriate legislation, the provisions of this article.

Article XV
[*Adopted 1870*]

Section 1.   The right of citizens of the United States to vote shall not be denied or abridged by the United States or by any State on account of race, color, or previous condition of servitude.

Section 2. The Congress shall have power to enforce this article by appropriate legislation.

Article XVI
[*Adopted 1913*]

The Congress shall have power to lay and collect taxes on incomes, from whatever source derived, without apportionment among the several States, and without regard to any census or enumeration.

Article XVII
[*Adopted 1913*]

Section 1. The Senate of the United States shall be composed of two Senators from each State, elected by the people thereof, for six years; and each Senator shall have one vote. The electors in each State shall have the qualifications requisite for electors of voters for the most numerous branch of the State legislatures.

Section 2. When vacancies happen in the representation of any State in the Senate, the executive authority of such State shall issue writs of election to fill such vacancies: Provided, that the Legislature of any State may empower the executive thereof to make temporary appointments until the people fill the vacancies by election as the Legislature may direct.

Section 3. This amendment shall not be so construed as to affect the election or term of any Senator chosen before it becomes valid as part of the Constitution.

Article XVIII
[*Adopted 1919; repealed 1933*]

Section 1. After one year from the ratification of this article the manufacture, sale, or transportation of intoxicating liquors within, the importation thereof into, or the exportation thereof from the United States and all territory subject to the jurisdiction thereof, for beverage purposes, is hereby prohibited.

Section 2. The Congress and the several States shall have concurrent power to enforce this article by appropriate legislation.

Section 3. This article shall be inoperative unless it shall have been ratified as an amendment to the Constitution by the legislatures of the several States, as provided by the Constitution, within seven years from the date of the submission thereof to the States by the Congress.

Article XIX
[*Adopted 1920*]

Section 1.   The right of citizens of the United States to vote shall not be denied or abridged by the United States or by any State on account of sex.

Section 2.   The Congress shall have the power to enforce this article by appropriate legislation.

Article XX
[*Adopted 1933*]

Section 1.   The terms of the President and Vice President shall end at noon on the 20th day of January, and the terms of Senators and Representatives at noon on the 3d day of January, of the years in which such terms would have ended if this article had not been ratified; and the terms of their successors shall then begin.

Section 2.   The Congress shall assemble at least once in every year, and such meeting shall begin at noon on the 3d of January, unless they shall by law appoint a different day.

Section 3.   If, at the time fixed for the beginning of the term of the President, the President-elect shall have died, the Vice President-elect shall become President. If a President shall not have been chosen before the time fixed for the beginning of his term, or if the President-elect shall have failed to qualify, then the Vice President-elect shall act as President until a President shall have qualified; and the Congress may by law provide for the case wherein neither a President-elect nor a Vice President-elect shall have qualified, declaring who shall then act as President, or the manner in which one who is to act shall be selected, and such persons shall act accordingly until a President or Vice President shall have qualified.

Section 4.   The Congress may by law provide for the case of the death of any of the persons from whom the House of Representatives may choose a President whenever the right of choice shall have devolved upon them, and for the case of the death of any of the persons from whom the Senate may choose a Vice President whenever the right of choice shall have devolved upon them.

Section 5.   Sections 1 and 2 shall take effect on the 15th day of October following the ratification of this article.

Section 6.   This article shall be inoperative unless it shall have been ratified as an amendment to the Constitution by the Legislatures of three-fourths of the several States within seven years from the date of its submission.

Article XXI
[*Adopted 1933*]

Section 1. The eighteenth article of amendment to the Constitution of the United States is hereby repealed.

Section 2. The transportation or importation into any State, Territory, or Possession of the United States for delivery or use therein of intoxicating liquors, in violation of the laws thereof, is hereby prohibited.

Section 3. This article shall be inoperative unless it shall have been ratified as an amendment to the Constitution by conventions in the several States, as provided in the Constitution, within seven years from the date of submission thereof to the States by the Congress.

Article XXII
[*Adopted 1951*]

Section 1. No person shall be elected to the office of President more than twice, and no person who has held the office of President, or acted as President, for more than two years of a term to which some other person was elected President shall be elected to the office of President more than once. But this article shall not apply to any person holding the office of President when this article was proposed by the Congress, and shall not prevent any person who may be holding the office of President, or acting as President, during the term within which this article becomes operative from holding the office of President or acting as President during the remainder of such term.

Section 2. This article shall be inoperative unless it shall have been ratified as an amendment to the Constitution by the legislatures of three-fourths of the several States within seven years from the date of its submission to the States by the Congress.

Article XXIII
[*Adopted 1961*]

Section 1. The District constituting the seat of Government of the United States shall appoint in such manner as the Congress may direct:

A number of electors of President and Vice President equal to the whole number of Senators and Representatives in Congress to which the District would be entitled if it were a State, but in no event more than the least populous State; they shall be in addition to those appointed by the States, but they shall be considered for the purposes of the election of President and Vice President, to be electors appointed by a State; and they shall meet in the

District and perform such duties as provided by the twelfth article of amendment.

Section 2.   The Congress shall have the power to enforce this article by appropriate legislation.

Article XXIV
[Adopted 1964]

Section 1.   The right of citizens of the United States to vote in any primary or other election for President or Vice President, for electors for President or Vice President, or for Senator or Representative in Congress, shall not be denied or abridged by the United States or any State by reason of failure to pay any poll tax or other tax.

Section 2.   The Congress shall have the power to enforce this article by appropriate legislation.

Article XXV
[Adopted 1967]

Section 1.   In case of the removal of the President from office or of his death or resignation, the Vice President shall become President.

Section 2.   Whenever there is a vacancy in the office of the Vice President, the President shall nominate a Vice President who shall take office upon confirmation by a majority vote of both Houses of Congress.

Section 3.   Whenever the President transmits to the President pro tempore of the Senate and the Speaker of the House of Representatives his written declaration that he is unable to discharge the powers and duties of his office, and until he transmits to them a written declaration to the contrary, such powers and duties shall be discharged by the Vice President as Acting President.

Section 4.   Whenever the Vice President and a majority of either the principal officers of the executive departments or of such other body as Congress may by law provide, transmit to the President pro tempore of the Senate and the Speaker of the House of Representatives their written declaration that the President is unable to discharge the powers and duties of his office, the Vice President shall immediately assume the powers and duties of the office as Acting President.

Thereafter, when the President transmits to the President pro tempore of the Senate and the Speaker of the House of Representatives his written declaration that no inability exists, he shall resume the powers and duties of his office unless the Vice President and a majority of either the principal officers of the executive departments or of such other body as Congress may by law provide, transmit within four days to the President pro tempore of the Senate and the Speaker of the House of Representatives their written declaration that the President is unable to discharge the powers and duties of his office. Thereupon Congress shall decide the issue, assembling within forty-eight hours for that purpose if not in session. If the Congress, within twenty-one days after receipt of the latter written declaration, or, if Congress is not in session, within twenty-one days after Congress is required to assemble, determines by two-thirds vote of both Houses that the President is unable to discharge the powers and duties of his office, the Vice President shall continue to discharge the same as Acting President; otherwise, the President shall resume the powers and duties of his office.

Article XXVI
[*Adopted 1971*]

Section 1. The right of citizens of the United States, who are eighteen years of age or older, to vote shall not be denied or abridged by the United States or by any State on account of age.

Section 2. The Congress shall have power to enforce this article by appropriate legislation.

Article XXVII
[*Adopted 1992*]

No law, varying the compensation for services of the Senators and Representatives, shall take effect, until an election of Representatives shall have intervened.

Sitting Congress cannot raise own salary

Table of Cases